CW00802201

THE MEDIEVAL
GREEK ROMANCE

First published in 1989, *The Medieval Greek Romance* provides essential information for the non-specialist about Greek fiction during the period 1071–1453, as well as proposing new solutions to problems that have vexed previous generations of scholars. Roderick Beaton applies sophisticated methods of literary analysis to the material, and bridges the artificial gap which has separated 'Byzantine' literature, in a form of ancient Greek, from 'modern Greek' writing, seeing the long tradition of romance writing in Greek as both homogeneous and of a high level of literary sophistication.

Throughout, consideration is given to relations and interconections with comparable literature in Western Europe. As many of the texts discussed are not yet accessible through English translation, the argument is illustrated by lucid plot summaries and extensive quotation (always accompanied by literal English renderings).

For its second edition, *The Medieval Greek Romance* has been revised throughout and expanded with the addition of a substantial 'Afterword', which assesses and responds to recent work on the subject.

Roderick Beaton is Koraës Professor of Modern Greek and Byzantine History, Language and Literature at King's College London, University of London.

THE MEDIEVAL GREEK ROMANCE

2nd edition, revised and expanded

Roderick Beaton

London and New York

First published 1989
by Cambridge University Press

Second edition published 1996
by Routledge
11 New Fetter Lane, London EC4P 4EE

Simultaneously published in the USA and Canada
by Routledge
29 West 35th Street, New York, NY 10001

© 1989 Cambridge University Press
© 1996 Roderick Beaton

Typeset in Garamond by
Solidus (Bristol) Limited
Printed and bound in Great Britain by
T J Press (Padstow) Ltd, Padstow, Cornwall

All rights reserved. No part of this book may be reprinted or
reproduced or utilized in any form or by any electronic,
mechanical, or other means, now known or hereafter invented,
including photocopying and recording, or in any information
storage or retrieval system, without permission in writing from
the publishers.

British Library Cataloguing in Publication Data
A catalogue record for this book is available from the British Library

Library of Congress Cataloguing in Publication Data
A catalogue record for this book has been requested

ISBN 0–415–12032–2 (hbk)
ISBN 0–415–12033–0 (pbk)

The originators, the exuberant men, are extinct and in their place subsists and modestly flourishes a generation notable for elegance and variety of contrivance. It may well happen that there are lean years ahead in which our posterity will look back hungrily to this period, when there was so much will and so much ability to please.

Evelyn Waugh

So then, if Zeus will not place our story among the stars, if Poseidon will not imprint it upon the waters, if Earth will not nurture it in plants and flowers, then, as though in unfading timbers and in adamantine precious stones, with Hermes' pen and ink and in language breathing the fire of rhetoric let our story be inscribed, and let some one of those who come after turn it into rhetoric and forge a golden statue hammered out of words as our imperishable monument.

Eustathios Makrembolites

In memoriam
David Bradley

1

CONTENTS

ILLUSTRATIONS

MAPS

FIGURE

PREFACE TO THE
FIRST EDITION

The Greek romances of the Middle Ages are tales of love, death and adventure. As such they may be seen as the successors to the first European prose fiction developed in Greek between the first and fourth centuries AD, and, more distantly, among the ancestors of the modern European novel. This study aims to explore this little-known territory of European literary history, and reveal the richness, the coherence and complexity, of a group of stories which ring the changes on a universal set of themes, but do so in a way specific to their own time and place. In the course of exploration we will discover that the adventures of the medieval Greek romance are as much the adventures of language and rhetoric as they are the adventures of the somewhat typecast heroes and heroines. In different ways all these works are suspended between nostalgic admiration for the creativity of an earlier age and a craving for permanence and fulfilment, not so much in the human happiness of the lovers (which for an orthodox Christian of the Middle Ages could never be permanent anyway) as in the approximation of the rhetorical *logos*, or discourse of the text, to the status of the divine *logos*.

There has been no systematic study of the Greek romances of the Middle Ages as a literary genre in any language, although the texts have been exhaustively quarried in the last hundred years by scholars in search of different kinds of historical, linguistic and cultural information. As a result, many of the questions addressed in this book may seem somewhat otiose to the Western medievalist used to relatively secure chronological and linguistic data, to consensus on editorial practice, and above all to the existence of modern scholarly editions. On the other hand there may be those working in the field of medieval Greek studies who feel that a study such as this is even premature, and should not be undertaken until better texts and more secure background data are available. In answer to the latter, I believe that it will be difficult to progress much further in the vexed questions surrounding editorial method for many of these texts until we can agree on the nature of the texts we are dealing with. One of the main aims of this book is therefore to propose a basis for such agreement. If the details of the argument at times arouse a puzzled sense of *déjà vu* in the specialist in the medieval literature of the West, this is the reason.

But in large measure this book is also addressed to the non-specialist, and particularly to scholars and students working comparatively on medieval literature. Here the main claim of the book is that the Greek romances represent a significant contribution to the European development of secular fiction in the later Middle Ages, and indeed occupy a special place in that development through their direct affiliations to the first European fiction, the Greek prose romances or novels of the first centuries AD. In concentrating on the Greek 'contribution' in this sense, I have given more weight to works originally written in Greek than to those known to have been translated or adapted from other languages. Cross-cultural connections between East and West are also given prominence, although I am uncomfortably aware that there may be specific questions which Western medievalists might have liked to see answered that I have been unable either to foresee or to accommodate satisfactorily within the scope of the present study.

This book has been a long time in the making, and personal debts to scholars, students and institutions mount up. Library research in Greece was facilitated by grants from the British Academy in 1981 and from the Hayter Travel Fund of the University of London in 1981 and 1984. Study leave granted by King's College for a term in 1984 and again in 1987 proved indispensable, and I am particularly grateful to the principal, Professor Stewart Sutherland, and to his predecessor, the late Lord Cameron of Balhousie, for making this possible during a period of enforced retrenchment. Among students I must mention with gratitude Sarah Ekdawi and Florentia Yannoullou, willing guinea-pigs for a new course at King's on 'Medieval literature in vernacular Greek', together with whom I first discovered many of the subtleties and the peculiar difficulties of the vernacular romances in 1982–3.

My debt to scholars and specialists in a variety of fields is too large to enumerate; but many of those whose names appear in the list of references are personal friends to whom I owe much in conversation and the unstinting flow of books and offprints. Where they find that I have disagreed with them in the ensuing pages I hope that they will respond in the spirit of open and continuing debate in which my own remarks are intended. Specific debts are owed to Simon Franklin and to Professor Robert Browning, who have taken trouble to give me access to the growing bibliography on the subject in Russian; to Elizabeth Jeffreys and Manolis Papathomopoulos for allowing me to read a portion of their forthcoming *editio princeps* of the *War of Troy*; and to Wim Bakker and Arnold van Gemert for a similar privilege in regard to their edition of the *Tale of Belisarios* which appeared during 1988. Special thanks are also due to the general editor of the series, Cambridge Studies in Medieval Literature, Professor Alastair Minnis, who read and commented on a draft of the whole book, and to Dr David Holton, who in reading the completed typescript saved me from a great many errors both great and small. It goes without saying that all remaining errors, inadequacies and omissions are my responsibility alone.

I should like finally to thank my wife, Fran, but for whose patience, support and sense of humour none of it, quite simply, would have been possible.

King's College London
April 1988

PREFACE TO THE
SECOND EDITION

The first edition of this book was written between 1984 and 1987, with some minor additions up to April 1988. By the time it appeared in late 1989, several independent and important studies of the subject were already either in print or well under way. The last few years have seen a long-overdue upsurge in scholarly interest in Byzantine literature, and the romances which are the subject of this book, although by no means typical of that literature as a whole, show the Byzantines, and their immediate Greek-speaking successors, at work simultaneously as continuators of the Hellenistic tradition and as forerunners of much modern literary fiction.

The present edition has been updated in order to take account of recent developments, in essentially two ways. First, I have carefully checked the whole text and silently corrected minor errors which had been pointed out to me by friends, colleagues and reviewers. I have also replaced references to older editions where new editions have become available, and where necessary revised accordingly the quotations in the text and references to line-numbers in the notes. Here and there I have altered the wording of the text, and deleted a small number of passages expressing opinions which I no longer hold (such divergences from the first edition are, however, signalled in the notes). Finally, throughout the text I have restored the Greek proper names cited to a form which may be more familiar to readers than the phonetic transcription I adopted in the first edition, and in Greek quotations I have also restored the traditional orthography with three accents and two breathing marks, in place of the simplified 'monotonic' system common in writing the modern language.

The most substantial addition to the book, however, is the Afterword, which presents, assesses and responds to developments in the field since 1987, and points out directions for future research. The references have also been fully updated (to the end of 1994).

Since the book first appeared a number of new debts have accumulated. The most important of these are to Francesca Rizzo Nervo and Yoryis Yatromanolakis, thanks to whose initiative *The Medieval Greek Romance* will shortly appear in, respectively, Italian and Greek translations. It was as a consequence of these initiatives that I first perceived the need for an updated edition of the book and began working on the present version. I am additionally grateful, in the preparation of this new English edition, to Niki Tsironi, who undertook the Greek version, and to Professor Athanasios Markopoulos, who read and commented carefully on a draft of it.

In the course of revision and of preparing the Afterword I have been helped in particular by Ruth Webb, who has kept me in touch with recent bibliography on the Hellenistic romance; by Gavin Betts, the first translator of any of the vernacular romances into English; Professor Stylianos Alexiou; Elizabeth and Michael Jeffreys; Suzanne MacAlister; and Tina Lendari, whose work on the manuscripts of *Libistros* has been invaluable although, in the spirit of the original edition, I have not, in the end, made use of her kindly given permission to quote from her edition-in-progress.

Finally I should like thank the Syndics of Cambridge University Press, the original publishers, for agreeing to the reversion of copyright which has made this new edition possible, and, more than anyone, Richard Stoneman, my editor at Routledge, who has given this book such a warm welcome and a new lease of life.

This edition was on its way to press when news came of the untimely death in February 1995 of Ole Smith. On the subject-matter of this book my differences of opinion with Professor Smith were – and are – fundamental. On reflection, it has seemed to me a more honest tribute to a scholar of unusual breadth of interests and tenacious productivity, to make no change to what I had already written in the Afterword. As a scholar, Ole Smith remains with us; his views and his arguments deserve to be discussed with no less rigour now than when he was alive.

King's College London
February 1995

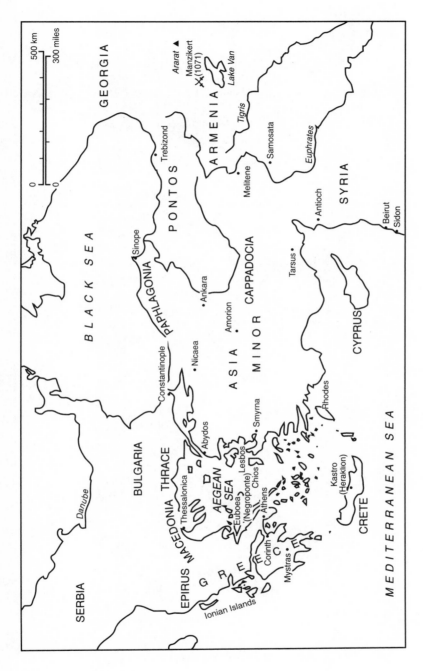

Map 1 The Greek-speaking world in the later Middle Ages

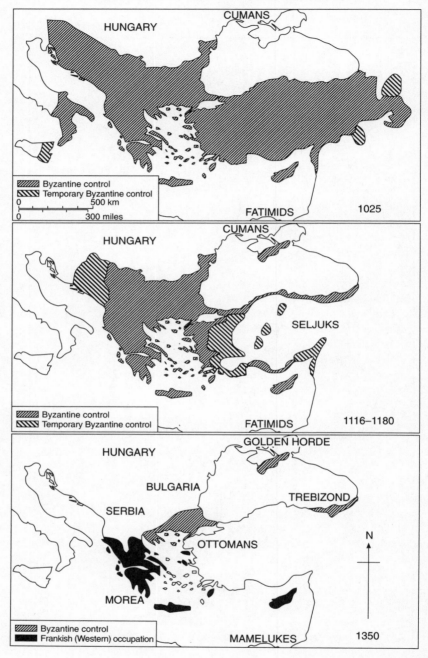

Map 2 The decline of the Byzantine empire

INTRODUCTION

There are sixteen Greek romances, written after 1100, which survive in whole or in part. All but one, the seventeenth-century *Erotokritos*, written in Crete in close proximity to the thought-world of post-Renaissance Italy, belong to the Middle Ages. In a Greek context the Middle Ages can be said to end with the fall of Constantinople to the Ottoman Turks in 1453, and activity in writing and copying romances in the medieval tradition ceases during the following century. All but one of these romances are in verse, and it is for this reason, as well as to emphasize the links between most of them and similar literature in the West, that I have adopted the generic term 'romance' rather than 'novel'. The distinction is in any case peculiar to English and particularly inappropriate when one is dealing with Greek fiction, whether ancient or medieval, in that no Greek generic term was ever proposed for this kind of literature before the nineteenth century.

It is for a similar reason that I have eschewed the term 'Byzantine' in my title. The modern name for the secular state of Eastern Christendom, which normally subsumes all medieval studies in the Greek field, has the effect of emphasizing the institutional and political differences between 'Byzantium' and the West. However, the story of Greek secular literature during our period has much more in common with what was happening elsewhere in Europe at the same time than at first sight appears. Above all, the new awareness in the twelfth century of a language community united by spoken Greek as well as by the literary inheritance from antiquity is closely analogous to the developments underlying the rise of the vernacular literatures in the West. And it is also significant that several of the later romances in this 'medieval Greek' tradition were written outside the reduced confines of the Byzantine empire; indeed, the medieval romance seems to have outlived that empire by up to a century.

It is, however, large-scale events of Byzantine history that have determined the chronological limits of this study. The defeat of the Byzantine armies at the battle of Manzikert in 1071 effectively began the long process of political and military decline and of intellectual reorientation which continued even after the end of the Byzantine empire in 1453 and played its

1

part in shaping the modern Greek nation in more recent times. In the aftermath of that defeat literary fiction, which had lain dormant (except in its ecclesiastical offshoot, the saint's life) since the fourth century, first began to be revived. At the opposite end of the chronological spectrum, the limit of 1453 is to be interpreted rather loosely: some of the texts discussed in Part II were almost certainly written a little after that date, and the intensive activity in copying, and presumably also in reciting, vernacular romances in the hundred years following the fall of Constantinople will be discussed in Chapter 12. However, this activity is best seen as a continuing response to the loss of the spiritual and cultural capital city; after the mid-sixteenth century the dominant position in Greek literary writing is assumed by Venetian-ruled Crete, and the romance tradition effectively comes to an end. Within this long period an important break is marked by another historical event, the capture of Constantinople by Western crusaders in 1204, and that date also divides this book into its two parts. The first deals with the revival and re-creation of the romance as a genre in the twelfth century, and discusses the four known texts written in the literary language during that century, as well as the 'epic', or 'proto-romance', of *Digenes Akrites*. The second explores the establishment of a common literary vernacular as the accepted medium for fiction, and presents the five original and six translated romances produced after the Latin interregnum of 1204–61 at Constantinople.

The medieval Greek romances have not been ignored by scholarship, as will be seen from the list of references at the end of this book. Individual romances, and both the learned and vernacular romances as groups, have been judged dismissively in the nineteenth and twentieth centuries; almost all serious studies of the romances have quarried them for historical realia, or for evidence of the development of spoken modern Greek or of the existence of a lost, and livelier, oral tradition of Byzantium. There has been no single study of the twelfth-century and the later romances together as a developing genre, and indeed few studies of either make more than passing mention of the other.[1]

A rare instance where the medieval Greek romance was seen as a link in the growth of modern fiction from its distant origins in the Hellenistic romances is provided by John Dunlop, whose *History of Prose Fiction* was first published in 1814. Dunlop devotes six pages to a summary and some trenchantly negative criticism of the only medieval Greek romance to be written in prose, *Hysmine and Hysminias*, and credits it with having influenced some Renaissance literature in French and Spanish.[2] Later, in 1876, Erwin Rohde, whose study of the Hellenistic romance is still cited as a classic, dismissed the same romance as a 'caricature' and deemed the vernacular romances unworthy of consideration on account of the 'barbarism of their speech'.[3] Nor were Greek attitudes during the nineteenth century any more favourable. In the memorable words of Adamandios

Koraes at the beginning of the century, the vernacular romance, *Belthandros and Chrysantza*

> makes revolting reading, on account of the mingling and juxtaposition of many words and phrases of ancient Greek with many words and phrases of the utmost vulgarity, in a word, on account of its repellent macaronism.[4]

On the opposite side from Koraes in the nineteenth-century controversy over the Greek language, one seeks in vain through the essays of Jean Psichari, who later in the century combed the vernacular romances for historical evidence in support of his championship of the spoken or 'demotic' language, for signs that he approved anything other than the language in which these romances were written.[5]

Modern attitudes, though less linguistically biased, are in the main little different. Not unrepresentative of the attitude towards the twelfth-century romances in the learned language is that expressed by Cyril Mango: 'It is true that the four specimens we possess are unbelievably tedious, but we are not now concerned with their slender literary merit'; while from a Greek perspective Constantine Trypanis has damned them as the 'nadir of Byzantine poetry'.[6] The distinguished German Byzantinist Hans-Georg Beck is condescending in the faint praise he gives to the 'push towards emancipation' in the face of Orthodox 'prudery' that he detects in these 'recondite' texts, which he probably wrongly believes to have been little read; while Herbert Hunger, who is one of the few historians to have worked closely with the texts, sees them as fulfilling 'a comparable function to film and popular novels and journalism in our own day'.[7] The most balanced comment on the twelfth-century romances comes from Robert Browning:

> Though the characters are rather wooden, and their utterances highly rhetorical, the authors show great fertility of invention and some psychological insight ... These middle Byzantine romances have long been brushed aside as artificial and boring by historians of literature, who often have not read them. Today there is a renewed interest in them, and in the eagerness with which their authors explored the techniques of fictitious narrative. The romances ... appear to have been composed to amuse and delight the refined upper strata of Byzantine society, a new task for serious literature to face.[8]

The romances of the twelfth century, because of their archaizing language, are never mentioned in histories of modern Greek literature, and even in the new Byzantinische Handbuch series of titles in the history of Byzantine literature, which supplements and updates the pioneering work of Karl Krumbacher, first published in 1897, they are assigned to a different volume from the vernacular romances.[9] Vernacular Greek literature of the period is regularly dealt with (chronologically following oral folk poetry collected in the nineteenth and twentieth centuries!) in histories of modern Greek literature;[10] and is well represented in the standard anthologies. There is of course a real problem in defining the point at which 'modern Greek' literature begins – a problem which this book, in ostentatiously straddling the traditional divide, cannot be said to have made any easier.[11] However, the dangers inherent in studying the vernacular literature of the period in isolation from the much larger corpus produced in the learned language have been well emphasized by Elizabeth and Michael Jeffreys:

> We are quite sure that it is not enough, as seems to happen in some Modern Greek lecture-courses and early chapters in literary histories, to confine research to texts which fall linguistically within the definition of Volksliteratur. Answers to the questions which we should like to put demand an examination of all the literature surviving from the period. Often a tendency discernible in popular poetry may be defined and clarified by observation of literature in more learned linguistic form.[12]

There is in any case more than a hint of dutiful lip-service in the attention paid to the romances and other early vernacular literature in modern Greek in these histories. Not one actually risks a positive evaluation of the texts, which are clearly invoked in order to claim a time-depth for modern Greek literature back to the twelfth century, rather than to introduce a category of texts with any expectation that they will actually be read. Indeed Beck, in the Byzantinische Handbuch volume devoted to *Volksliteratur*, even apologizes for giving full plot summaries of most of the texts on the grounds that 'hardly anyone ever reads them'.[13] Or, as Michael Jeffreys, who knows the vernacular Greek texts of the period as intimately as anyone, rather sadly concedes: 'It is not surprising that Byzantine vernacular literature has been analysed more than it has been enjoyed. The Greek vernacular was hardly used by writers of education and talent.'[14]

The most serious attempts before the late 1980s to come to grips with the *literary* as opposed to the linguistic or textual problems posed by the romances were made in the Soviet Union. A study of the vernacular romances by A. D. Aleksidze, which appeared in 1979, provided the first systematic attempt to apply Vladimir Propp's model of formalist analysis to any of these texts, with impressive results, particularly for *Kallimachos and Chrysorrhoe* and *Belthandros and Chrysantza*. Aleksidze admirably insisted on the unity of the vernacular romances and, as he also wrote on the learned romances of the twelfth century, would have been well placed to extend this unity to cover all the medieval Greek texts in the genre, although so far as I am aware he never did so.[15] A similarly rigorous literary-historical approach has also been applied to the twelfth-century texts by S. V. Polyakova (1979), and to the emergence of vernacular literature by T. V. Popova (1985). Elsewhere such approaches to the medieval Greek romance have been rare. Margaret Alexiou's 'reappraisal' of *Hysmine and Hysminias* (1977) still stands alone as a fully literary and critically aware reading of a single romance. More theoretically based applications of a formalist model have since then been proposed, for instance by Kechayoglou (1982) and Kapsomenos (1985). For developments since 1987, see the Afterword.

This introduction would not be complete without some mention of literary theory. As a contribution to literary history rather than a theoretical study, this book avoids as far as possible the technical lexicon (some will say 'jargon') and coded rhetoric of the embattled theoretical 'schools' of the late twentieth century. Where technical terms are introduced they are accompanied, at least on their first appearance in every chapter, by a note giving a concise definition and referring the reader to the appropriate theoretical 'authority'. Although this book does not pretend to apply any single theoretical model to its material, certain developments in the field of modern literary theory have contributed more than others, and this contribution is acknowledged at appropriate points in the notes. In particular I have found useful the model of narrative analysis put forward by Gérard Genette (1980), and the redefinition of literary history and of genre in medieval literature proposed by Hans Robert Jauss in two essays originally published in 1969 and 1972 respectively.[16] Central to the argument of the whole book is Jauss's belief that literature does not merely 'reflect' the historical process but is an active component within it; and that the act of literary creation is simultaneously a process of *reading* literary texts already in existence, and of responding to a unique and real situation in the historical world.

Part I
1071–1204

1

THE TWELFTH-CENTURY BACKGROUND

THE BYZANTINE EMPIRE IN THE TWELFTH CENTURY

In 1071 the Byzantine army under the Emperor Romanos IV Diogenes was defeated at Manzikert, in eastern Anatolia, by the forces of the Seljuk Sultan Alp Arslan. The emperor was taken prisoner, and the terms of the treaty under which he negotiated his freedom repudiated by his successor, Michael VII, who had usurped the throne during his absence. As a consequence of this defeat, during the next ten years the whole of central Anatolia, which had been the geographical and economic heartland of the Eastern empire since Roman times, came to be occupied by the Seljuk Turks, leaving only parts of the coastline in Byzantine hands. The same year also saw the Norman conquest of Sicily, and the loss to Byzantium of its last provinces in Western Europe. Thereafter the Byzantine claim to universal empire, despite the strident line proclaimed by the imperial court up until the fifteenth century, became progressively divorced from reality. The educated Byzantine of the late eleventh and twelfth centuries found himself having to think again about himself and his place in society, and the place of that society in the cosmos. The inheritance of the battle of Manzikert was to create 'a largely Greek state out of what had been a multilingual Empire'.[1]

The importance of 1071 as a watershed is agreed by modern historians of Byzantium, for many of whom it inaugurates the 'late' period of a tripartite division;[2] but its significance is evaluated more often in terms of the 'decline and fall' of an ancient civilization than of the emergence of a modern one. The map of the Byzantine empire between 1081 and 1204, as Anthony Bryer points out, reveals a geographically dispersed and strategically vulnerable spread of territory which happened to coincide to a very large extent with the areas of Greek colonization in the ancient world, and also with those areas where speakers of the *modern* language were to be found up until the population exchanges of the early twentieth century. In other words, the identity of spoken language and state that was to become a fundamental tenet of nineteenth-century nationalism throughout Europe became – by accident

– a reality during a formative period of medieval Greek history.

The significance of this fact is easily obscured because Greek had been, under the Roman empire, the unofficial *lingua franca* of the eastern Mediterranean, before becoming the official language of Byzantium in the sixth century. However, 'Greek' for most of this period meant a written language much of whose morphology, syntax and vocabulary, by the tenth and eleventh centuries, had to be learnt in school and perfected through arduous written exercises, whether the vernacular one spoke at home was the spoken Greek of the day or some other language. Although Greek in its written form was accorded special prestige, it did not in fact enjoy a monopoly even as a written language, let alone of speech, within the boundaries of the early and middle empire. The modern equation of 'Byzantine literature' with texts written exclusively in Greek gives a false picture of linguistic homogeneity, since literature was also produced within the Byzantine empire in Latin, Syriac, Coptic, Church Slavonic, Armenian and Georgian.[3] There is less documented evidence for linguistic diversity in the period between the eighth and eleventh centuries than there is for the earlier period, but it is clear that, although Greek was now the all but universal language of writing and education, many different spoken-language communities continued to flourish within the empire. The existence of Slavic speakers in large numbers in the Greek peninsula from the sixth century to at least the ninth has long been known, although the extreme view that Greek disappeared altogether as a spoken language, to be re-introduced later by learned circles in the capital, is no longer tenable. Slavic may not still have been much in use in the Greek peninsula by 1025, but the map of the Byzantine empire at the death of Basil II in that year shows many areas within its borders where it is scarcely possible that Greek could have been spoken as a first language by many of the inhabitants. Before 1071 there were many Byzantines whose mother-tongue was not Greek; after the sack of Constantinople by the fourth crusade in 1204 there were many mother-tongue speakers of Greek who lived outside the shrinking confines of the Byzantine state.

In other words the Byzantines of the twelfth century had something very like a national identity, in the modern sense, foisted on them; an identity, moreover, which Greek-speakers in later centuries never quite lost sight of, and which in the long run proved more enduring than the older Byzantine model of universal empire that was maintained at an official level until 1453. In the twelfth century this older way of looking at Byzantium and its role in the world was upheld by the emperors of the Komnenian dynasty and lent some credibility by their military and diplomatic successes. But this older worldview is, from that time on, an imperial overlay on an emergent political and cultural reality which is fundamentally incompatible with it. The latter worldview is perhaps historically manifested for the first time in the massacre of the Latins in Constantinople in 1182, and plays an increasingly evident role in the secular literature of the Palaiologan period, both within and outside the empire. But it is the interaction, perhaps even mutual irritance, set up between these two worldviews and their increasing lack of it, that motivates many of the striking cultural innovations of the twelfth century.

The defeat at Manzikert, and the chaotic decade of the 1070s, were followed by the accession to the throne of the tough military Emperor Alexios I Komnenos in 1081. For the next hundred years the Byzantine empire was ruled by Alexios (1081–1118) and his successors John II (1118–43) and Manuel I Komnenos (1143–80), until the collapse of the dynasty and of civil order in the final decades of the twelfth century. The crucial period of cultural transition that was the twelfth century in Byzantium is marked almost throughout by the firm and relatively stable rule of the Komnenian dynasty. This is not the place to examine the tangled question of the attitude of these emperors to the arts: suffice it to say that they may not have been either as philistine or as repressive of cultural innovation as they often appear from contemporary writings and in modern assessments. Authoritative, however, they certainly were, and a precedent with important implications in the field of literature was established as early as 1082, the year after Alexios' successful *coup d'état*. In that year the philosopher and rhetorician Ioannes Italos was publicly tried and condemned for heresy.

Italos had been the last and the least cautious of a distinguished line of eleventh-century teachers of rhetoric such as Ioannes Mavropous and Michael Psellos, who had revived interest in the speculations, and not just in the language and style, of the pagan philosophers. A modern study, broadly sympathetic to Italos, puts his case like this:

> [Italos,] while not deviating significantly from Christian dogma per se, argued a line of thought which often crossed over into the realm of dogma without the full context of a theological frame of reference. Rather, he bases himself extensively upon classical Greek philosophy, argues the pro and con of Greek philosophical propositions, and then adapts the points he discusses to a conclusion basically compatible with Christian teaching. In the course of his argumentation he proceeds syllogistically, which, repeatedly, involves him in assuming a philosophical hypothesis at variance with Christian teaching for the sake of argument, so that he can modify or disprove it.

The emperor himself intervened to make a show-trial of the proceedings, and to ensure that not just Italos himself but all who had been closely associated with his teachings should be anathematized.[4]

In this way the intellectual 'renaissance' of the eleventh century seems to have been checked. Rhetoric, which continued to flourish on a much increased scale throughout the century of the Komnenian emperors, was diverted into other avenues than philosophical enquiry. In consequence the

11

twelfth-century interest in classical Hellenism may lack the intellectual refinement of Psellos and his contemporaries but none the less builds on the achievements of the eleventh century to spread its activities much more widely (including the exploitation of the vernacular, which would hardly have had much interest for Psellos) but in less depth. It was against this intellectual background that literary fiction in the form of the romance, but also of Lucianic satire and a new genre of comic begging poetry, emerged in the mid-twelfth century.

The period of Byzantine history which is ushered in by the defeat of Manzikert and the trial of Italos has met with varying assessments at the hands of historians, both medieval and modern. It has been called a time either of renaissance or of reaction; the firm political and military grip of the three Komnenian emperors whose reigns span almost the entire period has been praised as genius and denounced as repression, and the crisis of identity which is here proposed as underlying the achievements, as well as the shortcomings, of the period has been robustly dismissed by one eminent scholar as a 'catastrophic failure to adapt to a changing world'.[5] The accession of Alexios I Komnenos in 1081 marked the beginning of a hundred years of stable government (by Byzantine standards at any rate) during which an abiding aim of imperial policy was to restate the traditional claims of universal empire (by military and diplomatic means) and of religious orthodoxy (by preventing the teaching of heretical doctrines). On the face of it Alexios and his successors, John and Manuel, succeeded: the frontiers were pushed back and the purity of religious dogma upheld. During this period the first real encounters between Byzantium and the West took place, as Western crusaders passed through Byzantine lands in 1096–7 and again in 1147, and as trading privileges within the empire were granted to merchants from Pisa, Genoa and Venice in the course of the century: contacts which, to begin with at least, were mutually beneficial.

In literature the romance suddenly appears in the mid-twelfth century, and alongside it satire, another fictional genre which had not been practised since late antiquity. It is surely a symptom of the times that both of these innovations have the outward appearance of revivals from the past, an appearance which, now as then, easily obscures the revolutionary act of reviving forms and conventions that had been so long out of use. Hellenistic satire and the conventions of the Hellenistic romance are re-appropriated by twelfth-century writers, after an interval of some eight hundred years. Like the outward image of Byzantium itself under the Komnenian emperors, these externals conceal a profound response to a changed world. It was during the same century that vernacular Greek (by this time, in effect, the modern language) was introduced into literature, although for the time being in a much more cautious and experimental way than in the West at the same period.

Both the nature and the significance of the innovative adaptation of long-discarded literary conventions in the Komnenian period become apparent if we define the phenomenon as a 'renaissance' in the terms of Hans Robert Jauss:

> One can line up the examples of how a new literary form can reopen access to forgotten literature. These include the so-called 'renaissances' – so-called, because the word's meaning gives rise to appearance of an automatic return, and often prevents one from recognizing that literary tradition can not transmit itself alone. That is, a literary past can return only when a new reception draws it back into the present, whether an altered aesthetic wilfully reaches back to reappropriate the past, or an unexpected light falls back on forgotten literature from the new moment of literary evolution, allowing something to be found that one previously could not have sought in it.[6]

The literary experimentation of the twelfth century seems largely to have ceased in the 1180s, a period of rapid disintegration following the death in 1180 of Manuel Komnenos.[7] There is no surviving fictional literature that can be dated with certainty to the hundred years following the sack of Constantinople by the Latins in 1204, although traditionally established genres of Byzantine writing continue unabated in the thirteenth century. Neither the romance nor the vernacular reappears for certain until the early fourteenth century, and it is only from that time that a form of the vernacular becomes the accepted medium for fiction (whether in the romances that are the subject of this book or in the satirical fables such as the *Tale of the Four-Footed Beasts*, the *Poulologos* and the *Tale of the Donkey*).[8] None the less, throughout those centuries when a vernacular literary idiom was being fashioned and was rapidly increasing in popularity, the romances of the twelfth century, written in the learned language, continued to be copied and read and, it will be argued, to influence writers.

LEVELS OF LANGUAGE AND LEVELS OF LITERATURE

We have seen that from 1071 onwards the spoken language of almost all Byzantines was for the first time Greek. To the resulting intellectual climate must be attributed two apparently contradictory trends in the literature of the twelfth century that have long been noticed: the simultaneous cultivation of a hyper-correct 'Attic' language in which the divorce between spoken and written Greek is pushed to an unprecedented extreme, and of the vernacular not just as a means of expression (as in the *Poems of Poor Prodromos* and Glykas' *Verses Written While Held Imprisoned*) but also as a source for literary material, as in the 'proto-romance', *Digenes Akrites*. In each case, what is sought, whether fully consciously or not, is an identity for the writer and his public as 'Greek', which may replace or co-exist uneasily with his received identity as citizen of God's earthly kingdom. In the case of the high Atticist, such as Anna Komnene, the search is for the authentication of that identity in a past as remote, and therefore as authoritative, as that of the Bible; in the case of the writers who experimented with the vernacular, of which the ones mentioned are only the most thoroughgoing examples, similar authentication is sought (usually playfully) in something shared as a lowest common denominator: the language of the street, and the names of trades and utensils in the poems attributed to Prodromos, the common heritage of proverbial wisdom in Glykas.

Between these extremes is a wide middle ground, a linguistic register modelled not on ancient Attic but on the by this time equally ancient *Koine*. The tradition on which this register drew was that of the Gospels, early Church Fathers and saints' lives, as well as of functional literature of an earlier period. No less a language of learning than the 'high style' of the Atticists, this register was prolifically exploited in the twelfth century for didactic and popularizing literature, especially that addressed for a reward to high personages when their comprehension was more important than their admiration.[9]

Twelfth-century writers show versatility, in some cases virtuosity, in their exploitation of different language registers. Theodore Prodromos, the most prolific writer of the age, uses all of them; so does the historian Michael Glykas; Konstantinos Manasses and Ioannes Tzetzes in different works use either the 'high' or the 'middle' register, apparently depending on whom they are addressing. A peculiarly Byzantine obsession (not unknown in modern Greece either) for transposing the same text from one register to another begins in the second half of the tenth century with the work of Symeon the Metaphrast, who supervised the rewriting of many of the older saints' lives in a more literary and less widely comprehensible linguistic idiom.[10] And after the twelfth century we find paraphrases in the other direction, from 'high' to 'middle' style, of the *Alexiad* of Anna Komnene and the *History* of Niketas Choniates. *Digenes Akrites* and the frequently copied 'Spaneas' poem, containing moral advice for a young man, are preserved in both 'middle-style' and 'low-style' versions, but in these cases we cannot be certain which is the paraphrase or when it was made.

This linguistic background is not as different from that found in the West at a similar period as at first appears. Histories of the modern literatures of Europe are by and large the histories of literature in the European vernaculars, and begin, as do the histories of modern Greek literature, with the earliest use of these vernaculars for literary purposes. But the ancient/ modern division according to whether Latin or the vernacular is used no more works to describe medieval literature in the West than does its counterpart for Byzantium. It is disputed whether Latin 'loosed the tongue of French' or the other way about, but what is not in doubt is that Latin poetry experienced as much of a renewal in the twelfth and thirteenth centuries as did poetry in the vernacular.[11] Nor in the beginning is any one kind of literature the special prerogative of the vernacular. But throughout the West, in each of the vernacular language areas, the same kind of diglossia as we observed in twelfth-century Byzantium was widely recognized. As E. R. Curtius puts it:

> The common man knows as well as the educated man that there are two languages; the language of the people and the language of the learned.... The learned language, Latin, is also called grammatica, and to Dante – as to the Roman Varro before him – it is an art language, devised by sages and unalterable.[12]

The principal difference, of course, lies between the 'two languages' usually found together in the West, and the two (or even three) registers of the same language which co-existed in Byzantium. As regards the Romance languages in the West, this distinction cannot have been clearcut until after the twelfth century, when these languages for the first time became fully distinct from Latin; while in those parts of Western Christendom where Latin co-existed with a Germanic or Celtic vernacular the relationship closely parallels that in non-Greek-speaking Byzantine provinces before 1071. If in the twelfth century the Holy Roman empire had been a centralized state whose boundaries had happened to coincide with the spread of Latin-based dialects, then the recognition of those dialects as distinct languages might have been considerably delayed. It is as much political and social considerations as purely linguistic ones that determine the point at which a divergent dialect or register gains recognition as a separate language.[13]

LITERACY, BOOKS AND READERS

We now know that the breakdown of urban institutions and the contraction of learning to a tiny, beleaguered elite in the early Middle Ages was as much a feature of Byzantine history as of Western European. Indeed the 'Dark Ages' of the seventh, eighth and ninth centuries in Byzantium may have been even darker than the corresponding and slightly earlier period in the West. Urban life and an urban-based economy seem to have disappeared almost entirely in the East, with the single exception of Constantinople, which hung on, to borrow a phrase of the late Lord Clark, 'by the skin of its teeth'.[14] The fact that, in all probability, only the centre remained to re-establish between the ninth and the eleventh centuries the centralized control it had always claimed enabled Byzantines, no less than modern historians, to assume a continuity in the social and cultural institutions of the Eastern empire which was largely illusory and almost entirely confined to the capital. In the West, on the other hand, since it is precisely centralized political institutions that have proved the most lasting casualty of the population movements of the fifth to seventh centuries, such an illusion could never have been sustained.

The spread of literacy, and the writing, production and dissemination of books, were among the institutions highly prized and well developed in the cities and towns of the Eastern Roman empire, and this was the milieu in which the Hellenistic romances seem to have been written and read. It used to be taken for granted that while such skills in the West were severely curtailed for several centuries, they continued to flourish uninterrupted in the East. In fact the learned tradition is continuous in both Latin and Greek, but the probability has recently had to be considered that literacy and book production were scarcely more widespread in Byzantium than they were during the Western Middle Ages. Modern scholarship provides a somewhat contradictory picture.

A lay reading public probably existed up until the seventh century and again in the eleventh and twelfth, when the reappearance of *belles-lettres* can plausibly be linked with the emergence of a new urban middle class; but this readership does not appear to have been very large, since so many of the texts were seemingly written for a single occasion, orally presented and then forgotten unless written up in a fair copy. If this is the reason why so many of them are preserved in only a single manuscript, then the book trade of the twelfth century cannot have been very lively.[15] Indeed it seems that much of the ceremonial poetry addressed to the emperor and members of the imperial family was composed for some kind of public performance, and then subsequently written out, so as to be read or at least preserved in manuscript form. In a far-reaching analysis of patronage in the twelfth century Margaret Mullett has drawn attention to the importance of audience and readers in Byzantine literature at this period; and has proposed that other types of literature as well may have been written for oral presentation before a *theatron*, a term whose precise significance in the twelfth century is problematic, but which certainly implies the presence of a 'live' audience. According to this analysis, the readership for *all* the non-ecclesiastical literature of the twelfth century may be equated with an audience or series of audiences before whom it was read aloud.[16]

An even narrower picture of the circulation of books and their readership is presented by Nigel Wilson. After the loss of Egypt in the seventh century, papyrus was no longer obtainable and parchment was exorbitantly expensive. Paper was cheaper and began to be used from the eleventh century on (a contributing factor in the increased literary production of that and the following century?) but Wilson can adduce little evidence that reading for pleasure was much practised, though he cites three private libraries that contained a copy of Achilles Tatios, one of which contained Heliodoros' romance as well. He too concludes that much belle-lettrist writing was produced to be read orally and written out only for vanity purposes, and ends by quoting Romilly Jenkins: 'No secular literature was written for a wide public, since no such public existed.'[17]

By contrast, Kazhdan and Constable consider the question of whether Byzantine literature as a whole was addressed to an audience or to a reading public, and conclude that, unlike ancient literature, with its emphasis on oral delivery and the secondary role of the written text, Byzantine literature 'was addressed primarily to the solitary reader'.[18] One may wonder whether the 'solitary practices' attributed by Kazhdan and Constable throughout their book to 'homo byzantinus' derive from placing overmuch credence on the testimony of the eleventh-century recluse Kekaumenos, who may have been somewhat paranoid. Finally Robert Browning has painted a lively picture, more consonant with that of Kazhdan than of Mango and Wilson, of a wide social spread of literacy and availability of education, which places telling but probably over-literal emphasis on the testimony of saints' lives.[19]

Certainly in late Hellenistic times, when the ancient romances were written between the first and at the latest the fourth century, the reading of books was a normal occupation among the kind of people who are also portrayed among the principal characters of these romances. It has even been proposed that 'the novels' rise would reflect merely the avid reading and prolific writing of the age, their demise the decline of a peaceful and cosmopolitan Greek world'.[20] In Achilles Tatios' romance *Leukippe and Kleitophon* the hero at one point pretends to be reading a book, apparently silently, so as to be able to peep under it at the heroine.[21] Interestingly, this must be one of the earliest pieces of evidence for the practice of silent reading in the ancient world, and implies that these romances themselves may well have been intended for the same kind of reception. The evidence for the surreptitious reading of (mainly ancient) romances copied so as to look like prayerbooks, between the fourteenth and the sixteenth centuries, need not be taken seriously;[22] but the minuscule format of some of these manuscripts certainly confirms that the reading of romances could be a private activity. Unfortunately we have no direct evidence for the kind of public that the medieval writers envisaged for their work; but it is scarcely possible that literature of entertainment, such as the romances, could have been produced and copied in the absence of a reading public of some sort. The 'proto-romance' of *Digenes Akrites* contains indications that it may have been written for oral delivery;[23] while the romances proper of the twelfth century give no clue to the kind of reception their authors envisaged for them.

EAST MEETS WEST?

The twelfth century has long been recognized as a period of new and closer, if not always amicable, contacts between Byzantium and the West. We have already noted in passing a number of parallels between the twelfth-century background in both halves of Christendom; now it is time to consider the question which sooner or later they inevitably raise: to what extent did innovations in either the East or the West contribute directly to developments in the other?

Parallels in intellectual life and attitudes evidently stem from the consolidation of higher education in Constantinople in the eleventh, and in parts of western Europe in the twelfth, centuries: the curriculum follows Hellenistic precepts in both instances, and the educational institutions of both East and West have been seen by modern historians as providing a necessary stratum of highly trained secular bureaucrats to fulfil the functions of increasingly complex state organizations, as well as satisfying the more abstract claims of philosophy.[24] The spread of secular, and particularly of vernacular, literature in the West from the twelfth century onward has been linked to 'overproduction' by these schools, whose graduates frequently failed to find employment at court or in the church and may often have turned their rhetorical and philosophical training to the entertainment of a nobility whose culture did not yet include the acquisition of these skills.[25] This argument has since been refined by Peter Dronke, who links it to the topos of the 'starving intellectual' and the revival of satire in the West at this time, and by Eugène Vinaver, who sees the development of the romance genre in the West as a secular equivalent to Biblical exegesis.[26]

In this case comparison between East and West offers a suggestive model by which we might try to supplement our understanding of the sudden revival of the secular romance in Byzantium. Certainly the 'starving intellectual' or 'begging' topos, and the revival of the same two genres, satire and romance, are as evident in Byzantine literature of the twelfth century as they are in Western.[27] There is good evidence in the Byzantine literature of the period for the existence of over-qualified and under-employed literati, although we should be wary of applying the Western model too rigorously to their activities. The centralization of the Byzantine empire meant that just about all of this educational and literary activity went on in the capital; job opportunities must have been better in the only medieval state to employ an extensive bureaucracy than they were in the West; and the picture of the talented clerk strumming a sophisticated lay for the delight of an unlettered nobility would have to undergo some adjustment to fit with what we know of aristocratic society in Constantinople. It would be unwise to attribute these parallel developments to influence in one direction or the other, since even if the parallel is fully accepted, the causes of similar phenomena at the same time in both halves of Christendom lie in an asymmetry between the educational aspirations of each society on the one hand, and the state of development of its economic and political institutions on the other.[28]

More specific parallels between literary developments in Byzantium and in the West in the twelfth century are tantalizing but cannot in the present state of our knowledge be ascribed to direct influence in one direction or the other. Such are the simultaneous appearance in widely separated parts of the West of the heroic narrative in verse, as the immediate precursor of the romance, and in the East of the heroic 'proto-romance', *Digenes Akrites*; the development in both East and West of the vernacular for literary purposes; and aspects of the story-material and ambience of both Eastern and Western romances. For the first of these, there seems to be no question of a direct relation; but for the second, influence from West to East has been suspected; while for the last, it has been suggested that an influence may have been at work in the opposite direction, from East to West.

It is well known that the establishment of the fictional genre of vernacular romance in Greek in the fourteenth and fifteenth centuries owes something to contacts with the West, which are assumed to stem from the presence of Western feudal courts in Greek-speaking lands between the fourth crusade and the Ottoman conquest. The extent and nature of these contacts will be discussed in Chapters 9 and 10. Greek-speakers in the twelfth century seem to follow their Western counterparts rather reluctantly in exploiting the vernacular for literary purposes: there are no texts wholly in the vernacular, and there is no equivalent in Greek, in that century, to the exuberant discovery of the vernacular as a new medium that is to be found in France at the same period. The possibility has been raised by Elizabeth Jeffreys that 'it was an awareness of the literary vigour of the vernaculars in the West that loosened Byzantine stylistic conventions'.[29] The terms of the proposal recall those used by Curtius and Dronke in the debate about the literary impetus behind the rise of the vernacular in the West, whether derived from above or below, from the learned tradition or from a hitherto unrecorded stratum of oral poetry; and it can no more easily be given an unequivocal answer in the case of Byzantium. Byzantine awareness of Western achievements in all fields was probably greater, during the century of the crusades, than Byzantine writers themselves admit. Manuel Komnenos was twice married to Western princesses and is frequently cited as having introduced the foreign sport of jousting to his court. It was also under the reign of Manuel (1143–80) that most of the literary innovations of the century seem to have been made, and after whose death they may well have ceased. There is some reference to Westerners and their ways in Prodromos' romance of the 1140s, *Rodanthe and Dosikles* (see pp. 72–3 below), and it has been suggested that Eustathios Makrembolites was acquainted, if not with the French *Roman de la Rose*, then with some of its predecessors in the tradition of courtly love poetry (see pp. 80–1, 211–12 below). But there is no real evidence for the kind of direct literary contact that seems to have taken place in the fourteenth and fifteenth centuries. That French 'loosed the tongue' of ancient Greek as well as of Latin in the twelfth century may be considered as a possibility but, even if true, there is no evidence that contact with the West had more than a superficial impact at that time.

Elizabeth Jeffreys has also proposed that simultaneous with this influence from West to East was another trend in the opposite direction. If the Greek twelfth-century romances were in existence by the 1140s, she argues, might they not have influenced the appearance of the French *romans d'antiquité* in the following decade? According to this view, the French romances (on the subjects of Troy, Thebes and Aeneas) may have been commissioned partly in order to emulate Byzantine literary developments and also to lay a Western counter-claim to universal empire based, as the Byzantine at that time was, on possession of a classical heritage. The key figure in this transaction is seen as Eleanor of Aquitaine, who accompanied the second crusade to Constantinople in 1147, and to whose later political ambitions Elizabeth Jeffreys links the commissioning of the French romances after Eleanor's return to France. The argument is certainly plausible, but not without difficulties, of which the greatest are the need to date at least two of the Greek romances to the years immediately preceding the second crusade, and the absence of firm links to connect literary works with particular patrons in Constantinople and France, or the visiting Eleanor with the 'circle' of her putative counterpart, the Sebastokratorissa Irene.[30] Finally, it should be mentioned that among German-speakers *Ruodlieb*, written in Latin around 1050, and *König Rother*, composed in Middle High German about the mid-twelfth century, include exotic journeys to the Mediterranean and may reflect Hellenistic or Byzantine influence.[31]

Another possibility that has been canvassed from time to time is that the oral sources for such Western romances as *Floire et Blancheflor* and *Pierre de Provence et la Belle Maguelonne* must have come if not from, then surely via, Greek-speaking lands.[32] More recently Deligiorgis has pointed out structural similarities between Eugenianos' romance *Drosilla and Charikles* and the French *Aucassin et Nicolette*, which in turn has clear links with later French romances with an 'orientalizing' strand: *Floire et Blancheflor* and *Paris et Vienne*.[33] The possibility that the origin of these Western romances of travel and adventure in the Eastern Mediterranean should be identified with the origin of their story-motifs in Arabic and Persian literature of the eighth to the twelfth centuries has been revived by Vincenzo Pecoraro, who further suggests that the fourteenth-century Greek romances which have neither Hellenistic nor Western models represent the belated trace of their passage through Byzantium from the Islamic world to the West some two hundred years earlier.[34] Certainly there is story material which the Byzantines took over from their Eastern neighbours (see p. 31 below); and this was in turn diffused to the West, but without ever gaining a place, among the Byzantines, in self-conscious literature. The diffusion of story-motifs is so widespread at all periods, and so difficult to trace conclusively, that it cannot reliably be used to identify the affinities of a given literary tradition.[35] The most that can be said for the moment is that cultural interaction between Byzantium and the West, and between the Islamic world and the West by way of Byzantium, may have played a part in the formation of the romance traditions of both halves of Christendom, but the precise nature and extent of this interaction cannot for the moment be determined.

2

THE LITERARY TRADITION

MIMESIS AND RHETORIC

The literature that will be of direct concern to us in this book represents only a small part of the corpus of Byzantine writing. Some 80 per cent of that corpus is reckoned to consist of theological works, and even of the remainder, the size of Beck's history of *Volksliteratur* (1971) and of the sections of Hunger's history of *Profane Literatur* (1978) in the authoritative Byzantinische Handbuch series, devoted to literature of entertainment, makes it clear that such literature represents no more than a tiny proportion of the whole. This chapter attempts to sketch in something of the context for the revival of literary fiction in the romances of the Komnenian period, in terms of generalizations about Byzantine literature as a whole, and of the theory and practice of rhetoric as these had developed by the twelfth century.

Byzantine literature in general has had no modern apologists, although particular areas have found qualified approbation. It seems to have had few overt *Byzantine* apologists either; a fact which at first sight seems more surprising, but merely stems from the special relationship which all Byzantine writers asserted in one way or another with the tradition of antiquity. It has even been suggested that Byzantine writers did not read the work of their immediate predecessors, but 'rather stood in a constant relation to their distant models'.[1] This is almost certainly untrue, at least for the romance, but one has the impression that the course of Byzantine literature more generally might have been little different if it had been. 'Timeless' it certainly appears; and the near-impossibility of dating unattributed texts which make no clear allusions to their period is proof that the obsessive antiquarianism of Byzantine rhetoric and literature is not something that one can dismiss as an annoying quirk, but is central to the literary concepts of the Byzantines.

If it is possible to generalize about the nature of literature in Byzantine civilization, it has usually been found easier to do so negatively: innovation was not highly prized, nor was the description or evocation of the visible world.[2] These negative characteristics could presumably be restated in positive terms, although the resulting formulation is likely to be cast in equally anachronistic language. The 'timelessness' that so offends the modern philologist could be redefined as an unparalleled success in the 'regaining' or 'suppression' of time that Marcel Proust and Claude Lévi-Strauss respectively have seen, in the twentieth century, as a fundamental instinct motivating artistic endeavour; and the non-referentiality of much Byzantine literature has been imaginatively restated by Hans-Georg Beck in terms of an exploration of the metonymic possibilities of language to produce a vast logically constructed whole which itself will be a metaphor for existence, or *analogia entis*, a restatement that presents uncanny points of resemblance with at least one recent theory of the modern novel.[3]

Byzantine literature was no more intended to be representational than was Byzantine painting. The characterization of Byzantine art by the poet W. B. Yeats, as a calculated turning-away from the 'blood and mire' of the contingent world towards the 'artifice of eternity', although based on remarkably little factual knowledge, has a striking validity for Byzantine literature too. This is not to deny any referential function to such writing; but references to the real world are characteristically (and annoyingly, to modern sensibilities) indirect.[4]

The techniques of literary expression by which Byzantine authors sought to achieve these ends are inseparable from the prescriptive legacy of late Hellenistic rhetoric. Originally the art of extempore speaking in public debate, rhetoric under the Roman empire came to be analysed and its techniques taught by sophists as the art of formal expression. With the role of public debate severely curtailed in both politics and the judicial process, the art of 'speech' which the sophists taught became primarily the art of written composition; and their cultivation of the already antiquated Attic language, which would have been barely comprehensible outside academic circles, drove a further wedge between public speaking as a practical art and the cultivation of literary style. Rhetoric for the sophists of the later empire and throughout the Byzantine period was of the type 'which emphasizes the role of the speaker and the process of learning to speak or to write primarily by imitation of models'.[5] Its attempts to analyse the written discourse of its chosen models into prescriptive terms, which then served as the basis for all education above the level of basic literacy, helped to fashion a literary movement in which the imitation of *words*, not the Aristotelian 'imitation of things', became paramount.

Modern judgements on the rhetorical prescriptions of the 'second sophistic' (roughly from the first to the fourth century AD) and of Byzantium are no more favourable than on their end products. The extreme position was taken up by Romilly Jenkins, who described the influence of rhetoric in the school curriculum as 'disastrous', and even attributed the reputation which the Byzantines acquired in the West, for trickery and double-dealing, to the practice of composing speeches for and against a given argument (*anaskeue* and *kataskeue*) in the classroom.[6] Several generations of writers and literary critics in the West today have been brought up on the assumption which Jenkins took for granted, namely that 'rhetoric' is equivalent to all that is false and artificial in a literature which at its best imitates 'reality'; but the analytical study of rhetoric, in the sense of the formal properties of discourse, has been revived in our century in ways that are sometimes reminiscent of Hellenistic and Byzantine scholarship, notably by the Russian formalists and subsequently by Paul de Man.

The area of the rhetorical curriculum in Byzantium which most concerns us here is the cycle of composition exercises known as *progymnasmata*. It was by means of these 'preliminary exercises' that, ever since the first century, the rudimentary arts of composition had been taught in schools.[7] The influence of this formal training is immense throughout Byzantine literature: everyone who learnt to read and write, alongside the grammar and syntax of the ancient language which was the sole medium for written expression, practised elementary composition in the form of these exercises. The cycle of (usually) fourteen different kinds of composition goes back to Theon in the first century AD, but the most influential textbook for the *progymnasmata* in Byzantium was that of the fifth-century rhetorician Aphthonios.[8] Aphthonios' prescriptions for each kind of exercise follow almost word for word those of Theon's influential successor in the second century Hermogenes; but the great advantage of Aphthonios for Byzantine schoolmen was that for each of the exercises described he appended an example which could be used as a model for imitation.

Not all the *progymnasmata* are equally important for our purposes, and it should suffice to single out those exercises which play an obvious role in the revival of the romance in the twelfth century. These are narrative (*diegema*), the character study (*ethopoeia*), and description (*ekphrasis*).[9]

The *progymnasmata* of Hermogenes were clearly conceived as part of a training in oratory, although from Aphthonios onwards this function seems to have been largely forgotten, so that the forms of discourse which Hermogenes thought indispensable to the orator in the course of time came to be regarded as the forms of discourse required for *literary* composition. Under narrative Hermogenes lists four types – mythical, fictional (*plasmatikon*), historical, and civil (*politikon*) – and goes on to exclude all but the last. But already by the time of Aphthonios the 'exposition of the facts in the case', an important part of political and judicial oratory, had been implicitly extended to any narration of past events resulting in a particular present situation. It is instructive that Aphthonios' example of narrative retains the form but breaks out of the context of courtroom oratory: he gives us the story of Adonis, offered as the explanation of why roses are red and have thorns.[10] Not surprisingly, later Byzantine exercises in narrative pick up the mythological theme and even playful tone of Aphthonios' example, so that *diegema* in the Middle Ages comes to mean primarily a mythological or fictional narrative. A comparable confusion in the West, where the *pro-gymnasmata* of Hermogenes were known, but not those of Aphthonios, seems to have given rise there too to the application of prescriptions originally intended for forensic oratory to narrative art.[11]

One of the most important and seemingly influential developments of these exercises in the twelfth century is the incomplete but florid and inventive series of *progymnasmata* by Nikephoros Basilakes.[12] The degree of interdependence between fictional narrative, when it reappears in Byzantium in the twelfth and again in the fourteenth century, and the rhetorical exercise of narrative (*diegema*) can be seen in the form of title used by Basilakes for his narrative exercises: Τὰ κατά ... followed by a proper name (the affairs of so-and-so).[13] The same form is also used in the three contemporary verse romances, as it had been almost a millennium earlier by Achilles Tatios. And in the fourteenth and fifteenth centuries almost all the fictional texts contain in their titles the word διήγησις (tale), which according to Hermogenes is distinguished from *diegema* only by scale and complexity.[14]

The origin of the character study (*ethopoeia*) in ancient oratory is the device, first practised by Lysias in the fifth century BC, of matching the style of an oration to the character of the litigant on whose behalf he addressed the court. In Theophrastos' *Characters* the description of character-types becomes a literary sub-genre, and Lysias' practice is now loosely linked to Aristotle's theory of *decorum*, in that a style of language is used to approximate to the character of the person described.[15] The character study is defined by Hermogenes as the 'imitation of the *style*' of the person who is supposed to be speaking, and an essential feature which distances it from Theophrastos' *Characters* and links it to its origin in forensic oratory is that it takes the form of the imaginary *speech* of the character, either to himself or to a silent audience, in a situation which is briefly outlined in the title of the exercise. Hermogenes even invokes the doctrine of τὸ πρέπον (*decorum*) to urge that one should always use the personal idiom that is fitting for the speaker and his situation. A young man has one way of speaking, he goes on, an old man another.[16] To these prescriptions Aphthonios adds brevity and clarity and the avoidance of plot or structure. But as with narrative, so with the character study, Aphthonios in his example removes the precepts of Hermogenes from the realm of oratory to place them firmly in the sphere of literature: he gives us a speech of Niobe on having lost all her children. The example which later Byzantines used as their model belongs exactly to the literary category that today we would describe as dramatic monologue in prose.[17]

What a sophisticated Byzantine of the twelfth century could do with this model is spectacularly demonstrated by the twenty-seven examples of the character study left to us by Nikephoros Basilakes.[18] All have headings in the form 'What x would say ...' in a given situation; nearly half are taken from classical mythology and the Bible respectively or in one bold instance, 'What

Hades would say on Lazarus being raised from the dead on the fourth day', from both. The last takes an episode from a life of three Syriac saints,[19] while another deals with an imaginary situation, ostensibly following the kind of model established by Nikolaos in the fourth century with his character-study on 'What a land-dweller would say on first seeing the sea' but actually a naughty allegory with close affinities to the world of the contemporary and later romance.[20]

Apart from those on Biblical themes, these are extended and highly witty pieces, which seem to have exerted a formative influence on Eustathios Makrembolites in *Hysmine and Hysminias* and share with that romance the device, traditional to these exercises, of using an unattributed first-person narration.[21] In all of them the idea of the plotless exposition of character through a speaker's own words has been taken much further; many contain almost as much of a narrative element as the exercises formally described as 'narrative', with the principal difference that these are narratives in the first person. They are also rich in the kind of wordplay that we shall also encounter in the romances, both in the learned language and in the vernacular, with an especial delight in the juxtaposition of words of similar sound for an effect that is often ironic.[22]

Two of the most daring of Basilakes' character-studies are 'What Danae would say, on being deflowered by Zeus transformed into gold', and 'What Pasiphae would say, on being made love to by the bull'.[23] The erotic subject-matter and its frankly erotic treatment are more risqué than anything we will find in the romance until *Kallimachos and Chrysorrhoe* in the fourteenth century, and their technique, which approximates closely to that of the interior monologue of the modernist novel, anticipates literary developments of the twentieth century. The verbs are chiefly in the present and perfect tenses, and the imagined words of Danae take us from the rueful apostrophe to her father on the first appearance of the shower of gold in the locked room, by way of mingled astonishment, to growing pleasure as the apparition of riches turns into the apparition of an immortal lover. As the piece reaches (literally) its climax, she reflects on Zeus' previous incarnations for carnal expeditions and exults that the king of gods and men loves her and is therefore in her power. Rapturously convinced that her fate will be different from that of all his other mortal conquests, she declares in a series of short phrases in quickening tempo that she loves him and gives herself to him wholeheartedly.

Eros makes another appearance, this time in person, in the bizarre scenario, a ludicrous extension of Aphthonios' tale of Adonis as an example of narrative, 'What Eros would say to a woodcutter on the point of cutting down Myrrha [metamorphosed into a tree] while she was pregnant with Adonis'.[24] Here Eros describes himself, with wings, bow and arrows, in terms common to the ancient and the twelfth-century romances, and boasts of his power over gods and mortals alike. Finally the character-study of the gardener who transplanted a cypress into his garden in hopes of its fruit and was disappointed, is fairly evidently an 'allegory of love' such as we find in the West in the *Roman de la Rose* (and to an extent in modern Greek folk-song) but is more limited in the medieval Greek romance.[25] The gardener evokes the beauties of the garden he tends in terms borrowed from the exercise of the *ekphrasis* (omitted in Basilakes' series), and takes a particular delight in the fruit of his apple trees. The apple tree he compares, as writers of Byzantine *ekphraseis* are wont to do, to a picture, but this is a picture in which Ἔρωτες (Cupids) peep between the branches, plucking the apples and disporting themselves. The apple, he says, is the more beautiful for being plucked by Cupids. The cypress which he transplants, and which is grammatically feminine, is beautifully slender and sways most gracefully in the breeze. But for all his hard work in carrying water to nurture it, it ungratefully fails to produce a single edible fruit. The gardener now goes about his tasks of watering the vegetable patch and other parts of the garden, but lets it be known that he is becoming tired of waiting![26]

The last of the *progymnasmata* with which we shall be concerned is the set-piece description or *ekphrasis*. According to Hermogenes, description ought to be clear and vivid: it should be possible, just by hearing the description, to conjure up 'almost' the appearance of the thing described. Many things are suitable for description: people, or things (such as a battle by sea or on land); stock situations such as war and peace; places; seasons. Description only becomes fully canonized as a separate exercise in Hermogenes' time, its functions having previously been distributed among myth, narrative, commonplace and encomium, but from now on it becomes firmly detached from these as an exercise in its own right. Aphthonios characteristically follows him, substituting animals and plants for Hermogenes' final category and echoes his prescription that the *ekphrasis* must 'imitate its object' as closely as possible. The example he gives, a description of the acropolis of Alexandria, is quite a long piece, highly metonymic in character, which begins with the generality of *acropoleis*, proceeds by way of the best-known exemplar, the acropolis of Athens, to Alexandria, the splendours of whose citadel are then enumerated in detail.[27] It is characteristic of Aphthonios that his example, while more or less consistent with his own and Hermogenes' definition – in this case, a description of a place – lends itself to imitation for a quality that is absent from the definition. Here the description, strictly of a place, is in fact primarily a description of works of art; and it is this latter aspect that comes to dominate the *ekphrasis* as a literary sub-genre in Byzantium. Indeed the *ekphrasis* seems to have become emancipated from the *progymnasmata* quite early on and is omitted, for instance, from Basilakes' series in the twelfth century. Many writers, on the other hand, who have not left rhetorical exercises, have left *ekphraseis*, and the form seems to have existed as a kind of sub-genre in prose and verse up till the seventh century and again after the tenth.[28]

Kazhdan and Constable have drawn attention to the *ekphrasis* as evidence for a Byzantine attitude that the ideal state of nature is to approximate to that of art. This attitude they find attested as early as the fourth century; and one of the few *ekphraseis* among the *progymnasmata* of the rhetorician Nikolaos, of that century, that is not devoted to a mythological personage, seems to apologize for its subject's being drawn from nature by its opening statement that 'Nature imitates the arts'. The subject of this description is a peacock.[29] It is remarkable how many Byzantine *ekphraseis* are either descriptions of works of art or describe people and things as if they were works of art. 'Nature' only begins to be mentioned in these descriptions as a shaping force in the twelfth century; but even in the romances of that century, in an obviously intended oxymoron, nature is credited with the functions of an artificer (τεχνίτης).[30] In describing an artwork the Byzantine author will follow the precepts of his models and praise it for its truth to life.[31] But as we shall see when we consider the *ekphraseis* in the romances, what is praised in these cases is most often the *artifice* by which the likeness to nature has been achieved.

REALISM AND THE INDIVIDUAL

If the legacy of Hellenistic rhetoric provides a little-changing substratum for all literature in both East and West up to and even beyond the end of the Middle Ages, undoubted innovations in the literature of the eleventh and twelfth centuries are the appearance of the author as an individual in his text, and a new kind of reference in literary texts to the contingent world, of the kind that later centuries were to dub 'realism'. Such an awareness and assertion of the self, and in parallel a new 'realistic' perception of the external world, have often been identified as central to the literary 'renaissance' of the twelfth century in the West.[32] Since then Robert Hanning has observed that 'one of the central motivating forces of the twelfth-century Renaissance was a new desire on the part of literate men and women to understand themselves as single, unique persons – what we would call *individuals*'.[33] The origin of this change he sees in the period of stability that began in the West in the eleventh century, and he then goes on to trace its effects in close analytical readings of the romances of Chrétien and his contemporaries towards the end of the twelfth century.[34]

Individuality, both in the author's relationship to his work and in the way in which human characters are depicted in that work, as well as a concomitant 'realism', have played an important part in much European literature written since the twelfth century; but one should be wary of reading the *individualism* of characters in a novel by, say, Dickens, or a 'realism' which is either representational or, in Emile Zola's term 'naturalist', into their counterparts in the twelfth century. The world of Chrétien's romances is not 'real' in either of those senses; the landscape of primeval forests peopled only by solitary knights, and of lonely castles with more than an aura of the supernatural about them, bears no more resemblance to twelfth-century France than does the political constitution of Arthur's court and the kingdom of Britain to the England (or France) of Henry II. Even when real places are introduced and an echo of real contemporary events, in *Cligès*, we are given none of the particulars by which we would recognize the terrain of an overland journey to Constantinople or even Constantinople itself.

The 'realism' of Chrétien, if that is the correct word for it, lies in his giving exterior form to an inner quest which is the real and evident subject of his romances. The quest, insofar as it is an inner and solitary one, places unprecedented weight on the concept of the individual, but it is rare for the heroes of Chrétien's romances to be presented fully as *characters* in the sense that we are used to in both ancient and modern literature. The same could be said in general terms of the four Greek romances of the twelfth century, different though they are from anything that was being written in the West at that time. At a general level, the discovery of the individual's subjective experience, as a space to be explored, animates the romances written in both East and West in the twelfth century and remains their central theme. But this 'individuality' is very different either from the 'individualism' or the literary 'characterization' of later centuries. The individual in the romances is rarely a unique 'character', in the sense that the term is used in modern fiction, perceived, that is, with all the particularity and concreteness of real people whom we would not be surprised to meet; rather, the heroes and heroines of the medieval romance represent generalizations of the self.

As we shall see more fully later, 'realism' too is likely to be something of a red herring in medieval Greek literature. Too often it has been equated with literalism, and texts have been read at face value which are full of literary warnings to the unwary, or else they have been underrated for their failure accurately to reflect the manners and customs of their time. Hardly any of the texts to be discussed in this book, any more than the romances of Chrétien, seem to have attempted that kind of verisimilitude (which is not to say that their authors were not, like Chrétien, concerned with reality). Although the undercurrent of innovation in twelfth-century Byzantine writers so ably documented by Kazhdan and Franklin does include the literary handling of the everyday and the particular, to use the term 'realism', with its connotations of nineteenth-century verisimilitude, may be to prejudge the nature of the literary experiments that were actually being made.[35]

3

THE 'PROTO-ROMANCE',
DIGENES AKRITES

PRECURSORS OF THE ROMANCE

The art of written narrative never ceased to be practised in Byzantium. We have already seen how *diegema* formed an integral part of the exercises in composition which played a basic role in the Byzantine school curriculum. Narrative skill at a more complex level is fundamental for two kinds of writing in which the Byzantines took an especial pride: historiography and hagiography. But in both of these, even though they may make abundant use of classical literary models, the techniques of story-telling are subordinated to a specific function. No emancipation of narrative discourse as an autonomous genre is possible.

The art of the historian continued to be practised throughout the Byzantine millennium with little or no sign of interaction with its fictional counterpart in the romance.[1] The same cannot, however, be said for hagiography. It has often been observed that precisely during the centuries in which the secular narrative of love and adventure was in abeyance, the saints' lives provided a narrative literature in which adventures continued to abound and the love of ordinary men and women for one another was replaced by the saint's love for God.[2] These parallels are not accidental. It is well known that early Christian apocryphal literature reflects the popularity of the romance in late antiquity, to the point of frequently appropriating its favourite themes. It seems to be by this route that some of the narrative topoi of the romance found their way into early saints' lives, where such themes as the quest of the hero, preservation of chastity against the odds, and voyages and encounters with pirates, were easily adapted to their new context.[3] At the level of rhetoric there is a further link between the late antique romances and the early saints' lives, in that the latter came to be based on the same rhetorical models as their secular predecessors had been: the hero or heroine of the saint's life, no less than the hero *and* heroine of the romance, is depicted according to the prescriptions for formal narratives of praise (the *basilikos logos*) of rhetorical handbooks.[4]

It is again probably not an accidental connection that after the burst of metaphrastic activity in the early eleventh century, in which older hagiography was recast into the 'high' style that also came to be used in the twelfth century for the romance, there is a falling-off in the production of original saints' lives.[5] Whether the decline of the saints' lives in the eleventh century is to be attributed to the same cause as the rise of an experimental secular literature in the twelfth, or whether the one is directly in some way the cause of the other, would be difficult to determine. It may be noted that one of the few saints' lives to be produced in the twelfth century was the work of Theodore Prodromos, who was also most probably the author of the first medieval Greek romance.[6] It is impossible not to see the revival of the romance in the twelfth century in terms of an increasing secularization and the search for a new identity among Byzantine literati in the generations that came after the defeat at Manzikert.

Throughout the middle Byzantine centuries, however, there does seem to have existed an undercurrent of fictional narrative, which gains in momentum towards the end of the period but never quite establishes itself as a self-conscious literary genre. It is presumably for this reason that the texts of this tradition are treated by Beck under the heading of *Volksliteratur*, although there is nothing markedly popular about either their language or their immediate sources. Under this heading can be grouped successive recensions of fables attributed to Aesop, of the Alexander 'romance' and the Greek bestiary *Physiologos*, which goes back to at least the fourth century. More innovative are the translations of oriental story material: the religious fable *Barlaam and Ioasaph* may have been translated from Syriac by John of Damascus in the eighth century; the Arabic *Kalilah va Dimnah*, like *Barlaam* originally a Sanskrit work, becomes in Greek *Stephanites and Ichnelates* at the end of the eleventh century; and the *Syntipas* group of tales, which has a partly Hellenistic background, was translated at about the same time from a Syriac version of an Arabic original.[7]

In the case of the Aesopian material, the Alexander story and the *Physiologos*, what we have is merely the elaboration, within a fixed framework, of a legacy from antiquity of relatively low prestige, but still the province exclusively of the educated; while in the translated material the structures are largely new, but a clear didactic function remains. It is not until the fourteenth and fifteenth centuries that some of this narrative tradition takes on a relatively 'popular' form and at the same time transcends the bounds of moral didacticism to take its place in an emergent fictional literature.[8] The popular Alexander story seems to have played a part, as we shall see, in the shaping of *Digenes Akrites*, and through that text its influence has been carried over into the later *Tale of Achilles*. Otherwise the contribution of these tales to the romance is confined to the inclusion of magical incidents in the stories of Prodromos' romance and in several of the later vernacular romances, and to the device of the narrative frame in the fourteenth-century *Libistros and Rhodamne*.

However, by far the most important precursor of the fully fledged revival

31

of the romance genre in the twelfth century is the 'epic' or 'proto-romance' of *Digenes Akrites*, to which we now turn our attention.

DIGENES: STORY AND VERSIONS

The space of little over a century saw the appearance in widely separated parts of Europe and the Middle East of a series of heroic narratives which have remarkably similar characteristics. In Western Europe the *Chanson de Roland*, the *Nibelungenlied* and the *Poema del Mio Cid* all deal with conflict between Christians and infidels at a historical period more or less remote from the composition of the texts that have come down to us, in or close to the twelfth century. All three are among the earliest examples of sustained narrative in the emerging vernacular languages of Europe; all three inaugurate an effectively new genre without literary precedent in the Middle Ages; all three narrate the exploits of a number of heroic male characters of whom one – Roland, Siegfried, Rodrigo – is shown as pre-eminent; and all are constructed according to the principle of 'bipartite structure', in which the action of the first half is only loosely connected to that of the second, a structural principle which seems first to have been adopted in *Beowulf* and carries over into the later romances in the West. To these three must be added the 'epic' or 'proto-romance' of Eastern Christendom, *Digenes Akrites*.

The setting is the frontier between the Christian empire of Byzantium, or 'Romania' as it is called in the text, and the Islamic world of eastern Anatolia and Mesopotamia. The historical world of the poem is a composite of conditions that existed at different periods between the ninth century and the early eleventh; the text was probably composed within a few years of 1100. Although there is some doubt about the language of the original poem, whether the 'middle' register or the vernacular, we can be certain that a vernacular *version* was already circulating by the mid-twelfth century and left its mark on the literary developments of the time. This text is the oldest piece of writing of any length to be written in a form of modern Greek, and so stands at the head of the literary tradition in the modern language, just as the Western exemplars do in their respective traditions. There is no precedent in Byzantine literature for the heroic genre,[9] although, as we shall see, *Digenes* does invoke literary precedents from late antiquity. The text narrates the deeds and physical prowess of a number of male characters, among whom the eponymous hero excels to an almost supernatural degree. Finally, the structure of the narrative falls clearly into two parts, each of which would form a coherent whole by itself: the first part tells the story of Digenes' parents and the birth of the hero; the second tells of the hero's life, from childhood to his early death.[10]

It should be mentioned that these twelfth-century Christian epics have their Muslim counterparts, also written down surprisingly long after the events they describe. The Arabic *Delhemma* and *Sayyid Battal* date from the twelfth century, the Turkish *Danishmendname* from the fourteenth (and presumably derives from Arabic sources). All three Muslim epics deal with frontier strife at the same historical period and in the same geographical areas as *Digenes*, and the name of Akrites can be discerned, although in a minor role, in all three.[11] There seems to be no possibility that these widely separated literary developments are directly linked.[12] The awareness of Western literature that is evident to some degree in all the Greek romances from *Hysmine and Hysminias* onwards is entirely absent from *Digenes*. There is equally little likelihood, and no evidence, that the Greek poem was known in the West in the twelfth century.[13]

Although *Digenes* is the only Greek vernacular poem of the Middle Ages to have been translated into English, the text remains scarcely known to English-speaking medievalists, to say nothing of the general reader, so it is worth providing a fairly full summary here.[14]

There was once a Syrian emir, who made a spectacular raid into Byzantine Anatolia, capturing towns, killing the men and taking the women prisoner. Among the prisoners is the (unnamed) daughter of a general. The girl's father had been exiled for some misdemeanour, so the distraught mother writes to her sons begging them to rescue their sister from dishonour, on pain of their mother's curse. The brothers ride up to the Arab's encampment, and the youngest challenges the emir to a single combat which is to determine his prisoner's fate.

A ferocious duel ensues; the emir gracefully concedes his opponent's heroic qualities and promises to return his captive to her brothers. However, they are at first deceived – and the details of this brief episode are indicative of the brutality of the world described in the poem. Directed to where they can find their sister, the brothers come upon the jumbled and mutilated remains of a large number of Christian girls, killed, their guide complacently tells them, 'because they would not do what we told them'.[15] Only after this horrific interlude does the emir admit to the brothers that he has kept their sister safe in his tent, has respected her chastity, and now wishes for nothing better than to marry her and convert to Christianity along with all his followers. The Arabs cross over into Byzantine territory and are received with rejoicing. A son is born to the couple, and will be named Basil Digenes Akrites – Digenes, fancifully rendered into English as 'Twyborn' or 'Twin-blooded', because he is born of two races;[16] Akrites (Borderer) because he will be pre-eminent among the aristocracy of the border regions (ἄκρα).

But trouble arises in a form which is exactly symmetrical to the main events told so far: it is now the turn of the emir's mother to write a letter to her son and threaten the powerful sanction of a mother's curse unless he should return, with his new bride, to Syria. The emir decides to pay a visit to his home, and shares his nostalgic longings with his wife, who readily agrees to accompany him. But the girl's brothers, forewarned by a dream, once again intervene to prevent her being taken outside 'Romania', and the emir goes alone after a touching farewell to his bride. His journey is hazardous, but he overcomes all obstacles, to reach Syria safely. After some lengthy attempts at persuasion on both sides (in which, incidentally, the anonymous author reveals a surprising degree of knowledge about Islamic beliefs and customs) the emir persuades his mother and all her fellow citizens to return with him and be baptized as Christians. The story of Digenes' parents (itself a miniature example of bipartite structure) now ends, about a third of the way through the poem, with repeated general rejoicing.

The story of Digenes himself begins with an invocation to love. The work of rival epic poets, among whom only Homer is named, is then dismissed as unworthy to be compared to the deeds of the incomparable hero; and the story so far is retold in a brief summary. The young Digenes is a precocious youth, and after a scant résumé of his early childhood we meet him again at the age of 12, when he successfully persuades his father and uncle (the two whose single combat early in the story had led to his father's conversion and his own birth) to take him on his first hunting-expedition. Having successfully proved his incredible physical strength in the face of bears and lions, Digenes is praised by his heroic mentors in terms that clearly imply a rite of passage into manhood. The hero's next exploit is to fall in love and to abduct for himself a bride. It is interesting, in passing, that sexual relationships in the world of the poem are invariably initiated in this way, a narrative feature which we shall find carried over into the twelfth-century romances. The girl (who is never named) is singing at her window as Digenes rides past. Love is at first sight and mutual, but she warns him that her father, like the father of Digenes' mother before him, is a general, and this one punishes all suitors with death. Digenes continues on his way, returning at night to abduct his bride-to-be. After massacring an army sent out in pursuit, but judiciously avoiding harming any of his future in-laws, he takes the girl to his home and they are married with the enforced consent of the general.

In an abrupt transition we learn that the hero has by now subdued the irregulars or bandits who roam the frontier areas and that his fame has even reached the emperor. The latter, named as Basil (presumably Basil II, who died in 1025), is campaigning in the vicinity and summons the young prodigy, promising to reward his prowess. But our hero replies with haughty courtesy that the emperor's retinue includes inexperienced soldiers, who might be tempted to 'say what they ought not', in which case he, Digenes, could hardly be answerable for himself. So, in a startling inversion of protocol, the emperor is summoned into the presence of the hero, who has pitched camp by the Euphrates and has a chance to display his spectacular powers of strength and courage in front of his overlord. Digenes, however, refuses any favours from the emperor, even the title of acknowledged ruler of the borders, on the grounds that all he wants is to live by himself with only his wife and retainers. The episode, which is only found in one of the poem's two earliest versions, concludes with the hero admonishing the emperor on how to use his power wisely.

The central part of the hero's story is now narrated in the first person, by way of a confession of the sin of adultery. This sin the otherwise uxorious Digenes committed twice: once with an unnamed Arab girl who had been deserted by her lover, and of whom he had taken advantage before compelling the unfaithful lover to marry her; and again with the warrior maiden Maximou, whom he had defeated in battle and who then had offered herself to him. The attempt (although only in one version of the text) by Digenes to expiate this sin by the further sin of murder provides a striking reminder of the stark moral world of the poem that we encountered earlier. Framed between these acts of adultery in Digenes' first-person narration is a series of adventures at a lonely oasis, in which the hero successfully protects his wife, saving her from capture by, in turn, wild beasts, supernatural beings and the irregulars or bandits of the frontier.

There is little now left for the hero to accomplish. By the banks of the Euphrates he builds a sumptuous palace and garden for himself and his wife and laments the death first of his father and then of his mother. While still young (one version specifies at the age of 33), he catches a chill which proves fatal. In a lengthy deathbed scene he recapitulates his exploits to his wife and retainers. His wife's prayer not to see the hero die but to die first herself is answered, and the two are laid to rest amid general mourning in a fine tomb by the Euphrates.

One of the many problems which have excited the attention of scholars from a variety of disciplines since the rediscovery of this poem in 1869 has been the existence of several manuscript versions, all of which tell substantially the same story, but with significant divergences in length, style and language. Matters have been further complicated by the existence of modern oral folksongs which tell of similar exploits set against a vaguely Byzantine and Middle Eastern background, and sometimes give their hero the name Akrites, Akritas or Digenes, and of prose reworkings of part of the story in Russian, which are thought to go back to the twelfth century. Work in the last two decades has shown that of the six extant Greek manuscripts only two can be regarded as direct witnesses to the original form of the poem.[17] The two oldest manuscript versions are known as E and G.[18] They differ so greatly in structure, style and language that each has to be discussed separately under these headings, before we can proceed to some cautious suggestions about the nature, and particularly the sources, of the lost original text of the early twelfth century.[19]

Version E

At 1,867 lines this is much the shortest surviving version of the story. The text, contained in a single manuscript of the fifteenth century, along with the fourteenth-century romance *Libistros and Rhodamne*, is notoriously corrupt, but has recently been shown to contain a number of readings which must go back to the early twelfth century;[20] and there is good evidence that this version, or one very like it, was already well known in Constantinople by the second half of the same century.[21]

As regards the structure of the story as told by E, the early pages of the manuscript have been lost and the story is taken up in the middle of the duel between the emir and the girl's brother. Narrative detail and particularly description are kept to a minimum, although we still find, in abbreviated form, the *ekphraseis* of Digenes' palace and garden. Minor episodes of the story, as summarized above, are omitted: Digenes' confrontation with the emperor, his first act of adultery and the murder of the warrior maiden Maximou that compounds his second sin; and the text ends with the simultaneous deaths of hero and heroine. One episode has been added: inserted before the preamble to the hero's youthful exploits and preceded by a few lines about his early childhood is an episode which begins:

'Εδὰ ἂς σᾶς ἀφηγήσωμαι περὶ τὰς ἀμωρίας του.[22]

Now I shall tell you about his youthful deeds/childhood pranks.

The lines which follow tell how the young Digenes heard about the exploits of the irregulars or bandits, the ἀπελάται (with whom he will later cross swords in order to defend his wife from them) and wanted to join them. He lay in wait for their water-carrier and persuaded him to take him to the bandits' lair. To be an *apelates* in this episode you had to be good at abducting other people's womenfolk and at striking with the mace. The first skill is not tested, but at the second Digenes of course excels, and apparently proves himself worthy to join the band, although the episode ends inconclusively.[23]

The inclusion of this episode is by far the most serious narrative inconsistency in the E version. Coming before the hero's first hunt at the age of 12, it marks an improbably early beginning to even this hero's precocious career, and it violates the logic of the narrative in that it comes *before* the rhetorical set-piece introducing the hero's youthful exploits. More conclusively, as has often been pointed out, it introduces the *apelatai* in a role which conflicts with the one that these same irregulars, named as Philopappous, Kinnamos and Ioannakes, will play later on in the story; and, in the E version as in the G, when Digenes later confronts them as his enemies there is no reference to his ever having met them before, let alone having once been one of their number. The interpolation can be explained if we assume that in this case, at least, G provides the better witness. In G, the preamble to the hero's early deeds includes, after

the airy dismissal of Homer common to both versions, the following allusion
to rival epic narratives of the writer's own time:

Φιλοπαππου̃ του̃ γέροντος, Κιννάμου καὶ ᾿Ιωαννάκη
οὐδ᾿ ὅλως ἔστιν ἄξιον τὰ αὐτῶν καταλέγειν,
οὗτοι γὰρ ἐκαυχήσαντο μηδὲν πεποιηκότες·[24]

Of old man Philopappous, of Kinnamos and Ioannakis
nothing that they did is worthy to be set down/recorded in song;
for these were boasters who achieved nothing at all.

Inspired by this hint, the scribe or redactor of the E version has decided to
supply, at just this point, an example of one of these 'rival' heroic tales, in
which Digenes appears in a relation to Philopappous and his cronies quite
different from that found elsewhere in our poem. The most interesting aspect
of the interpolation is that it shows that other heroic narratives of the eastern
frontier were still current in the twelfth century, presumably in oral form.

The mention of oral narratives provides a good starting-point for
discussion of the style of E. Its use of a high density of formulae, the almost
total absence of enjambment, and a 'paratactic' style (approximately half of
the poem's lines begin with the word 'and'), have repeatedly raised the
suspicion that oral processes, whether of composition or of transmission,
may have been at work to produce this version.[25] The most recent editor of
the text has shown satisfactorily that the corruptions of the manuscript are
not due to oral transmission, nor was the original text a transcription from
oral performance.[26] What we have in the E version is an early example, in
Greek, of the kind of text that Franz Bäuml has analysed in the medieval
German tradition and that we shall be encountering again in the vernacular
romances of the fourteenth and fifteenth centuries: a written text in which
techniques derived from oral poetry are used quite consciously but fulfil an
entirely different function from that which they served in oral poetry. In the
E version of *Digenes*, as in the *Nibelungenlied*, that function is, as Bäuml has
put it, no longer 'mechanical' but 'referential': 'the written formulaic text
inescapably refers the receiver to the oral-formulaic tradition' as the source
from which it derives not just the things it says (its story) but also its
authority for saying them.[27]

The verseform of both early versions is the fifteen-syllable accentual metre
known as 'political verse', whose rise to dominance will be described in
Chapter 6. The text as we possess it is metrically corrupt, but the basis of its
underlying metrical form can be clearly discerned in the verse form of later
vernacular literature and of folk poetry: with a strongly marked caesura, little
or no enjambment and the regular use of elision or synizesis to avoid hiatus
between adjacent vowel-sounds. The present state of the text, formerly
ascribed to scribal rendering of oral performance, has more recently been

attributed to the instability of the written vernacular at this period or to the hypothesis that the manuscript derives from a version in the dialect of Pontos.[28] To complicate matters further, the manuscript as we have it appears to have been copied in Crete in the fifteenth century, and intrusions from the linguistic idiom of the scribe have also been identified in the text.[29]

The language, finally, of the E version as we have it is extremely difficult to categorize, and the problem is compounded by the textual corruption evident in its metrical state. The basis is clearly the vernacular, but mixed to a disconcerting degree with elements of the 'middle' language register of the time. Although there may be a temptation to take the rough-hewn eccentricities of this vernacular *Digenes* as representative of the original poem, some allowance must certainly be made for the vagaries of manuscript transmission before the version we possess was copied in the fifteenth century.

Version G

The manuscript containing the G version, which is just over twice the length of E, is the oldest surviving witness to the start of the story; unlike E, this version is divided into eight books (of very variable length); and its account of events is consistently fuller, with extended rhetorical speeches by the characters (especially in the first part). As already mentioned, it includes three episodes absent entirely from E: the meeting with the emperor, Digenes' first adultery, and the murder of Maximou. The first of these is as likely to be an interpolation in G as an omission from E – either way, one may suspect, the result of a conscious decision dictated by political sensitivities. In G, the episode lengthens considerably the already disproportionately long fourth book and is introduced by a transition which is noticeably clumsy:

Πολλοὶ δὲ τῶν ἀπελατῶν τοῦτο ἀναμαθόντες,
συμβούλιον ἐποίησαν τήν κόρην ἀφαρπάσαι·
καὶ πάντας συναπέκτεινε καθυποτάσσων τούτους,
ὅπως τε κατεπτόησε πᾶσαν τήν Βαβυλῶνα,
Ταρσὸν ὁμοῦ καὶ τὸν Βαγδᾶ, τοὺς Μαυροχιονίτας,
καὶ ἄλλα μέρη ἱκανὰ τῶν δεινῶν Αἰθιόπων.
Ταῦτα τὰ κατορθώματα ὁ βασιλεὺς ἀκούσας ...[30]

Many of the irregulars when they learned of this
(*sc.* Digenes' marriage and retirement to live alone with his wife)
took counsel how to steal the girl;
and all of them he massacred, subduing them
as he also became the scourge of all Babylon,
together with Tarsos and Baghdad, the Blacksnowmen
and other well-defended places of the dread Ethiopians.
These achievements the emperor when he heard ...

The conflict with the irregulars over the girl, mentioned here, in fact comes much later as the subject of Book VI, and Digenes' forays further afield are briefly summarized again as a prelude to his settling down and building a palace by the Euphrates in Book VII.[31] As far as the logic of the narrative is concerned, although the meeting with the emperor provides an appropriate climax to the hero's younger deeds, the movement from the first hunt to the abduction of his bride and his marriage already serves that object, and there would have been a certain economy in moving directly from the celebration of the hero's marriage to his confession of subsequent adultery with which Book v begins.[32]

The other two episodes present in G but omitted from E have a more convincing function in the narrative structure. While E moves directly from the celebration of the hero's marriage to the account of his struggles to protect his wife at a lonely oasis (all of this narrated, without explanation, in the first person), G introduces the theme of adultery in the pious opening lines of Book v and then motivates the change into the first person by the hero's urge to confess his sin to a chance acquaintance.[33] The shift into the first person at this point in the narrative has been, surely rightly, identified as imitation of the *Odyssey*.[34] If so, then the naturalistic device whereby this shift is motivated must have played an important part in the structure of the original poem. At the level of narrative structure, there is a carefully achieved symmetry within the first-person narration as presented by the fifth and sixth books of G: two instances of adultery, the second more serious than the first, frame a series of exploits in which the hero undergoes a series of adventures whose common element is, by contrast, the protection of his wife. The episode of the murder of Maximou, which chivalrous editors have been reluctant to admit into the original composition, in this light forms a fitting climax to the hero's confession of his sins:

καβαλλικεύω παρευθύς, δῆθεν εἰς τὸ κυνῆγιν,
καὶ ταύτην δὲ καταλαβὼν ἀνηλεῶς ἀνεῖλον,
μοιχείαν, φόνον τότε γὰρ ἐκτελέσας ἀθλίως.[35]

I mounted at once, as though for hunting,
and catching up with her I pitilessly obliterated her,
(upon) adultery, murder then committing wretchedly.

The only significant omission in G is the episode of Digenes' youthful visit to the irregulars, the *apelatai*, which as I have already argued has been interpolated into the E version. Since Mavrogordato's authoritative edition of the G manuscript it has been assumed that this episode, despite its inconsistencies with the rest of the story, none the less had a place in the original poem. The principal reason for this is its inclusion in the manuscripts deriving from the fifteenth-century compilation, although in a different position in the story from that in which it is found in E. It has been ingeniously demonstrated by Suzanne MacAlister that the compiler had no more reliable authority for the inclusion of this episode than its presence in E. Being conscientious, however, he noted the inconsistency in its position before the proem to Digenes' youthful exploits in E and took advantage of a small lacuna in G to insert it later, between the first hunt and the hero's wooing of his bride. This explanation is substantially correct, and removes the last remaining suspicions that the fifteenth-century compiler may have known something about the original poem that we do not.[36]

However, there is no lacuna in G at this point. A re-examination of the construction of the fourth book of G provides an important instance of the careful formal structure which characterizes this version.[37] Book IV, it will be remembered, begins with an invocation to Love, followed by a contrast between the present poem and previous epics, and a résumé of the story so far.[38] The bulk of the book then divides into three substantial episodes: Digenes' first hunt at the age of 12 and successful passage from childhood to manhood;[39] his first meeting with the girl, whom he proceeds to abduct and marry;[40] and his meeting with the emperor, apparently after further adventures have spread his fame abroad.[41] The most important of these three, indicated by its relative length and by the way it is prepared for in the rhetorical preamble to the whole book, is the abduction. The subsequent meeting between Digenes and the emperor may not originally have been part of this close-knit narrative structure, but the hunt and the abduction belong together, with no room, in terms of the coherence of the discourse, for a break between them.

The style at the end of the episode of the hunt is far from realistic. Digenes' manhood once proved, the hero is suddenly described in terms of physical beauty that immediately remind one of the Hellenistic and later twelfth-century romances. On the site of his murderous tussles with bears and lions he is bathed by his father and uncle in a cool spring, then dressed in luxurious, bejewelled clothes, and changes his previous mount for a white horse with plaited mane and golden bells. As the youth prepares to ride home, anxious to display his newfound manhood to his mother, the imagery subtly but unmistakably points to a newly acquired sexuality:

�Ητον ὁ ἵππος τολμηρὸς καὶ θρασὺς εἰς τὸ παίζειν,
τὸ δὲ παιδίον εὔθιον εἰς τὸ καβαλλικεύειν·
πᾶς ὁ βλέπων ἐθαύμαζε τὸν ἄγουρον ἐκεῖνον,
πῶς μὲν ὁ ἵππος ἔπαιζε κατὰ γνώμην τοῦ νέου,
πῶς δὲ αὐτὸς ἐκάθητο ὥσπερ μῆλον εἰς δένδρον.
Καὶ ὥρμησαν τοῦ ἀπελθεῖν εἰς τὸν ἴδιον οἶκον·
οἱ μὲν ἄγουροι ἔμπροσθεν κατὰ τάξιν ὑπάγουν,
ἀπ' αὐτοῦ δὲ ὁ θεῖος του καὶ ὁ πατὴρ ὀπίσω,
καὶ μέσον ὁ νεώτερος, ὡς ἥλιος ἀστράπτων,

κοντάριν ἐμαλάκιζε μετὰ τὴν δεξιάν του
πρασινοαραβίτικον μετὰ χρυσοῦ διβέλλου.
Ὡραῖος ἦν εἰς ὅρασιν, τερπνὸς εἰς συντυχίαν,
μόσχος εἰς τὸ ἀνάβλεμμα ὅλος μεμυρισμένος.⁴²

The horse was headstrong and playfully bucked,
the boy was firmly mounted in the saddle;
every onlooker wondered at that young man,
the way the horse played obediently to the wishes of the youth
the way he sat like an apple on a tree.
And they launched out upon the homeward journey,
the retainers drawn up in front,
his uncle and his father behind,
and in the middle the young hero resplendent as the sun,
flexing a lance in his right hand
(that was) green of Araby with a pennon of gold.
Handsome he was to behold, delightful in speech,
in his look all fragrant with musk.

It is not his mother that the narrative is preparing for the hero to meet next.
The text continues, after the supposed lacuna:

Οἶκος ὑπῆρχε καθ' ὁδὸν στρατηγοῦ τοῦ μεγάλου ...⁴³

The house lay upon his way where the great general lived ...

and our hero launches into a love-song before he has even clapped eyes on
the girl, who is to be his next quarry. However abrupt the transition from a
naturalistic point of view, the logic of the text requires Digenes to begin his
wooing on the return journey from the hunt that has proved his manhood.
Indeed, a careful reading of the E version at this point, which does have a
lacuna (between E 791 and 792), reveals that by the time the hero has
returned home from hunting he has already met and fallen in love with his
bride-to-be.⁴⁴ The hunting of wild beasts is the necessary preliminary to the
no less predatory activity (in this poem) of winning a bride.

The narrative structure of the G version can now be summarized like this.
Books I–III contain the first part of the bipartite narrative common to both
versions, and the same bipartite structure is clearly duplicated within this first
part. These books contain the story of Digenes' parents, and the two
attempts to take his mother to Syria, both frustrated by the girl's brothers,
with a crucial role being played by the power of a mother's curse in both
episodes. The second and longer part of the bipartite narrative concerns
Digenes himself and is further divided into three unities. The first of these,
which takes up Book IV, relates the hero's early adventures. The second, in
Books V and VI, is in the form of a confession by Digenes himself of sins

committed, and of various contrasting exploits on behalf of his wife. The third, occupying Books VII and VIII, sees the hero settled in splendid and for the first time populous surroundings, and rounds off the story with the successive deaths of his kin and himself.

The style of the G version is consistently more elaborate than that of E, with full rein given to the rhetorical set-pieces common in eleventh- and twelfth-century Byzantine texts in the 'middle' and 'high' registers; a preference for long, complex periods; and a tendency, irritating to modern sensibilities, to interpose moral asides as apparently authorial comment on the action. The triteness of these, as well as of a twenty-nine-line prologue which is entirely out of character with the rest of the text, encourage one to believe that the asides, like the prologue, are the work of a monastic copyist, but it is as well to admit that the evidence for this is purely subjective.

The metre is again the fifteen-syllable 'political verse', though this time with frequent enjambment both at the line-ends and at the mid-line caesura, which contrasts with the norms of early vernacular writing and of oral folk-poetry (although of course the latter is only known from the transcriptions of much later periods). The most striking metrical feature of this text, which is unique in medieval Greek literature, is the high proportion of half-lines in an anapaestic/dactylic rhythm which cuts across the underlying iambic pattern. The first line of the poem in this version (after the prologue) illustrates this metrical deviation in a characteristic form, where the first half-line is regular and the second introduces the rogue rhythm:

$$\smile \ (/)\smile \ / \ \smile \ (/)\smile \ / \ \| \ \smile\smile \ / \smile \ \smile \ / \ \smile$$

³Ἦν ἀμιρᾶς τῶν εὐγενῶν πλουσιώτατος σ'όδρα⁴⁵

There was an emir among the nobles, mightily rich.

This metrical irregularity occurs in something between a quarter and a half of the lines of the poem in the G version; and despite exhaustive quantitative analysis of early examples of the metre, no other text has been found to exhibit such a consistent use of this feature.⁴⁶ Although this and other types of irregular stress are found in examples of vernacular 'political verse' up until the fifteenth century, the metrical practice adopted in the G version of *Digenes* cannot be fitted convincingly into any pattern of progressive development of the metre. I prefer to see it as a deliberate choice and therefore as a stylistic feature. The same accentual pattern often occurs in the Byzantine adaptation of the classical iambic trimeter, the metre used in the perfunctory introductory lines prefaced to the G version, and also in two of the later twelfth-century romances. But it is tempting to see the deliberate cultivation of this particular accentual pattern as an attempt to reproduce, translated into accentual terms, the metrical pattern with which the Homeric hexameter regularly ends. Homeric lines end with the pattern:

—⏑⏑—⏑

and many of them with the pattern, which corresponds to the 'political' line of G quoted above:

⏑⏑—⏑⏑—⏑

Finally, as is also illustrated by the same line, G (unlike E) regularly treats adjacent vowel-sounds as separate syllables. Hiatus replaces the elision or synizesis that is a feature of modern Greek pronunciation in general and of most versification in the vernacular at all periods; and this is a general feature of Byzantine writing in this metre which uses a learned language register.

This brings us finally to the language of G, which can broadly be categorized as the 'middle' register, with some pretension to the 'high' style and about the same number of concessions to the vernacular. It has been castigated as 'solecist', but this judgement is no less subjective than the abuse which modern purists (of various persuasions) have heaped on the mixed idiom of its rival, E.[47] Despite such variations the language of G is less inconsistent than is that of E; but in such a text linguistic consistency is no guarantee of authenticity. Transposition from one language register to another was already a common ploy for Byzantine men of letters by the twelfth century; disconcertingly there are some signs that both our surviving witnesses to the original *Digenes* may have been the product of some such transposition, in that each text contains a significant number of superior readings as well as of linguistic awkwardnesses.

THE ORIGINAL *DIGENES*

Although the original early twelfth-century poem is lost beyond recall, comparison of the extant witnesses can provide us with a good deal of information about the missing text. However, there are areas where some room for subjective preference between the available versions will probably always remain. First of all, we can be reasonably certain that where the evidence of the two versions is in agreement it is possible to extrapolate back to the original from which they derive. Where they disagree, careful comparison of both versions, and of each with the picture so far built up of the archetype, can furnish at least working hypotheses. I shall try to do this by turning now to consider the poem's sources, where the disagreement between the witnesses is one of emphasis only, not of substance; and from there to examine the nature of the poem, as presented by both witnesses.[48]

The sources of *Digenes* are of two distinct kinds. It has long been recognized that the tales of derring-do on the eastern frontiers of Byzantium derive from no literary source. Although the meticulous historical researches of Henri Grégoire and of others after him have revealed a wealth of precise historical and geographical references (in both versions of the poem), only minor background details of the story can be shown to have any basis in history.[49] Instead the material out of which most (but not all) of the story of Digenes and his parents has been fashioned must have been current in oral tradition, presumably in the regions in which the story is set, in south-eastern Anatolia and northern Mesopotamia. This supposition is strengthened by the existence of much shorter heroic ballads which distantly recall the same milieu as the medieval poem, recorded during the last two hundred years, and most fully elaborated among the Greeks of Asia Minor and Cyprus. A rare seventeenth-century transcription of such a ballad is unique in this tradition in that it gives the hero his full name, Digenes Akrites.[50] Another oral song, preserved in two manuscripts of the eighteenth century, 'The Son of Andronikos', also shares much of this background.[51] The importance of these modern songs as direct evidence of the oral sources of *Digenes* has been exaggerated in studies of Greek folk-poetry, and in much of the work of Stilpon Kyriakidis and Henri Grégoire, between the wars, on the medieval poem.[52] But some evidence does survive of the kind of oral source that must have been used in the original composition of *Digenes*.

The ballad known as the 'Song of Armoures' relates to the same world of Byzantine–Arab conflict around the Euphrates as is also described in *Digenes* and tells, in 'political' verse and vernacular language, of the efforts of the under-age son of a Byzantine warrior to rescue him from captivity at the hands of an Arab emir.[53] The story ends with the reconciliation of captor and captive, and praise for the young hero's precocious leap into manhood. Although the two manuscript witnesses to this ballad date from the fifteenth century, and in their closeness to each other cannot be the independent products of a still-functioning oral tradition, there is little doubt that the text they contain derives from an oral source, which probably was not much different in kind from the oral sources used by the author of *Digenes*. Further corroboration for the existence of such sources can be found in the reference in the G version of *Digenes* to epic tales about the *apelatai*, and very probably in the interpolation in the E version which, as I have argued, derives from such an oral tale. Finally there is the testimony of a tenth-century bishop to the existence in Anatolia at that time of wandering minstrels who would sing the deeds of famous men 'for an obol a time'. The importance of this testimony in demonstrating continuity in the folk-song tradition from Bishop Arethas' time to the present has been overemphasized by Greek folklorists, but there is no reason to doubt the truth of the statement as regards professional oral compositions of a type which could well have formed the basis for the story of *Digenes*.[54]

But were the sources of the original poem exclusively oral? Alexiou in his recent defence of the E version as the truest witness to that text thinks so but concedes references to the Old Testament and some degree of influence from saints' lives.[55] The G version, on the other hand, contains a significant number of allusions to the literary tradition, which have been duly

44

catalogued by editors.[56] Rather than focus on close verbal echoes, I shall point to instances where the literary tradition has played an evident role in shaping the structure of the narrative in the G version, but shall limit myself to cases where these structural elements are discernible in E as well.

Saints' lives

The overall plan of the narrative in both versions declares itself clearly enough as a kind of secular hagiography. Elements traditional to the Byzantine saints' lives which recur in modified form in *Digenes* are the extended treatment of the saint's parentage and the circumstances of his birth; his renunciation of worldly honours in order to live alone (often, as with Digenes in the central part of his story, in the desert); the progressive (and often precocious) revelation of his supernatural powers; the gathering of the followers about the saint's deathbed, and the latter's death without issue. Similarly, the blatantly unrealistic episode in the G version of the emperor's homage to the solitary hero derives from a topos common in saints' lives, in which an emperor will often make a detour to visit and pay homage at the cell of a famous holy man.[57] Although no specific saint's life has ever been picked out as the object of special reference in the construction of the tale of Digenes, one need not doubt that this broad pattern provided something of a blueprint for the author of this extended narrative about a secular hero.[58]

The Hellenistic romances

More or less direct echoes from the romances of Achilles Tatios and Heliodoros have been detected in the G version, the great majority of them occurring in the final two books. Although the presence of direct verbal reference to these texts in the E version has been denied by Alexiou, the influence of the Hellenistic romance is unmistakable in several episodes common to both versions. This is apparent first of all in the lengthy prologue to Digenes' youthful adventures, which, as already mentioned, takes the form of a rhetorical exposition on the theme of love. If E had been truly independent of the literary sources of G, one would have expected this passage not to appear there. However, the corresponding passage of E occupies only slightly fewer lines than in G, and closely follows their rhetorical structure.[59] Similarly, the final part of the hero's story, in both versions, is taken up with his ostentatious building programme on the Euphrates. The account of Digenes' palace and garden could hardly have been omitted since the story, in neither version, offers any other narrative material to fill the gap between the hero's conflicts to protect his wife, and his unheroic death. To be sure, the details of these buildings are greatly curtailed in the E version; but the conclusion is inescapable that the author responsible for the original arrangement of the narrative incidents deliberately chose a theme which is almost *de rigueur* in the Hellenistic genre.[60] The full-blown rhetorical *ekphraseis* in G point seemingly deliberately to the ancient romances as their source; their inclusion, albeit in summary form, in E betrays that this explicit reference to a literary precedent also formed part of the poem copied and adapted in that version.

The Alexander 'romance'

References to the popular Hellenistic 'romance' in which the deeds of Alexander the Great are turned from history into fable are frequent in G, where that hero is mentioned by name in three passages.[61] But the text's dependence on the Alexander story goes further than this: the choice of an unheroic ending for the tale of Digenes' deeds becomes easily intelligible as the *coup de grâce* of a narrative strategy which has deliberately sought to present the medieval borderer as an avatar of the legendary hero of Greek antiquity. Although this fundamental allusion is not made explicit in E, the details of the hero's death as given by that version are these: since all good things end, death one day came to the great Digenes Akrites, still described as νεώτερος (young man/hero). He fell victim to a fatal disease, called his companions and reminded them of all his heroic deeds. At the end of this speech he seemed to see an angel of fire in the sky, was greatly afraid and called his wife, to whom he announced his imminent death. She declared her desire to die with him, and the text ends with the two giving up the ghost together.[62] G additionally tells us that the fatal ailment arose from bathing;[63] and in a precise description of the symptoms echoes a rare technical usage common to Arrian's historical account and Pseudo-Kallisthenes' legendary one of Alexander's death after bathing in the river at Tarsos.[64] The hero's youth and childlessness are again emphasized in this version.[65]

Homer

Passing references to Homer as the ultimate precedent for epic narrative, and to Homeric characters, occur from time to time in G, although there is no reason to believe that the author (either of this version or of its original) knew the Homeric poems directly. Even to mention Homer, however, in a medieval poem devoted to local exploits sung in oral tradition is to claim some familiarity with the literary tradition, and some degree of legitimacy by appeal to it. Confirmation that one, at least, of these references belongs to the original poem comes from E, which bids us:

Βλέπετε, οἱ ἀναγινώσκοντες, τοὺς ἀριστεῖς ἐκείνους,
τοὺς Ἕλληνας, τοὺς θαυμαστοὺς καὶ ὀνομαστοὺς στρατιώτας,
<καὶ> ὅλα ὅσα ἐγίνουντα διὰ ἐκείνην τὴν Ἑλένην,

ὅτε ἐκατεπολέμησαν ἄπασαν τὴν Ἀσίαν,
καὶ πάντες ἐδοξάσθησαν διὰ περισσὴν ἀνδρείαν,
καὶ πάλιν εἰς ἐρωτικὰ ἄλλος τις οὐχ ὑπέστη.
Καὶ οὐ λέγομεν καυχίσματα ἢ πλάσματα καὶ μύθους,
ἃ Ὅμηρος ἐψεύσατο καὶ ἄλλοι τῶν Ἑλλήνων.[66]

Behold, o readers, those champions,
the [pagan] Hellenes, marvellous and renowned warriors,
and all that was done over that Helen,
when they waged war against the whole of Asia,
and all were glorified for outstanding bravery,
but none of them was proof against Eros.
And we do not tell idle boasts or fictions or fables,
things about which Homer told lies and others of the Hellenes.

This certainly does not imply very close acquaintance with the text of the *Iliad*; but the tale of Digenes is unmistakably here claiming its place in the prestigious literary tradition of which Homer stands at the head. The import of the passage is little different in the corresponding passage of G, which does not however mention Helen or the 'romance' elements of the Troy story but makes the no less bizarre claim (quite characteristic of this version) that Alexander the Great was a Christian.[67]

Finally, as already argued, the change to first-person narration for the central part of Digenes' story (common to both versions) may well be understood as an allusion to the story, although not necessarily to the text, of the *Odyssey*.

Given that these literary sources underlie both extant versions of our text, and in most cases have the character of deliberate pointers, what can we infer about the nature of the original poem? First of all we must recognize that that lost poem represented an attempt, presumably the first of its kind in Greek, to graft a self-consciously literary treatment upon material derived from oral tradition in the vernacular. Most of the story, but probably not its final part, was selected from oral traditional material, of the type mentioned in G in the disparaging reference to 'epic' tales of Digenes' rivals, the *apelatai*. In view of the nature of this source there is no need to suppose that all these tales related to the same hero or had previously been linked together to form an extended narrative. It is probably significant that the orally derived 'Song of Armoures' runs to only 197 lines, while the *apelatai* episode in the E version of *Digenes*, which I believe has been taken more or less directly from a similar source, runs to 78. Modern Greek ballads on heroic themes rarely contain more than 100 lines. However, the structure of the narrative of *Digenes* as we have it, with substantial space being devoted to the story of the hero's parents, and its ending with a series of literary references to the Hellenistic romances of ideal love and to the Alexander 'romance', has been dictated by literary precedents.

Confirmation of such a genesis for the twelfth-century poem comes from an examination of the hero's name. 'Akrites', literally 'borderer', is a common noun in Byzantine military usage, where by the eleventh century it meant an aristocrat given substantial privileges in return for keeping the disputed border territories under Byzantine control. As a proper name it clearly typifies this military and land-owning class; and as well as in our poem it appears in recognizable transformations in the Arabic and Turkish epics which derive from the same border conflicts. 'Digenes' is a different matter, however. Its very form (an adjective of the long defunct third declension) betrays its origin in the invention of someone with a literary and grammatical training. Indeed, one of the rare previous uses of the word is as a grammatical term meaning, of an adjective, 'possessing two genders'. 'Digenes', as the hero's name, is several times glossed in the G version of the poem as referring to the hero's 'double' birth. Thus the name of the symbolic hero of the eastern frontier is itself a composite of popular and learned traditions.[68]

So much we can infer about the lost *Digenes Akrites* with some confidence. When we come to consider its style and language we are on much shakier ground, and subjective preferences are difficult to eradicate altogether. What is striking about the style and language of the two versions is that each tends to follow more closely one or other of the poem's presumed original sources: E staying relatively close to the formulaic, paratactic style of the 'Song of Armoures', G going about half-way towards meeting the learned language of its Hellenistic models, introducing a metrical trick of style (as I have argued) as deliberate Homeric imitation, and using rhetorical language and elaborate periods in dialogue and description. When viewed from this angle, it is as though the redactor of each version had set out to regularize an original text which was either inconsistent or somewhere in between the registers and styles of our witnesses. This possibility becomes a serious probability when we compare *Digenes* with the other known vernacular texts of the twelfth century, discussed in Chapter 6, in which the vernacular is several times introduced into sophisticated literary texts in situations that accord precisely with the ancient rhetorical requirement of *decorum*. In the vernacular poems attributed to Prodromos, for instance, the narrator uses the language of the street whenever he presents himself as an impoverished wastrel, but this language is carefully contrasted with the passages in which the author directly addresses his patron in his own guise. May not the original *Digenes*, in a comparable way, have tended to follow the language and style of the sources it adopted for different parts of the narration? This would explain why the rhetorical speeches and descriptions of G are much fuller and more developed than are the corresponding passages of E, while at the same time the narration of action in E is much

48

more concise, and convincingly closer to what we know of the poem's oral sources, than are many of the narrative portions of G.[69] It is certainly worth noting that the handful of lines more or less common to both E and G all belong to the narrative parts of the poem, and in versification and language are closer to the norm of E than of G.

It remains to be determined when and where this remarkable literary feat took place. Neither version contains any clue to the identity, social milieu or place of abode of the writer. It has usually been assumed that he belonged to the same world that he described, and wrote somewhere on the eastern frontier before the loss of the Anatolian provinces in the years following 1071. However, the older view that the work is the result of progressive accretion, with portions being written in the ninth, tenth and eleventh centuries,[70] has given way to the realization that a single act of literary creativity must have taken place some time after all of the historical periods to which our texts at various points refer. Michael Angold has recently proposed the reign of Manuel Komnenos, which is surely too late; Stylianos Alexiou's proposal of the first decade of the twelfth century fits with what little evidence we possess. Angold, however, faces up to the most interesting consequence of accepting (in effect) either date: after 1071 there was no frontier in south-east Anatolia or northern Syria, and few Greek-speakers either. Angold daringly, and in my view rightly, proposes therefore that the poem was composed in Constantinople.[71] An element of conscious antiquarianism or nostalgia then enters into the original composition.

Digenes would not be alone among the world's heroic poems in being the work of an age which looked back with wonder and nostalgia towards its legendary past. Homer explicitly contrasts the valour and strength of the Achaean heroes with those of 'today'; and all the European and Middle Eastern epics of the Middle Ages glorify an age which had become similarly legendary by the time the texts were composed in the form in which we know them. In the case of *Digenes*, such an element of nostalgia provides an essential clue to why the poem should ever have been created in the first place. The writer of the original version need not have been – probably was not – a learned man; but in order to be literate he must have been practised in the rhetorical exercises in the learned language, the *progymnasmata*, that formed the basis of all Byzantine education, and had obviously taken the trouble to inform himself about the literary texts in the repertory on which it might be appropriate for him to draw. Why should such a writer choose to give specifically *literary* form to the oral tales of the eastern frontier which for several hundreds of years must have existed but remained beneath the notice of literature? The answer must lie in the Byzantine defeat at Manzikert in 1071 and the drastic change in attitudes that began from that time. The whole flourishing oral tradition on which *Digenes* was based must have been uprooted with the end of the conditions and the way of life that engendered them. It was then a matter of urgency – particularly, one would suppose, for those many Anatolian Byzantines who had lost their family homes at the time – to commit the traditions of their region to writing, to confer upon them the immortality conventionally associated with literature. Such an explanation accounts at a stroke both for the impetus in writing the poem at all and for the discrepancy between literary and oral styles and sources that can still be detected in its surviving witnesses. A comparable phenomenon can be seen in the Greek literature of the twentieth century, in the poems and novels of George Seferis, George Theotokas, Ilias Venezis and Kosmas Politis written in the wake of the expulsion of the Greeks from Anatolia in 1922–3. A more-or-less explicit element in the work of all four modern writers is the desire to preserve something of the traditions of a way of life that had been destroyed.

What I propose, then, is that *Digenes* was the work of a moderately educated writer, working in Constantinople within a generation of the defeat at Manzikert, whose overriding purpose was to preserve something of the heroic stories of his homeland by giving them literary form and linking them to the literary precedents of Homer and Hellenistic narrative. His poem was designed to appeal to a double authority: on the one hand to 'authentic' oral stories, on the other to the respected secular literary tradition of late antiquity in which interest was at that time beginning to be revived in the capital. Its original language and style may have been something of a hotch-potch, with the diverse sources not thoroughly integrated, so inviting the 'improvement' of later hands (a practice common enough in the Middle Ages, in both East and West).

A final problem is presented by the genre to which the original poem belonged. Hailed as the 'national *epic* of the Greeks' on its first discovery, it has also been termed a romance in whole or in part.[72] The generic ambivalence of the text is reflected in a certain uneasiness in the secondary literature devoted to the poem. Mavrogordato at one point declares that *Digenes* 'is not a romance, in spite of many borrowings from Hellenistic romances ... [It] is a heroic poem', only to contradict himself later: 'the poem of Digenes is in fact a romance';[73] and Beck's segregation of an epic 'Lay of the Emir' from the 'Romance of Digenes' has the ring of compromise. Trapp has used this model to affirm that the core of both parts belongs to the epic genre, and sees the romance elements as twelfth-century accretions, but this view will not stand given the importance of the romance elements in the poem's final episodes for the structure of the original poem. Alexiou also decides in favour of epic, principally on the grounds of the poem's historical and geographical realism and of the absence of a 'happy ending', such as we find in the Hellenistic romances,[74] although, as we shall see, there are later romances in vernacular Greek which end similarly to *Digenes*.[75]

The truth seems to be that the poem consciously initiates a movement from the harsh world of oral epic or heroic ballad, in which men prove their honour by fighting, and women are abducted, raped or brutally killed, towards the world of the romances that came to be written later in the same century, in which human, secular love transcends the workings of a cruel and capricious fate. The relation of *Digenes* to the romances which preceded it by almost a millennium, and to those which began to be written soon after it, is throughout an ambivalent one. Despite, or perhaps because of his infidelities, Digenes is devoted to his unnamed bride to the point of almost trying to subsume her existence within his own. His declared intention, soon after his marriage, is 'to live alone', but with his bride;[76] and there is a certain paradox in a lonely state which includes someone else. This loneliness of the hero seems, even more than the ending, to mark off the story of Digenes from both the earlier and the later romances. All the romances refer in their titles to two principal characters; and although the lovers are frequently separated from one another for long stretches of the action, the single overriding goal of each is to be reunited with the other. Although no ancient or medieval definition of the genre exists to help us, we may justifiably extrapolate from the evidence a governing principle for the Greek romance: it is the story of two characters, a man and a woman, for each of whom personal fulfilment is only possible through the achievement of lasting union with the other. The romance, with its 'snakes and ladders' structure of advance and retreat, is the story of how that union is teasingly deferred by the fickle hand of Chance, only to be brought about finally by an agency similarly beyond their control; and the story inevitably ends with the marriage of the pair. *Digenes*, by contrast, is (mainly) the story of a single, and solitary, individual who, like the heroes and saints of old, pits his will against his environment and gains honour among his peers. The women in Digenes' life, most of them not even named, are part of that environment; and fate or chance is not an issue in this story.

There remains in *Digenes* an unresolved tension between two types of plot structure and of admired behaviour: between the complementarity and duality of the principal roles in the romance on the one hand, and on the other the harsher conventions of the Alexander story, of the saints' lives and, presumably, of its oral sources, in insisting on the lonely self-sufficiency of its hero. But the elements already incorporated into *Digenes* from the Hellenistic romance in their turn throw a shadow over that solitary ideal. Catia Galatariotou has been the first to observe the real pathos in the hero's final retelling of his exploits to his wife as he is dying. All that he has done, he says repeatedly, he did 'so as to win you'.[77] At the end of the poem the purpose of heroic deeds is revealed, retrospectively, as having been to win a woman's love. And this ideal, romantic love that has hovered about the bloody battles and macho posturing of men-at-arms seems at the end of the text tragically unfulfilled. Digenes, I would like to suggest finally, is a romance hero *manqué*; the text an open-ended pointer towards the revival, in the middle of the twelfth century, of the genre of the romance proper.

4

THE RENAISSANCE OF
A GENRE

The obstacle to a radically new evaluation of the four twelfth-century romances has always been their evident dependence on models from late antiquity. So great is this dependence that even those classical scholars who have done most to rehabilitate the ancient romance tend to regard its twelfth-century counterpart as little more than a footnote.[1] For the same reason these romances have seemed unpromising material for the student of modern Greek literature, whose interest has been almost exclusively restricted to texts in the vernacular, and to the appearance of demonstrably 'new' story-material such as we find in *Digenes Akrites* and the later romances 'of chivalry'. These four romances, however, occupy a position in the history of literature which in itself should make them worthy of close study: they are among the first extended attempts to write secular fiction in medieval Europe, and as such their connections with the literature of late antiquity on the one hand and with later medieval European and modern literature on the other are of particular importance. Their sheer bulk (more than four hundred pages in Hercher's nineteenth-century edition) and the almost obsessive care with which they seem to have been composed are proof that they were of some consequence to their authors and first readers. Eustathios Makrembolites' romance, *Hysmine and Hysminias*, was copied in over twenty extant manuscripts, seventeen of them dating from between the thirteenth and the sixteenth century, a sign of a continuing readership which is matched by none of the more 'popular' vernacular romances composed during those centuries.[2] And the citation in the fifteenth century of passages of Konstantinos Manasses' romance *Aristandros and Kallithea* as texts *dulce et utile* for moral improvement is again proof of popularity of a kind. As we shall see later, all four of these romances exercised some influence on the vernacular writers of the fourteenth century; and there are good reasons, as we saw earlier, for seeking in them clues for the existence of contacts between Eastern and Western literature during the twelfth century.

Such attempts as have been made, in recent years, partially to rehabilitate these texts have focused on elements of realism, whether psychological or historical, and on departures from their Hellenistic sources; in so doing they have sought to appeal against the damning charge laid by Erwin Rohde as long ago as 1876, that the Byzantine romances slavishly imitate their ancient models while adding nothing of their own to the genre.[3] As we shall see when we come to consider the distinctive characteristics of each twelfth-century romance in the next chapter, there are certainly significant differences to be found in these texts, both from their ancient models and from each other. But these divergences fall far short of *Aktualisierungsversuch*, and no amount of special pleading can make a real case for their originality or realism in the modern sense.

The significance of the twelfth-century romances for their own time does not lie so much in isolated departures from their models as in the importance which these models came to acquire from being imitated in that way at that particular time. Given the whole Byzantine view of the world and of language which was the inheritance of the twelfth century (a world in which there is, literally, nothing new under the sun) the key to this revival of fiction and the beginning, in the East, of its modern development must be sought in what the Byzantine authors saw in the models they chose to imitate.

The five ancient romances which have been handed down to us entire (by these same Byzantines, be it noted) represent no more than a sample of a narrative genre which seems to have emerged in Hellenistic times, perhaps during the first century BC, and whose popularity up to the end of antiquity is demonstrated by numerous papyrus finds and by the extensive adoption of its favourite themes by Christian popularizing writers.[5] It was these five texts that principally represented ancient narrative fiction to the Byzantines of the twelfth century, and of these five pride of place was accorded to *Leukippe and Kleitophon* by Achilles Tatios and to the *Aithiopika* of Heliodoros.[6]

This is not the place to summarize the background and nature of the ancient romances, on which a growing number of excellent studies exists. Central to all of them is the quest of the solitary individual for salvation in a violent and irrational world ruled (actually or apparently) by Chance (Τύχη), through the love of another in its own likeness. The nexus of themes which we find associated with this quest serves as a common denominator for a broad range of human experiences and preoccupations and as such is sufficient to account for the popularity of the romance in antiquity and later. So fundamental, in this sense, are the plots of the romances that, although they have no organic relation to prior myth or religious belief, these self-conscious fictions through which the solitary individual seeks salvation against enormous odds readily acquired the status of myth and since antiquity have offered a starting-point alike for later literature (being taken up, for instance, by Shakespeare in his last plays) and for allegorical exegesis.[7] Early Christian writers were not slow to seize upon the allegorical possibilities of a journey or quest which might be equated with earthly life, and of an individual love which could transcend even death, as analogous to the soul's love for God; the more so since early Christianity itself emerged out of the same 'age of anxiety' as the romance.[8] But the allegorization of the ancient romances, whether by the Patriarch Photios in the ninth century or by Karl Kerényi in the twentieth, although it distorts a fictional text by reading it as something else, is surely also proof of the power of that text to generate an intellectual and emotional response to the fundamental questions confronted by its author and its earliest readers.

It is at this level that the ancient romances would have exercised their appeal for Byzantine intellectuals of the twelfth century. For Byzantines in the wake of the defeat at Manzikert it cannot have seemed self-evident any longer that the social and political order to which they belonged was divinely appointed to the role of universal empire. The uncertainties and the public anxieties which at the end of antiquity had been subsumed by Christianity, causing the secular romance to disappear,[9] reappear forcefully and in not dissimilar guises at the end of the eleventh century in the revival of pagan philosophy, in a renewed focus on the individual, and, closely related to both, in the rise of secular literature. The Byzantine romances of the twelfth century represent a renewed search for individual salvation through purely secular, human love; but the way to that salvation lies also in the ancient literary texts and their rhetorical techniques, which for Byzantines, both initiated and legitimized that quest.

In order to see in more detail how the Byzantine writers mobilized the resources inherited from antiquity in aid of their own twelfth-century quest for individual salvation and collective identity on the secular plane, we turn now to specific thematic elements of the ancient romance which are repeated or even exaggerated by its Byzantine successors; some of which, as we shall see, acquire radically new meanings by being repeated in the twelfth century.

The past

This is not the place to go into the complex question of the origin of the ancient romance and its precise relation to older genres; what is beyond question is the relationship of the type characterized by Harold Bloom as 'belatedness', which all the romance texts of antiquity betray with regard to older-established forms of literature.[10] Already, as Evelyn Waugh wrote of a different era, 'The originators, the exuberant men, are extinct and in their place subsists and modestly flourishes a generation notable for elegance and variety of contrivance'.[11] Just this attitude towards the literature of the past permeates the ancient romances, and their authors were at pains to legitimize the creation of an essentially new genre, prose fiction, by a wealth of allusion to the established canon. To what extent the romance is actually the descendant of any or all of New Comedy, Homeric epic, historiography or even mythology, is open to debate; but the texts themselves rely heavily on their allusions to and echoes of all these genres.[12] Just like the contemporary Lucianic satire, the ancient romance consists to a considerable extent of a collage of literary and mythological references; and, as with satire, we may suppose that this technique would have had a special appeal for Byzantine authors, for whom, as we have seen, the imitation of literary texts could be actually superior to the Aristotelian 'imitation of things'.

A new dimension is added to this 'belatedness' in the Byzantine romances in that an additional layer of potential allusion is afforded by the ancient romances themselves. The overall similarities of plot between each of the three Byzantine romances that survives complete and its ancient model have been somewhat exaggerated; but the opening flourishes of Prodromos' and Eugenianos' romances, respectively establishing sunset and sunrise as the prelude to an unprovoked attack by pirates, refer us immediately to the opening of the *Aithiopika* (and through it to the Homeric periphrases involving the chariot of the sun) and so declare the nature of the text that we are embarking upon; similarly, the matter-of-fact account of the natural and moral superiority of the narrator's fictional hometown, with which Makrembolites' romance begins, less pointedly refers us to the similar description of Sidon at the beginning of *Leukippe and Kleitophon*.

More or less direct allusions to ancient literature abound in all three complete Byzantine romances, and are often exploited for comic effect. The most spectacular series of such allusions comes in Eugenianos' romance *Drosilla and Charikles*, in the speech of over two hundred lines in which the yokel Kallidemos tries to seduce the heroine by persuasion and by a comically encyclopaedic recital of classical erotica.[13] In addition to Homer, he quotes or alludes to Heliodoros, Plato,[14] *Daphnis and Chloe* whose rustic setting seems to be parodied in this whole episode, Hesiod's fable of the five ages of man, Hero and Leander, Polyphemos and Galatea, Niobe, the Judgement of Paris, the story of Tantalos and miscellaneous amours of Zeus, Theokritos as parodied in *Daphnis and Chloe*,[15] and finally Semiramis in what may be an allusion to the lost *Ninos* romance. Eustathios Makrembolites, in *Hysmine and Hysminias*, also coyly alludes to the ancient romance tradition, and particularly to *Leukippe and Kleitophon*, as his hero–narrator, profoundly disturbed that his former erotic dreams have given way to nightmares in which he is caught by the girl's mother, fears that this may now really happen.[16] In the event his terrors prove groundless, but if the hero is assumed to know Achilles Tatios' romance, with its series of grimly prophetic dreams, as well as the author does and as the reader is expected to, then he has good grounds for being alarmed – and at the same time a false snare is set for the attentive reader. Elsewhere Makrembolites uses such allusions, like Eugenianos, for comic effect, putting a high-flown Homeric speech into the mouth of an uncouth character.[17]

Finally, the vast resource of Christian literature which separates the ancient, pagan writer of romance from his Byzantine counterpart is very occasionally, one might even say coyly, exploited by the latter: Kazhdan has pointed out the surely parodic adaptation of the New Testament phrase 'Whom God has joined let no man put asunder', now applied to the patronage of the lovers by Dionysos in *Drosilla and Charikles*; and he is probably right to see at least a new layer of allusion, if not actually of parody, in the references in the same romance to 'divine providence'.[18] The application of a Christian formula to the pagan gods may well have been intended to jolt the devout contemporary reader, although we should not forget that 'divine providence' also makes its appearance, in a genuinely pagan context, in the *Ephesiaka* of Xenophon and the *Aithiopika* of Heliodoros. In *Hysmine and Hysminias*, Christian allusion is used on at least one occasion in a context which reminds us of the often risqué adaptation of religious imagery to secular love in the Western romance: the narrator, in one of his erotic dreams, catches hold of the heroine's hand and comments: 'and yet in this too I conquer', an allusion to the conversion of Constantine the Great to Christianity, also brought about through a dream.[19]

In three of the five ancient romances the past also provides the literal setting for the action. Chariton's *Chaireas and Kallirrhoe* is the most explicit, placing its fictitious main characters at the fifth-century court of Hermokrates of Syracuse, a setting which according to Carl Müller may have been deliberately chosen to represent, for bourgeois writer and readership, the lost *Heroenzeit der bürgerlichen Polis* as the counterpart of the heroic age sung by Homer.[20] The historical setting of this earliest extant Greek romance is not in fact consistent, but is at least exploited in some detail;[21] and such evidence as we have for the early *Ninos* romance and the fragmentary *Metiochos and Parthenope* encourages the belief that the earliest European 'novel' was a form of *historical* novel.[22] Traces of a similar historical distancing can be observed in both Achilles Tatios' and Heliodoros' romances, which assume that Egypt is under pre-Hellenistic, Persian rule, although in other respects the cosmopolitan Greek world they evoke could be contemporary with their composition, except that the Roman empire under which their writers lived is never mentioned.[23] Only Xenophon's *Ephesiaka* and Longos' *Daphnis and Chloe*, in their very different ways, set their action entirely against the background of a timeless present. The three ancient romances which exploit a historical setting look backwards with an element of nostalgia to a lost classical or immediately post-classical period which can plausibly be considered as the 'golden age' of the Greek culture with which writers and readers alike identified themselves. The pastoral setting of *Daphnis and Chloe* is similarly that of a golden age, but here it is the timeless golden age of pastoral innocence first explored by Theokritos.

This projection into the past assumes still greater significance in the Byzantine romances. Just as none of the ancient romances makes the slightest reference to the contemporary reality of Roman rule, so none of the

Byzantine romances alludes (except in the sly asides already mentioned) to the coming of Christianity, to the existence of Constantinople, or to almost a thousand years of Byzantine history; and this is surely the more impressive omission. The action of all four Byzantine romances takes place against a very vaguely defined historical and geographical background, which in all of them is none the less recognizable as the pagan Hellenistic world in which the ancient romances were composed (but not exclusively set). The long debates about parthenogenesis on Olympos and about the likely attitude of the gods to human sacrifice in Prodromos' romance have to be read quite differently from the comparable passages in Heliodoros and Achilles Tatios when one reminds oneself that the author was a Christian writing in the twelfth century, and the same is true of the many apostrophes of the characters in these romances to gods in which neither author nor readers could have believed, as well as of the carefully worked-out details of fictitious ancient festivals in Makrembolites' romance. These are 'historical novels' in a sense which is only vestigial in the surviving ancient romances: they are attempts not just to revive past literature by allusion and imitation but to recapture, in the fictional world they create, the world of the past in which that literature took shape. And this effort is surely motivated by something more than the recondite pleasures of the antiquarian (although these play their part). It may be suggested that the hope of salvation, which the Byzantine author seeks through reactivating ancient fictions of individual love and impersonal chance, was no less to be sought through asserting his identity as the inheritor of that Hellenistic 'age of anxiety' in which these ancient fictions had flourished.

Love as tyrant

In all the romances, ancient and Byzantine, love offers the means of salvation for the individual and a hard-won harmony with a threatening environment. But love itself is not something freely chosen by the individual; nor is it initiated by the conscious will of the hero or heroine. Love in the romances is a cosmic force, before which individuals are powerless, and locked in perpetual conflict with the equally powerful and indiscriminate cosmic force of chance. In Chariton's romance a seemingly chance encounter between two young people was in fact, we are told, planned by Eros, and everything else in the story follows upon this initiative. Xenophon's hero, whose somewhat effeminate nature is encapsulated by his name Abrokomes,[24] dares to despise love and is punished by an enraged Eros with the devotion to Antheia which becomes the *raison d'être* for all his subsequent adventures. *Daphnis and Chloe* contains the fullest elaboration of the mythical deity of love as handed down by tradition: the child of Aphrodite who roams the world with bow, arrows and a flaming torch, and to whose power kings, the gods and even inanimate nature are not immune.[25] The tyrannous power of love and this

57

traditional iconographical representation are frequently alluded to in the romances of Achilles Tatios and Heliodoros, and repeated throughout the Byzantine romances.[26]

One could quite fairly extrapolate from all these romances a common view of the world in which the salvation that the individual seeks and at last finds in love is never to be equated with freedom. Love saves him from worse masters, but does not at the end leave him a free agent. By the same token, the various forms of literal bondage through which the heroes and heroines pass in all the romances have at least the potential to be considered as metaphors for the sway in which Eros holds them. This potential is rarely realized explicitly in the ancient romances, despite many references to love as a tyrant. The logical correlative to this, that the lover must be his slave, is spelt out for once in Melite's sustained assault on the hero's chastity in *Leukippe and Kleitophon*, when she upbraids him: 'How did you dare to spurn a woman in love, when you too are the slave of Eros?'.[27]

This possibility is recognized, and developed a little way, by Prodromos in *Rhodanthe and Dosikles*, in a passage where the heroine reconciles herself to slavery in a new household, by the argument that she has been a slave before alongside her fellow-slave Dosikles, and they were then the slaves not only of their piratical masters but also of Aphrodite.[28] Eugenianos too gives some room to this idea, inventing a new series of terrifying guises for the boy-archer.[29] Eugenianos is also the first writer to apply to Eros the attributes of temporal power in the Byzantine world, which, as we shall see in Chapter 10, were later to be developed as his dominant characteristics in the later vernacular romances. Kleandros in the sub-plot of that romance, congratulating himself on the successful abduction of Kalligone from her home, adds, addressing the girl: 'glory be to Eros the tyrant', an evident parody of the liturgical formula; elsewhere Eros is described by the imperial title 'lord of all'; and a lover describes himself as a 'wretched slave ... violently conscripted to love's service'.[30]

In Makrembolites' romance, however, the theme of love as enslavement takes on an entirely new dimension. Of the three parts of the romance, the first deals with the hero's subjugation to the god of love, who is now depicted, by means of a painting, as a stern young king on a splendid chariot surrounded by a court paying homage, and given the Byzantine imperial title Βασιλεύς (king/emperor); while in the third both lovers become the slaves of human masters before finally being delivered back into their state of willing bondage to love. There may be some attempt at synthesis here between the traditional Greek boy archer and the *Dieu d'Amor* of the emerging 'courtly love' literature of the West in the twelfth century;[31] but almost all the aspects of Makrembolites' treatment of love (probably excepting only the painting of the Court of Love described in Book II) can be seen as the development of a potential already present in the Greek tradition of antiquity and increasingly also in the other twelfth-century romances.[32] Presumably this is why the characters in the third part of the romance have so much to say about the reversal of their fortunes in making them slaves: there is a deliberate parallel between this reversal and that of Hysminias who, thinking himself a freeman and at first rejecting Hysmine's advances, found himself arraigned before the Court of Love in a dream and pressed into the service of Eros the King (Βασιλεύς), whose slaves he and Hysmine remain ever after.[33]

Love and death

The paradoxical nature of love is implied or explored in other ways too in the ancient romances, in particular in relation to death. Lovers among the minor characters frequently meet with unhappy ends which further highlight, and contrast with, the happy conclusion of the main story. But even for the principal characters, in their quest for salvation through mature and consummated love, the semblance of death, and a miraculous restoration to life, are constant requirements among the tribulations which they undergo.

The wanderings of Chaireas and Kallirrhoe in Chariton's romance are the consequence of the deathlike swoon into which the heroine falls when the hero, tricked by his enemies into believing her unfaithful, kicks her in the stomach. Kallirrhoe recovers to find herself buried along with a sumptuous treasure just as grave-robbers are opening her tomb, and this recovery from apparent death is at one point called 'regeneration'.[34] Xenophon's romance includes more than its share of hair's-breadth escapes, several of them miraculous, and at one point the heroine, Antheia, deliberately fakes death in order to escape a second marriage.[35] Later in the same romance the power of love over mortality is given a new twist, touching or morbid according to taste, in the tale of the fisherman who keeps his elderly wife's corpse mummified in his house and sees her even now as she used to be when he first fell in love with her.[36] Longos, in *Daphnis and Chloe*, is able to give this recurrent theme its most natural and least obtrusive form in the pastoral world of that romance. Here the succession of the seasons largely replaces the spatial wanderings and spectacular vicissitudes of the other romances, and it comes as no surprise to find the advent of spring described as 'the time of regeneration from the dead'.[37]

But it is Achilles Tatios and Heliodoros who go furthest in symbolically linking love, death and resurrection in their romances. Achilles effects a somewhat crude equation between love and death in the nightmare that wakes the heroine's mother in time to prevent the consummation of love and to send the lovers out upon their adventures: the mother dreams that her daughter's abdomen is being ripped open by an armed intruder. This garish symbolism is extended to resurrection from apparent death in the later episode in which Leukippe, in the hands of pirates, is seemingly eviscerated and buried before the hero's very eyes; an illusion subsequently explained by the use of theatrical props.[38] Not content with this, Achilles follows it up with a second illusory death of his heroine – and even has her killed a third time in a false report before either the hero or the reader has yet learnt the explanation for her second 'resurrection'.[39] The verb ἀναβιῶμαι (come back to life) figures prominently throughout the romance,[40] and the Ovidian myth of Pan and the nymph Syrinx, which introduces the long-awaited resolution of the plot, contains yet another allusion to the pattern of violent death, and regeneration through the power of love, which the romance seemingly tries to establish. Without implying any connection with 'mystery religions' or actual ritual, one need not doubt that Achilles seeks to interpret the nature of love and the progress towards its mature consummation as an initiation and a coming to terms with extreme possibilities of experience.

In the *Aithiopika* too the trials of the hero and heroine have the character of an initiation, perhaps in a more seriously religious sense. The same opposition that we observed in Achilles Tatios' romance reappears in the supposed murder of Charikleia in Book I, the actual murder of Knemon's Thisbe which follows, the tale of the priest Charikles, whose daughter was burnt to death on her wedding-night and for whom the heroine, Charikleia, seems to have been sent by providence as a substitute, the apparent resurrection of Thisbe and consternation of Knemon, an episode which is probably to be read as parody of Achilles Tatios, the minor but macabre scene of necromancy which so fascinated the Patriarch Photios,[41] the determination of the lovers to plead guilty to trumped-up charges so as to be united in death, and Charikleia's miraculous escape from the pyre in the eighth book. But all of these paradoxical reversals have been co-opted by Heliodoros into the service of a larger series of paradoxes.[42]

Turning now to the Byzantine romance, in Prodromos' *Rhodanthe and Dosikles*, death and resurrection first make an appearance in the elaborate illusionist spectacle laid on by the pirate henchman Gobryas to intimidate an envoy from a rival power.[43] Prodromos, as we shall see in the next chapter, places the emphasis here on the power of art which, by means of illusion, may even command nature; and the seeming death and revival of the heroine on two occasions later in the romance function as pointers rather to the power of narrative art than to the ambivalent nature of love.[44] In *Drosilla and Charikles*, on the other hand, Eugenianos makes use of the love–death equation in its characteristically modern Greek guise, in a love-letter which links Eros with Charon, and again in a love-letter attributes to love the power to bring life to the dead and slay the living.[45] In this romance too the heroine is mistakenly thought to be dead, although only once; and the themes of love and death are once more juxtaposed in the tragic outcome of the subplot, which mirrors the action of the main story.

Eustathios Makrembolites, in *Hysmine and Hysminias*, was evidently at some pains to tone down the vaudeville elements of his princpal source,

Leukippe and Kleitophon. The multiple 'deaths' of the heroine are reduced to one, and the manner of it is made more decorous and mythological. The uncouth shipmaster who has Hysmine thrown overboard to save the ship comically quotes Homer, and his victim is saved, like Arion, by a dolphin.[46] However, the conception of love as subsuming death and resurrection, which was given such prominence in his source, is twice revived quite explicitly by Makrembolites. Hysmine, whom Hysminias at first fails to recognize as a fellow-slave, identifies herself by a letter, in which she describes herself as: 'for you having tasted bitter death and finally a prisoner and a slave now...'[47] A little later he tells her his own sufferings, echoing her words and adding:

ἃ πάντα χαίρω παθών, ὅτι σὲ τὴν ἐμὴν ʿΥσμίνην ῎Ερως μοι πάλιν ἐξ ῎Αδου καινῶς ἀνεσώσατο.[48]

all of which I am glad to have suffered, because Eros has most strangely delivered you, my Hysmine, back from Hades.

Chance and the passive hero

With the single exception of Chariton's Chaireas, the principal characters of the ancient romances very rarely *do* anything. Action-packed though these narratives are, the actions narrated are almost always the actions of others or of impersonal forces, observed in their effects upon the hero and heroine. The example of Chariton, whose romance is the earliest of those that have come down to us, suggests that this may not always have been so. Chaireas has something of the quality of the Arthurian hero or of the later Greek Erotokritos, in that his sufferings at the hands of love are balanced and finally vindicated by his prowess in war. In the second part of the romance, the hero joins in a war against the Persian king who holds the heroine captive, and Chariton clearly seeks to demonstrate that the greatest warlike feats are those that are inspired by love: at the end of the crucial day's fighting Chaireas has beaten back the Persians by sea, while his rival for Kallirrhoe's love, Dionysios, fighting for the opposite side, has won the day on land.[49]

Elsewhere in the ancient romances we are hard put to it to discover a significant action initiated by a major character. Kleitophon, it is true, steals into Leukippe's bedroom and then, being caught almost *in flagrante*, has little choice but to leave home, with the heroine as a willing companion.[50] In Xenophon's *Ephesiaka* Antheia twice contrives to extricate herself from a tricky situation by an ingenious initiative,[51] although all Abrokomes' hair's-breadth escapes are attributed to chance or divine providence. Charikleia in the *Aithiopika* occasionally shows signs of a similar ingenuity in order to help herself,[52] but most of the human initiatives on behalf of the lovers in that romance are taken for them by the priest Kalasiris.[53] Otherwise the inactivity of the main characters in the face of chance and of a domineering god of love amounts in the ancient romances to the status of a theme, and as such is considerably extended in the romances of the twelfth century.

For understandable reasons it has not always been seen in this light. The Loeb editor of Achilles Tatios' romance is obliged to comment, at the point where the hero for the second time submits meekly to insult by his rival:

> The reader, bearing in mind Clitophon's behaviour at his previous meeting with Thersander (v 23), will by this time have come to the conclusion that the hero of the romance is a coward of the purest water. I do not know if Achilles Tatius intended to depict him so, or whether it is a fault in the drawing.[54]

This edition was first published during the First World War (in 1917), when the contrast between the moral attitude of the romance and public morals in England could hardly have been greater. But the passivity of Kleitophon, and of the other major characters in the ancient romance, goes far beyond moral weakness. Almost everything that happens in *Leukippe and Kleitophon* is the result of an accident, or a mistake.[55] Nor should we forget the various false events, such as the apparent deaths of Leukippe, in which an effect is not the result of its apparent cause, but of a more-or-less chance combination of different causes which could not have been deduced from the effect. At crucial moments, individuals in Achilles Tatios' romance do not rouse themselves to supreme feats, they 'resign themselves to chance'.[56]

So pervasive is this theme in the romances that we cannot seek to account for it by moral evaluation of particular characters, whether the moral judgement be our own or imputed to the author of the romance. The theme is fundamental enough to be reflected in the nearest to a generic term that ancient writers ever found for prose fiction: πάθος ἐρωτικόν.[57] These writers, it must be suggested, were at pains to create a world in which the initiative does not lie with the individual. It is an intentionally bleak world, whose antecedents are discernible in the attitudes to fate of Homer and the tragedians, but in which the individual has been scaled down and stripped of the supportive bulwark of the heroic code or the corporate institutions of the *polis*, both of which had included some familiarity between man and the divine. 'What is a human being to do in such a world?' is at least part of the question, in the terms of H. R. Jauss, to which the ancient romances are the response; and in their theme, already discussed, of human love finally but not easily triumphant we can discern their tentative answer.

It has already been suggested that the reappearance of the romance in twelfth-century Byzantium is a consequence of renewed intellectual anxieties which the writers of that period recognized in the ancient romances. The possibility that the world was governed by chance (or fate) was actively discussed in the mid-twelfth century.[58] The risk of condemnation for heresy offers yet another explanation of why the romance writers' exploration of a bleak world neither Christian nor Byzantine should have been carefully projected back into the pagan past, and further legitimized by the accepted 'imitation of authors'. At least one of the four writers of romance in the twelfth century, Theodore Prodromos, was actually called to defend himself publicly against a charge of misuse of ancient writers.[59]

In all four twelfth-century romances chance is very frequently invoked, often with highly disparaging epithets, as the mainspring of the action.[60] The helplessness of the individual before a destiny shaped by chance is greatly heightened in the twelfth-century romances as compared to their ancient models.[61] Salvation in these romances is never brought about through the characters helping themselves (as in Chariton's romance); and for the divine providence (πρόνοια) that in different ways oversees a happy end to the lovers' trials in Xenophon's and Heliodoros' romances is substituted the patronage of particular pagan gods (Hermes in *Rhodanthe and Dosikles*, Dionysos in *Drosilla and Charikles*) whose unreliability was a commonplace of Byzantine education, and is even openly suspected by the characters themselves.[62] In *Hysmin and Hysminias* the lovers are held in tutelage to the allegorical king of love, whose power to influence events is proved only at the end of the romance, and not before Hysminias has dared to accuse him of broken faith;[63] and the romance ends with the hero–narrator, recognizing that he has fallen foul of two such powerful gods as Zeus and Poseidon, placing his hopes for the eternal endurance of his love not in any divine power but in the art of the writer.[64]

The heroes of the three complete twelfth-century romances are all personable young men, well qualified for action. Dosikles in Prodromos' romance has had a military upbringing and is apparently already experienced in the arts of war;[65] Eugenianos' hero, Charikles, has the effeminate good looks and arrogant indifference to love of Xenophon's Abrokomes; but he has also been brought up to excel in the traditional pursuits of the Byzantine aristocracy, riding and hunting;[66] while Hysminias is an unexceptional young man of good family, chosen *by lot* to play the role of Zeus' herald in a religious ceremony, and taking himself and his duties very seriously. Each of these characters is responsible for conceiving and carrying out only one decisive action in the course of the narrative of which he is the protagonist, and in each case it is the same action: the abduction of the girl he loves.

This is surprising in that, although there are plenty of abductions planned and executed in the ancient romances, the hero never abducts the heroine from her family or protectors. Even in *Leukippe and Kleitophon* the two make separate decisions to flee together, and Kleitophon already had no choice but to go into exile, whether or not Leukippe accompanied him; and in the *Aithiopika* it is the priest and later mentor of Charikleia, Kalasiris, who plans and executes her abduction so as to bring her and Theagenes together. The abductions in Prodromos' and Eugenianos' romances are only very cursorily motivated by the intelligence that the heroine has just been betrothed elsewhere, while the pros and cons are more seriously debated in *Hysmine* and *Hysminias*, although the reason for the abduction remains the same.[67] The prominence of this single action in three texts which otherwise eschew action by the main characters altogether (an action which is further repeated in the subplots of Prodromos' and Eugenianos' romances) may be considered as a pointer not so much to contemporary mores as to the 'proto-romance' of *Digenes Akrites*, and provides the most direct evidence to link the romances of the mid-twelfth century with the pioneering role of that poem's anonymous author in reviving the genre at the beginning of the century. It is certainly striking that the young heroes of these romances, having once abducted their brides-to-be, are thereafter as powerless to avert the blows of chance as they were previously to resist the assaults of love.

In these romances the scale of the action has been considerably reduced, too, by comparison with their ancient models. In Prodromos' romance even the author seems at times to have forgotten his protagonists, as warring pirates and barbarians exchange the envoys and insults, and fight the battles, that will quite arbitrarily decide their fate; while the (traditional) preservation of their chastity and eventual reunion are the result of a chain of circum-stances subject to no other force than the author's imagination. In *Drosilla and Charikles* there are slightly increased causal connections between some of the episodes in the plot, and Charikles when faced, as Prodromos' hero had also been, with a threat to the heroine's honour, does not simply go to pieces as Drosikles had done but proposes drastic and far-reaching action. However, he adds, it is up to the gods to carry it out![68] In *Hysmine and Hysminias* the traditional action-plot is concentrated almost entirely into three of the eleven books;[69] at the only point in which Hysminias and his fellow-prisoners begin to plan an attack on their pirate captors they are forestalled by an army from the neighbouring town;[70] and the whole focus of this romance has been turned inward to the inner state of a hero who is manifestly not in control of his destiny.

It is now time to recall that the writers and first readers of these romances, for all the renewal of pagan anxieties and preoccupations revealed by their writings, were Christians. However great their classical learning or their possible scepticism with regard to the received ideology of their time, a fundamental place in their thinking was occupied by Christian doctrine and belief, according to which passive suffering in certain circumstances is not only a necessity but even a virtue. Christ had taught that most un-Hellenic of virtues, to turn the other cheek; and the supreme crisis in the gospel story, celebrated annually in the Easter liturgy, is called in Greek Τὰ Πάθη (what was suffered/experienced). Moreover, Prodromos and his contemporaries were writing secular, pagan romances for intellectual circles that had been brought up on saints' lives transposed into the same classicizing language as they themselves used, by Symeon Metaphrastes at the end of the tenth century; and many of those lives had themselves in their earliest form appropriated qualities and experiences from the ancient romance as attributes of the Christian saint. Given this perspective, the passivity of the Byzantine romantic hero is neither the moral cowardice that Sir Stephen Gaselee thought he detected in Achilles Tatios' Kleitophon, nor (simply) the demonstration of man's insignificance in the world when stripped of his traditional supports, but becomes a positive virtue. This is fully explicit in a key fragment from Konstantinos Manasses' romance *Aristandros and Kallithea*, in which a character *refuses* to act on the grounds that he would prefer 'rather to suffer and be damned than act and cause damnation'.[71]

In the twelfth-century romances a Christian fortitude is projected into a pagan world, and the question which (to echo Jauss's terms again) these texts presuppose turns out to be a startlingly modern one: what hope would there be for a Christian if the providence in which he believes were as fickle and illusory as that of the pagan gods of his ancestors? Part of the answer which these romances, no less tentatively than their Hellenistic predecessors, explore lies in the secular love of individuals for one another. But part is also to be found in the enduring quality of art.

Art and nature: description

With the exception of Xenophon's *Ephesiaka*, the ancient romances are self-conscious literary experiments in which the status of the text itself, both as work of art in relation to older masterpieces and as a fictional narrative creating a certain illusion of reality, is frequently brought to the fore. We have already noted the importance that the literature of the past assumes in the romances, and it is often through the prism of older literature or of the visual arts that the romance writer seeks to give his stories life. The rhetorical style, with its interminable speeches and descriptions, of Achilles Tatios and Heliodoros has long been the object of comment. It seems to have been for this above all that these romances were read and admired by Byzantine commentators such as Photios and Psellos. Modern classicists, on the other hand, in the wake of Erwin Rohde in the latter part of the nineteenth century, were until recently no less put off by the rhetorical embellishment of these two texts. Recent studies have begun to reappraise the self-conscious artifice of the whole literary movement of the 'second sophistic' to which the Hellenistic romance largely belongs, and have usefully pointed out that the romances of Achilles Tatios and Heliodoros differ from their predecessors by Chariton and Longos in this respect only in degree.[72]

The ancient romance is the product of an intellectual world in which the texts and the monuments of a past age were valued more highly than contemporary experience. Reality and authenticity were validated not by appeal to experience but by appeal to sources. For the 'belated' writer of this period, to make a character 'come alive' for his readers meant to compare him with a prototype in mythology, and better still with a picture or a statue of that prototype; in order to foster the illusion that the reader actually sees the scene described on the page, the writer must appeal to the techniques of representation used in the visual arts. It is a technique the opposite of realism as it was understood in the nineteenth century: nature is revered only insofar as it conforms to the laws of art, and not the other way about.

Some such assumption can be discerned in all the ancient romances. Chariton's heroine is compared to Aphrodite; the statue of the goddess in her likeness that Dionysios has set up at Miletos is at once recognized by the hero; later she is described as 'Nature's great achievement'; and the disappointed rival, at the end of the romance, contents himself with commissioning statues of her; while Chaireas is first described as 'like Achilles, the way sculptors and painters represent him'.[73] Even Xenophon describes his hero as too beautiful for a mortal, more like a god; and Antheia, his heroine, at her first appearance is dressed up in the likeness of the goddess for a festival of Artemis.[74] Heliodoros' Charikleia is similarly attired when we first see her amid the remains of a banquet turned slaughterhouse, and later we learn that when she met Theagenes she had been dressed as the priestess of Artemis. Her white skin and classical beauty have been inherited not from her Ethiopian parents but from a *painting* of Andromeda that had caught her mother's eye at the moment of her conception. In the same romance the hero, Theagenes, is first described as 'just how Homer depicts Achilles', introducing a visual metaphor for verbal description.[75]

But it is in the extended description, the *ekphrasis* of Hellenistic rhetorical exercises, that the relation between nature and art is most fully explored in the romances. Two of them actually begin with the set-piece description of a painting – *Leukippe and Kleitophon* with a picture of the rape of Europa, *Daphnis and Chloe* with a pastoral scene of Lesbos. The picture in Achilles' romance symbolically prefigures much of the action, as do the subjects of other paintings introduced later in the narrative;[76] in the proem to *Daphnis and Chloe* the narrator is explicitly inspired by the 'abundant τέχνη [art/skill/artifice] and erotic fortune' displayed by the picture, to 'copy it in writing'. Elsewhere the gardens which are described in all their varied splendour in these two romances represent nature tamed, selected and arranged by man, in an activity exactly analogous to that of the author in representing it in words, while Longos goes so far as to say, of the intertwined branches of the trees: 'their nature even seemed to be that of art'.[77] The same claim is made in a different context in the *Aithiopika*, where Kalasiris boasts that 'art can compel nature'.[78] Heliodoros, in his set-piece descriptions, eschews works of art for his subjects, but in constructing elaborate tableaux out of the scenes he describes sometimes gives the impression of describing a painting.[79]

Description in the ancient romance is about evenly balanced between the 'imitation of things' and the 'imitation of authors' (or works of art) first

sanctioned by Longinus. The nature of the text as illusion and in its relation
to other texts is undoubtedly a theme of some of their descriptions, as of the
other references to art or artifice mentioned. Given the direction in which
Byzantine literature as a whole developed from its Hellenistic roots, it is not
surprising to find this theme given greater prominence and a new significance
when it is taken up in the romances of the twelfth century. There is scarcely
a descriptive passage in any of the three complete romances that does not
bring into focus the artifice (literal or, in the case of natural descriptions,
metaphorical) through which the visual effect described has been achieved,
thus drawing attention to its own status as artifice. In *Drosilla and Charikles*
the description of the *locus amoenus* from which the lovers, in the opening
scene, have been snatched moves quickly from the natural parts of the
landscape to a detailed account of a fountain with a column surmounted by
an eagle, from whose mouth the stream of water flows, with statues by
Pheidias and Praxiteles all around;[80] while another *locus amoenus* in the
romance includes a 'golden plane tree much more splendid than that of
Xerxes'.[81] The heroine is described as a 'statue of Love',[82] and in the subplot
Kleandros says of Kalligone, in a letter to her: 'For nature ... has fashioned
you like a red-and-white iridescent statue'.[83] Later the classically educated
yokel Kallidemos compares the heroine first to a beautiful meadow[84] and
then to a bronze statue forged in a Hephaistian fire by a hard-hearted
craftsman.[85]

Prodromos in *Rhodanthe and Dosikles* describes his heroine as a
'hallowed statue' in the likeness of a goddess; her skin is the imitation of
snow, and the ensemble of her charms is described as πλάσις (creation, but
especially God's creation of the world).[86] Later the hero praises her colour:

> καλῶς γὰρ αὐτὴν καὶ κεκανονισμένως
> ἐσχημάτισεν ἡ γεωμέτρις Φύσις.[87]

> For this was beautiful and according to rules
> shaped by the geometer Nature.

In the banquet scene which is one of the achievements of this romance,
Nature is seemingly overruled by the will of the pirate chief 'by a single
word'.[88] The same scene also includes a spectacular set-piece description,
which with fine-toned irony is devoted to a cup that has just been broken:
the craftsmanship and the skill by which the illusion of a real scene had been
carved on this cup are praised at length, but the cup as a real object has
already disappeared. Art, it is implied, endures, and the claim is reinforced
when we recognize that the whole description is indebted to Achilles Tatios
who in turn was indebted to Herodotos: the real object becomes multiple,
remote, finally imaginary and ideal as we trace it back through these
successive layers, until what we are left with is art itself.[89] *Rhodanthe and*

Dosikles ends with another set-piece contrivance even more perverse by the standards of modern aesthetics. The two lovers and their two fathers embrace in a geometrical pattern seeming to consist of four bodies and a single head. The narrator digresses:

εἶδον κἀγὼ πολλάκις ἐν πολλοῖς πέπλοις ...
τοιοῦτον εἰκόνισμα καινοῦ ζωγράφου,
ὑφαντικῆς εὕρημα δηλαδὴ τέχνης·
μίαν κεφαλὴν εἰς τετρακτὺν σωμάτων
διαιρεθεῖσαν, ἢ τετρακτὺν σωμάτων
οἷον συνιζηκυῖαν εἰς κάραν μίαν· ...
    Τούτοις ὁμοιόσχημον ἤθελε γράφειν
ἡ τῆς χαρᾶς χείρ, ἡ σοφὴ γεωμέτρις,
τῶν πατέρων τὸ σχῆμα καὶ τῶν παιδίων,
ὅτε προσεπλάκησαν ἀλλήλοις ἅμα.[90]

I have often seen in many tapestries ...
such a depiction by an innovative artist,
the invention, that's to say, of the weaver's art,
one head into a tetraktys [*sic*] of bodies
divide, or a tetraktys of bodies
as though joined together in a single head ...
    Of just such a pattern would be made
by the hand of joy, that wise geometer,
the shape of the fathers and the children,
when they came together in a simultaneous embrace.

(The term 'tetraktys', which actually refers in Pythagorean number theory to the pyramid of integers whose sum is invariably ten, is here paraded as a pseudo-geometrical figure!)

Finally, the use made of *ekphrasis* and the antithesis between art and nature in *Hysmine and Hysminias* must be postponed to a discussion of the specific character of that romance. For the moment it will be enough to point to the description of the garden and fountain near the beginning, which further elaborates upon themes drawn from the corresponding description by Eugenianos;[91] to the series of descriptions of paintings which takes up a large part of Books II and IV; to the golden statue of Artemis with working bow and running water which, like Pan's syrinx in *Leukippe and Kleitophon*, affords an instant virginity test;[92] and to the closing pages of the romance, in which the salvation that has been sought throughout the ancient and the twelfth-century romances is equated with the permanence of 'a golden statue hammered out of words'.[93]

CONCLUSION

The five thematic elements isolated and examined here are all contributory factors to the artificiality or rhetoricity of the ancient romances, characteristics which until quite recently had earned for these texts the general condemnation of the few classical scholars who studied them. It is now much better understood that this brand of literary artifice is not a vice or a fault in the style and conception of the ancient romances; it is fundamental to their *raison d'être*, and so must be tackled on its own terms if the literary and historical significance of these texts is to be properly understood. By the same token, the innovative nature of the twelfth-century texts in the same genre, which represent a specific reception of these romances some eight hundred years after they were first composed, emerges from the new use to which thematic elements, characteristic of the Hellenistic genre, are put in the twelfth century. The past, both as object of literary allusion and as stage for the action narrated, acquires a new depth conferred by the lapse of almost a millennium: the deliberate distancing of the action in time, and the validation of cultural allegiances by reference to the Hellenistic world, are more unexpected and radical moves in twelfth-century Constantinople than was the equivalent but vaguer appeal of the Hellenistic romances to the 'heroic age of the bourgeois *polis*'.[94] Similarly the subordination of the individual to cosmic forces, principally Eros and chance, reactivates, in the new historical context of a Christian empire beginning upon its decline, the anxieties of individuals in the last centuries of the pagan world; while the transformation of the characters' traditional passivity in the ancient romances into Christian fortitude simultaneously transforms an inherited literary convention through re-appropriation in a different context. Finally, as the brief discussion of *ekphrasis* will have suggested, and as will be confirmed in the next chapter, the artificiality that modern readers have condemned in the Hellenistic romances becomes, in their twelfth-century reception, itself the means to salvation and the substitute for the true 'providence' that is notably absent at the level of story in the Byzantine romances. The salvation sought literally by the hero and heroine in these stories, and vicariously, it may be supposed, by their authors and first readers or audiences, is to be equated with, in the phrase of W. B. Yeats quoted earlier, 'the artifice of eternity'.

5

THE TWELFTH-CENTURY TEXTS

If the key to understanding the twelfth-century romances is to be found in the re-interpretations which they offer of their antique sources, this does not, however, mean that they are devoid of references to their own time or that their aims and achievements are uniform. Each of the four is a fully conscious attempt to work out, in a slightly different way, common problems of salvation in the world, and, in the text, of the rhetorical possibilities of the written word.

Theodore Prodromos, *Rhodanthe and Dosikles* (Τὰ κατὰ 'Ροδάνθην καὶ Δοσικλέα)[1]

Although none of the twelfth-century romances has so far been dated with any precision and it now seems possible that all four were composed within a few years of each other, it is commonly held that the initiative in the revival belongs to Prodromos.[2] Prodromos is now thought to have been born around 1100 and to have died either in the mid-1150s or shortly after 1170.[3] The romance is the largest of his many works, and it is tempting to assign its composition to the period between 1143 and 1149, when Prodromos seems to have been out of favour at the imperial court.[4] Although modern scholars tend to assume that the twelfth-century romances were little read,[5] the evidence of the manuscript tradition for all four contradicts this. Prodromos' romance has come down to us in four complete manuscripts, dating from between the thirteenth and the sixteenth century, and was excerpted in a further two, the second from as late as the seventeenth century.[6] This evidence for a continuing readership, as well as the scale of the work, suggest that *Rhodanthe and Dosikles* occupied a place of importance among the corpus of one of the most prolific and respected writers of the age.

The structure of the plot and its division into nine books, each with a certain thematic unity, is more tightly knit and more carefully balanced than we find in either Achilles Tatios' or Heliodoros' romances, to which it is indebted in about equal measure. Like the other twelfth-century romances which have come down to us entire, and like the second part of *Digenes*

Akrites that narrates the exploits of the hero himself, the romance is constructed out of three fairly equal parts. Books I–III are taken up with a complex double analepsis.[7] Prodromos, like Heliodoros, begins *in medias res*. Rhodanthe and Dosikles are caught up in an attack by pirates on the town of Rhodes and taken into captivity, along with many of the natives and a Greek from Cyprus, called Kratandros, whom Dosikles befriends. The remainder of the first part is taken up with an exchange of stories by Dosikles and Kratandros. The latter's tale is, like the story of Kleinias in Achilles Tatios' romance, a tragic foil to the main narrative. Kratandros tells how he was caught *in flagrante* in his mistress's room, and how in the ensuing mêlée she had been killed by one of the guards, in mistake for him. Dosikles then tells how he and Rhodanthe came to be in Rhodes. But this retrospective narrative, too, begins *in medias res* with the arrival of the pair in the town of Rhodes and their hospitality at the house of a local merchant and his family. The second book is entirely taken up with this second-degree analepsis, in which Dosikles, within his narrative to Kratandros, retells the story of his wooing and abduction of Rhodanthe as he had earlier told it to his hosts in Rhodes. The third book contains the conclusion of Dosikles' story, to the point where it links up with the beginning of the main narrative. The pirate chief Gobryas, whom we have already met in Book I as a capricious arbiter of life and death to his captives, now attempts to seduce Rhodanthe.

The second, and central, part of the romance curiously pushes the lovers into the wings, as most of the action is concentrated on the larger affairs of the pirates, on the outcome of which hangs the fate of the princpal characters. Gobryas, at the start of the fourth book, is threatening to make a human sacrifice of the hero and heroine. His superior officer, Mistylos, receives an ultimatum demanding tribute from one Bryaxes, king of Pissa, and the sacrifice has to be postponed. Book V, which occupies the central portion of the romance, scarcely mentions the lovers, as the pirate chief Mistylos and the king of Pissa exchange envoys and prepare for war. In Book VI a spectacular battle is fought, and the pirates who are holding Rhodanthe and Dosikles are beaten. At this point there intrudes into the romance a brutally realistic account of the atrocities associated with the sack of a town. At the end of the book we meet the hero and heroine again, an almost insignificant pair among the many captives loaded on to ships. Dosikles sees the ship carrying Rhodanthe sink, apparently with all hands, but Prodromos, unlike Achilles Tatios or Heliodoros, makes no attempt to keep the reader in suspense.

Book VII begins with the heroine brought ashore in Cyprus, where the action of the final part of the romance will be mainly set. Rhodanthe is now the slave of none other than the parents of Kratandros, the fellow-prisoner of Dosikles. In due course she tells her story to her mistress, Myrilla, whose recognition that her son must be in captivity in Pissa along with Dosikles provides the means to bring the two strands of the plot back together. Kratandros' father immediately sets out for Pissa to bring the young men back to Cyprus. In this way too the subplot of Kratandros' ill-fated love for Chrysochroe becomes part of the main plot. The scene of Book VIII moves back to Pissa, where the sacrifice of Dosikles and Kratandros, twice postponed at the hands of the pirates, is now about to be consummated by their new captor, King Bryaxes. The pair pull out all the stops in an impressive rhetorical display and manage to dissuade the king from his action. But then at the crucial moment help arrives in the form of Kratandros' father, who adds his rhetorical flourishes to theirs. In an amusing reversal of the conventions of the ancient genre, the king now loses patience and decides to send his victims to the stake after all. This fate is prevented only by a shower of rain borrowed from the least sophisticated and least rhetorical of the ancient romances, Xenophon's *Ephesiaka*.[8] Prodromos the rhetor seems here to be deliberately poking fun at his own profession: it isn't fine words that influence actions but the whims of the mighty and the caprices of chance.[9]

Reunited at the home of Kratandros' parents in Cyprus, the lovers face a final threat to their happiness in the form of their friend's mother, Myrilla, who conceives a hysterical passion for Dosikles and almost succeeds in poisoning Rhodanthe. This episode in Book VIII is symmetrical with that in the first part of the romance, in Book III, in which the heroine had been the object of the attentions of the pirate chief, Gobryas. The final book of the romance finds the lovers in a quandary: should they flee from Cyprus and the unwelcome attentions of Myrilla, at the cost of insulting their friend and host, Kratandros? The dilemma is resolved by factors outside their control: the fathers of the lovers turn up unexpectedly and announce that their respective families are now reconciled to the match. The romance ends by repeating briefly, in reverse, the journeys of the protagonists in its first part, this time from Cyprus to Rhodes, and finally home to Abydos.

There are several divergences from the model of the ancient romance which may reflect popular and/or Western influence. The most striking of these is the fact that *Rhodanthe and Dosikles*, like the romances of Eugenianos and Manasses, is written not in prose but, like *Digenes Akrites*, in verse. The verseform is the twelve-syllable accentual metre in which the rules of the ancient iambic trimeter are relaxed in favour of a four-stress rhythm which, as used by Prodromos, has considerable momentum as well as variety in the stress-patterns it produces. It is probably not coincidental that all the early romances in the West are also written in verse, as were the medieval epics, the *chansons de geste*, before them.

If the world of this romance is by and large the Hellenistic world in which its ancient predecessors had been set, a number of important differences signal preoccupations of Prodromos' own time. The military upbringing of the hero, and the details of the embassies and battles between the pirates and the Pissans, reflect recurrent preoccupations of Prodromos' occasional poetry written for the Komnenian court, which accorded a special place to the martial virtues. Pissa, Hunger argues, may well be Pisa, which had been granted trading privileges in 1111 and 1136, and there is no reason to disagree so long as we do not try to carry the identification any further than the name. Less convincingly, Hunger also sees an illusion to the attack on Corfu by Roger II in 1147 in the description of the sack of Rhodes with which the romance begins, on the grounds that the account of that attack by the historian Niketas Choniates shares many of its details and something of its expression.[10] But Choniates was writing more than fifty years after Prodromos' romance had begun to circulate, and it would probably not be the first time that a Greek historian drew on a source in literary fiction to fill out the details of a real historical event.[11]

Carolina Cupane has further demonstrated that in one episode, the conventional topos of human sacrifice by fire, inherited from Xenophon and Heliodoros and repeated in Book VIII, has become an ordeal by fire, which was a contemporary Western custom, regarded as exotic by the Byzantines. She has persuasively identified a particularly notorious instance of ordeal by fire in crusader-held Antioch that may have distantly provoked this episode in the romance.[12] In accepting this argument, one might shift the focus slightly, so as to emphasize the *congruence* between a contemporary exotic custom and a fictional topos as the motivating factor behind this contemporary allusion. There is probably a further (unflattering) allusion to Western Europeans in the name of the pirate 'satrap', Gobryas (Γωβρύας). Transliterated conventionally, the name looks impeccably ancient if not especially Greek. But this is one of the many instances where it is timely to remember that pronunciation in the twelfth century was similar to what it is today. Prodromos may well have been transliterating Geoffroi/Gottfried. Finally it should be mentioned that the word 'Hellene' appears in its revived twelfth-century sense of 'Greek', in a context that explicitly evokes a sense of 'national' solidarity. The hero's fellow-captive Kratandros is introduced as 'a Greek from Cyprus', and Dosikles responds rapturously: 'A Greek, the gods have saved me, this stranger, a Greek?'.[13]

In order to see how actual or suspected contemporary references in Prodromos' romance are subordinated to a specific artistic purpose, it will be useful to re-examine two passages which Hunger has interpreted as evidence of *Aktualisierungsversuch*. The decisive factor in the battle between the pirates and the Pissans in Book VI is the stratagem of Bryaxes, described in some detail, of sending an army of frogmen armed with metal hammers to knock holes in the hulls of the enemy ships. Hunger has seen in this episode a reference to real military technology in the twelfth century.[14] Certainly Prodromos' account has all the appearance of fact, especially when he explains that the hammers had to be small so as not to drag the frogmen down.[15] But like many Byzantine accounts of marvels, real or imaginary, this one is silent on the most important point: how did the frogmen breathe? Without discounting completely the possibility that Prodromos had seen or heard of real frogmen, one may hazard a quite different explanation for this passage. In Book IX of the *Aithiopika* the town of Syene in upper Egypt is besieged by Persians and forced into submission by a spectacular stratagem. Under cover of night the besiegers dig a deep, wide channel all round the outside of the walls and open the floodbanks of the Nile to let the water in. In language which Prodromos echoes frequently in his romance, Heliodoros relishes the paradox of the attackers' ships sailing up to walls which had been built for land defence: 'And it was the most novel of spectacles, a ship sailing between walls and a sailor sailing over land, and a boat passing over arable fields'. Nature is inverted by the artifice of the military strategist: the ingenious artificer who can turn land into water wins the day.[16] What happens in *Rhodanthe and Dosikles* is a simple inversion of the episode in Heliodoros. Again it is a reversal of nature that brings about victory, but instead of ships sailing above arable land we find the infantry going into action beneath the sea.

The fourth book of *Rhodanthe and Dosikles* is almost entirely taken up with the reception by the pirate king Mistylos and his henchman Gobryas of the envoy sent by Bryaxes from Pissa to demand tribute. The details of this narrative, like those of the speeches, preparation and fighting in the two books that follow, are irrelevant to the story of the lovers, who are absent from both scenes. But it would be a mistake to regard either episode as simply a digression. The subordination of nature to human artifice which we detected in the episode of the frogmen assumes far greater proportions in this earlier episode, to the extent that the 'digression' in fact sets out the dominant theme of the whole romance. The envoy is handed over, after a formal exchange of letters, to the 'satrap' Gobryas, who is to entertain him royally.

Artaxanes, the envoy, is intimidated from the first by the strange feast set before him. A roast lamb is brought to table and from its belly flies a flock of live sparrows.[17] Gobryas proceeds to explain that the laws of nature are subject to the will of his master, Mistylos, and goes on to enlarge upon his theme: not only can a roast lamb be 'pregnant' with live sparrows, but at Mistylos' command an army of the bravest men in the midst of a battle could find itself suddenly teeming with alien life and giving birth to little dogs (σκύλακες)! The literal-minded Artaxanes is already routed by this insinuation of male pregnancy, and the two debate its plausibility. The reader is presumably intended to decipher Gobryas' words as a punning allusion to worms (σκώληκες), to which the bodies of fighting men could indeed be said to 'give birth' – if they are killed. A young acrobat then appears, called Satyrion.[18] To Artaxanes' distress, the boy cuts his own throat with a sword, producing a great deal of blood in the process, but at a word from Gobryas he resurrects himself. The trick had been effected, we learn later, 'by dramatic illusion'.[19] The performance ends with Satyrion singing of the glory of Mistylos and with praise for the singer as craftsman (τεχνίτης).[20]

Hunger has drawn attention to the parallels between this episode and

Byzantine court ceremonial as we know it to have been two centuries before Prodromos' time, from the *Book of Ceremonies* and from Liutprand of Cremona, who recorded his experiences in the year 949 at the receiving-end of such tactics.[21] Prodromos himself wrote a large number of poems for ceremonial occasions at court and no doubt had seen foreign envoys subjected to such exhibitions of marvels. But beyond this fact there is probably nothing in Prodromos' story that reflects the details of such ceremonies in the twelfth century. For one thing, the perpetrators of the spectacle in the romance are a particularly nasty crew of pirates; and the allusions to Petronius' *Cena Trimalchionis* should be a sufficient clue that, if a contemporary Byzantine custom is alluded to, it has been subjected to a sinister transformation. It is also important to remember that this elaborate spectacle is cunningly undermined by its narrative context: just before this demonstration by Gobryas of the omnipotence of the pirate chief Mistylos, the same Gobryas has been scheming behind his master's back to win Rhodanthe for himself, even daring to promise Mistylos' daughter for Dosikles if he will aid the enterprise;[22] and in the following book it transpires that the opposing King Bryaxes can subdue nature to his will to more practical effect, in the episode of the frogmen and the subsequent destruction of the pirate fleet and the town.

The marvels of this episode of the romance do, however, have something in common with the real marvels of Byzantine court ceremonial in that they rely on an illusion which is imposing precisely because it parades its artificiality and hence the power of the emperor (or the pirate king) even over nature. Liutprand describes a tree of gilded bronze with singing birds made of the same material, a throne that can be raised and lowered, gilded lions that roar and an acrobatic performance that has some points of similarity with that of the acrobat Satyrion in Prodromos' romance. Byzantine accounts indicate that such things really existed in the first half of the ninth century and again in the tenth. It has been shown that the inspiration for these spectacular devices was almost exclusively literary: the Throne of Solomon in I Kings; the golden plane-tree at Sousa described by Herodotos, and the theoretical writings of Heron of Alexandria.[23] Rather than see Prodromos' marvels as a reference to contemporary Byzantine ceremonial practice, we may regard this episode, and indeed Prodoromos' romance as a whole, as a product of the same underlying impetus as had earlier generated the real marvels of the Byzantine court: the attempt to assert human artifice as superior to the works of nature.

This Gobryas in the story fails to do, and there are other comparable reversals in the romance: for instance, the failure of rhetorical argument to dissuade Bryaxes from carrying out a human sacrifice. But the power over nature which Gobryas claims for his master Mistylos is simultaneously claimed by Prodromos' text itself, and at this level there is no reversal. It is artifice, the 'dramatic illusion' of Prodromos' text, that prevails against a capricious and brutal chance to bring the lovers' wanderings to a happy conclusion. And the salvation that in different ways is sought throughout the Hellenistic romances is to be found, according to Prodromos, in the ingenuity of the intellect and its instrument, rhetoric, to transcend the limitations of nature and the caprices of chance.

Niketas Eugenianos, *Drosilla and Charikles* (*Τὰ κατὰ Δρόσιλλαν καὶ Χαρικλέα*)[24]

Eugenianos was a younger contemporary of Prodromos who survived him to write his epitaph. Like Prodromos he also wrote occasional poetry for the Komnenian court, and one of these pieces, an epithalamium dated to 1156–7, closely echoes the description of the heroine in his romance, and has been used as evidence to date the latter to the years immediately following.[25] The nature of its dependence on Prodromos' romance, and frequent allusions to it, suggest that it may have been written, as the title in one manuscript claims, in homage to Prodromos shortly after his death.[26] Certainly in his monody, or lament, on the death of Prodromos, Eugenianos records his debt to him and admiration for his 'master'.[27] If the death of Prodromos is correctly dated to 1156–8, this would confirm Kazhdan's dating of the romance to shortly after 1157; however, it is not clear what consequences follow if Prodromos lived, as Kazhdan now believes, into the 1170s.

It has long been recognized that Eugenianos' principal model is Prodromos' romance, although he also makes use of the pastoral tradition, and especially of Longos, in an entirely new way.[28] It should be noted that the initials of the hero and heroine, and hence of the title, repeat those of *Daphnis and Chloe*, but with the sexes reversed. In form Eugenianos follows Prodromos faithfully: there are again nine books, and the twelve-syllable accentual metre is again used. However, the organization of the material into books is less rigorous, and the intellectual opposition of art and nature is much reduced, as is the emphasis on military matters.

The contents of the plot can most concisely be summarized by listing the divergences from Prodromos' romance. In the subplot the love-story of the hero's fellow-prisoner, Kleandros, is not concluded before the main story begins as was the case in Prodromos' romance, but continues in parallel with the main narrative. In place of the circumstantial details of the merchants' dinner in Rhodes at which Dosikles related the beginning of his love for Rhodanthe, we have only a single analepsis by Charikles, considerably amplified by lyrical and satirical love-songs and a series of highly complex rhetorical love-letters from the hero to the heroine. After their capture in an enemy raid at the beginning, both hero and heroine end up as slaves in the Parthian court, and both are simultaneously the object of an intrigue in their captors' households. In place of the separate designs of Gobryas on the heroine and of Myrilla on the hero at opposite ends of Prodromos' romance, in Books III–IV Drosilla and Charikles are simultaneously subjected to the unwelcome attentions of the Parthian queen and her son. As a result of these intrigues the king is poisoned and the ensuing power vacuum prompts an invasion by Arabs. In this way the battle and subsequent change of masters, which is common to both romances, is indirectly a consequence of the lovers' fatal charms, thus bringing about a closer unity of the action than we find in Prodromos' romance.

Thereafter the plots diverge completely. Eugenianos' lovers are carried off by their new masters by land, not by sea, and it is Drosilla's accidental fall from a cart while travelling along a clifftop that separates her from Charikles. They then separately make their way to a village where Drosilla becomes the object of the pressing and comical attentions of the innkeeper's son, and the two are reunited in the hovel of the old woman Maryllis (a comical transformation of Theokritos' Amaryllis), where news come to Kleandros of the death of his mistress Kalligone. This means of weaving together the main plot with a tragic subplot is one of the most original departures made by Eugenianos, and produces the most striking effect of this carefully integrated narrative. By contrast to his models, in which the subsidiary pair of lovers is disposed of fairly soon after being introduced, Eugenianos delays the death of Kalligone in the subplot until almost the end of the romance.[29] As a result, the climax of one of the frankest love scenes between the principal characters in the ancient or twelfth-century romance, in which the claims of chastity seem to have been outweighed by the example of the sparrows in the trees and by the argument that 'who knows what Chance may bring?', is afforded by the irruption of their friend Kleandros upon the scene with the devastating news that the girl with whom he had hoped throughout the story to be reunited has died. So at the end of Eugenianos' romance the happy reunion of the principal pair of lovers is offset by the simultaneously tragic outcome of the subplot which has so far run parallel to it; and the death of Kalligone causes the bereft Kleandros shortly afterwards to die of grief.[30] It is neither accidental nor unimportant, we must suppose, that the final book of *Drosilla and Charikles* should begin with a funeral, intersperse rejoicing with laments, and end with a wedding. The lovers' adventures are brought to a close through the good offices of a merchant by the name of Gnathon who agrees, for a price, to transport them home in his ship. This mercenary *deus ex machina* seems intended as a deliberate counterbalance to the merchants depicted in Book II of *Rhodanthe and Dosikles*, among whom the hero – and possibly Prodromos as well – seemed very much at home. Eugenianos' attitudes generally appear more aristocratic than those of Prodromos in his romance, and the unflattering name, Gnathon, is also that of the homosexual parasite who intervenes at a comparable stage in the action of *Daphnis and Chloe*.

Kazhdan has argued that Eugenianos parodies the conventions of the genre in which he is writing. Certainly there is a new comic note in his romance, which makes its first appearance in the ribald songs of Charikles' contemporaries in Book III and reaches a crescendo in Book VI, in the yokel Kallidemos' absurdly literary wooing of Drosilla, and in the antics of Maryllis, who gets drunk and dances on the table as the lovers celebrate their reunion in Book VII. It is conspicuous, however, that the aspect of this scene that arouses most mirth among the onlookers is that the old woman ends by falling on her head and farting mightily.[31] But the subtler signs of parody that Kazhdan identifies cannot be conclusively proved.

In style this romance shows a marked development in the direction both of the lyricism and of the linguistic inventiveness of the later vernacular romances. The latter tendency is manifested in the coining of a significant number of compound words, which seems to have been a resource of the spoken language and, as we shall see in Chapter 6, is taken to extreme in the romances of the fourteenth and fifteenth centuries.[32] Eugenianos reasserts several strands of the genre that had been eclipsed by Prodromos and adds some new ones of his own: love-poetry is very pointedly restored, and we find lyrical elaborations of the theme of love and its associations in no fewer than six evocations of the garden or paradisal landscape,[33] as well as love-songs and love-letters and a whole new iconography of love. Nature, which Prodromos had rigorously subordinated to the intellect and its artifices, is also reinstated; and the second part of the romance, in which the lovers are reunited against a background of rustic nature and almost obey the example of the sparrows and their own natural instincts to break the rule of chastity, can be read as a fully conscious answer to Prodromos' intellectuality. Artifice is of course still present, not least in the telling of these 'natural' episodes, and this demonstration that artifice can aid the work of nature rather than violate it might, rather schematically, be considered as Eugenianos' principal contribution to the genre.

Konstantinos Manasses, *Aristandros and Kallithea* (Τὰ κατὰ ᾿Αρίστανδρον καὶ Καλλιθέαν)[34]

The author of this romance seems to have belonged to the same literary circle as Prodromos and the prolific allegorizer Ioannes Tzetzes, that was active around the middle of the twelfth century and may have been supported financially by members of the imperial family.[35] Between 1143 and 1152 Manasses wrote his most substantial surviving work, the influential *Synopsis Historike*, a world-chronicle in the long-established 'popularizing' tradition of Byzantine chronography, but the first of its kind to be written in verse. *Aristandros and Kallithea* may be contemporary with this work or may belong to the following decades. If the author is to be identified with the bishop of Naupaktos of that name who died in 1187, he must have been fairly young when he embarked on his chronicle. The most probable date for the romance is within a few years either side of 1160.[36]

Manasses' romance was the first of the four to capture the imagination of modern editors, who have devoted much ingenuity to reconstructing its plot. The results of these labours remain somewhat disappointing: the fragments which survive come from compilations of memorable moral precepts put together between the fourteenth and the sixteenth century, and represent the least interesting passages from a literary point of view.[37] The story seems to have followed Prodromos and Heliodoros in beginning *in medias res*, while in other respects, like Prodromos, Manasses prefers to follow Achilles Tatios.[38] Hero and heroine fall successively into the hands of at least three tyrannical masters, both are subjected to unwelcome attentions and trials of their constancy, and Aristandros narrowly escapes death on at least one occasion. Ending up in Egypt, the pair are finally set free in the course of a battle between barbarian forces and take ship for their native Greece.[39] New elements in the story seem to have been the role of the wicked eunuch,[40] a conventional enough figure in other Byzantine contexts but new in the romance; and the author's fascination with fabulous and exotic beasts, which seems to derive from Athenaios and Aelian.[41] This new contribution to the romance will reappear in the later vernacular texts, in the descriptions of the Ogre's Castle in *Kallimachos and Chrysorrhoe* and of the Castle of Eros in *Belthandros and Chrysantza*.

It is significant that Manasses was the first writer of romance to use the fifteen-syllable verseform, the so-called 'political' verse (πολιτικός στίχος), which from the fourteenth to the seventeenth century became obligatory in the vernacular romance, and which we have already encountered as the metre of *Digenes Akrites* and such early oral poetry as the 'Song of Armoures' (Chapter 3). The frequent appearance of hiatus in Manasses' metre suggests that, like other learned writers of the eleventh and twelfth centuries who used this verseform, he was not drawing directly on popular sources. But there is a good deal of circumstantial evidence to suggest that the 'political' verse was used in oral as well as in learned poetry by the twelfth century (see Chapter 6), so that Manasses' choice of it for a fictional narrative could be regarded as a literary gesture towards contemporary oral narrative – a gesture whose significance may have been recognized and taken up by writers of romance in the fourteenth and fifteenth centuries when they began to create a literary idiom based on the vernacular.[42] However, there are scarcely any direct hints of influence from popular tradition in the surviving fragments of *Aristandros and Kallithea*.[43]

Eustathios Makrembolites, *Hysmine and Hysminias* (Τὸ καθ' Ὑσμίνην καὶ Ὑσμινίαν Δρᾶμα)[44]

Traditionally dated to the 1180s, this would have been the last of the twelfth-century 'learned' romances to be written. It is the only medieval Greek romance to revert to the ancient medium for the genre, prose. Its author is otherwise known only as the composer of a brief collection of riddles and as the recipient of a letter written after 1180. Attempts to identify him with his comtemporary Eustathios of Thessalonike or with the somewhat later Eustathios who may have been the compiler of the fifteenth-century 'Z' version of *Digenes* have been generally discredited.[45] Makrembolites makes even fewer direct allusions to contemporary realia than Prodromos, and for the first time in the Greek romance the geography is entirely fictional. As in Prodromos' romance, however, the term 'Hellenes' is used in its twelfth-century sense to refer to the community of Greek-speakers: Hysminias finds himself in the hands of 'Greeks speaking the same language' and later the 'law of the Hellenes' is invoked, according to which Greeks may not be slaves.[46]

In these respects *Hysmine and Hysminias* belongs together with the other romances of the twelfth century. Attempts to date it more precisely, and to reconcile the very slender biographical indications linking the author to the period around 1180 with the literary-historical affinities of the text, have reached an intriguing impasse. A resolution of this problem must await a full study of the dating of all four twelfth-century romances. In a challenging series of articles, S.V. Polyakova has argued that Makrembolites' romance is the earliest of the twelfth-century romances, on which the *progymnasmata* of Nikephoros Basilakes and Prodromos' romance, both accepted as dating from the mid-century, drew as a source.[47] A significant number of links with the Old French *Roman de la Rose*, in the iconography of love and in the allegorical imagery of Hysminias' dreams, she further explains in terms of influence by the Greek romance on the French, and these conclusions have been accepted by Kazhdan and Epstein.[48] Against this Carolina Cupane has argued that the presentation of Eros the King in this romance represents a break with the earlier Greek tradition and reflects the influence, if not directly of the *Roman de la Rose*, then certainly of the emerging topos of the Dieu d'Amor which was well established in Old French and Provençal literature in the twelfth century. She further cites one case where Makrembolites apparently draws directly on a French text, the *Fablel du Dieu d'Amor*, of the late twelfth or early thirteenth century.[49] According to Cupane it is impossible that the courtly iconography of love in the West could have been influenced by Makrembolites, because it was already well established there in lyric poetry even before the twelfth century while it represents a new departure in the Greek romance.[50]

Two provisional comments can be made here. The first is that the evidence for Prodromos' and Basilakes' dependence on Makrembolites as presented by Polyakova is far from conclusive. The connections are plain to see, but in the present state of our knowledge there is nothing in the comparison of similar passages to prove conclusively which came first. On the other hand Cupane, who seems to accept the traditional dating of the romance to the late twelfth century, does not give sufficient consideration to the implications of Makrembolites' alleged dependence on the *Roman de la Rose*. Even assuming that he knew only the first part of that poem, attributed to Guillaume de Lorris, this text is unlikely to have been in existence before the first quarter of the thirteenth century.[51] If Makrembolites really did know the *Roman* and the *Fablel* as Cupane has argued, the consequence would have to be faced that *Hysmine and Hysminias* is a work of the thirteenth century and not of the twelfth. A less extreme proposal would be to suppose that the topoi of courtly love poetry, as it had already developed in the West, were introduced to Byzantium by the second crusade in 1147,[52] and first exploited in combination with traditional Greek themes by Basilakes in his *progymnasmata* (a possibility which will be taken up again in Chapter 10 and the Afterword).[53]

Hysmine and Hysminias is the only one of the 'learned' romances to have gained a place in a standard history of European literature. J. C. Dunlop, whose *History of Prose Fiction* was first published in 1814, was both scathing and patronizing, but also recognized, albeit grudgingly, the significant technical innovation of Makrembolites' use of first-person narrative:

> In the whole there is no decency, no probability, no invention, no happy disposition of incident. The author introduces the hero relating his own adventures; but one cannot discover whom he addresses, or why he is discursing.[54]

This was also the first of the medieval Greek romances to have been seriously examined in recent years as a work of literature.[55] Gigante has shown the extent to which covert allusions and quotations from a wealth of ancient authors go to make up the medieval text, a feature which immediately reminds us of Byzantine satire, but scarcely any less of Lucian and the ancient romance.[56] Gigante accounts for this with the suggestion that 'the whole romance is *nothing but* a literary game', although a little later he hints that an explanation of the romance's relation to its ancient models, along the lines proposed in the previous chapter, may be necessary.[57]

The humorous potential of the classical quotations and allusions, first identified by Gigante, was also recognized by Hunger, who further drew attention to the detailed psychology of the romance and the innovative use of erotic dreams.[58] These suggestions have since been taken up and developed with insight and originality by Margaret Alexiou, in the most thoroughgoing attempt so far to rehabilitate any of the twelfth-century romances as an achievement of serious literature. Alexiou pays careful attention to the departures of the romance from its evident model in *Leukippe and Kleitophon* by Achilles Tatios: notably in the much more consistent use of first-person narration (the 'frame-story' with which Achilles begins but neglects to end has been cut out so that everything in the text is narrated by Hysminias) and in the reduction of extraneous interest in the plot so that the narrator's point of view is never violated. As a result, she points out, we learn of Hysmine's adventures during the time that she was separated from the narrator only at the point where she tells her story to the assembled company in the final book. Another significant departure from his model noted by Alexiou is Makrembolites' psychological treatment of the main characters. The heroine's

> change from initial immodesty to later (relative) chastity has been criticized as inconsistent; but since she exists only as seen by Hysminias and not as a character in her own right, the inconsistency is not obtrusive ... Eustathios ... shows some insight into female behaviour as viewed by men.[59]

Alexiou identifies a similar realism in the detailed imagery of Hysminias' erotic dreams and concludes that:

> Eustathios' innovations in narrative technique, his bold eroticism, and his highly selective use of conventional episodes and stock devices, combine to add two new dimensions to the history of the romance: humour (even parody) and psychology.[60]

The popularity of this romance in the later Middle Ages, to which she draws attention 'is due to Eustathios' treatment of ancient models, which reflects a dynamic rather than a static attitude towards the past'.[61] Thomas Hägg, in his survey of the ancient romances, justly gives prominence to this reappraisal of *Hysmine and Hysminias* but adds the cautious 'reservation that perhaps this time the pendulum has swung a bit too far in the positive direction'.[62]

To the distinctive achievement of this romance as discussed by Gigante, Hunger and Alexiou a further element must now be added, and that is the theme of time and its relation to art, which goes a long way towards accounting for the ostentatious artifice of Makrembolites' style that remains a stumbling-block for any attempt to rehabilitate the romance according to modern aesthetic principles.

The narrative falls naturally into three distinct parts.[63] In the first the hero–narrator, Hysminias, is sent in the capacity of herald, as part of a regular religious festival, from his native Eurykomis to the neighbouring town of Aulikomis. He is housed there by one of the leading notables, whose house and garden are adorned with spectacular pictures and automata. His host's daughter, Hysmine, makes eyes at him and he at first rebuffs her. The bulk of this part of the romance is taken up with the description of a series of allegorical paintings – of Eros, the four cardinal virtues and the twelve months of the year – subtly interspersed with a series of dreams and waking encounters with Hysmine, in the course of which the hero falls irremediably in love with the heroine. This part ends with the return of all the actors to Hysminias' home town, Eurykomis, where the fictitious festival of the Diasia (festival of Zeus) is concluded by an act of reciprocal hospitality.

In the central part of the romance, which takes up Books VI–VIII, it is first of all learnt that Hysmine's father has arranged a marriage for her back in

Aulikomis, and she and Hysminias decide to elope. Their ship runs into a storm, and Hysmine has to be jettisoned to placate an angry Poseidon. Saved by a dolphin (as we learn much later), she becomes a slave in the Greek city of Artykomis. Meanwhile Hysminias is taken captive by pirates who are themselves overwhelmed by a Greek army, with the result that he too becomes a slave, in the neighbouring town of Daphnepolis. The second part concludes with Hysminias's anguish as the season of the Diasia comes round again: the festival is not celebrated in Daphnepolis, and he himself has exchanged the prestige of Zeus' herald for the condition of a slave. Another festival is shortly to be held, however, and his master is chosen for the role of herald.

The third part begins with Book IX, in which Hysminias' master takes him along on the ritual journey to Artykomis, to be entertained there by the very family in which Hysmine is also a slave. The narration at this point is full of ironic allusions to the parallel sequence of events in Book I, in which Hysminias had been the herald and he had first met Hysmine. At first he only half recognizes her in her new state, then she reveals herself by letter. For a time Hysmine is obliged to act the go-between for her mistress, Rhodope, who has fallen violently in love with Hysminias; but before this situation can become critical the intrigue is resolved by the arrival of the lovers' parents. After some wrangling the pair are set free, Hysmine proves her chastity, and all return to the heroine's home town of Aulikomis for the wedding.

Alexiou has pointed out that the time-scheme of the romance is strict and carefully devised.[64] The action of the first five books is principally concentrated into four days and nights during the festival of the Diasia, while the last three books narrate the events of six days and nights during the festival of Apollo at Artykomis. The adventures of the middle part of the romance are again principally concentrated into a small number of days, but in Book VIII a larger interval of time elapses, 'probably a year, assuming that the Diasia was an annual festival'.[65] In fact there is a dislocation at this point, since the anniversary of the Diasia has already passed before Hysminias' master is despatched to Artykomis for the festival of Apollo there, and Makrembolites for once does not specify how long an interval is involved:

Ὁ τῶν Διασίων ἧκε καιρός· καὶ κἂν Δαφνήπολις οὐ τιμᾷ τὰ Διάσια, κἂν οὐκ ἄγῃ πανήγυριν, ἀλλ' ἔμ' οὐ διέλαθε, καὶ τὴν μνήμην ἀνῆψε καὶ τὸν θρῆνον ἐξήγειρεν ...[66]

The time of the Diasia came; and for all that Daphnepolis does not honour the Diasia nor stages a festival, it did not escape my notice but kindled my memory and roused me to lament.

But since Hysminias' lament is overheard by his mistress, and recalled on the eve of his master's departure for the festival of Apollo,[67] we may assume that the second festival follows fairly closely upon the anniversary of the first.

So the action of the romance spans just over a year, with the events of the last part running in close parallel with those of the first, but with significant displacements in time, place and action. The second festival follows the same pattern as the first but not at quite the same point in the year; heralds make a ritual journey from one town to another but they are not the same towns (and neither in space nor in time is the extent of this displacement precisely revealed); and in the action Hysminias once again meets Hysmine in the course of this ritual journey, but this time both are slaves, a state which mirrors in displaced form their enslavement to Eros the King in Book III. The full significance of this careful structure will become apparent when we try to account for the presence of two passages which, according to modern aesthetic standards, have the appearance of digressions.

The first is the long *ekphrasis* in Book IV of the series of paintings representing the months of the year. These descriptions of seasonal activities derive from a tradition going back to antiquity and conform fairly closely to surviving Byzantine illustrations of the months from the eleventh to the thirteenth century as well as to an earlier literary realization by Prodromos.[68] Following a common Byzantine practice, the series begins with March, which is represented by a young man in armour (presumably suggested by the identification of the name of the month with the Roman god of war). The cycle of paintings includes various bucolic scenes and ends with the following, representing February:

Τέλος κρατῆρες πυρὸς ἐγεγράφατο καὶ φλὸξ ὡς ἀπὸ γῆς μέχρις αὐτῶν οὐρανῶν, ὡς μηδ' ἔχειν μαθεῖν εἴτ' ἐξ αἰθέρος εἰς γῆν ἐκχεῖται τὸ πῦρ ἄιτ' ἀπὸ γῆς ἐξῆπται πρὸς οὐρανόν. Καί τις ἀνὴρ ἐκατονταπέμπελος παρακάθηται τῇ φλογί, ὅλος ῥυτίς, ὅλος πολιὰ καὶ τὴν κεφαλὴν καὶ τὸν πώγωνα, διφθέραν ἐνδεδυμένος ἐκ κεφαλῆς εἰς ὀσφύν, τὰ δ' ἄλλα γυμνός, τὼ χεῖρε, τὼ πόδε καὶ τὸ πολὺ τῆς γαστρός. Ἐκτεταμένας εἶχε τὰς χεῖρας καὶ οἷον μεθεῖλκε τὴν φλόγα καὶ μετερρίπιζε καὶ ὅλην μετῆγε πρὸς ἑαυτόν.[69]

Finally braziers of fire were painted and a flame that seemed to reach from earth to very heaven, such that you could not tell whether the fire flows from the upper air to earth or from the earth reaches out toward the heavens. And an ancient man sits by the fire, all wrinkled, with hair and beard quite grey, dressed in a leather hide from head to waist, but the rest of him is naked – his hands, his feet and most of his abdomen. He held his hands outstretched as though to draw the fire and fan it and divert it towards himself.

The equation of the sequence of the months with the progress from youth to age is already implicit in the Byzantine iconographical tradition,[70] but in his depiction of February Makrembolites has added a detail all his own: the conventional brazier over which the old man warms his hands has become a great fire linking earth with heaven; and, rather daringly, it is not clear whether the origin of the fire is earthly or divine. In the context of the genre, this unprecedented image must represent love itself, which time and old age will put out of reach. Makrembolites goes on to make his point explicitly: Hysminias cannot concentrate on the pictures as his thoughts are all of Hysmine, until his friend Kratisthenes draws his attention to an iambic line inscribed above the heads of the figures:

τοὺς ἄνδρας ἀθρῶν τὸν χρόνον βλέπεις ὅλον.[71]

gazing at the men [in the pictures] you see the whole of time.

This message strikes home, and the hero and his friend together puzzle out the allegorical significance of each of the scenes. Of the explanations that follow, some refer only to the season of the year, others are no more than a gloss on the figure represented (e.g. March), but others hint that the successive seasons of the paintings correspond to the 'seasons' of life. This is quite explicit by the time we get to the last of the series, February, in which the 'harshness of winter' is 'no less than the chill of old age' (the transferred epithets further heightening the metaphor). Winter, moreover, in a quotation adapted from Hesiod, 'does not pierce the tender-skinned maiden, but bends an old man into a hoop'.[72]

This series of tableaux, and the ensuing discussion with Kratisthenes about what they mean, complete the process begun by Hysminias' encounter with the picture of Eros upon his throne.[73] It was Eros the King as represented in this picture that visited him in a dream and first commanded him to return Hysmine's love. Now this series of pictures warns him that love is not invincible to time: it is not enough to love only in dreams as he had done the previous night.[74] And on the night immediately following he declares his love in reality to an astonished Hysmine.[75]

There are other references in the romance to time and the seasons. The fathers of Hysminias and Hysmine, simultaneously lamenting their children's misfortunes, allude to their libations 'on behalf of children pitifully lost in the height of spring, in an ungarnered meadow and the midst of youth';[76] and there seems to be a conscious allusion to time in the repetition of elements from the first part of the story in the third part which takes place a little more than a year afterwards.[77] But the second of the two 'digressions', which comes at the very end of the romance, picks up this theme again and retrospectively explains why works of art should have played such a large part in Hysminias' initiation in the early books.

The narrative effectively comes to an end with the wedding and the narrator's impatience for night and the long-deferred consummation of his love. And suddenly this wait is frozen into eternity, as the narrator abandons his narrative and addresses a fervent prayer, instead, to love and the gods:

μὴ βυθὸς ἀμνηστίας κατεπικλύσῃ ταῦτα τὰ καθ' ἡμᾶς, μὴ χρόνος μακρός, μὴ ῥυτίς, μὴ λήθης κρατὴρ ἐν Ἅδου κιρνώμενος.[78]

may no abyss of forgetfulness engulf these experiences of ours, no wrinkle, nor duration of time, nor the cup of Lethe mixed in Hades.

Zeus, he fears, will hardly 'make his memory eternal' by inscribing it, like that of Herakles, among the stars. There is a characteristic pun here on πλανήτης as a planet and as a wanderer such as he and Hysmine have been. Zeus will not forgive him for having preferred the service of Eros to his. Poseidon might have granted them eternity, as he did to Ikaros by naming an island after him, but Poseidon will hardly forgive them either, after Hysmine's miraculous escape from his anger on the sea. Perhaps then 'Mother Earth' will afford them immortality by turning them into plants like Daphne or Hyacinth? Alas, no, lest she should be flooded by an implacable Poseidon:

Τοίνυν εἰ Ζεὺς οὐ καταστερίσει τὰ καθ' ἡμᾶς, εἰ Ποσειδῶν οὐ καταστηλογραφήσει τοῖς ὕδασιν, εἰ Γῆ μὴ φυτουργήσει τοῖς φυτοῖς καὶ τοῖς ἄνθεσιν, ἀλλ' ὡς ἐν ἀμαράντοις ξύλοις καὶ λίθοις ἀδάμασιν Ἑρμοῦ γραφίδι καὶ μέλανι καὶ γλώσσῃ πῦρ πνεούσῃ ῥητορικὸν τὰ καθ' ἡμᾶς στηλογραφηθήσεται, καί τις τῶν ὀψιγόνων καταρρητορεύσει ταῦτα καὶ ὡς ἀθανάτῳ στήλῃ τοῖς λόγοις ἀνδριάντα χαλκουργήσει κατάχρυσον.[79]

So, then, if Zeus will not place our story among the stars, if Poseidon will not imprint it upon the waters, if Earth will not nurture it in plants and flowers, then, as though in unfading timbers and in adamantine precious stones, with Hermes' pen and ink and in language breathing the fire of rhetoric let our story be inscribed, and let some one of those who come after turn it into rhetoric and forge a golden statue hammered out of words as our imperishable monument.

The romance then concludes with a brief epilogue in which the author, stepping out of the character of his narrator, recommends the book to his readers.

Makrembolites here gives the highest praise which even a Byzantine could muster to the art of rhetoric, equating it explicitly with the richest and most enduring monuments of nature and the visual arts. It is the art of rhetoric, and not the discredited mythology with which, in this passage, Makrembolites makes such fine rhetorical play, that can immortalize the human, secular love of the hero and heroine and preserve it from the fate that time, in the allegorical pictures of the months, promises to bring. This, finally, is why such a large part in the hero's initiation is played by works of art: he is also being initiated into the mysteries of that art upon which, as *narrator*, he will be required to draw in order to complete the process that begins with his falling in love and ends with his transforming that love into a permanent literary monument.

CONCLUSION

Once again the discussion of the twelfth-century romances, this time considered individually and without reference to their ancient models, has focused on the concept of τέχνη (art or artifice). Through the observation of how contemporary realia may sometimes be covertly assimilated in these texts, and the analysis of key passages, we have in effect discovered an important principle underlying the poetics of all four twelfth-century romances. These are not identical in each case, and indeed little can usefully be said about Manasses' fragmentary *Aristandros and Kallithea* under this heading. But Prodromos throughout his romance is bursting to tell us (indirectly of course) his views about art and nature, rhetoric and power. Of the three complete romances his is the most uncompromisingly intellectual: according to Prodromos, it is rhetoric and the author's inventiveness that confer permanence on the lovers' union and in a different way offer something stable and lasting to his readers as well. But this reassurance is tempered by touchingly ironic reminders that rhetoric is all too often impotent in the real world, a dilemma which the romance does not really resolve, and which is carried over into the many personal asides and complaints of Prodromos' ceremonial poetry – and indeed into the comic *Poems of Poor Prodromos* in the vernacular which are often attributed to him.

Eugenianos, by contrast, is lighter in weight, more 'romantic' in his treatment. But Eugenianos is scarcely less aware than Prodromos of his literary debts; and when these are not to Prodromos himself they are most significantly to the pastoral tradition. Beauty, both of people and of things, is more obviously extolled in this romance, but Eugenianos is far from indifferent to the artifice by which that beauty is represented (or created?) and given permanent form in the literary text.

Finally Makrembolites brings the new rhetorical trends of these romances to their most developed and integrated form. The plot of *Hysmine and Hysminias* owes far more to Prodromos' and Eugenianos' romances than to *Leukippe and Kleitophon* but has been reduced to bare essentials: the subplots, and most of the piratical escapades and battles (all of them hangovers from the Hellenistic romance) have been discarded in favour of a symmetrically constructed plot which consists largely of the inner experiences of the hero. By a brilliant stroke of invention, Makrembolites has given his romance the rhetorical form, not of *diegema* (narrative), but of *ethopoeia* (character study), and has drawn profitably on the risqué and inventive exercises in this genre by Nikephoros Basilakes that were discussed in Chapter 2. The result is that the text presents a twofold initiation – the hero is subjected to the mastery of love, but this is brought about through works of art, which then come alive in his dreams. The key to the romance turns out to lie in the succession of allegorical paintings described in Books II to IV: of love, the four cardinal virtues and the twelve months of the year. Through art Hysminias learns the power of love, the centrality of virtue and the rapacity of time. In the service of love and virtue he goes through trials of his love for Hysmine; in order to preserve it from the depredations of time, he vows to make their love imperishable in a book, in rhetoric. *Hysmine and Hysminias* surpasses the other complete twelfth-century romances in its restraint and control, combining a degree of Prodromos' intellectuality with the greater 'human interest' of Eugenianos. Its ending brings together the two levels on which, more or less consciously, all three of these romances had operated, as the longing of the lovers is satisfied not by their actual union (which in a sense they forgo) but by the promise of an immortality which is the gift of no god, pagan or Christian, but of the human artifice of rhetoric.

Part II
1204–1453

6

THE FIRST 'MODERN GREEK' LITERATURE

The brief period during which the boundaries of the Byzantine state coincided largely with the geographical spread of spoken Greek came to an abrupt end in 1204. In April of that year the knights of the fourth crusade, under the leadership of Baldwin of Montferrat, and urged on by the expansionist policies of the Republic of Venice, turned aside from their declared goal of the Holy Land and sacked Constantinople instead. After half a century of Latin rule, in 1261 the newly established Palaiologos dynasty regained control of their capital and held power with only a single brief interruption until the Ottoman conquest of 1453. But the empire as a political and economic entity never really recovered, and the political history of the final two centuries of Byzantium is one of continuous conflict, both civil and external, and of inexorably shrinking geographical boundaries and economic and military strength. Although Constantinople itself reverted to Byzantine control after a relatively short interregnum, and a number of territories, notably the greater part of the Peloponnese, were later regained by the Byzantines, for most of the period substantial Greek-speaking populations lived outside what was left of the Byzantine empire. In the thirteenth and fourteenth centuries Crete and Euboea (then known as Negroponte) belonged to Venice, as did Thessalonike briefly in the fifteenth century; the Dodecanese were ruled by the Knights Hospitaller of St John; Cyprus and parts of the Peloponnese by the dynasties of Lusignan and Villehardouin respectively; while Athens and Boeotia were fought over between French, Catalans and Florentines throughout the period. Epiros in the north-west, formally a 'despotate' within the empire and with dynastic links to Constantinople, was in reality governed for much of the period by the Italian Tocco family.

In Anatolia the Osmanli or Ottoman Turks succeeded the Seljuks of the eleventh and twelfth centuries as the dominant military force, and the Greek-speaking western coastline including Smyrna was in their hands by the mid-fourteenth century. During the civil war over the succession to Andronikos III, Turkish mercenaries were first brought across the Bosphoros by John Cantacuzene in 1342 and thereafter came to dominate most of Thrace and Macedonia.[1] By 1453 only the city itself and the outposts of Mystras in the west and Trebizond in the east remained. On 29 May of that year, after a bitter siege, the city fell to the Ottoman sultan, Mehmet the Conqueror, and the thousand-year empire of 'New Rome' came to an end. After 1461, with the surrender of the 'empire of Trebizond', the only extensive Greek-speaking areas not ruled by the Ottomans were Crete, the Ionian islands, the Dodecanese and Cyprus, all of which remained for the time being under Western control. Of these the Dodecanese were captured by the Turks in 1522, Cyprus in 1571 and Crete between 1645 and 1669. Only the Ionian islands (with the short-lived exception of Leukas) never formed part of the Ottoman empire. Not until the declaration of national independence in 1821 was there again a Greek self-governing state, and only after the enforced population exchanges with Turkey in 1922–3 did its boundaries again largely coincide with the geographical spread of the Greek language, as they had done, by an accident of history, in the twelfth century.

THE RISE OF VERNACULAR LITERATURE

The literary developments of this period of political confusion and fragmentation in many respects show a remarkable continuity from the intellectual and rhetorical interest of the twelfth century. The bulk of Byzantine literature from the final period is once again taken up with religious issues, the most important among them being the internal débâcle within the Orthodox Church provoked by Gregory Palamas and the Hesychast movement, and the powerful polemics for and against union with the Church of Rome (a move finally frustrated by the Orthodox rank and file). Court panegyric, scientific and rhetorical works, 'begging poetry' addressed to imperial patrons, as well as a small amount of satire, develop the more conservative aspects of such writing in the twelfth century. Much the most radical form of literary engagement with the changed world of Greek-speakers after 1204 is the sudden emergence in the early fourteenth century of the vernacular as the unchallenged medium for almost all literary fiction. The dominant role in this literary movement is played by the romance.[2]

The eleven romance texts will be introduced in detail in the next chapter and in Chapter 9, while a number of others in related genres will be discussed in the final chapter. In addition to the romances, the vernacular was used for two long chronicles in verse and one in prose, celebrating the deeds of Western dynasties. These are, respectively, the *Chronicle of the Morea*, about the Peloponnese,[3] the *Chronicle of the Tocco*, about Epiros,[4] both of them anonymous, and the *Recital concerning the Sweet Land of Cyprus* by Leontios Machairas.[5] The first of these, which can be dated to the first part of the fourteenth century, is one of the earliest vernacular poems that can be accurately dated in this period, and is generally agreed to be the closest surviving witness to the spoken idiom of the time. Since the *Chronicle of the Morea* is vehemently anti-Byzantine in its attitudes, it is generally supposed that its author was little influenced by the language and literary conventions of Byzantine 'high' literature;[6] it must be emphasized, however, that no writer at this time could have learnt the practicalities of writing Greek without some degree of contact with the language and rhetorical curriculum of Byzantine education, and traces of both can in fact be found in the text.

It is interesting that all three vernacular chronicles were written in Western-dominated regions; and their language as well as their attitudes offer a stark contrast to Byzantine historiography in the 'high' tradition, as we find it in the histories of Niketas Choniates in the thirteenth century and of the former emperor John Cantacuzene in the fourteenth. However, as we shall see, the rise of vernacular writing cannot be neatly restricted to Latin-controlled areas. The other main group of vernacular texts is made up of humorous political allegories drawn respectively from the worlds of quadrupeds, birds, fruit and fish. The last two, which are very brief, are among the few examples of vernacular prose at this period.[7]

It has long been realized that the 'vernacular' in which all of these texts were composed during the fourteenth and fifteenth centuries is far from being simply the spoken Greek of the time transferred to parchment.[8] In all the romances and other texts in the vernacular there are words, grammatical forms and syntactical constructions which have been borrowed wholesale from the learned language; and, more puzzlingly, a large number of variant forms co-exist in them. Many of these variants are today characteristic of different regional dialects, but most vernacular texts up till the mid-fifteenth century show no consistent features of a single modern dialect.[9] The exceptions are poetry in the Cretan dialect from about 1370 and, in the dialect of Cyprus, a translation of French lawbooks and Machairas' *Recital*. These reveal that some at least of the dialects of modern Greek were well developed by the end of the fourteenth century. Why, then, are recognizable dialect features avoided in the majority of texts until after the fall of Constantinople? Conceivably the mixed or 'common' language of these texts was the spoken idiom of the capital;[10] but it is more probable that the mixture of regional dialects, and of spoken with written vocabulary and grammar, represents an art-language or *Kunstsprache* evolved for literary purposes. The precise nature of this art-language will be discussed in detail in Chapter 11.

Characteristic of this 'common' language is an extravagance, that must surely be self-conscious, in the coining of new compound words. The combination of two lexical roots to produce new words is a regular feature of both ancient and modern Greek, although the modern language allows greater freedom in the types of root and the sequence in which they may be combined.[11] However, in vernacular verse texts of the fourteenth and fifteenth centuries this resource, which we saw tentatively emerging in the twelfth-century romances of Eugenianos and Manasses, is exploited with a reckless exuberance unparalleled at any other period and in any other kind of writing. To what extent this 'piling-up' was characteristic of spoken usage or was a peculiarity of the art-language of vernacular poetry, is difficult to tell. But a glance at some of the more recondite compounds thrown up in the romances assures us that these can only have been the proud creations of poets writing on this particular theme, to whatever degree they may have based themselves on a resource available in common parlance.

Libistros and Rhodamne, the longest of the vernacular romances originally written in Greek, contains the largest number of different compounds of the root *Eroto-*: approximately forty-six, together with a further ninety-one miscellaneous compounds which were sufficiently unusual or complex to be noted. Clear signs that this linguistic feature has acquired the status of a stylistic device can be seen in passages, almost always in descriptive writing (*ekphraseis*), where such compounds are grouped together, often entirely filling the half-line unit of the fifteen-syllable verseform. Here, with literal translation, is part of the description of the hero's bride-to-be in the *Tale of Achilles*:

> φεγγαρομεγαλόφθαλμος ἦτον ἡ κόρη ἐκείνη
> καὶ κοκκινοπλουμόχειλη, σελήνης λαμπροτέρα,
> μαρμαροχιονόδοντος, γλυκοστοματοβρύσις,
> ἀσπροκοκκινομάγουλη, γέννημα τῶν χαρίτων,
> κρυσταλλοχιονοτράχηλος, ὑπερανασταλμένη,
> στρογγυλεμορφοπούγουνη καὶ κάλλος εἶχεν ξένον.[12]

> Moon-great-eyed was that maiden ...
> and red-adorned-lipped, brighter than the moon,
> marble-snow-toothed, ‹a› sweet-mouth-fountain,
> white-red-checked, born of graces,
> crystal-snow-necked, ultra-tall,
> round-beautiful-chinned and a remarkable beauty.

The heroine of the translated *Phlorios and Platzia-Phlora* is first described, in terms whose content follows its Italian source closely enough, but whose expression draws on a resource peculiar to the literary Greek vernacular of the period:

> τὴν κρουσταλλίδαν τοῦ νεροῦ, τὴν παχνοχιονάτην,
> τὴν δενδροηλιόμορφην, μαυροπλουμιστομάταν,
> τὴν νεραντζοερωτοάκουστον, κρινοτριανταφυλλάτην,
> τραχηλομαρμαρόμνοστην, ροδοκοκκινοχείλαν,
> τὴν συντυχογλυκόλαλον, ἐρωτοεπαινεμένην ...[13]

> the crystal-clarity of water, hoarfrost-snow-white,
> tree-sun-beautiful[?], dark-adorned-eyed,
> orangetree-love-renowned, lily-rose-leaved,
> neck-marble-luscious, rose-red-lipped,
> speech-sweet-warbling, love-praised ...

94

It is presumably the opulence and strangeness of the language, rather than any visual reference, that is intended to convey the essential quality of the person described in these examples.[14] But any idea that the 'vernacular' literature of this period simply transferred the spoken language of the time into written form can be safely dismissed in the light of these examples.

Once the modern dialects began to oust the 'common' language of most vernacular texts during our period – in Crete and Cyprus at the end of the fourteenth century, elsewhere a century later – this linguistic characteristic quickly drops out of sight. Although still a productive feature of the modern language, unusual compounds are never again conspicuous in literature after the late fifteenth century.

The use of such an evidently stylized vernacular as the basis for literature had already, as we have seen, been tried in Greek before the fourteenth century. The 'proto-romance', *Digenes Akrites*, may well, in its original early twelfth-century form, have adopted the vernacular, at least for those parts of its narrative that derived from popular oral poetry; and we can be certain that a vernacular version of that poem was circulating in Constantinople by the middle of the same century. In 1149 Theodore Prodromos, author of the first Byzantine romance and of voluminous religious, ceremonial, didactic and satirical writings as well as of many letters, addressed a tongue-in-cheek plea for employment to the Emperor Manuel I. The revolutionary step of using everyday language for such a purpose is implicitly explained at two points in the poem: while the learned intermediary to whom a previous plea, in the learned language, had been addressed, is sluggish to act, the petitioner himself is in pain, wakeful and driven to make his predicament directly known to the emperor.[15] The unexpected use of plain language is implicitly intended to bring home to its recipient the urgency of the plea addressed to him. Then a few lines later Prodromos playfully warns the emperor that he himself is irreplaceable: you cannot set your jester to make vulgar mimicry or parody of the high-class entertainment provided by a Prodromos without realizing how much you are missing.[16] The joke of the piece lies in the fact that here Prodromos himself plays the part of the jester, the calculated vulgarity of the appeal designed, with barbed humour, to highlight the erudition of the neglected petitioner.

Prodromos is also most probably the author of a scattered series of similar pleas known collectively, from the persona of the narrator in two of them, as *Poems of Poor Prodromos*. The first of these, and probably also the second, predate the appeal to the Emperor Manuel and must have been written during the last years of the reign of John II (d. 1143), while the fourth was written or at any rate revised in 1172–3.[17] In each of these poems a racy fictional narrative with a strong satirical element is framed or punctuated by more formal appeals to the prospective patron in the 'middle' language register, which adopt the rhetorical style frequently found in poetry written for the Komnenian court.[18] All four contain more or less explicit comments on their author's choice of linguistic medium: in the first it is hoped that the mixture of playful anecdote with a serious purpose will bring the reward due to decorous amusement; in the second it is more robustly implied that a patron who allows his client to starve deserves no better than the linguistic equivalent of the crusts on which the poet has to chew; the third makes explicit the same appeal to immediacy as did Prodromos' poem of 1149; while the fourth additionally invites a contrast between the learning which the narrator has so painfully acquired and the speech of the humble tradesman in which he is reduced, as a last resort, to beg for favours.[19]

The vernacular was also used in a comparable way by another prominent intellectual at the court of Manuel I, Michael Glykas. Glykas seems to have been something of a rationalist for his time. An outspoken critic of Manuel's interest in astrology, he was imprisoned in 1157 and some time later wrote a historical work and a treatise on the divine mysteries, in which he rejected the idea of the resurrection of the flesh.[20] Shortly after his imprisonment, in 1159, Glykas addressed an appeal to the emperor, almost six hundred lines long, in which, like Prodromos, he punctuated racy and urgent anecdote, clearly aimed at entertainment, with more serious pleas in a higher language register. Unlike Prodromos, however, Glykas drew on a source in which he seems to have had a special interest, namely oral proverbial lore. Much of the vernacular parts of his poem is elaborated from popular proverbs, and Glykas is also known as the first Byzantine to have recorded a collection of proverbs which is still extant.[21]

The only remaining text to use the vernacular before the fourteenth century is the so-called 'Spaneas', a collection of fatherly advice found in widely divergent renderings in manuscripts from the late thirteenth century onwards. The evidence which for long was thought to connect the poem with the Komnenian royal family and the year 1142 has now been effectively challenged, and further work has shown that the versions we possess represent the linguistic transposition of older didactic literature, although their ultimate source is still the subject of discussion.[22] Whenever the transposition into the vernacular took place, the 'Spaneas' poem belongs to the phenomenon of linguistic transposition of which we have already noted examples from the eleventh century to the fifteenth, and probably played only a minor part in the development of the vernacular as a literary medium. The poem was widely read, however, and seems in some form to have served as a source for the advice of a father given in two translated romances, *Phlorios and Platzia-Phlora* and *Imperios and Margarona*, as well as being known to the Cretan poet Marinos Falieros in the first half of the fifteenth century.[23]

What is conspicuous about the literary appearances of the vernacular before the fourteenth century is that, with the possible exception of *Digenes Akrites*, all are closely associated with the imperial court and with the very circles in which the opposite, archaizing linguistic tendency was also cultivated. For all the popular flavour of the domestic scenes portrayed in the *Poems of Poor Prodromos* and the tapping of oral traditional sources in *Digenes* and in Glykas' 'Verses Written while Held Imprisoned', the impetus for using the vernacular in all these texts comes, as it were, 'from above'.[24] There is no question in the twelfth century of a 'breakthrough' of popular culture into writing.

The nature and origin of the literary vernacular as we find it in the romances of the fourteenth and fifteenth centuries raise complex questions which will be considered in detail in relation to the common elements shared among these texts, in Chapter 11. For the moment it will suffice to summarize the viewing of Hans-Georg Beck, that experiments in vernacular literature in the fourteenth century are initially, at least, a continuation of those in the twelfth. According to this view, the earlier texts of our period are the work of educated writers, self-consciously exploiting the possibilities of a new medium, while by the fifteenth century a new, genuinely popular literary stratum has begun to emerge.[25]

We know of no vernacular writing that was certainly produced during the thirteenth century.[26] In part this can be attributed to the chaos and readjustment following the sack of the capital in 1204. But we have no evidence of anything having been written in the vernacular for thirty years *before* that event either. The period of experimenting with the vernacular in the twelfth century turns out to have been quite short, and largely coincidental with the sudden re-emergence of the ancient fictional genres of satire and romance, all of which seem to reach a peak between about 1140 and, at the latest, 1180. This link between vernacular language and fiction is strengthened when we consider that the poems attributed to Prodromos and Glykas have much in common with the newly revived genre of satire, and the *Poems of Poor Prodromos* in particular make extensive use of fictional topoi. Although the twelfth-century romances make only small *linguistic* concessions to the vernacular, we detected the influence upon them of *Digenes Akrites*, which at the very least included a substratum drawn from the vernacular. It seems likely, then, that after the turmoil of the thirteenth century, or perhaps towards its end, writers began to look back to the short-lived period of experimentation in the twelfth century and to recognize a possibility already latent in the texts of that period. For this to happen a catalyst was doubtless needed, and this is the first clear sign of the Western influence that will be discussed in Chapters 9 and 10. As we shall see there, the idea that the vernacular should be the appropriate medium for fiction (and vice versa), the realizing of a potentiality latent in the experiments of two centuries before, may well have required the example of the Western vernaculars before it could come to fruition. And in that way modern Greek literature, as the counterpart of the modern literary traditions of Western Europe, may be said to begin.[27]

SIGNIFICANCE AND DEVELOPMENT OF THE 'POLITICAL' VERSEFORM

All the later romances, and most other literary texts written in the vernacular up to the end of the seventeenth century, are composed in the same verseform: the fifteen-syllable metre with iambic stress, and invariable caesura after the eighth syllable. Also invariable are the cadences at the mid-line caesura and the line end. The first is always a masculine cadence, ending on a strong beat (although it should be noted that this need not coincide with a primary stress marked by a written accent), the second feminine, ending on a weak beat:

$$˘ / ˘ / ˘ / ˘ (/) \parallel ˘ / ˘ / ˘ / ˘$$

It remains something of a puzzle why this metre came to be named, as it was by Byzantine authors from the twelfth century onwards, πολιτικὸς στίχος, (literally 'political verse'), and as such has come to be known in English too. One thing certain, however, is that it never had anything to do with politics. The adjective πολιτικός in the twelfth century seems to have meant 'down-to-earth', 'day-to-day', and hence, presumably, also 'prosaic'. The word seems to have referred to the private life of the citizen (πολίτης), if not actually to the dweller in Constantinople, commonly known as 'the City' (Ἡ Πόλις), and seems from long before the birth of the metre to have been contrasted with the grander sense of 'true poetry'.[28] A good deal of attention has been focused on this metre in recent years for two reasons: first, its historical origins have proved surprisingly elusive; and, second, its long history and extensive use, from the tenth century to the present day, have earned it the undisputed title of 'national' or 'native' metre of modern Greek poetry.

In the twelfth century we have already encountered the fifteen-syllable verseform as the metre of *Digenes Akrites* and of one of the romances in the 'high' language: *Aristandros and Kallithea* by Manasses. It is also the metre of all the vernacular poems of that century, as well as of the 'Spaneas' poem, which may be later. In addition it is prevalent in ceremonial poetry in both the 'high' and the 'middle' language registers and was extensively used by writers of the mid-century in exegetical works, mainly in the 'middle' register, apparently commissioned by members of the imperial family, from Tzetzes, Manasses and others. It is among these last writers that the metre is most commonly disparaged as πολιτικός, lowbrow, and not really appropriate for a writer of any erudition to use.[29]

In the fourteenth and fifteenth centuries vernacular poetry, almost without exception, was composed in this metre.[30] During the same period, while elements of the local dialect began to oust the 'common' vernacular in certain areas, the Western device of rhyme also made its first appearance in Greek poetry, and from the sixteenth century the most common literary use of 'political' verse is in the form of rhymed couplets. In the romances, however, with the exception of the *Theseid*, which was translated from an Italian rhymed poem, probably a little after the end of our period, and the sixteenth-century rhymed versions of *Apollonius* and *Imperios*, rhyme is unknown.

The question that has most aroused the interest of scholars is whether this metre, which established itself from the fourteenth century onwards as the natural medium for vernacular narrative, began life in an oral, popular medium, or was the invention of the learned. In favour of a popular origin is the fact that the fifteen-syllable metre, in its unrhymed form, is by far the predominant metre of Greek oral folk-poetry as recorded mainly in the nineteenth and twentieth centuries, but clearly deriving from a long tradition. Furthermore, there is surviving evidence for popular oral poetry in this metre going back to at least the mid-fifteenth century and probably also to the late twelfth.[31] Research into the earliest texts to use this metre has shown, on the other hand, that it had a considerable history in learned writing before the twelfth century.[32]

The reason that learned Byzantines were disparaging about this verseform was not necessarily because its native sphere was beneath their notice in the oral substratum of popular culture. There is no reason to doubt Maximos Planoudes, writing at the end of the thirteenth century, when he states contemptuously that this was the metre in which 'Ionian [= Anatolian] women' lamented their dead.[33] But a more fundamental Byzantine objection to the metre seems to have been that it was based on stress and not on quantity. To write in an accentual metre was to mark a decisive break with the literature of antiquity, when all Greek metres had been based on alternations not of stress but of the length of syllables. Quantity (that is, the systematic differentiation of syllables by their duration when pronounced) had disappeared from spoken Greek by the sixth century, but Byzantine authors continued to write verse mechanically applying the rules of quantitative metrics for another thousand years. In order to write verse which could *sound* metrical, as opposed to merely appearing so on the page, a Byzantine had to make some tacit acceptance of this change, and write in an accentual metre. The twelve-syllable metre of Prodromos' and Eugenianos' romances, and of the brief preamble to the G version of *Digenes Akrites*, was widely used in the twelfth century and later, because it could be made to *look*, more or less correctly, like the iambic trimeter of Attic tragedy, which generally contained the same number of syllables, although the lines would obviously have been pronounced according to stress. It was the absence of such a precedent for the fifteen-syllable line that left it exposed to the kind of disparagement we have noted: the ungrudging acceptance of something so innovative would have struck at the heart of the Byzantine concept of mimesis that we examined in Chapter 2.[34]

This is probably why Byzantine sources are silent about the origin of the verseform. An innovation of this sort was something to be tolerated for pragmatic reasons, rather than held up with pride. There is nothing, therefore, in the attitude taken by the sources to help us decide whether the origin of the metre was popular or learned. Modern scholarship has divided fairly evenly on the issue.[35] Starting from modern oral folk-poetry and working back towards its possible origins, the folklorists Stilpon Kyriakidis and Samuel Baud-Bovy proposed that the metre first emerged at a popular level, perhaps about the tenth or the eleventh century.[36] These arguments have had to be revised as more early evidence for the literary use of the metre has come to light. Since then Linos Politis and Johannes Koder have, for slightly different reasons, proposed that the new metre must have been the invention of an educated poet, probably writing in Constantinople at the imperial court. The most far-reaching proposal for a popular origin has been made by Michael Jeffreys, who offers a closely argued case for the derivation of the verseform from the acclamations in accentual verse used to greet triumphant generals in republican Rome. According to this proposal, the metre would have evolved from its Latin into its Byzantine Greek form at an oral level, in the course of imperial and related rituals over a period of almost a thousand years. Recently there has also been a revival of a proposal first put forward at the end of the last century, that the germ of the later fifteen-syllable metre is to be found in the Byzantine hymnography of the sixth century, when for the first time accentual stress came to be introduced into Greek verse.[37]

In all this, there are certain areas of broad agreement. First, the 'political' line acquired the form in which it has since become known not long before the tenth century; second, before that time there is no evidence for the metre in Greek, either in literature or in the scattered popular chants that have come down to us;[38] and, third, such little evidence as we have reveals that *accentual* verse at an oral level, in which line-lengths of seven and eight syllables, and trochaic as well as iambic rhythms, coexisted, was in use from the early seventh to the eleventh century. The most satisfactory reading of the available evidence so far proposed is this restatement, in 1981, by Linos Politis:

> The basis, the genetic nucleus [of 'political' verse] is popular, [in] the easy and malleable eight-syllable; but its broadening into a medium worthy to fulfil higher and more complex functions, presupposes some centre, some community, some common bonds both social and ideological .... The roots, the origin, yes, these are popular, but at the crucial moment came other auxiliary and more complex factors, and the final creation was the product of artistic initiative.[39]

In other words, the metre in which all of the later romances were composed already at its inception represented a compromise, or a meeting-point, between learned literature and popular oral tradition. The earliest 'modern' literature in Greek, in which literary fiction and vernacular language are for the first time fully integrated, is therefore couched exclusively in a verseform which, to the discomfiture rather than the pride of the Byzantine literati who used it, was their own novel creation.

7

THE ORIGINAL ROMANCES: THE TEXTS AND THEIR STORIES

During the last centuries of Byzantium, as in earlier periods when the romance had flourished, there existed no generic term specific to this kind of writing. From a historical perspective it is easy enough to identify a body of texts of the period which tell fictional tales of love and adventure and betray some generic affiliation with the twelfth-century love romances or the chivalric romances of the West, or in some degree with both. The contemporary term for such writing, which derives from the rhetorical exercises of the *progymnasmata* that were still being produced in the fourteenth century, is *diegesis* (διήγησις) or, less commonly, *diegema* (διήγημα, tale). But this term is applied to almost all narrative in the vernacular, and in the final chapter we shall be looking at some forms of narrative which reveal the influence of the contemporary romance without, in our own terms, being truly classifiable as romances. To what extent writers and readers, or audiences, were aware of the generic distinction we cannot be certain. There is, as we shall see, an impressive degree of cohesion among the romances of love and adventure, both thematically and stylistically, which suggests an implicit awareness of a common genre. But it may be that the writers of our period had a more open-ended concept of the genre in which they were working than is assumed here. Similarly, in the West the term *roman* at first meant 'anything written in a Latin-based [Romance] vernacular', and only gradually became a generic term.[1]

The romances of the Palaiologan period, so defined, divide naturally into two groups: those composed in Greek, and those translated or adapted from a Western language. The first of these groups, the five original romances, will be the subject of this and the following chapter and will be considered under three headings: text, story, and narrative structure. By the first of these I mean the texts of the romances viewed externally, and will include under this heading questions of authorship, date of composition, and textual transmission. This is in fact the aspect on which most of the available secondary literature has tended to concentrate. The distinction between story and narrative is adopted after Gérard Genette, who is one of a number of theoretical writers on narrative to emphasize the difference in kind between

101

narrative *content* (what is narrated) and narrative *discourse* (narrative as a linguistic construct, as text).[2] Genette proposes 'to use the word *story* for the signified or narrative content (even if this turns out, in a given case, to be low in dramatic intensity or fullness of incident) [and] to use the word *narrative* for the signifier, statement, discourse or narrative text itself'.[3] I shall not, however, make more than passing use in this and the following chapter of Genette's formalist/structuralist model for narrative 'grammar'. Under the heading of 'story' I shall give quite full plot summaries,[4] together with some comments focused on the fictional incidents narrated in the romances. Then in the following chapter, under the heading of 'narrative structure', I shall consider the romances as texts, in particular the arrangement of narrative incidents into a textual structure and, in the unique case of *Libistros and Rhodamne*, the development of a quite complex 'framing' device which allows for two stories to be told in parallel.

THE TEXTS: AUTHORSHIP, DATE, MANUSCRIPT TRADITION

The five tales of love and adventure that were originally composed in vernacular Greek are usually dated to the fourteenth and fifteenth centuries. All circulated anonymously in manuscript, and most of the extant witnesses date from a period of sixty or seventy years after the fall of Constantinople in 1453.[5] The manuscripts that we possess were therefore copied between one and two centuries after the probable dates of composition, and it is clear from the manuscript tradition that the literal accuracy expected of scribes when they were working with texts in the learned language did not apply to literature in the vernacular. This phenomenon (which is not confined to the romances but extends to the whole of vernacular Greek literature at this period) will be discussed in more detail in Chapter 11. In the meantime it will be sufficient to state the problem and draw such conclusions as we can about the authorship, date and place of composition, and the reliability of the textual witnesses for each of the romances.

The *Tale of Achilles* (Διήγησις τοῦ Ἀχιλλέως)[6]

This romance, like all the others except *Kallimachos*, is anonymous. It is the most difficult of all to date, even relatively to the other romances in this group. There are some slight indications that it may have been the first to be written, and for that reason I have considered it first, but this relationship with the other romances cannot be taken as proved. Let us now examine the evidence, such as it is.[7]

Achilles follows the model of *Digenes Akrites* quite closely, particularly in its apparent efforts to balance the macho heroism of an all-male world with the conventions and interests of the more literary romance. Its ending, with the death of the heroine substituted for that of the hero, also seems as if it is addressed to readers or hearers more familiar with that poem than with the conventions of the twelfth- or fourteenth-century romances. While not much can be read into this, it is at least possible that this romance represents a bridge from the mixture of heroic and romance elements in *Digenes* to the fully fledged vernacular romance as we find it developed in *Kallimachos and Chrysorrhoe*.

Digenes is the only vernacular text that we can say with absolute certainty was known to the author of *Achilles*. Although he must have known other romance texts (in particular *Hysmine and Hysminias*, from which the painted figure of Eros must derive) there is no other text of the fourteenth or fifteenth century that is unequivocally reflected in this one.[8] On the other hand there is an accumulation of evidence that other texts of this period may have drawn on *Achilles*, in particular the translation of the French *Pierre de Provence* (*Imperios and Margarona*) and, at least in its later versions, the *Tale of Belisarios*. Although, as we shall see in Chapter 11, the evidence for such links among vernacular Greek texts at this period has to be treated with great care, it is probable that the *Tale of Achilles* was quite widely known from the latter part of the fourteenth century onwards. On the other hand it was not certainly known to Meliteniotes, the author of the parodic romance *To Chastity*, which must have been written between about 1355 and 1395.

Finally a brief epigram, possibly dating from the thirteenth century, and containing a lament in the learned language in which Achilles mourns his dead wife, affords the strongest, but still far from conclusive, piece of evidence for an early date.[9] Although the text has no overt connection with that of the romance as it has come down to us, this would have been an unusual way to represent the Achilles of classical legend, and we have already seen several examples of writers in the learned language drawing on sources in the vernacular, from the twelfth century onwards. With the lines between popular and learned, and between the 'high' culture of Constantinople and developments in the vernacular (wherever they may have taken place), now less rigidly drawn than in the past, we may no longer discount this piece of evidence as inherently improbable.[10]

The *Tale of Achilles* has been preserved in three versions, of which the fullest is contained in a manuscript now in Naples, and dated to the third quarter of the fifteenth century.[11] Although we cannot tell to what extent this version may have been embellished in the course of transmission, this is the version that will normally be referred to here (by its initial letter, N). A less detailed version, following the main lines of N but often independent in wording, is contained in a late fifteenth-century manuscript in the British Library.[12] Another version, this time of the sixteenth century, exists in the Bodleian library, Oxford, and has been published no fewer than three times. This third version is generally accepted as being little more than a précis.[13] A new critical edition of all three versions was announced by Olef Smith in 1987.

Although the differences among these texts can tell us a good deal about the way such texts were copied and transmitted, we can be fairly confident that the N version gives us the substance if not the wording of the original poem. It seems certain, however, that the original ending has been lost. The Naples version has tacked on to it a short passage which suddenly shifts the action to Troy and borrows a number of lines, as well as its version of events, from Manasses' twelfth-century verse chronicle: Achilles is caught up in the expedition against Troy and is there murdered by Paris and his brother Deiphobos, who had treacherously proposed that he marry their sister. The heading to this episode in the manuscript, Γεναμένη ἐν Τροίᾳ (having occurred at Troy), as well as the prominent role of Paris in the lines that follow, makes it highly probable that these lines are the work of a scribe who expressly tried to link the *Tale of Achilles* with the romance of Paris, the Διήγησις γεναμένη ἐν Τροίᾳ or 'Tale having occurred at Troy', which, as we shall see, was the last of the original romances to be composed.[14]

Kallimachos and Chrysorrhoe
(Τὸ κατὰ Καλλίμαχον καὶ Χρυσορρόην Ἐρωτικὸν Διήγημα)[15]

There is no reason to doubt that this romance was written by Andronikos Komnenos Branas Doukas Angelos Palaiologos, the nephew of the first emperor of the Palaiologan dynasty, Michael VIII, between the years 1310 and 1340.[16] The evidence for this is contained, interestingly enough, not in the single surviving manuscript of the romance but in a verse epigram by the court poet Manuel Philes which praises Andronikos for his work and gives a sketchy but identifiable summary of the story with added religious exegesis. (This text is discussed in Chapter 12.) *Kallimachos* is the only vernacular text of this period (excluding those written in Crete under Venetian rule) whose author is known by name, and which can be dated with such relative precision. The fact that the evidence is external to the text as it has been transmitted, however, makes it likely that the anonymity common to literature of entertainment at this time is a generic convention rather than proof of a popular origin. Twelfth-century precedents can be seen in *Digenes Akrites* and the prose satire *Timarion*.[17]

Whether *Kallimachos* was the first of the vernacular romances to be written, or whether indeed Andronikos had other models to draw on that have not survived, we have no means of knowing. Certainly, as we shall see in Chapter 10, he knew the ancient and twelfth-century romances as well as, probably, *Digenes*. He may also have known the *Tale of Achilles* if, as I have suggested, that romance was already in existence. If he was singly or largely responsible for 'inventing' the new thematic and linguistic form of the romance which set the trend for the following century and a half, then he would certainly deserve a more important place in the histories of Byzantine and of modern Greek literature than he has yet been accorded. There is at any rate a degree of consensus in modern discussions of the romances that *Kallimachos* was followed, perhaps quite closely, by *Belthandros* and then by *Libistros*.[18] All three were certainly in existence before the latter half of the fourteenth century, as specific references to them are contained in Meliteniotes' parody, *To Chastity*, and clear generic allusions are also apparent in a scribal interpolation, now dated to the period 1354–74, at the end of the *Consolation concerning Ill and Good Fortune*.[19]

Kallimachos has come down to us in a single manuscript now in the university library at Leiden. The manuscript, which also contains an incomplete but otherwise seemingly reliable copy of *Libistros*, is believed to date from about 1520, that is, almost exactly two centuries after the composition of the poem.[20] In the absence of other manuscript copies we have no means of telling how much the copy that we possess is likely to have diverged from the original poem. In favour of its being a relatively close copy is its high proportion of learned linguistic forms and complex rhetorical periods, since the predominant trend in manuscript copying by this time was towards a more simplified diction. There are no examples in Greek vernacular literature, however, of a manuscript ever being copied with word-for-word exactitude, so that it would be naive to suppose that we possess the text exactly as written by Andronikos Palaiologos in the early fourteenth century.

The text as transmitted runs to 2,607 lines.

Belthandros and Chrysantza
(Διήγησις ἐξαίρετος Βελθάνδρου τοῦ Ῥωμαίου)[21]

On the date of this anonymous romance there is nothing to add to what was said in the previous section. Indeed there are no very convincing grounds for deciding firmly whether this romance or *Libistros* was the earlier. Like *Kallimachos*, *Belthandros* is attested in only one manuscript, again dating from a much later period. The Paris manuscript which contains the romance also contains a number of texts dating from the fourteenth and fifteenth centuries which use the more popular linguistic forms favoured in Crete and the Dodecanese, and it is probable that some of the elements of more popular speech and of oral folk-song found in *Belthandros* may not have been present in the original.[22] Older views that the original poem was translated from French,[23] or that the text as we have it has been substantially corrupted,[24] can now be safely set aside.[25] The romance is only half as long as *Kallimachos*, amounting to 1,348 lines.

Libistros and Rhodamne
('Αφήγησις Λιβίστρου)[26]

This romance presents the greatest difficulties of any of the original romances for modern editors. It has been preserved in five manuscripts which differ considerably in length, in the sequence of episodes, in language register and most of all in wording. These problems can of course be paralleled in other Greek vernacular texts (notably in *Digenes*, *Achilles*, *The War of Troy* and *Imperios*, as well as in other European vernacular literatures of the period), and their significance will be discussed more fully in Chapter 11. But where in the case of *Belthandros* we merely suspected that our sixteenth-century exemplar was not a faithful copy of the original, a comparative study of the five manuscripts of *Libistros* makes it abundantly clear that the original poem cannot have been exactly like any one of them.

Our fullest witness is a manuscript of the Vatican (Cod. Vat. gr. 2391) which was first described as recently as 1948 and unfortunately remains unpublished. Comparison of this manuscript with the remainder, however, reveals that a resourceful scribe or redactor has been at work here, adding rhetorical embellishments and giving to the text a linguistic flavour all his own. The manuscript itself was copied in Naples, probably shortly after 1500.[27] Of the remaining witnesses, compared in Lambert's still standard edition of 1935, the three oldest manuscripts all have gaps and transpositions in the sequence of episodes which make nonsense of the story, while the later and linguistically haywire Escorial manuscript preserves the story in its fullest and most detailed form.[28] Lambert's edition prints the uncorrected E text on the left-hand pages, with the corresponding passages of two other, older manuscripts facing. These are the Naples (N) and Leiden (S) manuscripts.[29] N is used up until N 979, equivalent to E 1128. From that point the Leiden manuscript (S), whose first thousand lines are missing, replaces it. Pending a new critical edition which will have to take into account the Vatican manuscript and the detailed corrections of Chatziyiakoumis, the best way to read this romance is to follow the right-hand pages of Lambert's edition, crossing over to the left wherever a gap appears on the right. References to the romance here assume this principle, and line-numbers are always preceded by the initial letter of the appropriate manuscript.

The E version, as well as providing the most faithful witness to the number and sequence of episodes, probably also gives the best indication of the length of the original poem. Its 4,407 lines approximate closely to the length of the twelfth-century verse romances, and make it much the longest of the later original romances. It is perhaps worth noting that the extra length, in comparison to the other contemporary romances, is gained not by the addition of the subplot of Klitobos' adventures, which, as we shall see in the next chapter, actually take up little space in the telling, but by the long sections which report the contents of love-letters, messages and songs.[30]

The *Tale of Troy*
(Διήγησις γεναμένη ἐν Τροίᾳ)[31]

There are good reasons for supposing that this was the last of the original romances to be written. It is more obviously dependent on specific sources than any other romance in this group. Indeed the author of this romance gives the impression of having cobbled his story, and even quite a lot of its individual lines, together from different parts of Manasses' twelfth-century chronicle and from the contemporary romance and related literature.[32] An additional source may well have been the fourteenth-century vernacular paraphrase of the *Iliad* by Konstantinos Hermoniakos, a poem which has been shown to derive closely from Manasses and from Tzetzes' *Iliad Allegories*.[33] Allusions to the Greek translation of Apollonius have also been noted.[34] For this reason, reinforced by the presence of a significant number of Italian loan-words,[35] there is a general consensus in placing the composition of this text later than that of the other original romances, between the mid-fifteenth and the mid-sixteenth century. If it was indeed the source for the interpolated ending of the N version of the *Tale of Achilles*, a date quite shortly after the fall of Constantinople seems most probable.

The poem's 1,166 lines are preserved in a single manuscript of the sixteenth century.[36]

Lost romances

Given the often precarious nature of the manuscript tradition for the romances that have come down to us, we should not be surprised to find that many more romances than these were in circulation during the final centuries of Byzantium. We have obviously no means of telling how many may have been lost, or how much they may have differed in style and content from those that have been preserved; but the titles and a hint of the content of two lost romances are listed among the contents of a sixteenth-century Greek library in Constantinople:

κ΄. ἱστορία τοῦ φραντζέσκου μετὰ τῆς μπέλας, καὶ ὅπως ἐπῆρε ὁ φραντζέσκος ἀπὸ τὸ σιδερόκαστρον τὴν μπέλα καὶ ἔφυγε ...

κγ΄. ἱστορία τοῦ γεναιοτάτου θησαίου βασιλέως ἀθηνῶν, καὶ ὅπως ἐπῆγε εἰς ταὶς ἀμαζόναις καὶ ἐπολέμησε καὶ ἐπαράλαβε αὐτὰς καὶ ὅπως πάλιν ἐπανῆλθεν εἰς τὰς ἀθῆνας καὶ συνεβασίλευσε μετὰ τοῦ ἀδελφοῦ αὐτοῦ ἀδριανοῦ ...[37]

xx. Story of Francesco and Bella, and how Francesco took Bella from the Castle of Iron and left [presumably with her] ...

XXIII. Story of the most valiant Theseus, king of Athens, and how he went to the Amazons and fought against them and took them over and how he returned again to Athens and ruled jointly with his brother Hadrian [!]

The same list also includes three known texts: the translated romance *Imperios and Margarona*; the original *Tale of Belisarios*; and the fifteenth-century Cretan poem on the Creation by Georgios Choumnos.

From the names of the protagonists, *Francesco and Bella* is more likely to have been translated from a Western source. But the *Story of Theseus*, as Lambros points out, can have had no connection with Boccaccio's *Theseid*, which was translated into Greek around 1500.[38] From the brief synopsis given, it is tempting to see this as an original romance drawing freely, and in an ahistorical manner, on traditional Greek sources after the manner of the *Tale of Achilles* and *Tale of Troy*.

Conclusion

Of the five original romances described in this chapter *Kallimachos*, *Belthandros* and *Libistros* can be dated with confidence to the period 1310 to about 1350.[39] *Kallimachos* we know to have been written by a member of the imperial family. It is most likely to have been written in or near Constantinople, and would certainly have circulated initially in the intimate circle of the Constantinopolitan court, of which Manuel Philes and most of the learned writers of the day were members. Some years later Meliteniotes wrote his parody *To Chastity* in the second half of the same century for the same court circle; and he alludes in that poem not only to *Kallimachos* but also to *Belthandros* and *Libistros*. We can be reasonably certain in concluding, then, that these two romances were also written and first circulated among the same group. In this respect there is a close parallel with the circumstances in which the twelfth-century romances were written, by a fairly close-knit group of writers connected with the imperial court and the intelligentsia. And indeed, as is generally acknowledged, these three romances show the closest affinities, of all the later romances, with their twelfth-century precursors.

The *Tale of Achilles* and *Tale of Troy* are much harder to place. Although diverging to a greater degree from the common narrative scheme of the original romances, they nonetheless share most of its essential features, and this can scarcely be accidental. The *Tale of Troy* is certainly late, and draws on an established tradition for its own rather curious purposes. But the *Tale of Achilles* could easily stand as a point of transition between the vernacular 'proto-romance' of *Digenes Akrites* and the developed form of the fourteenth-century vernacular romance as we find it in *Kallimachos*, *Bel-*

thandros and *Libistros*. The evidence for this, however, is suggestive rather than conclusive.

THE STORIES

The stories of the five romances are built upon a common and limited stock of narrative incidents. In each of them a royal prince, ignorant or scornful of Eros, sets out from his home. In a fabulous castle he first sees the princess with whom he is fated to fall in love. About half-way through the series of their adventures their love is consummated, but a setback follows. In two of the five romances the setback proves fatal and a happy ending is thwarted. In the other three, hero and heroine are separated for a time, one or both is believed dead but the pair are reunited after hair-raising adventures, with the aid of a woman helper who comes to a sticky end.

Even from this highly schematized description it is easy to see how these romances differ at the level of story from their twelfth-century precursors: the bourgeois hero and heroine of the Hellenistic romances and of *Hysmine and Hysminias*, and their aristocratic counterparts in Prodromos' and Eugenianos' romances, have become royal. The taboo on sex before marriage, rigorously maintained throughout all the earlier medieval romances, is flouted, frequently with gusto.[40] In this there may well be a deliberate throwback to the oldest surviving Hellenistic romance, Chariton's *Chaireas and Kallirrhoe*, in which the lovers are married at the beginning and then experience a series of trials before they can be reunited. The ending with the death of one of the lovers (the heroine in the *Tale of Achilles*, the hero in the *Tale of Troy*) is obviously contrary to the conventions of the older romance, although several of these had contained a subplot in which a parallel story ends in tragedy. The author of *Achilles* was clearly following the precedent of the twelfth-century 'proto-romance' *Digenes Akrites*; the ending of the *Tale of Troy* may have been suggested partly by the example of *Achilles* but is more obviously dictated by the use of the story of Paris and the sack of Troy as a basis. In the other romances the separation of hero and heroine and the apparent death (*Scheintod*) are traditional elements of the genre, although the magical means employed to this end in *Kallimachos* and in *Libistros* are not. Finally, the figure of the helper can be paralleled in several ancient and twelfth-century romances;[41] however, a specifically *female* helper who dies (and in the two romances just named is also a witch) has no real counterpart in the earlier tradition.

Let us now see how this scheme is worked out in detail in each of the five romances.

The *Tale of Achilles*

Despite its title, this romance has next to nothing in common with the classical legends surrounding this hero. The text begins, in the fullest version, with an invocation to the power of Eros reminiscent of the preamble to the young hero's adventures in *Digenes Akrites*. This is timely, because the story of the pagan Myrmidons which then begins concentrates exclusively on warlike deeds until the hero has proved himself fully in the field. Achilles, the long-awaited offspring of an unnamed king and queen, learns all the arts of letters between the ages of 4 and 8, before going on to specialize in feats of physical prowess. At 15 he takes part, disguised, in a tournament and vanquishes all opposition. Soon afterwards he is entrusted by his father with a military campaign against a neighbouring king who has invaded Myrmidon territory. With his hand-picked retainers about him, and chief among them Pantrouklos, he brilliantly relieves a besieged outpost and pursues his father's enemies back to their own castle.

As he approaches the castle on foot, his military victory assured but as yet innocent of love, he sees the women of the place looking down from the walls, and among them the daughter of the defeated king. He falls in love at first sight, and the harsh world of battles and male prowess gives place to a series of elaborate *ekphraseis* of the splendours of the girl, her palace and chamber (κουβούκλιν). Achilles is so smitten with love that he has a picture of Eros painted for him and in front of this picture he swears fealty to Love. The girl (who, like Digenes' bride, is never named) is at first haughty and rejects his letters. Eros himself appears to her in a dream, however, and Achilles' love is at last reciprocated. The pair first meet face to face when Achilles pole-vaults in full armour into her walled garden and they spend the night together. The following day he pays a more formal visit, at the head of his twelve retainers, to announce that he will abduct her at midnight. As earnest of his sincerity he strikes the wall and the whole ornate chamber collapses to the ground.

The abduction follows the pattern of Digenes' abduction of the general's daughter: the alarm is raised, the girl's brothers ride out in pursuit at the head of an army, the army is defeated but the brothers are spared to acquiesce in the wedding of the pair. A round of celebrations follows, given first by the groom's family, then by the bride's. A tournament is held in honour of the couple, and Achilles is victorious. But then, as in *Digenes*, the happy ending of the romance is diverted from its conventional course: after six years of happiness the girl falls ill. In long speeches she takes her leave, and Achilles mourns her, praying not to outlive her. The romance in its original form seems to have ended with the burial of the girl and the hero's inconsolable grief.

Kallimachos and Chrysorrhoe

The basic sequence of narrative incidents already outlined as common to all these romances is worked out by Andronikos Palaiologos against the stylized background of a never-never land of strange, folkloric marvels.[42] Once upon a time a king had three sons. Unable to decide which of the three should succeed him, he sends them out into the world to see which can prove himself worthiest to succeed. (This motif, as soon as it has served its function of launching the hero upon his adventures, is then forgotten.) The youngest of the three, Kallimachos, leads his brothers up a mountain, where they come upon an impregnable castle with monsters protruding from the ramparts. The less courageous elder brothers now take their leave, after giving Kallimachos a magic ring. The hero briskly pole-vaults over the ramparts to find the interior of the castle apparently deserted and opulently furnished. While he is admiring a painted ceiling of the heavens his gaze is drawn downwards to take in a nude female figure of indescribable beauty, hanging suspended by the hair.

The girl's gaoler, the ogre (δράκων) whose castle it now turns out to be, appears and beats his victim cruelly before the eyes of the hero, who has prudently concealed himself in a silver basin. He then manages to kill the ogre, thanks to a tip from the girl. She now introduces herself: she is Chrysorrhoe, daughter of a king, and sole survivor of a kingdom ravaged by the ogre in order to possess her. The two fall almost instantly in love and take a rapturous, healing bath before making love at the water's edge. For a time they live happily as lord and lady of the Ogre's Castle (Δρακοντόκαστρον).

But the wheel of fortune turns against them. The king of a neighbouring country, on a military expedition, spots the castle and is consumed with love for Chrysorrhoe, whom he has seen leaning over the ramparts. With the aid of a witch he abducts the heroine, leaving Kallimachos apparently dead on the ground outside the castle. Fate now takes a hand directly, in revealing the hero's plight to his brothers in a dream. They find his senseless body and revive him by taking from him a golden apple devised by the witch, which had the power to induce apparent death. The brothers fade out of the story for the second and final time, leaving Kallimachos to set out in search of his beloved. He comes upon a ploughman with shaved head and wearing a hair shirt and learns that this extravagant penance has been laid on the people of an entire country by its king, until such time as the bride he has abducted will yield to him. Kallimachos thus learns of Chrysorrhoe's whereabouts and her fidelity to him.

She, it turns out, is being held in a palace surrounded by a garden, where a swimming pool is constantly filled and refilled in order to quench the 'fire' of her obstinacy (which we and the hero, of course, recognize as the conventional symptom of her frustrated love for Kallimachos). The hero insinuates himself into the service of the palace as an under-gardener, and makes himself known to Chrysorrhoe by the device of hanging a ring in a tree. Claiming that her condition is much improved by sleeping unattended in a marquee in the garden, Chrysorrhoe manages to spend her nights in secret with Kallimachos, but the eunuchs set to guard her soon rumble this ruse, and the two are arraigned before the king for high treason.

As so often in the Greek romance of all periods, it is the heroine who takes the initiative at a crucial moment: in a carefully constructed speech Chrysorrhoe proves to the king's satisfaction that she is already the bride of Kallimachos, and the two are allowed to return to the Ogre's Castle, which they apparently intend to make their home. The witch, whose evil arts had only been used to serve the king's wishes, is made the scapegoat and summarily burnt (a fate more common, incidentally, in earlier romance than in Byzantine judicial process).[43] It may seem far-fetched to class the witch here as a 'helper', according to my general scheme, but two things that she does are crucial to the welfare of the hero and the happy outcome of the plot: first, she uses a device against Kallimachos which only *feigns* death, although she would have complied with the king's instructions just as well had she killed him; and, second, the apple which causes the feigned death is carefully inscribed with directions how to remedy its effect.

Belthandros and Chrysantza

The world in which the action of this romance takes place coincides loosely at certain points with the real political geography of Anatolia in the first half of the thirteenth century; but the most important of the hero's travels, like the whole of *Kallimachos*, take place off the map altogether.

Belthandros, a prince of the Romans (i.e. Byzantines), quarrels with his father and leaves home to seek his fortune, despite the entreaties of his elder brother. After leading his small retinue of followers safely through the bandit country of Turkish Anatolia he arrives near the southern coast at Tarsos. Close by, he comes upon a stream with a fiery star in its depths. He follows the stream and finds a sumptuous castle. Inside the castle, which he enters alone, he finds only statues and automata, and rooms richly painted and decorated. This is the Castle of Eros the King ('Ερωτόκαστρον). Among the statues in the ornate banqueting hall are two which together prove to be the twin sources of the mysterious river outside. From the eyes of a carved peacock held in the hand of a (probably female) statue pours a stream of tears that becomes the river; close to it stands a male statue, transfixed by a love-dart through the heart. From the wound pours a stream of fire which mingles with the tears of the other statue to produce the strange river of mingled water and fire that Belthandros had been following. Beneath the statues the hero finds inscriptions prophesying that he will fall in love with Chrysantza, daughter of the king of Antioch.

Belthandros is then summoned into the presence of the lord of the castle, to whom he makes terrified obeisance. Eros announces a beauty contest for the next day, at which Belthandros must give a wand to the most beautiful among forty princesses, whom he is destined to marry. The contest takes place, not without some plain speaking on the part of Belthandros and a number of the unsuccessful candidates. The wand is given to the most beautiful, and Belthandros turns to Eros to sing the praises of the winner. Abruptly at the end of this recital the princesses and Eros vanish 'like a dream'.[44] Alone again in the banqueting hall of the castle, Belthandros reads the prophetic inscriptions once more and resolves to seek out Chrysantza.

Arrived at Antioch, Belthandros offers himself as a vassal to the king and quickly becomes an intimate of the royal household. In due course he meets the king's daughter, and recognition is instantaneous and mutual: Chrysantza was the most beautiful of the forty princesses, to whom he had given the wand in the Castle of Eros. Two years pass before, overhearing her sighs of longing in a walled garden, he jumps the wall and the two spend the night together. The escapade has not passed unnoticed, however, and Belthandros is thrown into prison. Chrysantza, like so many heroines of Greek romances, devises a plan for his rescue. She lets her lady-in-waiting, Phaidrokaza, into the secret and asks her to pretend to the king that it was she whom Belthandros had been visiting the previous night. Phaidrokaza agrees, and further consents to go through with a formal marriage of convenience to Belthandros, so that the latter can continue to visit Chrysantza in secret.

This situation before long becomes unsatisfactory for the lovers, and they resolve to flee with Phaidrokaza and two of Belthandros' retainers. Furtively, during a storm, they steal away. The following day they come to a river swollen in spate. In the attempt to cross, the hero and heroine become separated and are thrown up, dazed and practically naked, on the far bank. Phaidrokaza and the retainers are drowned. Chrysantza, following the flight of a turtle-dove along the bank, comes upon the corpse of one of the retainers, unrecognizable from the river. Thinking it is Belthandros, she is about to fall on the dead man's sword, when Belthandros himself appears on the scene to forestall her. Shaken by the death of Phaidrokaza, for which Chrysantza holds them both responsible, the lovers make their way downstream to the sea. They cut a sorry figure when, destitute and in rags, they hail a ship, which Belthandros recognizes as belonging to his father's navy. He succeeds finally in making himself known to the count, who is on board, and who it turns out has been charged with finding Belthandros to inform him that his elder brother is dead. His father, the hero now learns, is ready to welcome him as his heir. The lovers are married amid royal celebrations back in Belthandros' native city, which must be Constantinople although it is not named, and he and Chrysantza are proclaimed king and queen.

Libistros and Rhodamne

This romance is unique among the vernacular Greek texts of the period in telling two stories in parallel: the love-stories respectively of Libistros, the main hero, and of his friend and confidant, Klitobos, who is also the narrator. The way in which the writer has interwoven these stories to create a text of some complexity will be discussed in the next chapter. For the moment I shall merely summarize the main events of both stories, in the order in which they are supposed to have occurred. As this sequence differs drastically from the order in which the fictional events are presented by the narrative, I have given each episode a number, arabic for Libistros' adventures, roman for those of Klitobos. This will facilitate reference back to the story in the next chapter, where the complex interweaving of story elements to produce the narrative will be discussed.

Libistros, a prince of a 'Latin' land called Libandros, first hears of the power of love after an incident while hunting (1); that same night he dreams that he is ambushed by winged and armed Cupids (Ἔρωτες) who arraign him before the throne of Eros, the King of Love and ruler of a palace and domain peopled by allegorical figures. Eros accepts the hero's submission and pronounces that his fate will be to love and marry Rhodamne, daughter of King Chrysos (Golden) of Argyrokastron (Castle of Silver). Before he wakes, the whole subsequent course of his adventures has also been prophesied to him (2). This dream is followed by another, in which he dreams that Eros the King introduces him to Rhodamne; so great is his erotic excitement, however, that he awakes before he can embrace her (3).

Libistros then sets off on his travels, to find the Castle of Silver (4). After two years of wandering he and his band of retainers pitch camp under its walls, and are curiously observed by the inhabitants, including Rhodamne, from the ramparts (5). The castle is triangular in shape, and the wall on each side is surmounted by a series of allegorical statues, representing the Virtues, the twelve months of the year, and the attributes of love (6). One of the hero's henchmen gains entry to the castle, where he wins the confidence of the eunuch set to guard the heroine's seclusion (7). Mutual love is gradually established through a lengthy exchange of letters, Libistros attaching his to arrows and firing them through the window into Rhodamne's bedchamber (κουβούκλιν), she replying through her eunuch and Libistros' henchman (8). At length, after an exchange of rings effected in the same way, Rhodamne consents to a secret meeting which takes place when she leaves the castle to go hunting with her kinsmen (9). The two make love and swear fidelity (10). But there is an obstacle: Rhodamne has already been betrothed to one Berderichos, king of Egypt. Her father is sufficiently impressed by Libistros' appearance, however, to propose a tournament in which the two suitors should compete for his daughter's hand. Libistros defeats his rival, who leaves in dudgeon for Egypt, and hero and heroine are married with much ceremony (11).

114

The pair live happily for two years (12), at the end of which time the defeated rival, Berderichos, reappears on the scene, this time in disguise. With him is a witch, who enables him to abduct Rhodamne, leaving Libistros apparently dead by means of a magic ring (13). Revived to find his bride vanished, the hero leaves his adopted home and sets out alone to recover her (14). After two years of wandering, he falls in with another wanderer in a similar plight: this is Klitobos, the protagonist of the second story and narrator of both (15 = IV). Together with Klitobos, the hero comes upon a hovel in which lives the witch who had provided the magical means for Rhodamne's abduction. She has been cast off by her former master and is willing to reveal all, and even to summon up daemonic aid for Libistros, in return for a promise of clemency (16 = V). The hero solemnly binds himself to these terms, and he and Klitobos set out on magic flying horses which carry them across the sea to Egypt (17 = VI). Rhodamne meanwhile has been granted a stay of consummation by her captor, during which time she has been running a country inn, at which she asks all comers for news of Libistros. To avoid too great a shock to her, Klitobos volunteers to find her at the inn and explain the situation (VII). That done Libistros arrives and the three ride off together, back across the sea on the old woman's magic horses (18 = VIII). They return the horses and Rhodamne, on learning of the witch's part in her abduction, demands that she be put to death immediately. This, despite his earlier promise of clemency, Libistros does (19 = IX).

The reunited pair make their way back, along with Klitobos, to the Castle of Silver, reminding each other along the way of the letters and songs they had exchanged during their bizarre courtship and recalling yet others (20 = X). Klitobos' single state casts a blight on the company, however, and Libistros rewards him for his constant help and companionship with the hand of Rhodamne's sister, Melanthia (21 = XI). Libistros and Rhodamne rule happily over her father's kingdom (22).

The second story is that of Klitobos, the son of an Armenian noble from the fictional province of Litavia.[45] He has the misfortune to fall passionately in love with the king's daughter (I). She, however, is already married to a powerful Persian. During her husband's absence she returns Klitobos' love, but the king notices what is going on and has Klitobos thrown into prison, where his rival on his return is about to have him put to death (II). He escapes thanks to the resourcefulness of the girl Myrtane, but has to flee the country and forsake all hope of ever being reunited with her (III). Some time after this, in his wanderings, he meets Libistros, who is also in search of a lost love (IV = 15), and his doings become part of the latter's story for a time (V–XI = 16–21). After his marriage to Rhodamne's sister he lives happily with her in the Castle of Silver for several years (XII). But on the death of his wife he becomes homesick for Armenia and takes leave of his friends in order to return there (XIII). He arrives to find his beloved Myrtane now a widow, and begins to tell the story of his own and Libistros' adventures in the hope of

pleasing her and regaining her favours (XIV). The story as told by the text
ends with the end of its own narrating (XV). We do not know whether
Klitobos and Myrtane lived happily ever after.

The *Tale of Troy*

The full Greek title of this poem, also known in English as *Troas* and *A
Byzantine Iliad*,[46] is Διήγησις γεναμένη ἐν Τροίᾳ [,] ἅπας ὁ ἀφανισμὸς ἔνθε
ἐγίνη, or literally 'Tale which took place at Troy: all the destruction [that]
there took place'. Despite this title it owes little to Homer and nothing at all
to the Greek translation of the French *Roman de Troie*, the *War of Troy*. In
essence it does for Paris what the *Tale of Achilles* had done for that hero:
namely to weave a romance around a legendary name, with limited respect
for the background from which the characters were originally drawn. The
Tale of Troy is in reality the romance of Paris.[47]

The tale begins with Hekabe's prophetic dream and the birth of Paris,
familiar from the classical tradition. There follows a series of expedients
designed to prevent the destruction foretold should Paris grow to manhood:
the infant Paris, like Moses, is put out to sea in a basket, to be found and
brought up by shepherds; later, like the *heroines* of many romances, he is
secluded in a splendidly decorated tower. All these expedients are unavailing,
and in due course, like the heroes of the other romances, Paris sets out from
home in search of adventure but is shipwrecked and taken in by some monks
on an island. The beautiful Helen keeps vigil in a lonely castle, and all the
heroes of the world have come by land and sea to lay siege to her beauty.
Menelaos prevails, but no sooner is he married to her than he has,
conveniently, to depart on an expedition. Paris, in the guise of his monastic
hosts, succeeds in entering the castle, but then impresses the retainers there
by his courtly bearing and feats of arms. Before long he and Helen have fallen
in love, and the pair live clandestinely as man and wife in the castle, until it
transpires that Helen is pregnant. They therefore escape by sea and turn up
shortly afterwards, to no one's enthusiasm, back at Troy.

Thus ends the first part of the story, with the union of the lovers. The
setback common to all these stories now makes its appearance in the form of
the expedition of the Greeks against Troy, and the individual fates of Paris
and Helen are taken over by larger events whose course is already determined
in the poet's sources. The Greek heroes arrive in their ships, Achilles sulks
in his tent and is then treacherously killed by Paris and his brother
Deiphobos. Paris himself is now eclipsed by Achilles as an actor in the story;
and his death comes about as part of the Greeks' revenge for the treacherous
murder of that hero. After the immolation of Priam and his daughters on the
burial mound of Achilles, the romance of Paris ends with a lament for the
passing of the glory not of Paris but of his victim, Achilles.

8

THE ORIGINAL
ROMANCES:
NARRATIVE STRUCTURE

We have already seen that the fictional stories told in each of the romances are founded upon a restricted and recurrent group of events and situations (a prince's quest, the initiation into love, the separation of lovers through actual or simulated death, and so on). When the story told belongs to fiction rather than to history, the selection of events and situations to narrate, and their arrangement into a pattern, or 'plot', belongs not to the world of the imagined events themselves, but to the activity of the author in creating his literary text or *narrative*. For the purposes of this section it is not so much the recurrent events that we will be considering as the formal pattern or narrative structure created in each of the romances by the choice and arrangement of events to be narrated, and also the manner of their narration.

In discussing each of the romances in turn, considered this time from the point of view of narrative, I shall concentrate principally on the techniques used in each case to order the events of the fictional story into a coherent formal pattern, but I shall also point out more briefly other characteristics of language, style, specific techniques of story-telling, and narrative inconsistencies. Rather than attempting to be exhaustive, I aim to demonstrate, through selective presentation of the narrative techniques and structures present in these romances, what rewarding material they offer for further detailed study along these lines.

The *Tale of Achilles*

The romance begins with a brief prologue on the power of love, reminiscent in style and in its relation to what follows of the preamble to the youthful exploits of Digenes. This is balanced by what may be termed an epilogue, again parallel to the final part of *Digenes Akrites*, in which the hero's bride dies, he wishes to die with her and finally is left lamenting.[1] The main portion of the narrative falls into three parts. The first, in which the declared theme of love is conspicuous by its total absence, recounts the parentage, birth, youth and military prowess of the hero.[2] A new phase of the narrative, as well as of the fictional life of the hero, begins when, after his victory, he visits the

117

castle of the king he has defeated and first sets eyes on his adversary's beautiful daughter. Here the whole style and tone of the narrative change; by contrast to the first part, the narrative of Achilles' wooing which now begins, and includes the long *ekphraseis* of the girl and her palace, focuses entirely on a feminine world of beauty and of the submission to that world of the hero in his moment of victory. This second part culminates in the explicit love-making of the pair.[3]

Summarizing the progress of the narrative rather schematically, then, the first part ends with the hero's victory in war, the second with his winning the favours of the girl he loves. The third part interweaves the two kinds of 'combat' in which the hero has learnt to excel: his victory in love must be consolidated by feats of arms.[4] In order to marry the daughter of a hostile king, Achilles must abduct her and defend his action by force, and the wedding itself is celebrated by a tournament.[5] Although the texts as we have them present minor inconsistencies, the structure of this narrative is clear and coherent. It is the only one of the later romances whose structural organization falls into three parts rather than the bipartite patterns we have already noted in the case of *Digenes Akrites*, but there is a foretaste in this romance of the sensitivity to proportion that we shall discover in the other texts, in that the breaks in this narrative of approximately 1,800 lines come at intervals of about 600 lines, thus dividing the text into more-or-less equal sections. These three parts, which schematically present war and love first in terms of antithesis, and then of synthesis in the final part, may perhaps owe something to the tripartite structure of the twelfth-century romances, and especially to Makrembolites' *Hysmine and Hysminias*, as well as to the second part of *Digenes Akrites*, in which the adventures of the hero are similarly divided.

Kallimachos and Chrysorrhoe

The language in which this romance is written contains a much higher proportion of learned forms, superimposed on a vernacular base, than we find in any of the other romances of this period (except the translated fragment *The Old Knight*). This mixture of language levels has been subjected to an exhaustive study which reveals that for all its evident distance from the speech of any single epoch, the language of *Kallimachos and Chrysorrhoe* forms a coherent, functioning system.[6] In keeping with the learned elements of the language in this romance is a preference for long and often quite complex rhetorical periods, which fluently overrun the limits of the fifteen-syllable line. Despite this, the mid-line and end-line caesuras are generally respected. Although the influence of rhetorical conventions from the earlier romances is evident – in the *ekphraseis*, in Chrysorrhoe's courtroom speech, in frequent anaphora and alliteration – these are throughout subordinate to the function of telling a story.

A prologue establishes an attitude to the events described which will be reiterated in different words many times in the course of the romance: nothing in life is without its share of sorrow, and indeed joy and sorrow are inextricably linked. This, the prologue continues, is certainly the nature of 'the bittersweet pangs of love'[7] – as you will learn, the narrator continues, if you read on. The sentiments of this prologue are repeated several times in the body of the text. The main narrative falls explicitly into two parts, of which the second begins with a brief reprise of the prologue.[8] The first part contains the hero's adventures from setting out with his brothers to establishing himself and Chrysorrhoe as lord and lady of the Ogre's Castle;[9] the second, the abduction of the heroine and the adventures which lead to their permanent reunion and return to the scene of their first love.[10] These 'halves' are far from symmetrical in extent; but the author was not indifferent to the claims of formal symmetry. Overlaying or in counterpoint to this bipartite structure is another: the midpoint of the narrative, which falls well into the second thematic 'part', is the point at which the planned abduction of Chrysorrhoe is actually carried out,[11] and it is this episode that also shifts the scene of the action (which has been predominantly at the Ogre's Castle up to this point) to the new setting of the foreign king's palace, where the action will eventually be resolved. Furthermore the action before and after the midpoint of the narrative consists of a quest by the hero which ends in union with the heroine, and in each case begins with the appearance of Kallimachos' shadowy brothers.[12] Although it may be far-fetched to suppose that authors at this period actually counted the lines of their texts, the positioning of this crucial episode, and of the decisive change of scene that goes with it, around the exact centre of the romance's 2,607 lines betrays a careful regard for proportion on the part of the author, and this is a characteristic that we will find repeated in others of the original romances.[13]

A connection and a parallelism between the two parts of this romance are reinforced in subtler ways too. Kallimachos in the second part compares his 'service' to Chrysorrhoe in liberating her from the ogre to his new servile role as under-gardener, which he hopes will lead him to her once again.[14] This role in turn had been foreshadowed earlier in the romance at the point where the foreign king first sees the pair leaning out of the Ogre's Castle, and Kallimachos is described (interestingly, in terms of technique, through his rival's eyes), as:

ὁ καὶ τοῦ κάστρου βασιλεὺς καὶ τῆς δεσποίνης δοῦλος
καὶ τῶν χαρίτων κηπουρός, τῆς καλλονῆς δραγάτης
καὶ τρυγητὴς τῶν ἡδονῶν τῆς ἀσυγκρίτου κόρης.[15]

... the castle's king and slave of his mistress
and gardener of the graces, keeper of beauty's vineyard
and the one to pluck the delights of the matchless girl.

This imagery is taken up in a playful exchange that takes place when Kallimachos introduces himself to Chrysorrhoe in his disguise. How dare he, a paid servant, offer roses from the royal garden to her, its mistress? The disguised Kallimachos replies:

Ἐκεῖνος λέγει· « δέσποιναν ἐσὲν ἡ τύχη γράφει,
ἐμὲ δὲ πάλιν ἔδωκεν τὸ νὰ τρυγῶ τὰ ῥόδα.
Αὐθέντης εἶσαι τῶν φυτῶν, ἐγὼ τοῦ κήπου φύλαξ.
Ἂν πέσῃς εἰς τὸ στρῶμάν σου βασιλικῶς ἐπάνω,
παραμονὴν τὸν μισθαργὸν καὶ φύλαξιν εὑρήσεις
καὶ τρυγητὴν τῶν ῥόδων σου καὶ τῶν φυτῶν δραγάτην ».[16]

He says: 'it is written by fate that you should be the mistress,
but to me is it given to pluck the roses.
You are lord of the plants, I guardian of the garden.
Should you lay yourself royally upon your bed,
in the paid servant you will find protection and guarding
and one to pluck your roses and be the vineyard-keeper of your plants.'

In more serious vein the same imagery is reiterated in the resolution of the story, in Chrysorrhoe's courtroom speech in defence of Kallimachos. Her carefully constructed argument, which wins the day, derives from the second book of Kings: if a man should sow a vineyard and tend it, is it right for a powerful neighbour to muscle in and seize the harvest?[17]

Imagery then plays an important part in the narrative organization of this romance and provides the means for a deliberate interweaving of the two parts of the story, which in terms of incident are only weakly connected.

The narrative follows the chronological order of the events narrated with only two minor exceptions. One is a recapitulation which exposes a small discrepancy in the narrative that is more likely to be due to the transmission of the text than to the original author.[18] A second allows for a shift in focus, so that the events of Chrysorrhoe's abduction, told in the main narrative from the viewpoint of Kallimachos or with the witch as the focal point, can be presented from the point of view of the victim herself.[19] The author's skill in manipulating the point of view from which events are supposed to be perceived has already been noticed, in passing, in the scene where the king spies the hero and heroine on the walls of the Ogre's Castle. There is another instance of this in a minor episode in which Kallimachos learns how the king's people regard their ruler's problems with his abducted bride. His informant's discourse is subtly modulated as it progresses, from indirect to direct speech.[20] But the most spectacular example is the *coup de théâtre* achieved when Kallimachos in the story, and the reader in the text, first perceive the heroine: the narrative follows the hero's gaze as he takes in the sumptuous paintings of pagan deities on the roof of the ogre's chamber. Only then does he observe the naked female figure hanging suspended by her hair; and the narrative makes the reader an accomplice to his shock of realization. This is no part of the décor: the girl is real.[21]

Belthandros and Chrysantza

The action of this romance, no less than that of *Kallimachos*, falls into two parts. The first, which takes place entirely in the realm of the fantastic, consists of the hero's discovery of the Castle of Eros, his submission to Eros the King and his choice of Chrysantza from among the forty beautiful princesses; the second narrates his courtship of Chrysantza in the real world, their secret life together, their elopement, separation and narrow escape from death. These two main parts are framed by an introduction and epilogue in which the hero first sets out from his home and family and finally returns there with his bride. The contrasting character of the two main parts which make up this romance has excited its share of critical comment and aroused speculation as to whether the text as we have it is a reliable copy of the original.[22] In fact there is a similar contrast in *Kallimachos*, whose first half is largely set in the similarly fabulous Ogre's Castle, with a move to a more realistically represented court environment in the second. A closer look at the organization of *Belthandros* will show how carefully this whole tale, too, has been constructed.

The mathematical centre of this romance's 1,348 lines occurs just after the hero has awarded the wand as a prize to the most beautiful of the princesses, who will of course turn out to be Chrysantza.[23] Eros the King summons him again and demands to know the outcome of the contest,[24] upon which Belthandros launches into a long and ecstatic *ekphrasis* of his chosen bride-to-be, which brings the first part of the romance, set in the Castle of Eros, to an end.[25] The rest of the narrative is symmetrically arranged around this central climax, so that the two halves of the narrative reflect each other as in a mirror.

On either side of this central point we find Belthandros voluntarily offering obedience to an overlord: the symbolic figure of Eros in the first half, the real king of Antioch, who is Chrysantza's father, in the second.[26] Moving further from this central point we find it framed by adventures in a palace within a castle which combines wonders with a sense of danger: respectively the interior in the Castle of Eros and the court of Chrysantza's father.[27] In the first the hero is initiated into the nature of love symbolically, in the second literally. One might even note a correspondence between the blood which flows from the (male) statue wounded by love in Eros' Castle and the heroine's blood on the sheets which, in an unexpected access of realism, are displayed on the morning after the hero's sham-wedding to Phaidrokaza.[28]

The symmetrical principle is also applied slightly differently in a parallelism and antithesis between the *final* episode in each half of the narrative. The episode of the beauty contest which concludes the first part, and the escape from Antioch which concludes the second, are both introduced by brief descriptions of night. Night in the Castle of Eros is presented as a time for enchantment and union heralded by a flying representative of Eros:

> Καὶ τότε νὺξ ἀσέληνος δέχεται τὴν ἡμέραν
> καὶ τὸ γυρεύειν χάριτας Ἐρωτοκάστρου ἄλλας.
> Ἔρως εἰς ἦλθε πρὸς αὐτὸν ἀεροπτεροδρόμος.[29]

> And then a moonless night took the place of day
> [time] to seek further charms of the Castle of Love.
> A Cupid came to him flying on wings through the air.

The second nocturnal adventure begins with an identical image, but the properties of night this time are destructive; here the counterpart of the winged Cupid is the birds, and the movement they represent, in being *separated* from their mates, is the exact opposite of the bringing-together initiated in the previous extract:

> Ἡ νὺξ ἐκείνη ἀσέληνος ὑπῆρχε καὶ σκοτώδης
> καὶ ἀστραπόβροντο πολύ, ἀλλὰ καὶ ἀνεμοζάλη·
> ἐκ δὲ τοσαύτης τε βροχῆς καὶ τοῦ νεροῦ τὴν βίαν
> καὶ τὰ πουλιὰ τὰ ταίρια των ἐχάσασι τὴν νύκτα.[30]

> That night was moonless and dark
> and filled with thunder and lightning, a tempest too;
> by such a downpour and the force of the rain
> even the birds were parted from their mates.

Moving still further from the centre of the narrative, we find that the two palaces (of Eros and of the king of Antioch) are separated from the hero's familiar world by a river. In the first half it is the discovery of the mysterious river of fire and water that leads Belthandros from Tarsos, which he had reached on leaving home, into the realm of Eros.[31] Correspondingly, when the pair finally decide to elope from Antioch, before they can live together openly as man and wife they have to cross another river, which robs them of all they possess and almost even of their lives.[32] The first river Belthandros followed *upstream* to discover the Castle of Eros;[33] the second the lovers after their harrowing adventure follow *downstream* to the sea.[34] The first river, described in terms of beauty and wonder, leads away from the real world towards the union of the lovers; the second, presented as a destructive, frightening force of nature,[35] is in this romance the mechanism for the traditional separation and apparent death of the lovers.[36]

Continuing our centrifugal progress outwards from the midpoint of the romance, we find that outside the balancing frame of the two rivers,

Belthandros' journey from home is carried out by land, while the return journey is effected by sea.[37] The hero, finally, in the introductory part of the narrative is alienated from home and family and ignorant of love; on his return at the close of the narrative he is restored to his father's affections, hailed as king and married to his ideal princess.

The symmetrical structure of the narrative can be illustrated by a diagram.[38] The vertical columns with the arrows show the sequence of narrated events, beginning at the top of the left-hand column and ending at the top of the right-hand, while the thematic correspondences between the two halves of the narrative can be seen by reading horizontally.

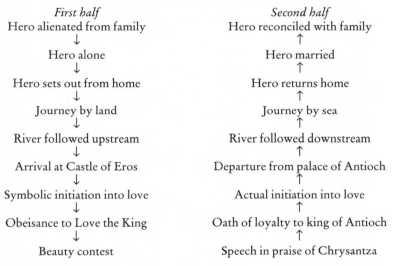

First half	*Second half*
Hero alienated from family	Hero reconciled with family
↓	↑
Hero alone	Hero married
↓	↑
Hero sets out from home	Hero returns home
↓	↑
Journey by land	Journey by sea
↓	↑
River followed upstream	River followed downstream
↓	↑
Arrival at Castle of Eros	Departure from palace of Antioch
↓	↑
Symbolic initiation into love	Actual initiation into love
↓	↑
Obeisance to Love the King	Oath of loyalty to king of Antioch
↓	↑
Beauty contest	Speech in praise of Chrysantza

As in *Kallimachos*, the coherence of this complex narrative scheme is achieved very largely by the use of imagery. This is particularly evident in the case of the two rivers which frame the two main episodes of the narrative. The first river, which leads the hero to the Castle of Eros, is described as an amplification of the rhetorical figure of oxymoron:

> Ἐνῷ δ' ἐκεῖ περιέτρεχε μὲ τὰ παιδόπουλά του,
> εὕρηκεν μικροπόταμον καὶ εἰς τὸ νερόν του μέσον
> νὰ εἶπες οὐρανόδρομον ἀστέρα ἔχει ἔσω·
> καὶ κεῖται μέσον τοῦ νεροῦ καὶ μετ' ἐκεῖνο τρέχει.
> Ἔπιασε τὸ ἀναπόταμον ἐκεῖνος καὶ γυρεύει,
> τὴν κεφαλὴν τοῦ ποταμοῦ ἐπεθυμεῖ γνωρίσαι,
> τὴν φλόγα μέσον τοῦ νεροῦ, πόθεν καὶ κεῖνον τρέχει.[39]

While he was going about there [at Tarsus] with his retainers
he found a little river and within its waters
you'd say there was a heaven-wandering star in there;

that lies within the water and with it flows along.
He set off upstream in search,
anxious to learn the river's source,
and whence the fire within the water also flows.

The answer to the riddle is of course the paradoxical nature of love, which traditionally both refreshes like water and burns or consumes the sufferer like fire; and the result for Belthandros of following the river to its source is his initiation by Eros the King. The twin sources of the river, as we saw, were a pair of statues in the banqueting hall of the Castle of Love, each bearing a caption prophesying the future love of Belthandros and Chrysantza. The statues (of a weeping woman holding a peacock and of a man pierced through his heart by an arrow) together are allegorical representations of love as the union of opposites: male and female, water and fire.[40] The peacock which the female statue holds is a traditional Byzantine symbol for eternal life; and the water of the river, emerging from such a source, is clearly suggestive of the water of life, even perhaps of the power of love to confer immortality. The other statue, which represents the source of the river's fiery component in the blood gushing from an open wound to the heart, correspondingly represents the dangers of love and its potential for destruction. At the level of its imagery, Belthandros' initiation is more far-reaching, and more suggestive of the complex nature of love as perceived in this text, than is anything overtly said or done in the Castle of Eros.

When the river reappears as an image in the second part of the romance, it is in keeping with the shift from the symbolic and fantastic to the relatively realistic that the imagery used to describe it should appeal to nature rather than to rhetoric. But this river too has an ambivalent role in the narrative: it represents the way to safety and happiness for the lovers but at the same time strips them of all they possess, almost even of each other. That this river too, like the previous one, is intended to connote the ambivalent, and potentially destructive, nature of love is borne out by other instances of fire-and-water imagery in the romance. 'Death by water', the fate suffered by Phaidrokaza and the companions, and only narrowly escaped by Belthandros and Chrysantza themselves, had specifically been wished on the hero by the runner-up in the beauty contest. The disappointed suitor's curse explicitly links drowning with the 'fire' of love:

« Ὦ ἀδικώτατε κριτά, εἰς τὸν Θεὸν ἐλπίζω
νὰ πέσῃς μέσα στὸν βυθὸν τῆς ἐρωτοαγάπης·
καὶ εἰς τὸ ρεῦμα τοῦ νεροῦ νὰ πνιγῇς, ν' ἀποθάνῃς,
ὅτι καὶ τὴν καρδίαν μου ἀπέκαυσας διόλου ».[41]

O most unjust judge, I pray to God
that you may fall into the abyss of love;

and in the water's current there be drowned and die,
because you have burnt up my heart altogether.

The same imagery is more simply repeated in Chrysantza's soliloquy which betrays her love for Belthandros and which he overhears:

καὶ μάκρυνε τὸ τέρμενον δυὸ χρόνους καὶ δυὸ μῆνας
ὁποὺ βαστῶ τὴν φλόγαν σου κρυμμένη στὴν ἀγκάλην.[42]

and the time has increased to two years and two months
in which I've held your flame concealed in my embrace.

A vital component binding the episodes of the romance together is the consistent exploitation of imagery of fire and water as representative of the ambivalent nature of its central theme, namely love.

As in *Kallimachos*, the sequence of the narrative throughout follows the temporal order of the events as they are supposed to have happened. Occasionally, though, the narrator or one of the characters makes a reference back to events which have already been recounted, and here two minor inconsistencies may be observed in the text as it has been transmitted. In his journey across Anatolia at the beginning of the romance, Belthandros successfully beats off an attack by robbers and turns them to flight. On the return voyage at the end of the romance he briefly recounts the sum of his adventures to his father's eunuch (in the text, in the form of reported speech). Touching on this point, he now says that he killed the robbers.[43] The other concerns the prophecies which Belthandros read on the statues in the Castle of Eros. There are two of these, inscribed beneath the carved figures from which flows the river of water and fire; their message, that Belthandros and Chrysantza are destined for each other.[44] The hero's reaction when he reads these prophecies is perhaps disproportionately negative,[45] a fact possibly explained by a reference back to this prophecy at the point where he and Chrysantza are separated by the stormy river:

Καὶ τότες ἐπληρώθηκε τὸ μοιρογράφημά του,
τὸ ὅπερ ἐθεάσατο ἐν τῷ Ἐρωτοκάστρῳ.[46]

And then was fulfilled what fate had written for him,
which he had seen in the Castle of Eros.

Had this part of his adventures in fact been prophesied to him then, his adverse reaction might have been more understandable. Either something has dropped out of the earlier part of the narrative, or these two lines are an interpolation, perhaps inspired by the example of *Libistros*, where in a comparable situation the hero's adventures are prophesied to him in full.[47]

Libistros and Rhodamne

This is the first original, fictional text in Greek to make full and consistent use of the technique of the frame-story (*Rahmenerzählung* or *conte à tiroirs*), which plays such a conspicuous part in the medieval story-telling of the Islamic world. It is also a rarity in Greek fiction up to this time in its use of a first-person narrator. As we shall see in Chapter 10, the text declares its lineal descent from the two earlier first-person narratives in Greek fiction, *Leukippe and Kleitophon* by Achilles Tatios and *Hysmine and Hysminias* by Eustathios Makrembolites.[48] Achilles Tatios, however, had begun with a frame (the narrator meets Kleitophon on a visit to the city of Sidon, only to become a silent narratee as the latter tells his tale) which is forgotten at the end of the romance. The conclusion of Kleitophon's narrative fails to return us to our starting-point or to tell us what has become of him and Leukippe so as to leave him, apparently alone, telling his story to strangers in Sidon. Makrembolites had resolved this problem by doing away with the frame altogether and making the entire text the first-person narrative of the hero, Hysminias. But the author of *Libistros* has gone one better than either of his predecessors: the text begins and ends with a realistic frame, in which Klitobos is imagined as telling the whole story, of his own and Libistros' adventures, before an audience which includes the Princess Myrtane, whose favours he hopes by this means to regain. Such a frame, in which the act of story-telling becomes itself an event in the story, is reminiscent of the classic Arabic and Persian collections of tales of which the *Thousand and One Nights* is the best-known example. Certain of these collections had been circulating quite widely in Greek translation since the eleventh century.[49]

Despite its greater complexity, the organization of this romance follows the same principle of symmetry as we have already observed at work in the organization of the narrative in *Kallimachos* and *Belthandros*. At its outermost ends we have the frame, which means that the narrative both begins and ends at the same point in time, allowing only for a difference of the time taken for the recital of its contents by the fictional narrator, Klitobos. This narrator begins, in order to entertain the Princess Myrtane, by announcing that he will tell the story of the adventures in love of his friend Libistros.[50] The end of the text brings us back to the same point, but the reader now knows that Myrtane, to whom the whole narrative is fictionally addressed, is the girl that Klitobos has loved and lost: the tale itself, a love story, is his gift to her and ends with the plea that, like its hero and heroine Libistros and Rhodamne, he and Myrtane should live happily ever after and die simultaneously.[51]

Within this frame the whole story is told in the first person by Klitobos. Klitobos' narrative, however, begins *in medias res*. While wandering as an exile he came upon the sorrowing figure of Libistros, who then told him *his* story. The main narrative is in this way divided into two parts. In the first Klitobos becomes the narratee as he (fictionally of course) reports the actual words used to him by Libistros. This part contains Libistros' story up to his meeting with Klitobos, including his marriage to Rhodamne and her abduction, and takes up a little over half the total extent of the narrative.[52] The second part is told by Klitobos direct, as he himself becomes an actor in the adventures which lead to the restitution of Rhodamne and the return of the pair to the Castle of Silver.[53] The first part of Libistros' adventures, told by him to Klitobos, takes up some 2,500 lines in the E text (2,200 in N); the second, narrated direct by Klitobos to Myrtane, takes up about 1,700 in E (1,400 in N).[54]

These two parts of the main narrative are not merely differentiated by the change of narrator. As in *Kallimachos* and *Belthandros*, the first part tells of the hero's initiation into love in a spectacular castle, and as in *Belthandros* the fantastic palace of Eros (this time visited in a dream) is duplicated in the scarcely less fantastic Castle of Silver which is Rhodamne's home. This part ends, after the hero's marriage to the heroine and her subsequent abduction, with the meeting of Libistros and Klitobos, with which it also began. It is interesting to note, however, that the exact mathematical centre of both the E and the N text is occupied by the scene of Libistros' first waking meeting with Rodamne and their love-making in a meadow.[55]

The action of the second part, narrated by Klitobos, runs in parallel to that of the first. The friends are launched upon their quest by a dream which reveals Rhodamne's whereabouts,[56] just as Libistros had first seen Rhodamne and had been initiated into love in a series of dreams.[57] The chain of events in both parts of the narrative is set in motion in a similar way. Libistros' courtship of Rhodamne begins when, out hunting with his falcon, his arrow shoots and kills one of a pair of turtle-doves, and its mate, to his astonishment, hurls itself to its death upon the corpse.[58] From this small beginning the hero's curiosity about love is aroused, and that very night he dreams of his initiation in the palace of Eros. Similarly symbolic imagery from the world of birds also sets him and Klitobos on the track of the abducted Rhodamne: the substance of Klitobos' dream just mentioned is that a black eagle swept up a partridge in its talons, but on being threatened by the hero's bow set it down unharmed.

In both parts a two-year quest is involved; the stages of the return journey towards the end of the second mirror the progress of Libistros' search, as told to Klitobos at the beginning of the first;[59] and in both we are treated to a series of love-letters and songs (recalled and elaborated by the lovers on their homeward journey).[60] One of the series of songs with which the lovers while away the time on their homeward journey expressly draws attention to this symmetry, as the hero celebrates the happiness with which he retraces the route earlier taken in sorrow.[61] Finally, both parts end with a wedding: of Libistros and Rhodamne in the first, of Klitobos and Melanthia in the second.

Klitobos' own story is interspersed with the main narrative in a way which shows careful regard for this overall two-part structure. After the prologue, Klitobos tells how he met Libistros wandering in search of Rhodamne. In doing so he begins his narrative in the middle not just of Libistros' story but also of his own. Of the events of his own life that had led up to his meeting with Libistros he tells us (and Myrtane) at this point only:

> Ἤμουν καὶ ἐγὼ ἐκ τὴν χώραν μου διωγμένος διὰ πόθον,
> θλιμμένος ἐκ τὸν ἔρωταν, καμμένος διὰ ἀγάπην,
> ἐξέβηκα ἀπὸ λύπης μου καὶ κόσμον περιεπάτουν
> διὰ κουφισμὸν καὶ ἀνάπαυσιν τῶν πόνων μου τῶν τόσων·[62]

> And I too had been driven from my country by love's desire,
> grieved by Eros, scorched by love,
> I had set out through grief and was wandering the world
> for respite and relief from so many pains.

We shall hear no more of Klitobos' sufferings, however, until the conclusion of Libistros' narration, which takes up the entire first part of the romance. We are reminded of his presence, however, by a whole series of asides, and direct addresses to him as 'friend', with which Libistros' narrative is sprinkled,[63] and by a strategically placed interruption. After the narration of Libistros' third dream, which had followed his arrival outside the Castle of Silver, Klitobos correctly anticipates the reader's bafflement with Libistros' description of the triple-faced King of Love and interrupts to seek elucidation.[64] Shortly afterwards we are reminded of the narrative frame (in this case Libistros' narration to Klitobos in the meadow) by the injunction that it is time for bed. The hero's adventures at the Castle of Silver must wait for morning.[65]

At the end of the first part of the narrative Libistros asks Klitobos to reciprocate by telling his own story, and this he does in the space of just fifty-four lines.[66] Tantalizingly, however, he leaves off his narration with a 'cliffhanger': while he is imprisoned for his illicit love of Myrtane, her husband plots to have him put to death.[67] Libistros fails to notice the omission,[68] and the first part of the narrative concludes at this point. In the second part the principal focus of the narrative is again directed towards the affairs of Libistros and Rhodamne, but Klitobos himself takes part in the action, of which he now becomes the narrator. About half-way through this second part he has an opportunity to remind us (and his fictional audience) of his own concerns and to supply the missing part of his own story, as he introduces himself to Rhodamne in her guise as innkeeper. To her he repeats the salient facts of his story, much as he had previously told them to Libistros.[69] This time, however, he makes good his earlier omission: it was the secret intervention of Myrtane that saved his life and enabled him to exchange his imprisonment for exile from his country, during which he fell in with Libistros.[70]

The placing of this component of the story in the sequence of the narrative is surely not accidental; nor is it dictated only by considerations of the text's formal proportions. Klitobos' life was saved, in his own story, by the initiative of that story's heroine (a state of affairs common enough in the genre, as we have seen). But it is significant at the *psychological* level of the narrative that he chooses to suppress this aspect of his adventures when relating them to another man, Libistros, but prominently gives Myrtane her due when telling the story to a woman, Rhodamne. Indeed a close parallelism is established between the two heroines, the one about whom Klitobos narrates and the one to whom he narrates – especially when it is remembered that this narration about Myrtane to Rhodamne is itself part of the whole story about Rhodamne narrated by Klitobos to Myrtane! By delaying the revelation to his fictional audience, which includes Myrtane herself, of his mistress's active role in saving his life, he also places his affirmation of gratitude closer to the time when the narrative will, according to its own fiction, come to an end, and the narrator can be expected to claim his reward from Myrtane. Finally, the conclusion to Klitobos' story comes at the end of the whole narrative, in his marriage to Rhodamne's sister, followed by her death and his return to his native Armenia and to Myrtane, so completing the parallel with the main story of Libistros' adventures.[71]

By contrast to the broad extent of Libistros' story in the narrative, it is interesting to notice that the subsidiary story of Klitobos is told in four chunks of between forty and ninety lines each, two of which also provide the prologue and epilogue to the whole narrative. If we add to these the passage (of about the same length) in which Klitobos interrupts his friend in the first part of the narrative, and Libistros postpones the rest of his story until the following morning, a further pattern becomes discernible: Klitobos' interventions are separated in all but one case by the space of approximately eight hundred lines. As the single exception is a gap of 1,700 lines, it is even possible that the original text might have contained a further intervention somewhere in the middle of it. The placing of Klitobos' appearances in the narrative on his own account, that is when he tells his own story or interrupts Libistros' narrative, rather than acting as narratee and confidant of the hero, can best be shown diagrammatically:

Content	Line nos (E)	No. of lines (E)
Prologue (meeting of K and L)	N 1–34 + 1–55	70
[MAIN NARRATIVE: LIBISTROS]	57–834	777
K's question, narrative suspended	837–83	46
[MAIN NARRATIVE: LIBISTROS]	884–2587	1703
Dialogue, K's story (1)	2588–2668	80
[MAIN NARRATIVE: KLITOBOS]	2669–3493	824
K's story to Rhodamne (2)	3493–3582	89
[MAIN NARRATIVE: KLITOBOS]	3583–4360	777
Epilogue	4361–4407	46

But even this scheme is considerably simplified, as it makes insufficient allowance for the predominance in this romance of directly reported speech. Since much of this speech consists of narrative or contains narrative elements, the result is to produce a series of frames or, in the terminology of Genette, of narrative *levels*.[72] The first of these levels (and here I briefly part company with Genette) is the level of the text itself. This is the level of the *real* narrator, who is of course not the fictional Klitobos but the author who is truly responsible for everything that is said in the text. At this level a historical individual (about whom in this case we know nothing at all) addresses a public through the conventions and expectations built into the genre in which he chooses to write.[73] Nothing contained in the text of *Libistros* itself is directly attributable to this narrator; however, the existence of this narrative level is assumed by any reader who is untroubled at not finding himself included in the group addressed by the fictional narrator, Klitobos, in the prologue and epilogue. As this level is not directly present in the text, I shall call it 'narrative level 0'.

Below this level,[74] comes the fictive narration of Klitobos, addressed to a specific, and equally fictive, audience. Klitobos' narration, which I shall call 'narrative level 1', spans the whole extent of the narrative as given to us by the text. 'Narrative level 2' is the level at which, *within* Klitobos' fictional narrative, someone else takes over the business of narrating; that is, whenever he is reporting not events but someone else's report of events. This happens throughout the entire first half of the narrative after the prologue, when Klitobos reports Libistros' story as the latter had told it to him, with the exception of the brief passage of dialogue mentioned earlier. The *telling* of Libistros' story belongs, with everything else reported direct by Klitobos, on level 1 (this is what Genette terms a 'narrating instance'). Everything that happens within that story, however, belongs to level 2, that is, is subordinate to the narrating instance in which Libistros narrates to Klitobos. This second level makes a number of reappearances in the second part of the narrative, notably when the witch gives her account of Rhodamne's abduction to the two friends; when Rhodamne tells her story to Klitobos at the inn in Egypt; when he responds by telling his own and Libistros' stories to her; and when Libistros and Rhodamne recall to each other and to Klitobos, on the homeward journey, events from their courtship.

A third level is introduced whenever a narrator at the second level reports events which had in turn been reported to him.[75] This happens in the first part of the romance, that is in Libistros' narrative, when the hero's confidant reports to him how his first love-letters, fired on arrows into the castle, have been received,[76] and in several of the letters themselves which in whole or in part consist of narrative. In the second part this happens when Klitobos, in his narration to Rhodamne, goes on to repeat the substance of Libistros' story as earlier told to *him*, by way of preparing her for the hero's imminent arrival upon the scene.[77]

In the first part of the narrative a fourth and fifth level even appear: Libistros' confidant relays to him the account of events within the castle given him by the eunuch who guards Rhodamne,[78] but part of this narration in turn consists of Rhodamne's narration to the eunuch of the events of a dream in which she had been visited by Eros.[79] These lines represent the nadir of the narrative levels exploited in this romance: Rhodamne narrates her dream to the eunuch, who narrates it to Klitobos, who narrates it to Myrtane – and all of this is *really* narrated by the author, who lies perfectly concealed within his text, to us, his readers.[80]

The use and arrangement of so many narrative levels also involve complex distortions in the temporal sequence of the narrative, for which Genette has coined the term 'anachronies'.[81] Almost all the anachronies in *Libistros* are of the same kind and are the result of the distribution of the narrating function among a number of narrators at different levels. If we take as our yardstick the (fictional) temporal point at which Klitobos tells his story to Myrtane, with which our text both begins and ends, it is immediately obvious that the story told as the text unfolds does not move forward in time from its starting-point but instead takes a number of backward leaps. Such distortions in the conversion of story time into narrative sequence, equivalent to the more widely used but less rigorously defined term 'flashbacks', are called by Genette 'analepses'.[82] The whole narrative of *Libistros*, in fact, consists of a series of analepses. Indeed each time a new narrative level is introduced we are faced, by definition, with an analepsis in relation to the previous level, since a new narrator is bound to relate events which have already happened at the moment when he is introduced to narrate them.[83]

Only at one point is a different kind of temporal distortion introduced: Libistros' first dream concludes with a prophecy which outlines all the main events of his and Rhodamne's lives (but naturally not Klitobos') right up to the time of their dreams.[84] Such an anticipation of events not yet narrated is termed by Genette a 'prolepsis'.[85] The prolepsis here has been inserted into a double analepsis (Klitobos has begun his narrative by going *back* to the time of his first meeting with Libistros; Libistros in turn goes *back* in time to the beginning of his adventures in order to narrate them to his friend). But the prolepsis has a reach[86] that goes far beyond the narrating instance of either of the analepses into which it has been inserted. In relation to Libistros telling his story to Klitobos, the parts of the prophecy dealing with his marriage to Rhodamne and the latter's abduction have already proved true. But at the end of his narration (the second-level analepsis) Libistros *does not know where Rhodamne is*.[87] In fact it requires Klitobos' dream to convince the hero that the prophecy may have contained a clue to her whereabouts.[88] This, it will readily be admitted, is one of the narrative's less plausible expedients. Finally, by the time that Klitobos tells his story to Myrtane (the narrating instance of level 1), most of the rest of the prophecy has also been proved true; but the prophesied deaths of the hero and heroine still lie in the future. By contrast, the narrative at no point contains a clue as to how the story of Klitobos and Myrtane will end, after the conclusion of the narrative that contains it.

The main analepses of the narrative can be shown schematically by reference back to the stories of the two principal characters as retold in chronological sequence set out in the previous chapter. There the events of Libistros' story were numbered with an arabic sequence, those of Klitobos' story in roman. The brief 'titles' of narrative incidents given here refer to that summary.

Line nos	L's story	K's story	Event
N 1–26	–	XIV	Narration to Myrtane
N 27–34 + E 1–79	15	IV	Meeting of L and K
81–161	1	–	L first hears of love
162–610	2	–	Dream: Castle of Eros
611–85	3	–	Dream: Rhodamne
686–834	4	–	Journey to Castle of Silver
835–83	15a	IVa	Dialogue of L and K
884–1171	5–6	–	Castle of Silver described
1172–1380	7	–	Contact established
1381–1840	8	–	Exchange of letters
1842–2216	9–10	–	Exchange of rings; meeting
2217–2515	11	–	Tournament; wedding
2516–21	12	–	Two years of marriage
2522–51	13	–	Abduction of Rhodamne
2552–83	14	–	L sets out
2584–2606	15b	IVb	Dialogue of L and K
2607–68	–	I–II	Love for M; imprisonment
2669–2923	16	V	Encounter with the witch
2924–3075	17	VI	Crossing to Egypt
3076–3141	–	VII	K and R at the inn
3142–3447	(12–13)	–	R's story to K
3448–92	–	VIIa	K and R at the inn
3493–3530	–	I–II	K's story repeated to R
3531–46	–	III	K's release from prison
3547–82	15c	IVc	Meeting of L and K retold to R

3583–3635	(1–17)	–	L's story retold to R
3636–3711	–	VIIb	K and R at the inn
3712–3910	18	VIII	Reunion; escape from Egypt
3911–24	19	IX	Death of the witch
3925–4201	20	X	Return journey
4202–4316	21	XI	L marries K to R's sister
4317–60	22	XIa	Reunion at Castle of Silver
4361–76	–	XII–XIII	Death of wife; leaves for home
4379–4407	–	XV	Concludes story to Myrtane

The chronology of the fictional events of the narrative is worked out with remarkable consistency, as it really requires to be for such a complex narrative to maintain its coherence.[89] Libistros' journey to the Castle of Silver takes two years; his marriage to Rhodamne lasts for two years before her abduction, and during that same interval his rival plots to win her.[90] It then takes him a further two years to find her again; and these and many other shorter intervals are specified repeatedly throughout the narrative. Only in the details of this last interval does a slight degree of confusion enter. Rhodamne tells Klitobos at the inn that it is for two years that her 'innkeeper' (that is, Libistros) has been missing;[91] and after the lovers' reunion they remind each other that their separation has lasted for two years.[92] However, when Libistros and Klitobos encounter the witch and charter her flying horses, she says that only a year and a half have passed since the abduction.[93] It is then at most a matter of days before Klitobos finds himself in Rhodamne's company at the inn.[94] There she tells him (as the witch has already done) that she has been granted a four-year remission by Berderichos in which to live unmolested as an innkeeper. She reckons that it is eighteen months since her abductor left the country, but for an unspecified period before then he had pestered her mercilessly.[95] The discrepancy, which is trivial enough, has probably occurred because the interval of a year and a half is mentioned twice. On the second occasion, in Rhodamne's narrative, it is consistent with a total interval of two years, but this is not also compatible with the witch's story. The only purpose in labouring this point at all is to illustrate how generally conscientious the author is in establishing a clear and consistent chronological sequence, so that the multiple anachronies of his narrative are clearly bound together into a coherent whole.

Although in length and in complexity of narrative organization this romance far surpasses its peers, in its use of imagery, and particularly of imagery as a means of providing a broader coherence and unity of structure, it lags far behind *Kallimachos* and *Belthandros*. The 'triple-form-faced' figure of Eros the King and the symbolically triangular Castle of Silver (which will be discussed in Chapter 10 in another context) are ingeniously contrived, as is the complex interweaving of the two narrators and their respective stories. But these are the contrivances of a more mathematical, more abstract mind

133

than those that devised the striking visual symbols of a girl suspended by her hair, naked, from a painted ceiling, or a river of fire and water emanating from a magical Castle of Eros. The author of this romance may be considered as a latter-day Prodromos, rather than a latter-day Eugenianos.

The *Tale of Troy*

By contrast with the original romances which preceded it, this text contains few signs of ingenuity. It maintains the bipartite structure characteristic of these romances, in that there is a clear break, as well as a shift in the focus of the narrative, after line 763 (out of a total of 1,166 lines). Up until this point the story has been of Paris' childhood, exile from his home, and temporary guise as a monk, which enables him to take advantage of Menelaos' absence and gain access to Helen's castle and affections. The second part, which traditionally puts an obstacle in the way of the lovers, is more closely derived from Manasses' account of the Trojan war, although some of the details derive ultimately, if not very accurately, from Homer.[96] The conventions of the romance recede somewhat in the second half, and there is no equivalent here to the balanced correspondences between the two parts that we found in the last three texts discussed. The nearest would be a parallel between Paris' concealment among the monks in the first part and the similarly unheroic transformation in his *alter ego* Achilles (who will ultimately usurp his central place in the text) into a woman while sulking in his tent.[97] These acts of transvestism in each half of the romance may be seen in relation to Helen's disguise *as a man* when she and Paris flee her native castle and head for Troy, at the transition from the first to the second part of the narrative.[98] This act of transvestism may derive from the minor episode in *Digenes Akrites*, where the daughter of a Syrian nobleman, Haplorrhabdes, narrates to the hero how she had eloped with her lover in male disguise.[99] But it is interesting to note that transexual disguise, sometimes alternating with disguise as a monk, plays a significant role in a number of ballad-types in Greek oral poetry.[100]

Overall, then, this is an episodic, cento-like text, which clearly fails to impose much consistency on the material from which it derives. There is no likelihood that successive redactions or the interference of copyists have been responsible for the shortcomings of the *Tale of Troy*. Rather, a writer much less sure of his craft than the authors of the romances so far discussed seems to have tried with only limited success to create a unified story by combining popular history with the form and conventions of the romance.

9

TRANSLATIONS AND ADAPTATIONS OF WESTERN ROMANCES

There are six romances in Greek written before the sixteenth century which were translated more or less closely from Western originals. The term 'romances of chivalry', commonly applied today to all the later Greek romances, can only properly be applied to this group (and even here with the exception of *Apollonios*).[1] Although not unknown to the authors of the original romances, as we shall see in the next chapter, the world of Western chivalry first enters the Greek romance around the year 1350, when the compendious *Roman de Troie* by Benoît de Saint-Maure was translated into Greek.[2] There is an interesting irony here, in that the chivalric world of the medieval West first became known to Greek readers through a work which had in its turn superimposed the manners of this world upon an ancient *Greek* story.[3] Nor is this merely a random curiosity of literary history: as we shall see, the Greek translators of Western romances were highly selective in the originals they chose to translate, and all their sources have some sort of connection with the fictional or historical world of older Greek literature.

In this chapter I assume that the reader will have at least a nodding acquaintance with the original stories drawn on by Greek translators and have not summarized their plots. Nor have I attempted to extend the scope of this study generally by introducing detailed comparisons between Western and Greek versions of the same story, preferring to emphasize what does not seem previously to have been noticed, namely the principles determining the choice of originals to translate, with their important implication that the translators also knew something of the native Greek tradition of the romance. For several of the translations quite detailed, if sometimes mechanical, comparisons with their sources have already been undertaken, and these are referred to in the notes; for others, notably the *War of Troy* and *Apollonios*, such studies are, at the time of writing, being undertaken thoroughly for the first time by the current editors of the texts. A full study of the Greek *Theseid* in relation to its source by Boccaccio must await a complete edition of the text.

The *War of Troy*[4]

The Old French original from which the Greek version was translated was one of the three *romans d'antiquité* written in the mid-twelfth century. Together with *Enéas* and the *Roman de Thèbes*, the *Roman de Troie* by Benoît de Saint-Maure retells an ancient story from Latin sources, investing it with an atmosphere and attitudes belonging more naturally to the feudalism of the period when these romances were written.[5] In the development of French vernacular literature they follow the appearance in writing of the *chansons de geste*, with their probably oral substratum, and narrowly precede the development of the courtly romance in the writings of Chrétien de Troyes of the 1170s. It is worth remarking that in generic terms the *romans d'antiquité* are scarcely romances at all: *roman* in their titles refers to the vernacular in which they were written, rather than to their content.[6] All three might be more precisely termed 'popular history' with a strong admixture of fiction, related to the romance proper in the preponderance of love and war as recurring themes. The possibility that the impetus behind the writing of these Old French romances derived from Byzantine attitudes to antiquity, and the Byzantine revival of the romance in the 1140s, by way of the second crusade is intriguing but cannot definitely be proved.[7]

The 30,316 octosyllabic lines of the French are rendered into 14,369 lines of Greek 'political' or fifteen-syllable verse.[8] The Greek *War of Troy* is therefore as long as all the original and most of the other translated romances put together. Despite its prodigious length, it seems to have been the most read and copied of all the vernacular Greek romances, if the number of surviving manuscripts (seven) can be taken as a reliable guide.[9] Although, given the relative lengths of the French and the Greek lines, the translation is not much shorter than the original, there is a natural tendency for the second half of the Greek fifteen-syllable line to act as a 'filler' or amplification of the first, so that in practice the Greek version represents a considerable reduction of the French. Generally omitted or abbreviated are elements of the exotic, and descriptions of marvellous objects, speeches, and blow-by-blow accounts of battles.[10] A more interesting omission is any mention of the Judgement of Paris, an omission repeated in the independent *Tale of Troy*. In this it seems fairly certain that the translator was influenced by the example of Manasses' widely read chronicle, in which this episode was also suppressed.[11] Corroboration for this significant link between the translation and twelfth-century literature in Greek can be seen in a number of instances where the translator has quoted direct from Manasses' account of the Trojan war instead of, or as well as, translating the sense of the French.[12]

Although problems of dating are no less fraught in the case of the translated romances than in that of their counterparts originally written in Greek, it seems fairly likely that this was the earliest of the five extant translations, perhaps made about 1350.[13]

Phlorios and Platzia-Phlora[14]

As its title betrays, this is a fairly close translation of the well-known late medieval story of *Floire et Blancheflor*, which seems first to have been written in French and subsequently translated into most of the European vernaculars. The Greek version, in 1,843 fifteen-syllable lines, of which two manuscripts survive, was translated from a Tuscan verse rendering, *Il Cantare di Fiorio e Biancifiore*, which dates from the first half of the fourteenth century.[15] The date of the Greek translation cannot be determined with any precision but is generally thought to lie within the second half of the fourteenth century or at the latest the early years of the fifteenth. It has been plausibly suggested that the Italian text found its way to a Greek-speaking land at the hands of the humanist and friend of Boccaccio, Nicola Acciaiuoli, who visited the Frankish-held Peloponnese from 1338 to 1341.[16] How much time would have had to elapse between the arrival of the Italian manuscript in the Peloponnese and the Greek translation we have no means of knowing.

There are few divergences between the Greek and Italian versions in the story they tell. No attempt has been made by the Greek translator to Hellenize the characters or the settings. Fiorio becomes Phlorios (Φλώριος), Biancifiore becomes Platzia-Phlora (Πλάτζια-Φλώρα).[17] The heroine's father is a knight of Rome, the hero a prince of Saracen Spain, and the action takes place largely in Spain, with a shift to Cairo ('Babylon') in the second part, after Platzia-Phlora has been sold to slave traders so as to concentrate the young prince's mind on higher things. Even the curious details with which the story ends – the conversion of the Saracen king and queen and all their subjects to Christianity, and the election of Phlorios' father (or is it himself?) as king of Rome – are faithfully reproduced without regard for the different cultural horizons of the poem's Greek readers. The Christianity to which the Muslims are converted is the 'Catholic faith of the Orthodox Romans'.[18] Although this phrase would in most Greek contexts refer to the orthodox religion of Byzantium, the choice of wording in Greek seems to have been dictated by nothing other than fidelity to the text of the original. It is in any case clear that 'Romans' in this work are citizens of Rome.[19] It seems highly likely therefore that the translator and his first readers or audiences belonged to the Catholic ascendancy of the Peloponnese – a situation which can be paralleled in the case of at least two original writers in Greek in Venetian-held Crete: Marinos Falieros (on whom see pp. 200–4 below), and Markos Antonios Foskolos in the seventeenth century.

Only in the very last line of the translation is there any overt allusion to the new cultural context of the romance in its Greek version:

καὶ ἐβασίλευσε εὐσεβῶς στὴν πρεσβυτέραν Ρώμην.[20]

and he ruled piously in the *elder* Rome [my italics].

Here at last there is an awareness that the language in which the poem has now been cast is that of 'Romans' in a different sense. The Byzantine empire had for centuries presented itself to the world as the 'empire of New Rome'. The significance of this final line is that it acknowledges, as the Italian poem obviously had no need to, the existence of more than one 'Rome'. We cannot tell, however, whether the attitude implied here is disdainful to the Byzantines or, from a Byzantine point of view, conciliatory to the West.[21]

In any case we can be certain that the translator was well versed in the vernacular Greek poetry of his day. Many tricks of style, such as the use of extravagant compound words in description and occasional clear echoes of oral folk-poetry,[22] are characteristic of original poetry in the vernacular. If, as seems likely, the translator was working in the Frankish-held Peloponnese, he may well have known the *Chronicle of the Morea*; and certainly the simplified style that he favours, with an absence of complex sentences and with fewer learned elements than we find in most of the original romances, brings *Phlorios* closer to the style of that poem. There is no sign that the translator knew or at any rate drew on any Greek literature in the learned language, although he does insert into the episode of the hero's leave-taking from his parents a series of moral precepts which derive from the didactic poem known, in its vernacular form, by the title 'Spaneas'.[23]

Imperios and Margarona[24]

This romance adapts its source much more freely than does either of the two previously discussed. Indeed, at 893 lines in Kriaras' edition, it is shorter than all the romances except *Apollonios* and the fragmentary *Old Knight*. *Imperios* is perhaps better regarded as a summary than as a full reworking of its original. Its source, it is now agreed, is the French prose tale *Pierre de Provence et la Belle Maguelonne*. This was another story widely diffused throughout the European vernaculars, but not until the late fifteenth and sixteenth centuries. The Greek adaptation of the source is a good deal freer than those into other languages, and suspicions have been raised on a variety of grounds that it may actually predate the oldest French version which has come down to us.[25] This bears a date of 1453, which makes it likely that the Greek version dates from after the fall of Constantinople and, strictly speaking, falls outside the chronological limits of this book. But the French manuscripts which include this date also carry the implication that the text had been translated from another language, so that the source of the Greek may have been an older redaction in French, or possibly in Catalan.[26] Any idea that the Greek version was the source for the French can fairly obviously be ruled out on the grounds that the characters' names and the principal geographical settings all belong to the West. The suggestion has, however, been put forward that the nucleus of the original story is to be sought in history rather than in the world of fiction, and that this early version of the story may have been brought to Greece by Catalans in the thirteenth century.[27] Tantalizing though these possibilities are, they must be regarded as inherently improbable, given the close generic ties of all the known versions with the romance.[28]

If the kernel of this romance belongs to fiction rather than to history, and its earliest version is, if not French, then certainly Western, none the less there are elements of the story and its setting that seem oddly at home in a Greek context. The story of a royal pair who fall in love after the hero's victory in a tournament, exchange rings, are (or attempt to be) united in secret, are then separated as one of the lovers is unwillingly transported to Egypt, and finally reunited after trials to reign as king and queen, is in essence also the story of *Floire et Blancheflor*, and of another late medieval French romance, *Paris et Vienne*, which provided the basic source for the later Cretan romance, *Erotokritos*, written under the influence of the Italian Renaissance by Vitsentzos Kornaros in the early seventeenth century.

It has been proposed from time to time that all three of these French romances, which include episodes of travel in the exotic eastern Mediterranean, derive from a tradition originating in or transmitted by way of Byzantium.[29] It should be said at once that there is not a shred of evidence that these stories were current in Greek before the romances that we have were translated from their Western versions. However, the same source in the *Thousand and One Nights*, the tale of Qamar-ez-Zaman, has been proposed as the ultimate origin both of the Imperios/Pierre story and for *Floire and Blancheflor*.[30] Such an origin would accord well with the historical geography especially of *Floire*, which is largely set in Muslim Spain, and is only cursorily assimilated to a Christian readership in the unmotivated and unhistorical mass conversion with which it ends. But these elements, as well as evidence for the incorporation of local Provençal legend into *Pierre*,[31] make it much more probable that any such basis of Arab story material entered Christian Europe from the West rather than from the East.

However, the probable origin of the story-material used in these Western romances does bear a special interest for the history of the Greek romance. Why should all three of these atypical Western romances have been translated or adapted into Greek, among so small a number of such adaptations? One reason must have been that the world of the eastern Mediterranean to which the characters are transported in the second half of each of them was familiar – not so much from real life, in which commerce with Egypt was presumably negligible in the fourteenth and fifteenth centuries, but from the Hellenistic and twelfth-century Greek romances. Not just this part of the setting, but the overall plot structure of these romances would have struck a chord with Greek writers at all conversant with romance literature in their own language: boy meets girl, the two are betrothed, separated and reunited after trials that prove the constancy of their love. These are elements common to all the Greek romances from *Chaireas and Kallirrhoe* in the first century AD to the original vernacular romances of the fourteenth century. And here the suggested Arabic origin of these common story elements can help us to account for what otherwise would be a remarkable coincidence. It is well known that the *Thousand and One Nights*, as a kind of encyclopaedia of medieval story-telling, itself drew on a diversity of sources, of which the Hellenistic romance was one.[32] In this way, without implying any far-fetched continuity of a Greek narrative tradition for which no evidence exists, it is possible to trace how a *type* of story came to be transmitted and modified from a Hellenistic origin, first in an Arabic, then, by way of Muslim Spain and Christian Provence, in a French narrative genre, before being finally re-adapted back into Greek by writers who recognized its distant affinity with the revived romance tradition in their own language.

In any case *Imperios and Margarona* enjoyed undoubted popularity. It is preserved in whole or in part in five manuscripts, of which the earliest is the Naples manuscript that also contains the fullest version of the *Tale of Achilles*. But, more important for its continued reception in and beyond the sixteenth century, it was the only one of the Greek romances to be recast in rhymed form and printed in a series of popular editions in Venice, from 1543 onwards.[33]

Apollonios of Tyre[34]

This is the only one of the translated romances which has no chivalric elements. Instead its story goes back by a direct tradition to late antiquity. The single manuscript contains the heading: 'Translation from Latin to [vernacular] Greek'.[35] In fact its immediate source seems to have been a fourteenth-century prose version in Italian. The Greek version, somewhat abbreviated in 850 lines, can be only very approximately dated to the period 1350–1450. Its most interesting feature, in which it is at variance both with the Western tradition of the original Latin text and with the Greek romances in general, is its obtrusively Christian setting. The action is said to have taken place after the ascension of Christ and the mission of the apostles;[36] the reunion of Apollonios and his daughter takes place during celebrations of a feast dedicated not to Zeus but to Christ, at Easter, and appropriately enough the 'resurrection' of the hero's long-lost wife follows in terms which invite comparison between the traditional restoration to life found in the Hellenistic romances and the Resurrection.[37] Needless to say, the sojourn of the hero's wife at Ephesos is located not at the ancient temple of Artemis, as in the Latin original, but at the more obscure nunnery in the same city, of the protomartyr Thekla.[38] The only literary allusion infiltrated into the text is explicitly to the Psalms.[39]

The motive behind this translation may plausibly be linked to that already identified for the other translations and adaptations so far discussed. *Apollonius* in its earliest known form was a Latin romance of the third century AD which drew on the Hellenistic genre, particularly in its theme of far-flung adventures and the separation of lovers. Its structure, with the incestuous relationship of Antiochus and his daughter at the beginning reduplicated by Apollonius' quest and reunion with his own daughter at the end,[40] has affinities with that of the Hellenistic romances, in which an initial experience of love at first sight is reaffirmed and validated only after separation and trials. Whether the third-century Latin text was actually based on an older romance in Greek does not for our purposes greatly matter.[41] Once again there is no need to suppose that the fourteenth- or fifteenth-century Greek translator knew anything more than we do about the ultimate origin of his source. It was enough for him that its themes, structure and geographical setting were familiar from the Greek romances already known to him.

Later, at the close of the fifteenth century, a new translation of this romance, this time into rhyming couplets, was made from the fourteenth-century Italian version of Antonio Pucci, and published, between 1524 and 1526, in Venice. This later version, which enjoyed enormous popular success and was reprinted many times up until 1805, interestingly betrays no knowledge of the earlier, unrhymed translation. A new critical edition of both Greek versions of this romance has been announced.[42]

Boccaccio's *Teseida*

Probably the latest in date of the translated romances, the Greek *Theseid* has been dated to the second half of the fifteenth century or even the early sixteenth.[43] This puts it after the fall of Constantinople, and so makes it the only absolutely certain instance of a medieval romance being translated in Western, by this time almost certainly Venetian, territory. The most likely place for the translation to have been made is Crete; and insofar as its language and style show clear awareness of earlier romances in Greek, the Greek *Theseid* affords useful proof that some at least of the Palaiologan romances were known in Venetian Crete up to at least the late fifteenth century. This text also itself constitutes something of a bridge between these romances and the developing and distinctive literature in Cretan dialect produced under the influence of the Italian Renaissance. Like the later rhymed version of *Imperios*, the *Theseid* was printed in Venice (although only once, so far as is known, in 1529) and as a result must have reached a wider public than could have been possible for any of the earlier romances.

Only the first book has so far appeared in a modern edition.[44] Here, as with the *War of Troy*, we are dealing with a faithful but reduced copy of the original, one which makes fluent and sometimes creative use of the inherited resources of the traditional fifteen-syllable verseform in Greek.[45] Although the regular couplet rhyme, which had been in use in Cretan dialect poetry since the late fourteenth century, is not used, the stanzaic format of the Italian *ottava rima* is retained, with a single pair of end-rhymes in the final two lines. Throughout the text we find minor elements introduced into the Greek version which recall oral folk poetry or the earlier Greek romance (or both). Such is the description of a storm which mirrors the internal turmoil of a character[46] and the use of coined compound words, which we identified earlier as characteristic of the literary language of the Palaiologan romances.[47] The most interesting intrusion comes at the beginning of the story proper, after the versified preface, where a standard way of beginning a Greek romance has replaced the original.[48]

Boccaccio's tale of Theseus, duke of Athens, and the rivalry of the knights Palamone and Arcita for the hand of Emilia, written in 1339-40, is an exemplary story of late medieval (literary) chivalry. As such it became the tale put by Geoffrey Chaucer into the mouth of his 'verray parfit gentil knight' in *The Canterbury Tales*. But by Boccaccio's time the classical revival in Italy was already beginning, and the characters and setting of his romance belong ostensibly to pagan Athens. Duke Theseus owes his name and that of his dukedom to classical mythology, but little else. Of the real protagonists of the story, the male rivals Palamone and Arcita have names that look Greek, although the heroine, Emilia, does not. It has been proposed that Boccaccio knew, or had at least heard of *Digenes Akrites*, and that he derived the name of the more warlike of his rival heroes from 'Akrites'.[49] The incidental similarities between the stories of Akrites and Arcita are not really striking enough to sustain the hypothesis that *Digenes* influenced Boccaccio, and the main theme of the *Theseid*, the rivalry between a knight of Venus and a knight of Mars, corresponds to nothing else in medieval Greek. However, the possibility that the name and something of the warlike reputation of Akrites were known to Boccaccio cannot be discounted. In any case, there is no indication that the Greek translator of the *Theseid* knew of any such specific connection of his original with an earlier Greek text. But the Greek setting, subsumed into an entirely Western world of chivalry, might well have reminded him of precedents such as the *War of Troy*, and would certainly have provided sufficient motivation for his choice of poem to translate.

The Arthurian cycle

All the translated romances so far discussed were in their original, Western form atypical of the genre as it evolved in the West, in that they possessed some resemblance to the ancient and earlier medieval Greek genre; and it was for this reason, I have suggested, that they came to be translated into Greek. But these were not the only Western romances to be transplanted to Greek-speaking lands; evidence that the stories of the Arthurian cycle also circulated there, without having any direct impact on the chosen subject matter of Greek writers and translators of romance, affords added proof that the translations so far discussed were picked neither at random nor in the absence of any wider choice.

As early as the thirteenth century, on two royal occasions, recitations from the 'matter of Brittany and the Round Table' and the adventures 'of Lancelot, Tristan and Palamedes' took place before the Lusignan kings of Cyprus.[50] Nor is this dissemination of Arthurian material confined to Cyprus. The claim of Alain de Lille, in the late twelfth century, that the fame of Arthur of Britain had already spread to the Orient, and specifically to Egypt and Constantinople, as well as to Antioch, Armenia and Palestine though doubtless exaggerated, none the less deserves to be taken seriously.[51] For Greek-speaking lands we have the testimony of an Italian pilgrim who stopped off in 1395, on his return journey from Jerusalem, at Venetian-held Negroponte (the modern Chalkida in Euboea). While there he learnt that the story of Gawain's rescue of the daughter of Morgan le Fay, and subsequent marriage to her, was well known to his hosts, and had even come to be attached to a local landmark. (It may be significant that his informants appear to have belonged to the Venetian colonial garrison rather than to the local population.) The account contains sufficient detail to enable us to identify the source of the story current in Euboea: a fourteenth-century Italian compilation in *ottava rima*.[52]

Further evidence is provided by the discovery of some pages of the French prose *Tristan* reused in the binding of a manuscript of the mid-fifteenth century. The manuscript itself gives an additional clue to the social circles in which Western romances circulated in Greek-speaking lands. It is a collection of Latin–Greek lexika, the property of one Bartolomeus de Columpnis, who records in a mixture of Latin and Greek his departure with the manuscript from Chios in August 1454, the year after the fall of Constantinople to the Ottomans. The owner of the manuscript is almost certainly to be identified with the amateur antiquarian Bartholomaeus de Columnis *de Chio*, who is known to have possessed a manuscript of Quintilian and as the author of an epigram in Greek.[53] It was presumably the ancestors of this bilingual representative of the Genoese ascendancy in Chios who had earlier brought the Tristan romance to that island.

It seems, then, that Arthurian material was quite widespread in the Western possessions in the Aegean, particularly among the colonial rulers. One fragment, containing an episode from an Arthurian romance translated into Greek, survives. This is the 307-line text known conventionally as *The Old Knight* (the manuscript has no title).[54] The story tells of the arrival of an elderly knight at King Arthur's court, together with a beautiful maiden. Without declaring his identity, he challenges the knights of the Round Table to single combat; the girl is to be the prize for the victor. All the knights, and even Arthur himself, are beaten and the old knight proclaims the superiority of the First Table in the bygone days of Arthur's father. The knight then succours a beleaguered widow alone in a castle, before sending a letter to

King Arthur disclosing his name. At this point the Greek fragment breaks off, just before the conclusion of the tale, in which we learn that the old knight is named Branor le Brun.

This somewhat inconsequential tale makes a relatively late appearance in the French Arthurian corpus, in a compilation of the late thirteenth century, as one of two preliminary accretions to the romance *Guiron le Courtois*, also known as *Palamedes*.[55] The Greek translation is quite free, introducing an element of humour and of Homeric allusion quite foreign to either the Western or the Greek genre, and altering some of the details.[56] There is insufficient evidence to decide whether its immediate source was in French or in Italian.[57] As to the date of the translation, this must fall some time between the first appearance of the story in French at the end of the thirteenth century and the date of the single manuscript, *c.* 1425–50.[58] It is tempting to suppose that the date of the manuscript is also, in this case, the date of the translation.

In language and style this fragment seems entirely independent of the other Greek romances, original or translated. Although it uses the unrhymed fifteen-syllable verseform, its language is marked by studied and often awkward archaism, with only a few concessions to the vernacular.[59] Strangely, however, for a text in this relatively 'high' linguistic register, its syntax is elementary, with a point of punctuation at the end of most lines. The absence of enjambment at the line-ends is in contrast to what happens at the mid-line caesura, which is less clearly marked than is common at this period (even in the 'middle'-language register of Meliteniotes, for example) and occasionally violated in a way which is unprecedented in the metre before the twentieth century:

Μή πως αὐτός ἀναδειχθῆ βελτίων τοῦ πρεσβύτου
καὶ τὴν νικῶσαν ἀληθῶς λήψεται. Τῆς τραπέζης
οἱ δαιτυμόνες καὶ στερροὶ τοῖς ὅπλοις κηρυχθέντες,
ὁ δὲ Τριστάνος ἐν αὐτοῖς ἀρτιφαὴς ὑπῆρχεν.[60]

Lest he should be revealed superior to the old [knight]
and truly take the prize. Of the table
the denizens [were] stoutly proclaimed in arms,
and Tristan was a bright newcomer in their midst.

This curious poem, long neglected,[61] has been re-examined by A. Garzya, who credits the translator with greater originality and seriousness of purpose than had been assumed,[62] and we now have a valuable detailed comparison of the Greek and French texts.[63] The latter's conclusion that the text is a political allegory contrasting the vanquished 'old order' of Byzantium (represented by Branor) and the new feudal order (represented by Arthur's court) deserves further consideration. There is no sign either that *The Old*

Knight was influenced by the Greek romance or that it exercised any direct influence upon it. It has been suggested that references to 'Palamedes' as a literary authority in the *Tale of Achilles*, *Imperios* and the *Tale of Troy* prove that this and other Arthurian tales in which Palamedes appears were required reading in Greek at this time, but this proposal has no basis in fact.[64] There is indeed no reason to suppose that any more than the isolated episode of *The Old Knight* was ever translated into Greek: the six leaves of the extant manuscript cover all of the episode except its beginning and end, which would have contained sufficient material for one lost folio at either end, to make up a normal quire of eight.

But the ghost of Palamedes continues to hover. In *The Old Knight* he is the first of King Arthur's henchmen to enter the lists and fights bravely; his defeat rouses the ire of Gawain, who only in this Greek version is his friend, to avenge the slight to his honour.[65] Furthermore the French romance into which the episode of Branor le Brun was interpolated was also originally entitled *Palamedes*, although its real hero is Guiron le Courtois, and the romance seems to have been better known under this name.[66] The literary origins of this pagan 'perfect' knight, supposedly from 'Babylon', are obscure; but he seems first to have entered the Arthurian tradition in the French prose *Tristan*, written *c.* 1225–30, and actually plays no more than a minor role in this romance and in *Palamedes/Guiron*.[67] The fact that this episode was placed first in a compilation which may well have borne the apparently Greek title *Palamedes*, and itself gives relative prominence to that hero, suggests that the same principle may have determined the choice of an original here as for all the other translations into Greek from Western romances.

10

GENEALOGY

No literary text is produced or read in a vacuum, and one of the tasks facing the historian of literature is to disentangle the networks of relationships which combined to establish a framework for the new literary text at the time when it was produced, so as to give it some 'meaning' for its first readers. Such literary interrelations are commonly known in modern theoretically based studies by the term 'intertextuality,'[1] a term which usefully frees them from the mechanical model of 'influence' or 'imitation', according to which only the 'original' elements of a work were deemed worthy of praise or attention, but which in its application often fails to be rigorously historical. This chapter assumes a view of textual relationships which draws broadly on T. S. Eliot's theory of originality and tradition;[2] on the theory of literary development of the Russian formalists as refined by Jauss; and on the concept of intertextuality as it has evolved through the writings of Kristeva, Barthes and others. The consonance between the Byzantines' own view of mimesis, discussed in Chapter 2, and aspects of these modern theories should also be borne in mind.

The term 'genealogy' (after Nietzsche) has recently resurfaced with a variety of nuances in theoretical discussions of historical relationships among literary texts. I use it here in order to emphasize that, contrary to what is regularly implied in traditional studies of literary 'influence', it is not the 'classic' or 'influential' works of the past that initiate the relationship; rather, the potentiality latent in these works has to be activated, selectively, by later writers.[3] The traditional dominance of the concept of 'influence' actually inverts the true relationship, in which the older work, although obviously prior, is none the less inert until acted upon in the present. The metaphor of genealogy, finally, must be understood primarily in the sense of the procedure by which family relationships are retraced and reconstructed, starting out from the present; but at the same time its organic metaphor does not exclude a (metaphorically) 'genetic' reading of literary tradition.[4]

There are three networks of relationships, 'genealogical' in this sense, which can be seen to have played a part in the genesis and development of the fourteenth- and fifteenth-century Greek romances: relationships with the older romances (and to a small extent with other texts) in Greek; relationships with the Western medieval romance; and relationships with oral tradition. The last of these is much the most complicated and cannot be discussed in the same terms as the first two, because we have hardly any oral 'texts' dating from the period before the romances were composed. The question of an 'oral background' to the romances, and to other vernacular Greek literature of the period, must be postponed until the next chapter, where it will be put into the context of a wider discussion of the common or traditional elements which link the vernacular texts with one another. The subject of this chapter will be purely literary interrelations and will of course be confined to relations with older texts. The relations between the romances and contemporary or subsequent literature, that is, their reception, will be the subject of the final chapter.

It goes without saying that the genealogy of the translated romances presents far fewer problems than does that of the original group. Indeed the discussion in the previous chapter of the treatment and selection of their Western originals has already dealt with this question. So the discussion in the present chapter will focus predominantly on the original romances.

THE TWELFTH-CENTURY AND HELLENISTIC ROMANCES

It is generally agreed that the original romances as a group reveal an awareness, in varying degrees, of the older examples of the genre in the learned language. Andronikos Palaiologos, the author of *Kallimachos and Chrysorrhoe*, undoubtedly knew *Drosilla and Charikles* and *Hysmine and Hysminias*, as well as Heliodoros' *Aithiopika* and, more surprisingly, Chariton's *Chaireas and Kallirrhoe*;[5] the relatively close relation between *Libistros and Rhodamne* and *Hysmine and Hysminias* is again not in doubt, and aspects of it have been examined in detail.[6] Although contrary views have been expressed,[7] H. and R. Kahane have persuasively argued that *Belthandros and Chrysantza* too is a work of some erudition.[8] The *Tale of Achilles* draws extensively on *Digenes Akrites* and to a smaller degree on Eugenianos' and/or Makrembolites' romances.[9] As for the *Tale of Troy*, no one has yet accused its author of erudition, but as well as drawing heavily on the other romances of its time this poem made fundamental use of Manasses' twelfth-century Chronicle and even contains a few, rather muddled, echoes of the *Iliad*.

There can be little doubt, then, that the authors of the original romances were well read in the secular literature of the twelfth century.[10] What use did they make of these precedents? To answer this question, we shall look first at debts to their twelfth-century precursors that are more or less common to the original romances, before turning to examine the particular use that each one made of the older literature available.

The continued cultivation of the rhetorical exercise of *ekphrasis*, or set-piece description, is the most commonly mentioned link between the vernacular romances and those of the twelfth century.[11] The most frequently described items in the later romances are: the heroine, the exterior of a castle, an interior with painted rooms and statues, and a bathhouse. The scope of the *ekphrasis* is more restricted than in the earlier romances, but in length and rhetorical elaboration the *ekphraseis* of the vernacular romances are frequently spectacular. In line with the mainstream Byzantine theory of rhetoric is their technique of representation, which is not really visual at all but, rather, by the richness and contrivance of the language offers a metaphor for the richness and contrivance of the object to which it corresponds. It is certainly not accidental that almost all these *ekphraseis* are devoted to works of art or architecture; those which are not, namely the *ekphraseis* of the heroines, frequently describe a human form *as if* it were a work of art.

In the *Tale of Achilles* the long *ekphrasis* of the unnamed girl gives her the attributes of a statue and a painting;[12] Chrysorrhoe is likened to a statue of Aphrodite and a few lines later is said to be a likeness of that goddess, in a direct verbal allusion to *Hysmine and Hysminias*;[13] Chrysantza is praised by her future lover as having been 'made' by nature in the garden of the graces.[14] And in the description of manmade objects great prominence is given, as in the twelfth-century romances in particular, but also in the Hellenistic romances, to the artifice with which these have been constructed. The *Tale of Achilles*, exceptionally, borrows religious imagery in a way that might well have seemed risqué to a Byzantine listener, to describe the statues of the heroine's garden as 'non-manmade statues of the Lord'.[15] Elsewhere the ingenuity of the craftsman is praised in terms which, as in the twelfth-century romances, reflect back quite deliberately on the technique of the author of the romance himself. The *locus amoenus* in which the innocent Libistros is surprised, in his dream, by armed Cupids is described as 'made by an artist's hands';[16] the allegorical statues of the twelve months ranged along one wall of Rhodamne's castle are the work of an 'extraordinary stone-and-jewel-carver.[17] The *ekphrasis* of the bathhouse in the Ogre's Castle in *Kallimachos* begins as a narrative of what the craftsman (τεχνίτης) did to make it.[18] Inside the Castle of Eros in *Belthandros* are a series of artfully created automata.[19] Indeed in the grounds of this castle is a remarkable garden in which nature is quite explicitly made to resemble art:

> Ἄνωθεν βλέμμαν ἔρριψεν ὡς πρὸς τὰ δένδρη τάχα
> καὶ δένδρων εἶδε καλλονὴν καὶ ἰσότηταν εὐμόρφην
> καὶ τὴν κορμοανάβασιν εὐκολωτάτην πάνυ,
> ὅτι νὰ εἶπες ἐκ παντὸς ὅτι ρουκανοτέκτων
> ἐρρουκανοετούρνευσεν, σταθμίσας ἔπηξέν τα.[20]

148

He raised his eyes in the direction of the trees
and saw the beauty of the trees and their shapely evenness
and the ascent of their trunks unimpeded altogether
such that you'd say a lathe-turner had turned
them on his lathe, and fixed and put them there.

The use of the *ekphrasis*, and the insistence in these descriptions on the superiority of artifice and rhetoric over nature, are only the most obvious of the rhetorical devices of the earlier romances that are taken over and continued by the vernacular writers. Despite the change of linguistic register, many of the rhetorical figures elaborated by twelfth-century writers of romance remain in use: anaphora, for instance, with a series of parallel phrases, usually expostulations, introduced by a repeated opening word or phrase. The most extravagant of these is to be found in *Libistros*, where no fewer than thirty-two parallel phrases are introduced by πῶς; (how?).[21] But the most effective occurs at the moment where Kallimachos, after surveying the painted roof inside the Ogre's Castle, has his first sight of Chrysorrhoe, suspended like part of the strange decor by the hair. The narrator himself affects horror at what he has to tell us:

'Εν μέσῳ γάρ, ἀλλὰ πολὺν ὁ λόγος πόνον ἔχει,
ἐκ τῶν τριχῶν ἐκρέματο κόρη μεμονωμένη
– σαλεύει μου τὴν αἴσθησιν, σαλεύει μου τὰς φρένας –
ἐκ τῶν τριχῶν – αἳ φρόνημαν παράλογον τῆς τύχης –
ἐκ τῶν τριχῶν ἐκρέματο κόρη – σιγῶ τῷ λόγῳ,
ἰδοὺ σιγῶ μετὰ νεκρᾶς καρδίας τοῦτο γράφω –
ἐκ τῶν τριχῶν ἐκρέματο κόρη μὲ τῶν χαρίτων.[22]

For in the middle, but telling it brings much pain,
by the hair there hung a maiden all alone
– it shakes my senses, it shakes my reason –
by the hair – alas the unreasoning will of fate –
by the hair there hung a maiden – I cannot speak,
behold I lower my voice, with leaden heart I write this –
by the hair there hung a maiden full of graces.

Alliterative wordplay occurs in all these romances, although I have not attempted to quantify it. An example picked at random comes from the *Tale of Achilles*: the king (Achilles' father), receives a letter from his son:

τὴν γοῦν γραφὴν ὁ βασιλεὺς ὡς ἔλαβεν εἰς χεῖρας
χαρὲς ἐχάρην τὴν ψυχήν, χάριτος ἐπληρώθη.[23]

the letter as the king took in his hands
he joyfully rejoiced, he was filled with joy.

One of the most sophisticated examples of this kind of wordplay is to be found in *Libistros*, where the narrator, Klitobos, arrives at an inn in Egypt on his quest to find his friend's lost wife, Rhodamne, and asks for a bed for the night. The innkeeper will shortly turn out, of course, to be none other than Rhodamne herself. The wordplay turns on the fact that ξενοδόχος (inn-keeper) means literally a 'receiver of strangers'; and she parries his request with a play on words that hints that she no less than he is a stranger here, and nothing is quite what it seems:

> ἐμπαίνω ἀπέσω θαρρικά· «Μὴ ξενοδόχος;» λέγω,
> «μὴ ξενοδόχος ἄνθρωπος, μή, μὴ μονὴ νὰ μείνω;»
> Ἀκούει με ἡ παράξενος, ἐβγαίνει καὶ θεωρεῖ με·
> «Λάλει τὴν ξενοδόχισσαν, μή, ξένε, ξενοδόχον·
> οὐκ ἔχει ἡ ξενοδόχισσα πούποτε ξενοδόχον,
> ξένη ἔνι καὶ ἡ ξενοδόχισσα, ξένε μου, ἀπὸ τὸν τόπον
> καὶ ἀπὸ τὴν χώραν τὴν θεωρεῖς καὶ ἐκ τὸ ξενοδοχεῖον.»[24]

> I enter [the inn] boldly; 'Is there an innkeeper?' I say,
> 'is there any keeper of the inn, or any room to room in?'
> The marvellous [girl] hears me, comes out and looks at me;
> 'Call her a woman-innkeeper, not, stranger, an innkeeper;
> for the woman-innkeeper has no innkeeper to keep her inn,
> for the woman-innkeeper is a stranger too, stranger, in this place
> and in this land where you see her and in this inn.'

We have already noted some of the thematic links between these and the twelfth-century romances, as well as the main differences. Other links that should be briefly mentioned are the frequent invocations to the uncertainty and malevolence of fate;[25] the fake death of the hero or heroine, the recovery from which is sometimes called a 'resurrection',[26] and the movement from an early experience of love at first sight to its maturing and testing through a series of adventures and wanderings.

If we turn now to the later original romances individually, we find each writer discovering and developing particular possibilities latent or explicitly present in the older literature in the genre. In the case of the *Tale of Achilles*, as we have already seen, the principal precursor is *Digenes Akrites*, and there are probably intentional allusions to that poem in the proem in praise of love; in the warlike and sometimes rather boorish behaviour of the hero; in the paucity of proper names; in the manner of the hero's abduction of the heroine; and in the death of one of the protagonists at the end.[27] The fact that Achilles has a painting of Eros made for him before which he then prostrates himself, in his efforts to woo his bride, indicates a knowledge of *Hysmine and Hysminias* (where the painted figure of Eros the King first appears in the

Greek romance) or, depending on when *Achilles* was written, conceivably also on *Libistros and Rhodamne*.[28]

In the case of *Kallimachos* the links are much more clearly with the learned romance than with the heroic world of Digenes. The author has here declared his admiration for Chariton's romance by splitting the name of the latter's heroine, Kallirrhoe, into two and attaching the first part to his hero, the second to his heroine. The fact that the hero's name, Kallimachos, is also that of a Hellenistic poet may well also have suited his purpose in declaring the literary affiliations of his poem. The heroine's name further makes allusion to Prodromos' romance, in which Chrysochroe had been the name of the heroine in the tragic subplot. The only other proper names in this romance point clearly in the same direction. The hero's brothers, who are each named only once are called Nikokles and Xanthippos.[29] A further significant allusion to Chariton's romance occurs in the trial scene, in which the heroine bravely proves that she belongs rightfully to her husband before a foreign king who has seized her against her will. By just such a forensic display, in very similar circumstances, did Chariton's Kallirrhoe plead for her husband before the king of Babylon. It may even be suggested that it was Andronikos Palaiologos' initiative in looking back to what we now know to have been the oldest of the extant ancient romances, instead of to the more rhetorically elaborate romances of Achilles Tatios and Heliodoros, as his twelfth-century predecessors had done, that had a decisive effect in establishing the distinctive form of the later vernacular romances. *Chaireas and Kallirrhoe*, unlike any of the other ancient romances, mixes warlike adventure and 'sufferings in love' (πάθος ἐρωτικόν) about equally; and Chaireas, like the later medieval heroes, had to prove himself a warrior before he could be happily reunited with his bride.

It is tempting to see a literary origin also for the extraordinarily vivid image of the hero's first sight of the heroine, suspended by her hair and tormented by the ogre. The verb κρέμομαι (be suspended) used here, and its derivatives, are common in the romances of the twelfth century and again of the fourteenth century in the sense of 'to hang upon, to be in a state of erotic suspense or desire',[30] a usage which goes back to Achilles Tatios.[31] Niketas Eugenianos, in *Drosilla and Charikles*, is certainly aware of this sense of the verb, as the innkeeper's son, in his attempts to seduce the heroine, accuses her of 'tyrannizing one whom you hold in suspense'.[32] There is probably an intentional element of wordplay when the same author on two occasions describes a hero first setting eyes on a girl and falling in love with her, when she is leaning out of the window.[33] It may be further significant that in the first of these cases the girl's name is Kalligone, one of several names of this type in the older romances which may have determined the choice of the name Kallimachos for a romance hero. It seems quite likely that Andronikos Palaiologos developed his striking image for a heroine's plight from the coincidence of two

quite conventional elements of the older romance: the meaning of the verb
κρέμομαι in an erotic sense, and the use by Eugenianos of the same verb to
describe a girl leaning out of a window in an erotic context.

A similar creation of a powerful visual image out of a purely rhetorical
precedent can be seen in the Ogre's Castle itself, which in *Kallimachos*
occupies the place in the structural scheme of the romance elsewhere taken
up by a castle, or palace, of Eros. Although the ogre is very different from
the allegorical figure of Eros the King in *Libistros* and in *Belthandros*, and his
actual function is the inverse of that of Eros, his castle is decorated with
pictures of Eros, and it is here that the hero and heroine are initiated into
love. One reason for this bold transformation can be traced back, again, to
Eugenianos' romance. In one of the love-songs with which Book II of that
romance is liberally strewn, Eros is called an 'ogreish spawn' which like a
serpent gnaws away at the entrails of the lover.[34] Reference to the precedent
of Eugenianos suggests that the folklore of dragons with which Andronikos
filled out his image of the Ogre's Castle is actually subservient to a symbolic
purpose.[35] According to this reading, the ogre represents the obsessive, all-
consuming, even sadistic element of sexuality (Eros), and his cruel treatment
in suspending the heroine by the hair an imaginative visual metaphor for
κρεμασμός, the suspense or anxiety of desire.

Finally the erotic foreplay of Kallimachos and Chrysorrhoe in the bath is
surely inspired by the very similar proceedings described in *Hysmine and
Hysminias*.[36] It is entirely characteristic of this author's use of elements
picked up from his predecessors that what could, under the conventions
governing the genre in the twelfth century, take place only in a dream is
transposed to actuality in *Kallimachos*.

Belthandros and Chrysantza has drawn on Makrembolites' romance for the
dominant role given to Eros the King in the first part of the narrative.[37] Other
specific correspondences point towards *Drosilla and Charikles* as its most
influential precursor. The gryphon in the garden of the Castle of Eros, from
whose mouth a stream gushes forth to be collected in a basin that never
overflows,[38] has been likened to a similar figure in Hysmine's garden, but this
in turn derives from Eugenianos.[38] Also from Eugenianos comes the description of Xerxes' plane-tree with golden singing birds,[39] and quite possibly the
hero's initiation into love alongside a river.[40] The river itself, with its
paradoxical mingling of the elements of fire and water symbolically representing the paradoxical nature of Eros, is once again an elaboration in visual terms
of a rhetorical figure drawn from the twelfth-century romances, in this case a
refrain which is repeated in both Prodromos' and Eugenianos' romances:

Ὦ πῦρ δροσίζον, ὦ φλογίζουσα δρόσος.[41]

O cooling fire, o fiery coolness.

152

A rare allusion in *Belthandros* to the story of Leander (his statue is in the collection of the Castle of Eros) may also have been suggested by Eugenianos, who puts a résumé of the Ovidian story into the mouth of Drosilla's peasant wooer Kallidemos,[42] although there is also an implicit allusion to this story in Prodromos' romance, where the lovers' home town is named as Abydos.

When we come to *Libistros* the overall resemblances to Makrembolites' romance are easily recognized. A hero, initially scornful of love, is arraigned in a succession of dreams before Eros the King, to whom he dutifully swears allegiance in future; the allegorical paintings with captions, representing Eros and his court, the virtues and the twelve months of the year are duly reproduced in *Libistros*;[43] but the most important link with the older romance is in the use in *Libistros* of first-person narrative. The name of the narrator, Klitobos or Klitobon (Κλιτοβός/Κλιτοβών), alludes clearly enough to the first-person narrator of Achilles Tatios, on which Makrembolites had also drawn in his romance; and the interchange of narrative levels between the heroes of two interlocking love-stories, discussed in Chapter 8, is an elaboration of the device first explored by Prodromos and Eugenianos, whereby we learn the earlier part of the hero's adventures when he swops stories with a confidant in a similar plight. The conclusion of Klitobos' narrative and of the whole romance also reveals some dependence on the ending of *Hysmine and Hysminias*, although the narrative situation is quite different: Klitobos has told the whole story in order to gain his long-deferred object of reunion with his beloved Myrtane. Although there is no real equivalent here to the subtlety of the 'open' ending of Makrembolites' romance, Klitobos ends with a comparable plea to that of Hysminias, namely that someone someday should write the full story of *his* sufferings in love as he has now told that of his friend Libistros.[44] Since such a 'romance of Klitobos' is not in fact what the real author has given us, there is a certain pathos and indeed 'openness' in this ending where the narrator's plea has been only partially fulfilled by the author.

Another twelfth-century text known to the author of *Libistros* was *Digenes Akrites*. After the abduction of Rhodamne, and after Libistros has told the whole story up to this point to Klitobos, the latter has a dream which helps the two of them to work out the heroine's whereabouts. In this dream a high-flying eagle, as black as a crow and prodigious in size, swept up a red partridge in his talons and bore it aloft.[45] Just such a dream, with the same imagery of a bird of prey and a partridge, revealed the proposed departure of Digenes' mother with her husband back to his native Syria and in just the same way the dream proved the means to the frustration of the plan.[46]

These are not the only allusions of the fourteenth-century original romances to their predecessors in the twelfth century, but they should suffice to confirm the impression that, despite the decisive shift from the learned register to the vernacular, the writers of romance at this time made conscious and innovative use of the models available to them in their own language. Two general conclusions can be offered here, although more detailed work will be required to substantiate them fully. First of all, only the *Tale of Achilles* makes systematic use of the vernacular proto-romance *Digenes Akrites*; only *Libistros* makes comparable use of Makrembolites' romance, although both these texts appear to be known to all the fourteenth-century writers of romances. Eugenianos' *Drosilla and Charikles* may well turn out to have been more generally influential in the fourteenth century than has been recognized, and this would not be surprising in view of its tendency towards lyricism and down-to-earth explicitness in its treatment of its theme. By contrast, there are no certain allusions to Prodromos' more intellectualized romance. Too little remains for comparison of Manasses' fragmentary *Aristandros and Kallithea*, but we know from the excerpts that have come down to us that it circulated in Constantinople in the fourteenth century. It is quite likely that the image of the wheel of fortune which we find from time to time in the fourteenth-century romances derives from there (although of course it was a commonplace of Western literature by this time), and that some of the exotic elements of the vernacular romances may also have had their forerunners in that romance.

EAST MEETS WEST

The six romances that were translated into Greek from Western European language during the fourteenth and fifteenth centuries provide ample proof that Western literature of entertainment was neither unknown nor without interest to Greek writers. It seems probable that most if not all of the translations were made in Western-held lands, while the original romances, with the likely exception (on the grounds of date) of the *Tale of Troy*, were written within the Byzantine empire. This in turn almost certainly means in Constantinople. But the stylistic similarities shared by almost *all* Greek vernacular writing of the period, which will be the subject of the next chapter, show that these two groups cannot have existed in isolation from each other. One would therefore expect that Constantinopolitan writers would be aware of developments in the Western romance of the twelfth and thirteenth centuries.

The term 'influence' that is most often used in discussions of this subject in fact suggests a more passive dependence of the Greek writers of the romance on their Western peers than can really be sustained.[47] There are two ways that the interrelations between the Greek original romances and Western literature can be examined. The first, which seems in fact to be the less productive, is also the one that has received the most attention: this is the teasing-out of verbal references to Western customs, or to 'Latins', and the identification of foreign loan-words in the texts. The other, which has been pioneered by Carolina Cupane, looks at literary topoi and shows how Greek models have been subtly adapted to come closer to their Western counterparts.

Allusions to 'Latins'

Direct allusions to 'Latins' and their customs in the five original romances are severely limited both in number and in scope. Some items of specialist vocabulary, such as ϱέντα (lists; a kind of tournament), λίζιος (liege-man), καβαλάϱης (horseman; not, in these romances, a knight), undoubtedly derive from Western feudal usage. But the tournament had been introduced to Byzantium by Manuel I in the mid-twelfth century and formally entered literature with Niketas Choniates' detailed description in the early thirteenth century of a competition which had taken place in 1159.[48] The term λίζιος too, though in a slightly different sense, referring to vassal states, also occurs in Choniates' history,[49] and in fiction Hysminias had already been made a quasi-feudal vassal of Eros the King in Makrembolites' romance.[50] Falconry, which is mentioned in *Belthandros*, has been taken to be a Western institution, but was in fact an approved sport of Byzantine emperors at least as far back as the mid-eleventh century.[51]

Other overt references to 'Latins' or 'Franks' and their ways are slightly more revealing. To have one's hair 'in the Frankish style' is a term of praise in the *Tale of Achilles* and in *Libistros*,[52] and the same is true of a Frankish or 'Latin' style of dressing.[53] Libistros himself is even described as 'of Latin race'.[54] Although there are no Latins in *Belthandros*, the reference to the real places of Tarsos and Antioch, in a vaguely defined historical setting in which the Anatolian interior is populated by Turks, implies a reference to the crusader outposts in those towns. The most that can be deduced from these passing references is that Latins and their ways were to some degree fashionable.[55] It would not be too fanciful to suppose further that in such allusions the writers of these three romances, at least, were acknowledging their own respect for their Western peers in the romance genre.

That such a respect existed, although veiled in the texts in a characteristically Byzantine way, is more clearly demonstrated by an examination of two topoi that are extensively developed in the vernacular Greek romances.

Eros the King

Carolina Cupane has traced the development of the dramatic personification of love from Makrembolites' romance, through *Belthandros and Chrysantza* to *Libistros and Rhodamne*.[56] This line of dependence is demonstrated in detail and is absolutely persuasive. Her main thesis, however, is that with *Hysmine and Hysminias* we find a radical break with the Hellenistic and earlier twelfth-century iconography of the god of love; she argues that the 'prodigious youth, his entire body naked', armed with bow and torch, his legs ending, incongruously, mermaid-like, in wings, and seated on a throne amid the vassals of the earth, is none other than the Dieu d'Amor of twelfth-century French literature, and in particular of the *Roman de la Rose*.[57] The new iconography of Eros in the fourteenth-century romances as 'king of kings', a forbidding youth rather than the chubby cherub of the Hellenistic romances, surely does owe something to the French tradition. But it is entirely characteristic of the way in which Western precedents are taken over by the Greek writers of romance, that this representation of Eros the King (Ἔρως Βασιλεύς) does not represent such a sudden and radical break with earlier Greek tradition as Cupane proposes.

First, as Cupane herself acknowledges, the tyrannical power of Eros, the boy-god of love, over gods, men and the animal world is well established in Hellenistic and earlier Greek literature.[58] Much of the 'new' character of Eros as despotic ruler in Makrembolites' romance is already present in *Drosilla and Charikles*, where it is clear that Eugenianos is simply exploiting and making explicit elements of the traditional Greek mythology of Eros. In that romance Eros is given the unprecedented title 'lord of all'; described as 'absolute tyrant over mortals', he is waited on by the Graces; he is even hailed in a similar role in the adaptation of the religious formula 'glory be to Eros the tyrant'.[59] The same phrase recurs in Manasses' fragmentary *Aristandros and Kallithea*: 'there is nothing which Eros the tyrant will not dare', in a passage which also refers to a lover's vassalage in terms that anticipate the 'feudal' submission of Hysminias in Makrembolites' romance: 'and having become a slave by the hands of Eros'.[60] It is a smaller step than Cupane would have us believe from these rhetorical elaborations of the traditional attributes of Eros to the more fully visualized and developed iconography of Makrembolites and the fourteenth-century romances.

Makrembolites' representation of Eros may indeed, as Cupane has argued, draw on the twelfth-century French tradition, but it is worth pointing out that Eros the King in the Greek romances is always given the trappings and the power of *secular*, not divine, authority. And in the vernacular romances which take up Makrembolites' pictorial representation, he is never called a god, but always given the Byzantine title of King/Emperor (Βασιλεύς). In Makrembolites' romance and in *Belthandros* and *Libistros*, the two later romances in which Eros appears in person, the king of love is depicted with all the appurtenances of Byzantine imperial might. Eros as king/emperor, as opposed to a *god* of love, is a distinctively Greek invention; and moreover this Eros never entirely loses the wings, bow and torch that proclaim his descent from the Hellenistic boy Cupid, although the wings in particular, visually realized according to Makrembolites' description, actually risk being more absurd than impressive.

By the time we come to *Libistros*, Cupane has suggested that the 'Western' representation has come to take precedence, relegating the traditional boy archer to a subsidiary role.[61] The truth is more complex. Libistros meets Eros the King face to face once in each of three dreams. In the first the hero is arraigned before the throne of a remarkable, and again visually unimaginable, figure:

Ἔρως τριμορφοπρόσωπος κάθεται εἰς τὸν θρόνον,
τὸ πρῶτον του τὸ πρόσωπον ὥσπερ μικροῦ παιδίου,
ἁπαλοσάρκου, φοβεροῦ, καὶ εἶχεν ξανθὴν τὴν πλάσιν,
τοῦ νὰ τὸν εἶδες, ἐκ παντὸς χέρια καλοῦ ζωγράφου
τεχνίτου τὸν ἐστόρησαν, ψέγος οὐδὲν βαστάζει·
τὸ δεύτερον ἐφαίνετον ὡς μέσης ἡλικίας,
νὰ ἔχῃ τὸ γένιν στρογγυλόν, τὴν ὄψιν ὡς τὸ χιόνι·
καὶ τὸ ἀπὸ ἐκείνου πρόσωπον γέροντος εἶδες ὄψιν,
σύνθεσιν, σχῆμα καὶ κοπὴν καὶ πλάσιν ἀναλόγως·
καὶ τὸ μὲν πρῶτον πρόσωπον εἶχεν ἐξ ὁλοκλήρου
τὰ χέρια, τὰ ποδάρια καὶ τὸ ἄλλον του τὸ σῶμα,
τὸ δὲ ἀπὸ ἐκείνου πρόσωπον μόνον ἀπὸ τοὺς ὤμους.[62]

Eros triple-form-faced sits upon the throne,
his first face like that of a small child,
tender-fleshed, terrible, and blonde of aspect,
to see it, [it was] quite [as though] the hands of a fine painter
[and] craftsman had painted it, it bears no blemish;
the second appeared as though in middle age,
with rounded beard, the complexion like snow;
next you could see an old man's face,
in composition, form and profile, aspect, all in proportion;
and while the first face had in its entirety
the hands, the legs and the rest of the body,
the other face [was] only from the shoulders [upwards].

Cupane has suggested a number of possible, but fairly distant, parallels for this 'triple-form-faced' king of love.[63] His literary pedigree becomes apparent when this description is set alongside the second appearance of Eros the King. In the second of his dreams Libistros finds himself in a beautiful meadow, where he is met by the king of love, who holds in one hand the traditional bow of the Hellenistic Eros, but in the other, Rhodamne.[64] The description of Eros here at first sight contradicts that of the 'three-form-faced' king, and for this reason Cupane concludes that here the hero meets 'not the God [sic] of Love in all his regal splendour, but only one of his three manifestations'.[65] The text is quite explicit, however, that this is indeed 'Eros the King', and again makes reference to the three 'ages' combined in the single figure.[66] Despite their apparent disparities, the two descriptions are carefully consistent. Examination of the relevant passage reveals that the middle-aged and the old face are in some way superimposed; and this must be the significance of the curious adjective 'triple-form-faced' – not 'with three faces', but 'with three facial forms'. The full figure is entirely that of an infant, but on its shoulders it bears two distinct faces, one of which combines two further aspects, that of the mature and that of the old man. It is in this sense that 'triple-form-faced' Eros can also be described in the first description and throughout the second, as having *two* faces.[68]

Shortly before he meets Rhodamne in reality, on his arrival outside the Castle of Silver, Libistros has yet a third dream, in which Eros awakens him from sleep to encourage him in his endeavours.[69] Eros is not on this occasion described, but this third dream provides the opportunity for the narratee of this part of the story, Klitobos, to remind us of his presence and so punctuate the long second-degree narration by Libistros that makes up the whole first part of the romance. Klitobos admits to being as mystified as the reader must surely be about the 'three faces of Eros', and asks for elucidation.[70] The style of the question, and still more of Libistros' answer, is reminiscent of theological discussions of the nature of the Trinity. The text of this explication, as transmitted, is largely unintelligible, and it is of course possible that some such effect was intended.[71] But it does emerge clearly that all three faces are part of the essential nature of the king of love, and correspond to different aspects of his symbolic role.[72]

The genealogy of this composite figure of Eros can now be worked out. Two of his faces derive from the traditional description of the boy or infant Eros 'with the face of an old man' as depicted in *Daphnis and Chloe*; the third, that of the grown youth 'in the prime of life', is the grown youth (μειράκιον) of Makrembolites' romance. What the author of *Libistros* has done is to superimpose this facet of the iconography of Eros, that was new in the twelfth century, upon the already paradoxical figure envisaged by Hellenistic writers of romance. At the same time he has conflated the 'grown youth' of Makrembolites' romance (who may or may not derive from the Western Dieu d'Amor) with the Western tradition of the God of Love, which was certainly known to the author of *Libistros*. Eros the King, in this romance, is not merely a three-in-one figure with parodic overtones of the Trinity. He combines the dual aspect of himself already traditional in Greek with a third, that of the grown youth, which by the time of *Libistros* has considerable currency in the West. In the process, the nameless author has ingeniously incorporated into the iconography of Eros the lesson on time learnt by Hysminias. In this romance, Eros himself encapsulates the three 'ages of man': infancy, maturity, and old age. It is little wonder that Klitobos, in the story, is so bewildered!

The castle

It is once again Carolina Cupane who has recognized the importance of this innovative element of description in the later romances and demonstrated how, in *Kallimachos*, *Belthandros* and *Libistros*, and in the allegorical poems derived from the romance (*To Chastity* by Meliteniotes, and the anonymous *Consolation concerning Ill Fortune and Good Fortune*), an element of purely Western derivation is deliberately integrated into the Byzantine genre.[73]

Cupane identifies the first appearance of the walled castle in medieval Greek in the description of the palace built by Digenes for his wife and retainers on the banks of the Euphrates.[74] Here the details in G of the walled garden and in E of a castle with walls and battlements are mere adjuncts to a series of descriptions derived from the Hellenistic romance.[75] What is described is essentially a palace and a garden, as in the older romances; the fortifications could be seen as simply a realistic addition, given the belligerent environment in which Digenes lives.[76] By contrast, the Ogre's Castle in *Kallimachos*, and the adventure-seeking hero who dares to explore it, are both fundamental structural elements of that romance, and in clear relation to the knights errant and strange castles of Chrétien's romances and the Arthurian tradition.[77] Then in *Belthandros* and in *Libistros* the mysterious castle as the focal point of a hero's adventures is linked with the allegorical presentation of Eros the King, derived from Makrembolites, to produce the Castle of Eros, in which the hero is arraigned before the king, and his future service to love is foretold to him.[78]

The essential element of Cupane's argument, that the central motif of these romances is a mysterious castle borrowed wholesale from the Western romance but fully and creatively homogenized with the earlier Greek tradition, is of great importance for our understanding of the way in which these original romances relate to Western narrative literature. The significance of the castle, however, may be even greater than Cupane allows us to suppose.

First of all, the castle appears in a very similar role in all five of the original romances. As well as in the examples discussed by Cupane, it is in a similarly fortified and similarly described castle that Achilles and Paris respectively have their first experiences of love.[79] In *Belthandros* and in *Libistros* the castle is specifically the domain of Eros the King; in the castles in *Kallimachos* and in the *Tale of Achilles*, Eros is prominently featured in a painting there;[80] in the *Tale of Troy* Helen's castle is besieged by all the eligible princes of the world, who fight tournaments to determine who is to win the owner as his bride.[81] The link between the castle and the central theme of love is securely established in all five romances, and is taken a degree further in Meliteniotes' parody, in which Chastity is the name of the lady surrounded by extravagant machicolations and other obstacles.[82] That this link is not fortuitous can best be seen by an examination of the Castle of Silver in *Libistros*, in which Rhodamne lives.

The ruler of this castle and father of the girl is named Chrysos (Golden); the castle is called Argyrokastron (Castle of Silver), which although a real name has an obviously symbolic rather than geographical significance.[83] The construction of this castle is no more realistic than its name: it is triangular, with twelve towers on each wall, the towers in turn surmounted by statues of allegorical figures; moreover the building appears 'seamless', you could not tell where one 'stone is joined to another.[84] One reason for the improbable architectural form of the castle may have been the author's desire to describe the same three groups of allegorical figures as Makrembolites had done in *Hysmine and Hysminias*, namely the virtues, the months of the year and the flunkeys in the service of Eros ('Ερωτιδόπουλα). But surely it has more to do with the triple nature of Eros the King as described earlier in the romance, symbolically equating the 'real' castle in which Rhodamne lives with the composite symbolic figure of Eros in Libistros' dream. The link is in fact made explicit, as the hero's account of the castle to Klitobos begins with a reminder of the point at which he had left off narrating the previous evening: with his explanation to Klitobos of the 'three faces of Eros'.[85]

Libistros and his hundred retainers arrive outside the Castle of Silver after a two-year quest. They pitch camp and the hero proposes to spy out the land, identify the chamber (κουβούκλιν) where the girl lives, and find a means to parley with those inside.[86] A confidant advises him how to gain access to the girl:

> γράψε εἰς σαγίτταν γράμματα· ὅταν ἴδῃς ἀπέχει
> ἀπό τὸ πανεξαίρετον τῆς κόρης τὸ κουβούκλι
> ὅτι προκύπτει ἡ ἐρωτικὴ κἂν μία τὸ νὰ μᾶς βλέψῃ,
> ποῖσε ἀφορμὴν ὅτι θεωρεῖς πουλὶν εἰς τὸ κουβούκλιν,
> καὶ τόξευσέ το ἀχαμνὰ καὶ πρόσεξε νὰ πέσῃ
> ἀπέσω εἰς τὸ κουβούκλιν της τῆς κόρης ἡ σαγίττα,
> καὶ τέως νὰ δώσῃς ἀφορμὴν καὶ ἀρχήν εἰς τὴν ἀγάπην,
> καὶ νὰ ἴδῃς τὸ ἐπιχείρημα τὸ πῶς νὰ τὸ ἐμπέσῃς.[87]

> Write letters on an arrow; when you see without
> the ravishing chamber of the girl
> the loved one leaning out, if she should glance but once in our
>   direction,
> pretend to see a bird upon the chamber,
> and shoot low down and make sure that [the arrow] falls
> inside the maiden's chamber,
> and so you will take the initiative and make a start in love,
> and see how to get deeper into the enterprise.[88]

Libistros complies and the next eight hundred lines are taken up with an exchange of letters conducted, on the hero's side, by firing arrows into the girl's bedchamber. It is of course in precisely this way that Eros is said to make his mischief and create desire by firing his arrows into his victims' hearts; the castle, symbolically, is nothing but a physical extension of Rhodamne herself. This identification is confirmed a little later by one of Libistros' love-letters, which elaborates upon the conceit of the (male) lover's heart as a castle.[89] Particularly revealing are the lines:

παρ' οὗ ὅτι αἰχμαλωτίζομαι διὰ πόθον ἐδικόν σου,
παροῦ τὸ κάστρον τῆς ἐμῆς προδίδεται καρδίας
ἀπὸ τὸν δήμιον ἔρωταν, ὡραία, τὸν ἐδικόν σου ...
τὸ κάστρον τῆς καρδίας μου μόνη νὰ τὸ ὑποτάξῃς,
καὶ αὐθεντικὰ νὰ τὸ διαβῇς τὸν πύργον τῆς ψυχῆς μου.[90]

but I am held prisoner by desire for you,
but the castle of my heart is betrayed
by the love of you, my beauty, that slays ...
May you alone subdue the castle of my heart
and set foot as lord and master in the tower of my soul.

The same metaphor is also explicit in the *Tale of Achilles*, where in a similar context the hero's bride-to-be addresses her first love-letter to him:

τὸν πύργον τῆς καρδίτσας μου, τὸν ὑψηλὸν καὶ μέγαν,
τὸν ἐκαυχούμην πάντοτε κανεὶς νὰ μὴ χαλάσῃ,
Ἔρως σαγίτταν ἔσυρεν καὶ ἐκατεχάλασέν τον
καὶ εἰς πόθον τῆς ἀγάπης σου ἤφερεν τὴν ψυχήν μου.[91]

the castle of my heart, so high and great,
that I did ever boast no one should sack,
Eros has drawn an arrow and sacked it utterly.

This metaphor is maintained with remarkable consistency through the other original romances of the period. I have already suggested that elements of the Ogre's Castle in *Kallimachos* may be metaphorical extensions of traditional abstract qualities of love. In *Belthandros* this aspect is clearer still, since the whole elaborate edifice of the Castle of Love, as Cupane puts it, 'exists only for Belthandros, was built for him, is the castle of his adventures and his destiny.'[92] It fulfils no other purpose than the initiation of the hero whose destiny is carved in stone beneath the statues from which flows the fiery river, symbolizing the paradoxical nature of love.[93] Elsewhere, in the *Tale of Achilles*, which Cupane does not discuss, the hero subdues a sumptuous castle by force before being smitten with love for its princess, whom he abducts after pole-vaulting with his javelin into her walled garden and demonstrates his virility by knocking down the chamber in which she had been secluded.[94] It may be of significance that in *Kallimachos* too the hero gains access to the castle in this suggestively symbolic way and Belthandros also leaps a wall for the same purpose, although without the aid of a javelin.[95] By contrast, Paris in the *Tale of Troy* enters Helen's castle in the guise of a monk, and at first represents himself as a poor wanderer.[96]

The conclusion must be that if the visual depiction of the mysterious castle is new in the Greek romances of the fourteenth century and derives from the West, the metaphorical role which it fulfils has a long tradition in Greek behind it: we have already encountered the seclusion of the heroine as a standard convention in *Digenes Akrites* and the twelfth-century romances. And the metaphor of fortifications as the extension of a girl's sexual defences, made famous in the West by the influential *Roman de la Rose* in the early thirteenth century, is already present in Greek almost a century before that poem was written. Nikephoros Basilakes, who lived around the middle of the twelfth century, puts the following reproach into the mouth of a girl who has been seduced and abandoned (and the metaphor can be traced back to the *Greek Anthology*):

Ἔρωτι συμμάχῳ χρησάμενος καὶ τὴν γλῶτταν ἔχων ἐλέπολιν, κατ' αὐτῆς δὴ σωφροσύνης κατεπεστράτευσε, πολιορκῆσαι θέλων τῆς παρθενίας μου τὴν ἀκρόπολιν καὶ καταστρατηγῆσαι τῆς σωφροσύνης αὐτῆς.[97]

Using Eros as his ally, and his tongue as his siege-engine, he led a campaign against my very chastity, wishing to besiege the citadel of my virginity and to lay low my chastity itself.

The same metaphor is extended by Makrembolites in one of Hysminias' erotic dreams, and since there are a number of correspondence between this romance and Basilakes' rhetorical exercises, it is quite likely that the author of *Hysmine and Hysminias* was drawing on this source here rather than on the *Roman de la Rose* or the Western tradition which preceded it:

Γίνομαι καὶ περὶ τὸ στέρνον τῆς κόρης· ἡ δ' ἀντέχεται μάλα γενναίως καὶ ὅλη συστέλλεται καὶ ὅλῳ σώματι περιτειχίζει τὸν μαστὸν ὡς πόλις ἀκρόπολιν, καὶ χερσὶ καὶ τραχήλῳ καὶ πώγωνι καὶ γαστρὶ τοὺς μαστοὺς καταφράττει καὶ περιφράττει.[98]

I make a pass at the girl's chest; she puts up a spirited resistance and draws herself in and with her whole body defends her breast as a city does a citadel, and with her hands and neck and chin and stomach she fences and cordons off her breasts.

At about the same time (the early to mid-twelfth century) Prodromos also drew on this metaphor in a different context, in a scathing attack on an illiterate pretender to letters, to whom he sarcastically enumerates the feats his opponent still has to perform before he can 'capture the citadel of learning'.[99] Once again, in a complex and subtle synthesis of Eastern and Western traditions, the Byzantine element turns out to be more tenacious than at first sight appears.

CONCLUSION

The genealogy of the original romances of the fourteenth and fifteenth centuries is twofold. Obvious generic links and evident allusions betray their affinity with their predecessors of the twelfth century and, beyond them, of the Hellenistic period. Although overt references to Western realia or literary models are rare and of limited significance, a re-examination of the topoi identified by Cupane reveals that the authors of the Greek romances had some knowledge of the Western genre and consciously assimilated elements deriving from it, as 'catalysts' in extending the possibilities of the Greek genre in new ways. The extent of this awareness, and the means by which Byzantine writers of romance came to know the work of their peers in the West, cannot for the time being be determined. However, the evidence (discussed in Chapter 12) that the court poet Meliteniotes was well versed in a variety of Western vernacular genres, as well as in the original Greek romances, confirms that such an awareness existed in fourteenth-century Constantinople.

11

ORALITY

So far we have looked only at links between the Greek romances and literary texts which we know beyond doubt were in existence at the time when our romances were written. But it will already have become apparent that there is much common ground linking the later vernacular romances with one another. Here we cannot in most cases trace the relationship between texts in such a satisfactory way. One reason for this is uncertainty as to the precise chronology of the romances; another is the absence of definite evidence as to where and for what type of readership or audience they were composed. One influential approach to this question in recent years has been to invoke the processes of oral tradition in the composition and/or transmission of the romances. In investigating this issue it will be necessary to re-examine the elements of common ground that exist among all the later Greek romances, and the theories that have been advanced to account for them, before going on to propose a new explanation for these phenomena.

The common elements linking several, in some cases all, of the romances, whether original or translated, are of two kinds. Common themes linking the original romances, and a common quest among Western originals for those touching on aspects of the Greek tradition in the translated romances, have already been discussed. These elements have attracted much less attention, however, than have more obvious correspondences at the level of common wording, particularly in single lines or short groups of lines. I shall return to thematic resemblances later in this chapter. In the meantime we must begin with the verbal similarities which have been noticed among different romances, and the explanations proposed to account for them.

THE THEORIES

These explanations fall into three groups. The first, which develops earlier suggestions is today justly associated with the names of Michael and Elizabeth Jeffreys.[1] According to the Jeffreys the romances, along with most other vernacular Greek texts of the fourteenth and fifteenth centuries, preserve in varying degrees traces of an oral tradition of extended narratives in the fifteen-syllable metre, which would have provided the only model available at the time for composition in the popular language. The common elements in the romances are therefore traditional, and betray the oral origin of the language and verseform in which they are written (but not of the stories or the texts themselves). The second explanation is more conventional. Giuseppe Spadaro[2] has proposed that all the verbal correspondences among romance texts (and some others) can be accounted for in terms of literary borrowings among a close-knit and under-talented group of writers. The third possibility has been studied in less detail and has been tried systematically only for a small group of texts. First seriously proposed by Schreiner, it has been applied with immense devotion to detail by Arnold van Gemert and Wim Bakker.[3] According to these scholars the common elements are due to scribal interference: when the same copyist has written out more than one vernacular text in the same manuscript, he will tend to repeat lines or expressions originally belonging to one text when copying another.

The Jeffreys' theory

The possibility that the textual discrepancies among different versions of vernacular Greek texts preserved in more than one manuscript were the result of oral transmission was first explored by Michael and Elizabeth Jeffreys in a detailed study of the variant manuscripts of *Imperios and Margarona*, carefully compared with one another and with the poem's French original.[4] Subsequently, in a computer-aided study of the early fourteenth-century *Chronicle of the Morea*, Michael Jeffreys demonstrated that the proportion of exactly recurring short phrases in that text corresponded closely to the results of similar studies of oral epic poetry as studied in, predominantly, Bosnia, by Milman Parry and Albert Lord, as well as in the Homeric poems and other medieval texts in which oral processes had been suspected.[5] In this way the variations between manuscript versions of the *same* text came to suggest a model which would also account for the many elements repeated both within a single text and across two or more different texts. At the end of this paper and in another of the following year, Michael Jeffreys went on to link textual variation and the use of apparently oral formulae with another characteristic of this vernacular literature, namely its mixed language, and to propose that, like the mixed language of the Homeric poems, this too may have been the product of a centuries-old oral tradition.[6] Then in a paper of 1979 Elizabeth and Michael Jeffreys together undertook a similar but less rigorously quantitative study of the unpublished *War of Troy*, in which they identified a significant proportion of recurring phrases and phrase-patterns which they proposed were 'formulaic', in the sense classically defined by Milman Parry as 'a group of words which is regularly employed under the same metrical conditions to express a given essential idea'.[7] In the conclusion to that article the Jeffreys suggested that 'the *War of Troy* is a transitional text between oral and literary composition'.[8]

In a series of articles since then the Jeffreys have continued to argue for the position adopted in their earlier work, responded vigorously to criticism and occasionally allowed a slight readjustment of emphasis.[9] A note of caution is sounded, for example, when the conclusion on the *War of Troy* just quoted is rephrased in an article of 1983: 'We would attribute them [*sc.* changes between different manuscripts] to a tradition of copying within a psychological framework based on oral modes of thought ... with little emphasis on verbal accuracy in copying;[10] and again: 'The oral tradition intervenes only to relax the definition of accurate copying aimed at by the scribes'.[11] Michael Jeffreys, in returning to the subject of his 1973 article, the *Chronicle of the Morea*, made a broader plea for understanding the mechanisms of this kind of text:

> We must learn to read them, so far as practicable, with the eye of the first reader, and still more to hear them with the ear of the first listener, before going on to other critical tasks. In this attempt, I believe that the decoding of the mixed language, if it can be done, will help us a great deal.[12]

At about the same time Constantine Trypanis, in his compendious survey of Greek poetry from Homer to Seferis, went much further, in presenting all the vernacular texts of the period as the products of oral tradition, and work by Hans Eideneier on a somewhat different tack has proposed criteria for identifying traces of oral *transmission* in texts of the period, without presupposing that they are necessarily also written in an oral traditional style.[13] Two recent editors of vernacular texts have gone so far as to propose, with Trypanis, that at least some of their manuscript witnesses represent independent recordings from oral tradition.[14]

Spadaro's theory

The greater part of Giuseppe Spadaro's work was carried out and published, like that of the Jeffreys, in a succession of articles published in the mid-1970s. The two theories can be seen as the product of a parallel development, although now that both have been formulated for some years they have taken on a more antagonistic character, and are certainly seen by their proponents as mutually exclusive. Spadaro's careful comparison of texts goes back to 1966, when he successfully demonstrated the close dependence of *Phlorios and Platzia-Phlora* on the extant Italian version of the *Cantare di Fiorio e Biancifiore*. Having thus overturned the arguments of Schreiner that *Phlorios* had been influenced in the course of transmission by *Imperios and Margarona*,[15] Spadaro then turned his attention to the many common lines and expressions linking these two Greek romances, in order to argue that the author of *Imperios* was intimately acquainted with the Greek text of *Phlorios*.[16] In another article he began to look for evidence of similar dependence among a group consisting of two romances, the *Tale of Achilles* and *Imperios*, and the stylistically similar *Tale of Belisarios*.[17] A subsequent article extends across a much larger canvas, adding to the texts already considered *Kallimachos*, *Belthandros*, *Libistros*, the *Tale of Troy* and the reworking of the Belisarios poem, dated to shortly after 1499, by the Rhodian poet Emmanuel Georgillas or Limenites.[18] Other articles in this interrelated series link the *War of Troy* with the *Theseid* and with the *Tale of Achilles*, and return to the *Tale of Belisarios* and *Tale of Achilles*.[19] Spadaro's conclusions have been usefully summarized by the Jeffreys in the form of a diagram (Figure 1).

An important component of Spadaro's theory is the lack of talent which he ascribes to the vernacular writers. It is because they are either too lazy or too uninspired to invent lines of their own that they appropriate those of their peers; the term 'plagiarism' occurs frequently in Spadaro's writings. This is how Spadaro sums up the abilities of these writers:

> A good proportion of the poets of medieval Greek literature in the vernacular composed their works without possessing true poetic inspiration, without having great resources of expressive means. This is why they were constrained to go in search of motifs, of points of departure, of half-lines, of lines, of ready-made phrases which they could then insert with naive artistry and without much compunction into their compositions.[20]

Contamination by scribes

This is the likeliest explanation for the interpolated ending of the *Tale of Achilles* in the Naples manuscript, which draws directly from *Imperios*, *Belisarios* and in all probability the *Tale of Troy*. However, the most detailed work which has so far been done to determine to what extent common elements among vernacular Greek texts may be due to scribal interference has focused on the *Tale of Belisarios* and to that extent has not been central to the romance. Arnold van Gemert and Wim Bakker have devoted meticulous attention to the transmission of this poem, of which four redactions can be discerned in the surviving manuscripts. Central to their argument is the belief that the substantial number of lines and phrases shared between this poem and the *Tale of Achilles* (and to some extent also with *Imperios*) do not belong to the original composition, which they date fairly closely to the decade before 1400, but are due to the scribe whose work was copied to produce the extant Naples manuscript, of the second half of the fifteenth century, in which all three texts are preserved.[21]

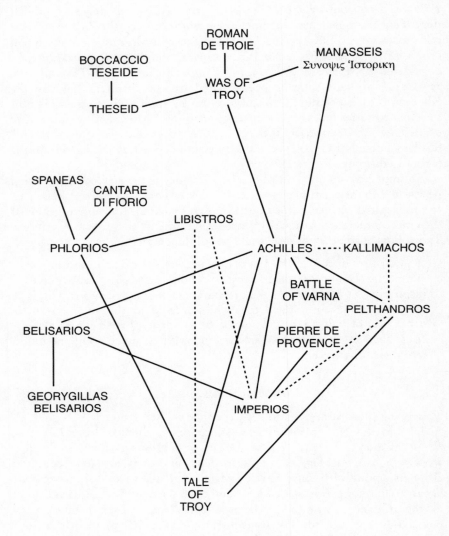

Figure 1 Diagrammatic representation of the main connections among romances and related texts from the fourteenth to the sixteenth century, extrapolated by E. and M. Jeffreys from the articles by Spadaro discussed here. The Jeffreys comment 'The evidence for this table has been gathered from all Spadaro's papers cited . . . We have found it impractical, for reasons of space, to document each of its connections'.[22] (I am most grateful to Elizabeth and Michael Jeffreys for permission to reproduce this diagram here.)

CRITIQUE OF THE THEORIES

It must be said at once that each of the explanations that have been proposed for the incidence of common lines and expressions in the romances is supported by evidence that is not easily explained away. For this reason alone one cannot help feeling that none of them is adequate to provide a total explanation of the phenomenon. The strengths and weaknesses of each theory must now be examined.

Scribal contamination is strongly supported by two general features of the manuscript tradition. First, when the same text is preserved in more than one manuscript there is not a single case in the whole of medieval Greek vernacular literature of a text being reproduced exactly. The variations, which are almost always at the level of wording rather than of changes to the story, are in many cases attributable, without much argument, to copyists. The second, complementary, characteristic is that when more than one text is preserved *in the same manuscript* we find common elements throughout the manuscript, at the level of verbal expression, which may not correspond with other manuscript versions of the same poems. The most striking case of this is the Naples manuscript, which contains the *Tale of Achilles, Imperios* and *Belisarios*. Another is the Escorial manuscript, which contains the verbally garbled but otherwise quite reliable versions of *Digenes Akrites* and *Libistros*. The intervention of copyists in the transmission of these texts is therefore not in doubt; the particular contribution of van Gemert's and Bakker's work, presented in its fullest detail in their edition of the *Tale of Belisarios*, is to demonstrate that within the group of texts in the Naples manuscript the direction of 'influence' from one to another is not consistent.[23] This proves that some of the correspondences noted by Spadaro cannot be due to the *author* in every case, but must also be due to mutual interference among texts which were being copied together.

The greatest weakness of this explanation for the common elements is that it has been the least developed theoretically. The empirical evidence is sound, and it must be accepted that to some degree such common elements are due to manuscript copyists. But beyond that we are in effect thrown back on one or other of the Jeffreys' or Spadaro's accounts of how these common elements come to be transferred from one text to another. Is the scribe in this case in the position analogous to that of the oral singer? Could he, in an extreme possibility, even be recording the performance of an oral singer with his characteristic stock of formulae? Such an explanation is easily compatible with the Jeffreys' model of a scribe who recognizes the characteristics of a fluid oral poem in the text he is copying and therefore reproduces it not word-for-word but after the manner of an oral singer, replacing formulaic expressions in his text with similarly formulaic expressions from his own repertory. Or are the scribes, like Spadaro's talentless authors, driven to forage through the other texts they have copied, in order to find a suitable phrase to replace something perhaps unsatisfactory in the original before them? It is in fact no easier to envisage precisely *how* elements of one text found their way into another at the hands of scribes than to understand how the texts in their original form came to share so many common elements of expression. One thing is certain: that contamination by scribes can account for only a small proportion of the correspondences listed by the Jeffreys and Spadaro. It therefore seems probable that whatever mechanism operated in the larger sphere of the composition of the poems was also at work on a smaller scale at the level of the scribe.

There is in fact a danger of building too much on the theory of scribal interference, which is already apparent in the work of Bakker and van Gemert. A criterion that they have adopted for distinguishing successive redactions of the Belisarios poem is the quantity and quality of assimilation from other texts, which they attribute exclusively to scribes or redactors rather than to the author of the poem. One may detect in this a tendency towards circular reasoning: common elements with other poems are proof of interpolation, common elements exist between one text and another, therefore the common elements in our text must have been interpolated. In the case of the Belisarios poem this may well prove to be true, but it will not work as an explanation for the vast majority of verbal similarities which link the romances and other vernacular Greek texts.

Turning now to Spadaro's proposition, the evidence presented is much less homogeneous than it seems at first sight. The impression of a single, consistent argument has actually been enhanced by the honourable efforts of Spadaro's opponents, the Jeffreys, to present his conclusions in a more systematic way than he himself has done.[24] The dependence of *Imperios* on the Greek text of *Phlorios*, which is the subject of Spadaro's 1975 article, is proved by a volume of evidence which in both quantity and quality cannot be refuted. In terms of quantity the sheer number of correspondences between the two texts is unmatched by that for any other pair of texts considered by Spadaro except for *Belisarios* and the *Tale of Achilles* (where, again, a direct relationship at the level of the copyist is confirmed by van Gemert and Bakker). Although not all these correspondences are equally persuasive in themselves, and some must surely be what Spadaro himself calls, rather loosely, 'commonplaces', none the less the quantity of data puts the argument on quite a different level from the arguments in Spadaro's subsequent articles. As to quality, there is one crucial case where Spadaro has demonstrated incontrovertibly that *Imperios* reproduces at least one line from *Phlorios* which derives from the original of the latter poem and has no counterpart in the French text of *Pierre de Provence*. That this evidence is also accepted by the Jeffreys is of considerable importance.[25] The existence of even one proven case of literary borrowing, as opposed to re-use of traditional formulaic expressions, demonstrates that oral-traditional factors cannot be the *sole* cause of the common elements found among the romances, and that some form of literary interaction must also have been at work.

Spadaro's comparative work on the *Tale of Achilles, Belisarios* and *Imperios* is at variance with the conclusions of Michailidis and of van Gemert and Bakker in that he sees the interaction as having taken place at the level of composition rather than of the compilation of the Naples manuscript.[26] But once again the volume of correspondences, which is much greater than anything found to link other specific texts (apart from *Phlorios* and *Imperios*), is highly suggestive of a direct link between at least the *Tale of Achilles* and *Belisarios*, whether this be due to writer or to scribe.[27] However, in the wider-reaching comparisons of his later articles, although some of the parallels cited are striking, neither in quantity nor in quality are they persuasive that direct links existed between any other pairs of texts on a scale comparable to those previously demonstrated between *Phlorios* and *Imperios* and between the *Tale of Achilles* and *Belisarios*.[28] The weakness of these somewhat miscellaneous arguments, and the need to consider a kind of relationship between texts that is radically different from the 'plagiarism' proposed by Spadaro, can be demonstrated by looking in detail at the opening passages of a number of romances, to some of which he has drawn attention.

Spadaro cites the opening of the Greek *War of Troy* alongside the corresponding passage by Benoît:

Ἦν τις Ἑλλήνων βασιλεύς, εὐγενικός, ἀνδρεῖος,
πλούσιος καὶ πανευτυχής, χώρας τῆς Μυρμιδόνος·
οὗτος ὑπῆρχεν ὁ πατὴρ τοῦ λαμπροῦ Ἀχιλλέως.
Εἶχεν δὲ καὶ αὐτάδελφον ἐν τῇ Πελοποννήσῳ·
Τελαμόνιος ἐλέγετο τὸ ὄνομα ἐκεῖνος.   5
Οὗτος ὁ Τελαμόνιος εἶχεν υἱὸν ἀνδρεῖον,
τὸν Ἰασοῦν τὸν πάγκαλον, εὐγενικὸν καὶ μέγαν·
εἶχεν μεγάλην δύναμιν, εἶχεν μεγάλην γνῶσιν
καὶ εἰς πολλὰ βασίλεια διὰ πολλὰς ἀνδρείας
ἀκουστὸς καὶ ἐγνώριμος ὑπῆρχεν εἰς τοὺς πάντας.[29]   10

There was a certain king of the Hellenes, noble, brave,
rich and blessed with good fortune, of the land of Myrmidon [*sic*];
this man was the father of the renowned Achilles.
He also had a brother in the Peloponnese;
Telamonios was this man's name.
This Telamonios had a son who was brave,
the handsome Jason, noble and great;
he had great strength, he had great understanding
and in many kingdoms for his many acts of valour
was famed and renowned on all sides.

The French text from which the Greek derives is as follows:

> Peleüs fu uns riches reis,
> mout proz, mout sages, mout corteis:
> par Grece alot sa seignorie
> a del regne ot mout grant partie ...
> Icist reis aveit un suen frere ...
> Eson ert par non apelé;
> en Penelope la cité ...
> Icist Eson un fil aveit
> qui Jason apelez esteit,
> de grant beauté e de grant pris
> e de grant sen, si com jo truis.
> Grand force aveit e grant vertu,
> par maint regne fu coneü.[30]

Spadaro goes on to note that the Greek lines, translated from the French in the mid-fourteenth century, are followed closely in the interpolated *ottava* near the beginning of the Greek translation of Boccaccio's *Theseid* and in the opening of the *Tale of Achilles*.[31] Both these correspondences he accounts for in the same way, and uses them as evidence that not only the Greek translator of the *Theseid* but also the author of the *Tale of Achilles* knew the translation of the *War of Troy*. A closer look at the evidence reveals that the same explanation will not do for both cases.

The case of the *Theseid* is scarcely controversial but its implications are important. Spadaro quotes the interpolated lines and indicates the correspondences with the *War of Troy*. In reproducing them I have indicated correspondences in a different way from Spadaro, underlining portions of text which correspond exactly to the previous extract and following each line with the line number in brackets of the *War of Troy* where the correspondence can be observed. I have also been slightly more rigorous than Spadaro in determining the degree of similarity which counts as a correspondence:

> Ἦν τις Ἑλλήνων βασιλεύς, εὐγενικός, ἀνδρεῖος,   (1)
> πλούσιος καὶ πανευτυχής, τῆς πόλεως ᾿Αθήνας·   (2)
> οὗτος ὑπῆρχεν ὁ λαμπρὸς καὶ βασιλεὺς Αἰγέος·   (3)
> εἶχεν υἱὸν πανέμνοστον, φριχτὸν εἰς τὴν ἀνδρείαν·   (6)
> Θησέος ὠνομάζετον, εὔμορφος ὑπὲρ μέτρον·
> εἶχε μεγάλην δύναμιν, εἶχε μεγάλη γνῶσιν,   (8)
> καὶ εἰς πολλὰ βασίλεια ἔδειξε τὴν ἀνδρειάν του·   (9)
> εἰς φήμην, δόξαν καὶ τιμὴν ἦλθε 'κ τὴν προθυμιάν του.[32]

There was a certain king of the Hellenes, noble, brave,
rich and blessed with good fortune, of the city of Athens;
this man was the renowned and sovereign Aegeus;

He had a son most handsome, terrible in valour;
Theseus was he named, good-looking beyond measure;
he had great strength, he had great understanding
and in many kingdoms showed his valour;
renown, glory and honour he won for his keen spirit.

What we have here is much more than a reliance on traditional formulae, especially since the translator of Boccaccio was not obliged to resort to his own tradition in this way. The interpolated passage in the *Theseid* is as close a paraphrase of the opening of the *War of Troy* as could have been possible given the different name and genealogy of the hero to be introduced, and given also the formal constraint of the eight-line group corresponding to the *ottava* of Boccaccio's original. The greater difference from the *War of Troy* shown in the wording (but not the meaning) of the last line is evidently due to the further formal constraint in this poem that the last two lines of the Greek *ottava* should form a rhyming pair. While we cannot altogether exclude the possibility that the entire passage was traditional and called up by the translator of the *Theseid* from his own stock of oral formulae or knowledge of the oral poetry of his day, this explanation signally fails to explain why he should have chosen to do so in a long poem which contains no other significant interpolations. There is no question here of reliance on oral tradition and every sign, on the contrary, that an allusion to an older Greek poem which, like this one, was a translation of a large-scale work, in another language, was the result of deliberate choice. Thus far we may agree with Spadaro. However, the argument just put forward, for conscious allusion rather than plagiarism as a last resort, militates against his model of enforced dependence, just as much as it does against reliance on oral tradition.

Spadaro next goes on to compare the opening passage of the *War of Troy* with the *Tale of Achilles*. Here the narrative proper (after a prologue in manuscript N) begins in two versions with the lines:

Εἷς τῶν Ἑλλήνων βασιλεύς, εὐγενικὸς καὶ ἀνδρεῖος,
πλούσιος καὶ πανευτυχὴς ἐν χώρᾳ Μυρμιδόνων.[33]

One of the kings of the Hellenes, noble and brave,
rich and blessed with good fortune in the land of the Myrmidons.

Although the rest of the passage has no direct verbal correspondences to the opening of the *War of Troy*, it is worth noting that the king in question will shortly turn out to be the father of Achilles, with whom the passage from the *War of Troy* also began, and that the same qualities of bravery and nobility are extolled here too. Spadaro argues that, since the passage in the *War of Troy* derives closely from the French original of that poem, this passage must

173

therefore have been imitated by the author of *Achilles*, and not the other way round.[34] Although he has noted a number of other similarities on which he bases his case for the dependence of the *Tale of Achilles* on the *War of Troy*, this one is the most substantial, with its direct appeal to the French text of Benoît. But if we leave out of account the more systematic correspondences to the later *Theseid*, which have now been satisfactorily explained, the correspondence between the *Tale of Achilles* and Benoît's French text turns out to be entirely illusory. Lines 1–2 of the Greek *War* and lines 20–1 of *Achilles* (N) are all but identical; line 3 of the *War*, to which there is no corresponding line in *Achilles*, refers to Achilles by name. But Benoît makes no mention of Achilles at this point. The Greek translator has followed him in introducing Jason as the nephew of Peleus, but the references to Achilles and to 'Myrmidon', which is clearly mistaken for the name of a place, and the syntactical structure 'There was a certain (τις) ...' do not derive from the French. The conclusion to be drawn from a careful application of Spadaro's own methods is in fact the opposite of his. The translator of the *War of Troy* drew upon *Achilles* in the very first lines of his poem, and this is clearly shown by his misunderstanding of ἐν χώρᾳ Μυρμιδόνων ('in the land of the Myrmidons') as referring to a placename: χώρας τῆς Μυρμιδόνος ('of the land of Myrmidon').

There are other instances in which Spadaro's method has been invoked to support contrary conclusions.[35] The point I wish to make here is more fundamental. The full sentence with which the *Tale of Achilles*, after the prologue, begins is as follows:

Εἷς τῶν Ἑλλήνων βασιλεύς, εὐγενικὸς καὶ ἀνδρεῖος,
πλούσιος καὶ πανευτυχὴς ἐν χώρᾳ Μυρμιδόνων,
ἐρωτικός, πανευειδής, ἀγέρωχος τὸν τρόπον,
εἶχεν γὰρ νέους μαχητὰς καὶ διαλεκτὰ φουσσάτα,
πρὸς μάχας καὶ παραταγὰς ὅλους δοκιμασμένους,
ὅλους καλούς, εὐγενικούς, ὅλους ἀνδρειωμένους·
ποτέ του γὰρ οὐκ ἤθελεν, εἰς ὅλον τὸ φουσσάτον
ἄνδρα νὰ ἰδῇ πολεμιστὴν ἐξ ἀφανῶν γονέων,
εἰμὴ ἐκ γένους ἔκλαμπρου, πάνυ πλουσιωτάτου.[36]

One of the kings of the Hellenes, noble and brave,
rich and blessed with good fortune in the land of the Myrmidons,
a lover, good-looking, indomitable in his manners,
had young fighters and hand-picked armies,
for battles and battle-lines all well trained,
all good, noble, all courageous;
for never would he consent in all his army
to see a man a warrior [if he came] of low-born parents,
but only [if he came] of excellent stock, the richest.

It is instructive to compare this passage, as Spadaro does not, with the comparable jumping-off points of the other original romances. *Kallimachos* begins, again after a brief prologue, like this:

> Βάρβαρος γάρ τις βασιλεύς, δυνάστης ἐπηρμένος,
> πολλῶν χρημάτων ἀρχηγός, πολλῶν χωρῶν αὐθέντης,
> τὴν ἔπαρσιν ἀβάσταγος, ἀγέρωχος τὸ σχῆμα,
> τρεῖς παῖδας ἔσχεν εὐειδεῖς, ἠγαπημένους πλεῖστα,
> εἰς κάλλος καὶ εἰς σύνθεσιν ἐρωτοφορουμένους
> καὶ τ' ἄλλα πάντα θαυμαστούς, γενναίους εἰς ἀνδρείαν.[37]

> There was a certain barbarian king, a proud ruler,
> commander of great riches, lord of many lands,
> intolerant in his pride, indomitable in appearance,
> three good-looking sons he had, that were very dear to him,
> [who were] in beauty and in bearing clothed in love
> and in all else marvellous, courageous in valour.

Very similar in structure and in some of its key words is the opening, again after a prologue, of *Belthandros*:

> Δυνάστης ἦταν βασιλεὺς Ῥοδόφιλος, ὁκάτις
> (τὸ ὄνομα ῥωμαϊκὸν) χωρῶν ὑπεραπείρων.
> Τυραννικῶς αὐθέντευεν ὡς φυσικὸς αὐθέντης
> καὶ τοὺς ἐκεῖσε γύρωθεν ἐδέσποζε τοπάρχας.
> Εἶχε καὶ παῖδας εὐειδεῖς, ἠγαπημένους δύο.[38]

> There was a king [and] ruler, a certain Rodophilos
> (the name is Greek) of countless lands.
> Tyrannically he ruled as to the manner born
> and held sway over all the local governors round about.
> He had good-looking sons, two, that were dear to him.

Even the *Tale of Troy*, derivative though it is, can usefully be cited:

> Ὁ βασιλεὺς ὁ Πρίαμος, ὁ θαυμαστὸς ἐκεῖνος,
> ὁ δυνατὸς καὶ ἰσχυρός, ὁ πλούσιος καὶ μέγας,
> καὶ τῶν Ἑλλήνων ἀρχηγὸς καὶ βασιλεὺς εἰς πάντας,
> εἶχεν ἀνδρείαν ἐπαινετὴν καὶ παρρησιὰν καὶ δόξαν.
> Υἱοὺς πολλοὺς ἐποίησεν, ὥσπερ Ὅμηρος γράφει,
> εἶχεν ἡ Τροία ἔσωθεν ἄρχοντας ἐπηρμένους,
> εὐγενικοὺς καὶ πλουσίους καὶ θαυμαστούς, μεγάλους.[39]

> King Priam, that great [man],
> the powerful and strong, the rich and great,

commander of the Hellenes (*sic*!] and ruler over all,
had renowned valour, power and glory.
Many sons he made, as Homer writes,
there were inside Troy proud courtiers,
noble and rich and wonderful, great.

Only *Libistros* among the original romances has no parallel passage, as the
first-person narrative of Klitobos introduces us directly to the hero without
reference to his parentage.

The common elements among these four passages from original romances
and two from translations can now be briefly summarized. The formula
'there was a certain / there was one …' is invariable. The king in question is
in all the original romances the father of the hero (in the *War of Troy* the
uncle, and in the *Theseid* the benign patron of the rivals in love, Theseus).
This king is either a 'Hellene', which, as we have seen, meant primarily a
pagan, and in context refers to the remote world of ancient mythology, or,
in *Kallimachos* a 'barbarian', a term which, although in semantic opposition
to 'Hellene', refers us equally outside the world of contemporary Christendom. The kings are invariably praised for the same qualities: power, wealth
and pride, and key words associated with these concepts recur throughout
the examples.[40]

In the light of this evidence it becomes even more difficult to sustain
Spadaro's argument that the *Tale of Achilles* follows the *War of Troy* at this
point. But even the counter-argument that the direction of influence was the
other way around loses some of its force when Spadaro's examples are set
against comparable passages in four of the five original romances. The
evidence of these passages confirms one of the Jeffreys' objections to
Spadaro's method, namely that it does not present *enough* evidence, thus
singling out random instances of correspondences which are in fact far more
frequent than even Spadaro's long lists of lines and phrases suggest.[41] It is
difficult to escape the conclusion, after examining all the passages just
quoted, that this manner of beginning the narrative part of a romance was
traditional in the Greek vernacular genre and for that reason was deliberately
incorporated into the two most ambitious works of translation into Greek
undertaken in that genre, the *War of Troy* and the *Theseid*. Further
comparison with *Digenes Akrites*, which also begins with a description of the
hero's father, provides a strong clue as to where this tradition may have
started:

Ἦν ἀμηρᾶς τῶν εὐγενῶν πλουσιώτατος σφόδρα,
φρονήσεώς τε μέτοχος καὶ ἀνδρείας εἰς ἄκρος.[42]

There was an emir among the nobles, mightily rich,
possessed of wit and bravery to the limit.

A vital question that remains to be resolved, of course, concerns the precise meaning of 'traditional' in this context; and with this question it will be timely to move on to a critique of the Jeffreys' arguments.

Of the theories advanced to account for the common and repetitive elements found throughout the vernacular Greek literature of the period, that proposed by Elizabeth and Michael Jeffreys is by far the most comprehensive and sophisticated. By postulating an older tradition of extended oral narrative to which original writers, translators and copyists alike had recourse in their respective tasks, they have been able to propose a single solution which will account simultaneously for several distinct characteristics of these texts which have puzzled scholars. The theory of an 'oral-traditional background' accounts at a stroke not just for the common elements recurring both within and between texts, but also for the degree and kind of manuscript variation found and for the mixed language register with its juxtaposition of learned and spoken elements. Attractive though the theory is as a complete package, there are obstacles to accepting it without modification. In particular, as the Jeffreys have formulated it, it requires acceptance of two far-reaching hypotheses for which no supporting evidence exists. These are, first, that a tradition of extended, epic-style narrative in Greek had flourished for centuries before the vernacular texts came to be written, and gradually disappeared as the new medium of writing superseded it; and, second, that this tradition, like the oral tradition that preceded the written Homeric poems, had lasted long enough and in a sufficiently cohesive form to have created as part of its formulaic stock an accumulation of linguistic forms from many different epochs. While neither of these hypotheses can be proved to be false, there is an evident lack of economy in a theory which depends on such a large basis of hypothesis. A complementary weakness of the Jeffreys' theory is that while it relies to this extent on evidence for a hypothetical oral tradition, it leaves out of account the close literary connections between the original romances and older literature. Indeed, in focusing their attention on some of the most textually problematic works of the period, the *Chronicle of the Morea*, *Imperios*, and the *War of Troy*, they have tended to concentrate their efforts on texts which were probably created in the Frankish-ruled Peloponnese, at the expense of the original romances written (almost certainly) in the Byzantine capital, but belonging no less to the same linguistic and textual tradition.

A more specific difficulty concerns the nature of the 'oral formulae' which the Jeffreys have identified in the *Chronicle of the Morea* and *War of Troy*.[43] Doubts have been raised as to whether repeated half-lines such as ὁ πρίγκιπα Γυλιάμος ('Prince Guillaume'), or ἐκείνην τὴν ἡμέραν ('that day') from the *Chronicle of the Morea*, are sufficiently memorable or distinctive to have played a significant part in a fully functioning system of oral-formulaic composition,[44] and the same objection could be extended to all the thirty-eight examples of 'formulae' quoted by the Jeffreys as occurring twelve or more times in the *War of Troy*.[45] Particular exception has been taken to repeated phrases included in these lists which contain linguistic archaisms and which the Jeffreys have further proposed as evidence for the mixed language of the texts as an oral-traditional *Kunstsprache*. A. Mohay objected that the often-repeated phrase μετὰ χαρᾶς μεγάλης ('with great joy'), which could not have been used in common speech later than the tenth century, since by that time the ancient prepositional construction had fallen out of use, must be the result of learned influence in the fourteenth-century texts.[46] And Hans Eideneier, who believes that many of these texts were transmitted, but not composed, by oral means, has made similar objections to μικροί τε καὶ μεγάλοι ('both small and great'), which for obviously metrical reasons retains the archaic particle.[47] It may be accepted without difficulty that many of these phrases, particularly those which contain archaic linguistic elements, are 'traditional'; some of them even survive as clichés in speech today. But in order to be 'traditional' do they also have to be oral?

One way of tackling this question is to look for parallels between the vernacular texts and the oral tradition of ballad-type poetry which was extensively collected from all over the Greek-speaking world in the nineteenth and twentieth centuries. There are two difficulties which have to be admitted in trying to do this. The first is that most of our evidence for this *modern* oral tradition comes from a period much later than that of the romances and may well have been influenced, directly or indirectly, by the very texts that we are examining. And the second is the difficulty in many cases of distinguishing whether elements in the texts that do seem to echo the oral tradition belong to the original writer or to the copyist. The justification for proceeding despite these difficulties is that we have good evidence for the continuous existence of a ballad-type tradition in the fifteen-syllable metre from at least the twelfth century, and surviving evidence from that century and from texts of the fifteenth and seventeenth centuries shows that the structural characteristics and many of the formulaic systems of the songs collected in the nineteenth and twentieth centuries were already in existence at a much earlier period.[48] Even if the modern oral tradition has absorbed influences from the romances and other vernacular texts, these are more likely to be thematic than verbal; and it is striking that the cliché-formulae of the vernacular texts, such as μικροί τε καὶ μεγάλοι ('both small and great') and ὁ θαυμαστὸς ἐκεῖνος ('that marvellous man') are avoided throughout the oral ballad tradition.[49] The advantage of looking at correspondences with the modern song tradition is that it allows us, if only very approximately, to gauge the dependence of the vernacular texts on an oral tradition which we can be reasonably sure was functioning when the texts were composed.

Resemblances between the romances and oral folk-songs collected in more recent times have frequently been noted.[50] Examples of half-line or whole-line phrases in the romances which can be closely paralleled in the later oral tradition are, however, surprisingly few.[51] It is difficult to quantify these correspondences to oral folk-poetry entirely satisfactorily, as many less striking parallels could undoubtedly be added. The conclusion to which they point is that formulaic expressions from the oral tradition crop up from time to time in the romances, but with nothing like the frequency or the centrality of truly functional oral formulae. They are much more credibly to be understood as nods towards tradition of a kind already seen throughout these texts in their allusions to their literary precursors. One may assume without much difficulty that some will have been the almost unconscious insertions of later scribes; others, particularly those in *Libistros* which are found in more than one manuscript, presumably belong to the original poem. They can be ranged alongside other sorts of allusions to the same tradition which occur with comparable frequency in the texts: allusions, for instance, to ballads or tales of dragon-slayers in *Kallimachos*, to Charon or Charos as the anthropomorphic representative of death,[52] and to nature, in the topos of the 'pathetic fallacy', participating in human emotions.[53]

Using only this very limited evidence and making no attempt to quantify it, we may confirm, but in a much more restricted sense than the Jeffreys have done, that there is an oral background or substratum to the romances, but that the formulaic repetitions that they have noticed are conspicuously not part of it. If such a large number of repeated phrases cannot be traced back to an oral tradition *which was certainly known to the authors of the romances*, where, then, have they come from? A more than adequate explanation for this phenomenon has been proposed by Franz Bäuml, whose work has already been mentioned in the discussion of *Digenes Akrites* in Chapter 3. According to Bäuml's model, almost all the Greek vernacular texts would fit into the category of poems like the *Nibelungenlied*, in which a writing poet capitalizes on his audience's knowledge of and respect for traditional oral poetry and consciously alludes to it in order to legitimize a kind of art which may in fact signal a major break away from traditional forms.[54] To this extent the writing poet will freely invent formulae, as well as drawing on traditional ones. The crucial difference between this kind of poem and one which derives direct from oral tradition is that the formulae are not functional, or only vestigially so. The poem has not been composed out of the traditional oral building-blocks of formulae and formula-systems, but has been composed *using* them. But the most important contribution of Bäuml's analysis to an understanding of the Greek romances is that it removes the element of the poet's *dependence* on his repeated lines and phrases, which is as much a component of the Jeffreys' theory as it is of Spadaro's. The possibility that formulaic phrases were the creation of writing poets for whom and for whose audiences oral tradition represented a form of 'authority' also removes one of the most cumbersome components of the Jeffreys' theory: the hypothetical lost oral tradition of Byzantium.

But Bäuml's analysis will only take us part of the way. It has served to put a distance between the vernacular texts and their oral background, limiting the nature of that background to something much closer to the oral legacy of more recent times whose existence need not be doubted. More fundamentally, it has shown that such elements in the literary texts as do derive direct from oral poetry are not integral to them: they are not in any important sense 'traditional'. Earlier the question was put, do the clichés which are in some sense evidently *traditional* to vernacular literature also have to be *oral*?

We have now effectively separated the 'oral-traditional background' sought by the Jeffreys into quite distinct components. The oral elements are allusions to the 'authority' of oral tradition, not part of a 'traditional style, which has been transmitted by orally composed songs' or 'the written remains of a style which developed for oral and ephemeral purposes'.[55] Correspondingly, most of the 'traditional' elements which link one romance with another are not oral at all, but literary. 'Traditional elements' include all the repeated phrases and phrase-patterns identified by the Jeffreys and most of those picked out by Spadaro, with the exceptions noted above where a close link between two specific texts could be satisfactorily proved. They also include the recurrence of variations upon larger-scale units, such as we identified in the opening sentences of the main narrative in the original romances, and such indeed as the recurring story-pattern discussed in Chapter 7. The possibility that such traditional links are the result of textual rather than oral processes is of course fundamental to Spadaro's theory. There are two arguments, however, which the Jeffreys also accept, which prove that this kind of process could be a reality in the fourteenth and fifteenth centuries.

First, among all the multifarious evidence for some sort of link between *Phlorios* and *Imperios*, there is one uncontested case, already discussed, where the translator of the latter drew directly on the Greek translation of the former. Once this is accepted,[56] it is no longer possible to argue that the scarcity of texts and difficulties of copying at this time would have prevented writers from knowing the work of their predecessors and contemporaries unless through oral circulation.[57] The second argument derives from Elizabeth Jeffreys, who has pointed out a number of lines in the *War of Troy* which follow more or less verbatim the verse chronicle written in the twelfth century in the middle language register by Konstantinos Manasses.[58] Since it is inconceivable that any part of Manasses' long chronicle ever circulated as an oral poem, the conclusion is inescapable that the translator of the *War of Troy* knew the twelfth-century Greek chronicle well and chose to follow its wording in the few cases where Manasses' account of the Trojan war coincided with that of the French poem before him. Whether he had previously memorized that part of Manasses' chronicle before beginning his task, or actually had the *Synopsis Historike* open on the desk before him as well as the *Roman de Troie*, either way it speaks volumes for this translator's attitude to the Greek literary tradition that he found it important to consult and even to allude Manasses at all.

If we have still to explain satisfactorily the mechanism through which lines of one text come to be embedded in another, I propose that the examples of the use of *Phlorios* made by the translator of *Imperios*, and of Manasses made by the translator of the *War of Troy*, will prove to be better pointers to the nature of the 'tradition' linking all these texts than will recourse to an oral tradition of a type whose existence cannot be proved.

A NEW PROPOSAL

Any new theory in this already much-contested area will have to meet exacting standards. The following proposal is put forward not so much as a rival to those just examined but rather as an attempt at synthesis. I begin from the small area of agreement between the Jeffreys and Spadaro. First (as the Jeffreys deserve full credit for emphasizing time and again), we are not dealing with oral but with written texts. Second, there is a proportion of lines and phrases repeated both within texts and from one text to another which strikes a reader used to dealing with classical or with modern literary texts as so high as to demand explanation. Third, the rival explanations offered begin from the premise that the writers and translators of these poems were lacking in literary skills and so were compelled to make the best use of their limited resources.[59] The first two of these observations can easily be accepted; the third, as the reader who has followed the account of the romances given in this book so far will surely be ready to agree, is wide of the mark.

We cannot now deny the technical competence and the subtlety of the writers of most of the original romances in devising the structure of their narratives, in filling them out with complex, even ingenious, rhetorical devices, and in alluding in direct and indirect ways to the Greek and Western literary traditions. And this brings us back to a point made at the beginning of this chapter: that the common, or 'traditional', elements linking the romances go far beyond the verbal correspondences on which the three theories discussed have concentrated. The adoption of a common narrative scheme in all five original romances, and the degree of consistency shown in all the translated romances, in choosing Western material in some way linked to the Greek tradition, even in going out of their way to incorporate elements of that tradition into their translations, presuppose a community of interest and a commonality of purpose much more than an absence of originality. Indeed, as we saw in the first part of this book, originality in modern terms had no place in the medieval Greek literary tradition; or, rather, it is paradoxically and somewhat defensively buried under the apparent guise of imitation.

It is consistent with that tradition that the writers and translators of romances in the fourteenth and fifteenth centuries, whether working in Byzantine Constantinople or in Western feudal courts in Greece or the Aegean, should have valued a style of writing which constantly proclaims its allegiance to 'authorities', particularly Greek ones. An obvious 'authority' of this kind was to be found in the Greek literature of the twelfth century; another in the Greek oral tradition; yet another, much less overtly displayed, was to be found in the fictional literature of the medieval West. But perhaps the most important 'authority' of all at such a time of political and cultural transition was the example of one's peers working in the same vernacular language. Quite simply, the writers of vernacular romance imitated one another because their predecessors in the twelfth century had also done so. By using the diction of their contemporaries and immediate precursors, the writers and translators were *creating* a new tradition in the vernacular, not preserving for lack of better resources the last gasp of a disappearing oral tradition.

The shared elements among the romances, then, are the effect of two closely interrelated causes. One is the consciously felt need to create a tradition of literary fiction in the vernacular: would-be writers devoted careful attention to some, at least, of the work of their predecessors and learnt, like popular writers today, to exploit the clichés and plot-conventions of the genre.[60] But the other is, as the Jeffreys have demonstrated, the deference shown by literary writers exploiting a linguistic register which was still predominantly the medium for oral discourse towards the 'authority' of traditional oral poetry. As a result, as well as incorporating elements of plot and diction from the oral tradition, they tended like oral poets to repeat ready-made phrases in their texts and to take over other such phrases from other texts. Many of these phrases, however, betray, by their linguistic or sometimes their metrical form, that they were not first coined in the vernacular.

Two important problems remain. How are the variations among manuscript copies to be accounted for, and how did the mixed language of the vernacular texts come into being? The first is part and parcel of the complementary phenomenon whereby different texts copied by the same scribe show signs of mutual contamination. In accounting for both phenomena it is necessary to bear in mind our earlier observation that whatever mechanism was found to operate at the level of 'borrowing' by scribes was likely also to apply to 'borrowing' by the first authors of the poems. Here I find Hans Eideneier's proposal persuasive, with the difference that where he writes of *Dichtersänger* and oral transmission I believe that we are dealing once again with purely textual interaction. Arguing against the Jeffreys, Eideneier points out that during the fourteenth and fifteenth centuries vernacular literature never acquired the institutional prestige of literature in the learned language, and as a result its transmission was left in the hands of individuals who had a personal stake in it, that is, whose motive for copying may well have been to make a small contribution of their own, and who were not restrained from doing so by institutional pressures.[61]

In other words the scribe was not being paid to produce a copy, as was the normal state of affairs where manuscripts in the learned language were concerned, but rather embarked on his own initiative on creating a new text of a poem which had come into his hands. In some cases he may have been a professional copyist working under conditions quite different from those he would normally encounter; in others (judging simply from the reported appearance of different manuscripts) he was probably an amateur with a less sure knowledge of the learned language; either way his position is in some respects analogous to that of an oral singer recreating a traditional song with each rendition. It is probable that such copies were often made with a view to reciting or even singing aloud in public rather than for silent reading; what is important is that in the vernacular tradition the function of a copyist overlaps with that of the author (who is indeed himself, as we have seen, something of a 'copyist' in his allusions to the work of others).

This ambivalent nature of the scribe is better documented in the study of Western vernacular literatures, where it has even been suggested that the function of 'author', in a literary, secular sense, was derived from a fusion of two older medieval functions, those of scribe and of oral performer.[62] There is at least one instance in the West (where of course manuscript variation is as normal in the transmission of vernacular texts as it is in Greek) where a scribe steps out of his silent role to draw attention to himself and the way he has acted upon his text. Gui de Mori, an obscure thirteenth-century cleric who copied the French *Roman de la Rose*, explains in the verseform of the original what he proposes to do in making his copy:

> However, having taken care that the [work's] intended meaning and subject matter will neither be worsened nor destroyed by me, I will add so much of my own composition to it, taking out some things and putting in others, that it will be more accessible and more enjoyable to listen to.[63]

There is another way too in which the practice of the copyist in this tradition may have come close to that of the original author. At a later period and in a different environment, but still one in which it was normal for vernacular literature to be copied in manuscript and orally performed, the playwright Markos Antonios Foskolos copied out in his own hand the text of the tragedy *Erophile* by Georgios Chortatses, which had been written half a century before. This manuscript has only quite recently come to light and has not been edited;[64] however, Foskolos' own play *Fortounatos*, of which, unusually, we possess an autograph manuscript, is a variation on the theme, characters and situations of another play by Chortatses, the comedy *Katzourbos*.[65] Foskolos' comedy stands in a very similar relation to that of Chortatses as does Eugenianos' romance to that of Prodromos, or *Libistros* to *Hysmine and Hysminias*, or indeed as most of the original fourteenth-century romances do to one another (given that the relative chronology cannot be certainly established). 'Imitation' in Foskolos' play is inseparable from parodic or playful inversion and is liberally laced with allusions which pay homage, just as we found the writers of romance doing, to his 'source': for instance the foundling hero, who throughout the later play is known as 'Fortounatos' and gives the work its title, is discovered at the end to be truly named Nikoletos, the name of the hero in Chortatses' play. One can readily suppose that in Foskolos' day an aspiring poet would expect to learn his craft by copying the manuscripts of his predecessors.

If this practice is transposed back to the fourteenth and fifteenth centuries, it may be suggested that the writers of romances learnt their craft by copying whatever texts in the same idiom could be found. In his capacity as scribe, an aspiring author would naturally 'improve' his texts in a minor way as he went along. Then when he came to write (or translate) a romance of his own, some of the phrases and narrative details he had picked up from his copying would be carried over into his own work, while other characteristic hallmarks of his own personal style, now developed more fully, would already have been transferred to the texts that he had copied. Such a process provides the most plausible explanation, I believe, for the interpenetration of texts preserved together in the same manuscript that van Gemert and Bakker have studied, as well as for some of the verbal correspondences across a much wider range found by Spadaro and the Jeffreys. By the time he had copied an entire poem, the scribe or would-be author would have become conversant enough with its characteristic tricks of style not to have to turn back to the manuscript in order to reproduce them. But he might also recall more vaguely a particularly memorable passage and go back to it in the manuscript to copy it directly when faced with a similar context in his own writing or translating. This is the most likely explanation of the interpolations from *Phlorios* in *Imperios*.

The mixed language of the romances, if it is not the product of a long oral tradition, also requires a different explanation. Hans-Georg Beck has been prepared to accept it as 'spoken common Greek',[66] and proposes that its inconsistencies in the texts are due to the inexperience of learned writers (and scribes) in handling the vernacular;[67] while for Kriaras the appearance of the vernacular can only be due to a 'breakthrough' by writers deficient in the exacting skills of Byzantine literacy.[68] Against Beck the Jeffreys have argued that 'it seems strange . . . that men trained in the linguistic exercises of classical grammar and rhetoric should fail for some centuries to present the forms of everyday speech with any consistency'.[69] They have also taken issue with Robert Browning's proposal that the language of the *Chronicle of the Morea* may be 'the result rather of a lack of feeling for the language [on the part of a Hellenized Westerner] than of conscious effort to raise his style above that of everyday speech', preferring their own solution that the mixed forms derive from an oral-traditional *Kunstsprache*.[70]

The weakness of Beck's, Browning's and Kriaras's accounts lies in the assumption tacitly made by all three scholars of a negative *evaluation* of the mixed language of these texts. Such an evaluation, anachronistic in terms of modern linguistic methods, is the unconscious inheritance of the polemical debate about the modern Greek language which set the terms for discussion of the medieval vernacular from the late eighteenth to the early twentieth century.[71] The Jeffreys are surely right to view the alleged linguistic incompetence of the poets with suspicion, but in their objection to Beck they too have perpetuated a characteristic preoccupation of the language debate of the nineteenth and early twentieth centuries: the demand for consistency.

The Jeffreys theory of an oral-traditional *Kunstsprache* juxtaposes the antithetical conclusions of Jean Psichari and Georgios Chatzidakis at the end of the nineteenth century. The former had shown that the language of the vernacular texts evolves in the direction of modern spoken usage throughout the period, the latter that all the linguistic changes observable in the texts had in fact taken place in speech several centuries earlier. Although none of the texts is internally consistent, and all in effect mingle the spoken and literary registers, there is a consistent tendency observable in those texts whose relative chronology can be determined, and more evidently still in the manuscript tradition up until the sixteenth century, for the vernacular element progressively to displace literary and learned components of the language and sometimes also of the style.[72] This trend is readily compatible with the Jeffreys' theory of a special 'art language' which does evolve historically, but under different constraints from those governing the development of spoken usage. But the trend from a more learned and literary usage to one that is simpler and closer to spoken forms, and which increasingly adopts elements of oral folk-poetry, is surely in the wrong direction if the *origin* of this linguistic idiom is to be sought in oral tradition.[73] As time goes on the written texts come to show *more*, not fewer, spoken and oral-poetic elements. In order to posit an oral basis for this whole tradition, learned elements included, the Jeffreys have had to propose the preservation of a large number of linguistic fossils from earlier periods in the oral idiom of the thirteenth and fourteenth centuries; the validity of some of these, as we have seen, has been disputed. Given the large proportion of demonstrably literary elements of style and genre as well as of language in the original romances, elements which become progressively attenuated in the manuscript tradition and are less in evidence in later texts like the *Tale of Troy* and many of the translations, it would be more economical to suppose that the archaic linguistic elements derive from a literary rather than an oral source. My proposal is that the language of the romances and other vernacular texts is indeed a *Kunstsprache* but that its basis is literary, not oral. As Chatzidakis first proposed, it is neither more nor less than an 'artificial literary language'.[74]

This brings us back to Beck's proposal, which seems so far as it goes the most plausible yet advanced: that the initiative for exploiting the vernacular in the fourteenth century came 'from above' and was followed in the fifteenth century by a period of popularization. This view is entirely consistent with the likely literary consequences of the breakdown of political institutions in the Greek-speaking world, both Byzantine and Latin, after the late fourteenth century. The linguistic inconsistency of this literary language does not have to be explained by resource to oral tradition. As Beck himself argues, for writers trained in the learned tradition 'there was no stylistic example, no consistent usage and no recognised master'.[75] One need only think of the slow progress towards a written standard (and often even slower progress towards a standard orthography) of the Western vernaculars to appreciate the problems which such writers faced. In particular, they were no longer, like Prodromos and Glykas in the twelfth century, using the vernacular for the purpose of pastiche. Learning to write in the vernacular is a very different matter from simply speaking in it; and if one were to learn to write *Greek*, whether one lived at Constantinople or in the service of the Villehouardin dynasty of the Peloponnese, there was only one way to do it. As Browning has observed, 'in learning to read and write a man was exposed to the classical tradition'.[76] Since the only kind of Greek that existed on the page was a form of the ancient, learned language, nobody who set out systematically to transfer the vernacular to a written medium could ignore the precedents, the linguistic forms and the clichés of literary usage.

Far from representing the 'written remains' of a once flourishing, and by implication also more lively, oral tradition, the language of the romances is more probably the product of a conscious effort on the part of successive writers to forge a new literary idiom out of the disparate elements available to Greek-speakers at the end of the Middle Ages. The inconsistencies for which their texts have so frequently been, from different points of view, condemned, is proof merely of the magnitude of the task that faced these writers and of the heterogeneous nature of the resources available to them. That they failed to create a stable and enduring literary register in modern Greek, while the parallel endeavours of a Chrétien, a Dante or a Chaucer in the West have been crowned with the acclaim of scholars in our time crediting them with the creation of a national language, is purely a matter of history.

The initiative in the development of *written* (as opposed to spoken) modern Greek had already passed by the end of the fourteenth century to the Venetian colony of Crete, where a similar process, but based this time on the dialect of the region, continued without interruption until the mid-seventeenth century. The language of the plays of Chortatses and the Renaissance-influenced romance *Erotokritos* is still to a degree a mixture of learned and popular elements; in all these texts linguistic archaisms co-exist with formulaic expressions, and imagery derived from the oral tradition; but in these texts the process of integration begun by Andronikos Palaiologos, and before him by the anonymous author of the original *Digenes Akrites*, was brought a stage further to create a literary vehicle whose full subtlety, complexity and range have only recently been recognized.[77] The extent to which the Cretan tradition drew on the medieval romances will be touched upon in the next chapter.

CONCLUSION

The results of the somewhat involved, interlocking arguments of this chapter can now be briefly summarized. Certain close connections between specific pairs of texts can be accounted for in terms of direct literary borrowing or even deliberate allusion; in a number of other instances the intervention of scribes in repeating lines or expressions from one text to another, and also in making minor 'improvements' to their texts, is beyond doubt. Spadaro's theory has been endorsed to the extent that it proposes a literary rather than an oral cause for the frequent interrelations among the romances and other texts, but his theory of 'plagiarism' is insufficient to account for a wider and more systematic network of relations than his method reveals. In this respect the Jeffreys' more conceptually sophisticated explanation has been followed. However, the Jeffreys exaggerate the significance of *oral* factors as the basis for the *traditional* elements found in the romances. Instead, these elements are due to the conscious attempt, by writers well versed in twelfth-century Greek and some Western medieval secular literature, to create a fictional tradition in their own language. Such a tradition would have been seen simultaneously as a legitimate offspring of Byzantine and ancient fiction on the one hand, and, on the other, as a counterpart to the vernacular fiction that had already developed in the West. Formulaic characteristics of the romances are to be accounted for by the appeal of an emergent literary tradition to the 'authority' of previous Greek poetry in the vernacular, that is, of oral poetry.

The precise extent of the dependence of vernacular literature upon the precedent of oral poetry cannot be determined fully, as we have little direct evidence for the kind of oral poetry that flourished in Greek in the fourteenth and fifteenth centuries. While this dependence may well have been greater than I have been suggesting (for the sake of clarity in developing the argument), it is not, according to this view, essential to assume that the oral resources available to the writers of the romance were profoundly different in character and scope from the oral poetry recorded in Greek in more recent times. The repetitive elements that link one romance text with another result from the way in which writers learnt their craft, which certainly involved reading, and very probably also copying, of manuscripts in the same tradition; there is a precedent for this in the close interrelations which link the twelfth-century romances with one another and with those of Hellenistic times. The roles of author/translator and of copyist are not clearly differentiated, so that copying a text involves a greater or lesser degree of rewriting, while writing or even translating a text of one's own comes to involve a degree of copying from other texts of the same kind.

Finally, the mixed language or register which is characteristic of these texts is explained by the attempt of a succession of writers – in the beginning at least, of educated background – to create a new medium that would be at once literary and vernacular. The inconsistencies of the texts as transmitted are due to historical factors which prevented this development from reaching its logical conclusion, as a parallel and later development did in Crete in the seventeenth century. The most radical component of the view expressed here and throughout much of the rest of this book is the belief that the writers of vernacular romances were not talentless imitators using whatever meagre expressive means were to hand, as both the Jeffreys and Spadaro have proposed, but were fully conscious craftsmen working with means and towards objectives not easily recognized by us today.

12

RECEPTION

We have seen that the authors and translators of the Palaiologan romances were fully literate, self-conscious craftsmen. The previous two chapters have situated the texts of this period in relation, first, to those of their predecessors in the genre and, second, to one another and to what can be inferred about contemporary oral tradition. The focus of this chapter will be on the impact of the Palaiologan romances on other Greek literature of their time and subsequently.[1]

The impact of the vernacular romances on other kinds of writing up to and beyond the fall of Constantinople has been little considered, except to a small degree in studies of the Cretan literature that was produced in the wake of the Italian Renaissance.

In the sections that follow I shall be considering only narrative writing. The absence of the love-lyric from Byzantine literature is well known. Love-poetry in the vernacular did, however, flourish, mainly in the Aegean archipelago, for a brief period between the mid-fifteenth and the mid-sixteenth century. These poems have generally been assumed to be either of popular or of Western inspiration, but it is worth noting that they flourished during precisely the brief period when most of the surviving copies of the romances were made, and disappeared at the same time as manuscript copying of these texts also ceased. Much work remains to be done to establish the literary context for these poems before the possible contribution of the romances to their development can be properly assessed.

The miscellany of vernacular love-poetry published by Pernot from a manuscript of the sixteenth century and the so-called 'Alphabet of Love' are generally taken to be of popular inspiration, although the use of rhyme shows a connection with the literary experiments undertaken in Crete and Cyprus by writers aware of Italian poetry of the Renaissance.[2] Seven brief love-lyrics, attributed in a late fifteenth-century manuscript to Theodore Prodromos, are probably not much older.[3] The last of this group is syntactically in the form of a single conditional period, of which the protasis takes up the first ten lines, and the apodosis the remaining five. This (unrhymed) poem almost certainly represents the first surviving attempt by a Greek poet to translate, paraphrase or imitate a sonnet. A rare group of original love-lyrics in the learned language, but in the fifteen-syllable metre of the romances and other vernacular poems of the period, is also known from the turn of the fifteenth century.[4] Finally, a set of highly sophisticated love-poems in the Cypriot dialect, composed around the middle of the sixteenth century, consists of translations and imitations of minor Italian poets who wrote after the manner of Petrarch.[5]

Byzantine court poetry

There are two texts in the learned language emanating from the court at Constantinople which engage directly with the vernacular romances that have come down to us. Both have been mentioned previously in connection with the date and authorship of *Kallimachos and Chrysorrhoe* and with the dating of both *Belthandros* and *Libistros*. The first is the 'Epigram on a Book of Love [written] by the Emperor's Cousin' by Manuel Philes.[6] The epigram is in the form of a recommendation of the book to a young, noble addressee.[7] From the summary it gives of the main points of the plot,[8] there can be no doubt that the 'book of love' in question is *Kallimachos and Chrysorrhoe*. The small discrepancies between Philes' résumé and the romance as we know it might possibly be due to the transmission of the text of the latter, but Philes is selective in choosing those elements of the plot that will sustain his allegorical reading,[9] and it was probably in this spirit that he added lion-slaying to the hero's list of accomplishments.[10]

The epigram offers a reading of the romance as moral allegory. The real purpose of the text, in Philes' reading, is edification, although superficially it deals with love.[11] The father with whom the story of Kallimachos begins is the heavenly Father, the test to see who will inherit the kingdom an allegory for the trials of earthly life, especially the temptations of the flesh, which according to Philes are to be avoided.[12] The ogre is linked to Satan and also (presumably through his treatment of Chrysorrhoe) to rampant sexuality.[13] The ring given to the hero by his brothers (Philes seems to imply rather that it came direct from the father) is the token of betrothal to the 'spirit';[14] the union of soul and body (or of mortal man to the realm of the spirit), of which the ring is the harbinger, is put at risk by 'pleasure-seeking urges';[15] and the loss of Chrysorrhoe through the machinations of the hostile king in the romance is attributed here to the hero's haste in succumbing to the pleasures of the flesh.[16] The heroine is a symbol when present of temptation, when absent of 'salvation'.[17] Deprived of salvation, the didactic allegory continues, one should efface and humble oneself in black robes until the ring, 'divine grace',[18] affords the means of reunion with one's 'mate',[19] by which the soul is meant. In this way a return to one's 'good homeland of incorruptibility', i.e. Paradise, can be effected.[20] Philes finally returns to extended admiration for the skill of the author in mingling the pleasurable with the edifying in his tale, and in representing so much of human life in his narrative,[21] and concludes by naming this exemplary individual as Andronikos Palaiologos, cousin to the reigning emperor.

By modern standards of critical exegesis this reading is considerably flawed, and indeed Philes' activity as a reader has not been taken very seriously by modern commentators. Börje Knös, who has given more careful attention to this text than anyone, does not rate it highly as literary criticism:

> Philes' summary is very faulty, fragmentary and incoherent, and the omissions that he has made here [sc. in the summary] and in his interpretation of the book in question are even more marked.[22]

Beck has suggested, quite plausibly, that this allegorical résumé was meant as a kind of respectable 'alibi' for a risqué secular author, whom Philes was implicitly defending from allegations of profanity.[23] Certainly Philes seems somewhat wilful in the contradictory values he assigns to the hero's love for the heroine in his reading; and there is nothing in the text of this, or indeed of any of the other romances of this period, to support his assumption that the turn of fate that separates the lovers is the *moral* consequence of their intemperate love-making. Many of the romances do, however, begin or end with an address to their public which invokes the *dulce et utile* formula that is also the starting-point for Philes' allegorical reading of this one.[24] Nor should we forget that romances in Greek had been read allegorically since at least early Christian times, or that the rise of the genre in the West has been linked to the practice of biblical exegesis by means of allegory. However implausible Philes' reading may appear as a total interpretation of the text in all its aspects, it has considerable historical importance as the earliest recorded reading of such a text *which belongs to the same milieu as the text itself.*

There are even indications that the possibility of a reading on this level was envisaged by the author and built into the text. The romance ends in a way that conflicts with the pagan setting consistently used in the story up to that point. The lovers return after their ordeal to the Ogre's Castle:

> Ἰδοὺ καὶ τοῦτο φθάνουσιν, καὶ πάλιν εὐφροσύνης
> ἀρρήτου καὶ γλυκύτητος μόνοι κατατρυφῶσιν
> καὶ μὲ χαρίτων τοῦ Θεοῦ, αὐτοῦ τοῦ λυτρωτοῦ μας,
> εὑρέθησαν εἰς τὴν χαρὰν καὶ τὸ καλὸν τὸ πρῶτον,
> ἀπαλλαχθέντες τοῦ κακοῦ καὶ τῆς πικρᾶς ὀδύνης.[25]

> And lo they reached the place, and once again of happiness
> passing words, and sweetness take their fill alone.
> and by the graces [sic] of our Lord, of Him our Saviour,
> they were restored to their first happiness and good,
> set free from evil and from bitter pain.

Although it should be noted that Kallimachos does not in fact return to inherit his father's kingdom, preferring to take Chrysorrhoe back to the scene of their first love, this return is depicted in terms of redemption in a religious and now specifically Christian sense that seems to presage the interpretation given to it by Philes. In the context of the romance as a whole this ending seems not so much an anachronism or narrative inconsistency as a carefully placed bridge back from the remote world of the story to the spiritual concerns of the world in which that story is told. Indeed the use of the plural 'graces', which belongs to the language of love, in the context of divine 'grace', is risqué but by no means blasphemous. It subtly implies a movement from the erotic 'graces' of the secular entertainment now drawing to a close to the more serious concerns, assumed to be shared by author and audience alike, with the 'grace of God'.[26] It may be that Philes as an actual reader of this romance does greater, if admittedly partial, justice to his subject, in terms of a reader's expectations in the fourteenth century, than is immediately apparent today.

The work entitled *Verses of Meliteniotes: To Chastity* is *sui generis* in Byzantine literature.[27] Indeed it has even slipped through the net of the comprehensive Byzantinische Handbuch series of histories of Byzantine literature, seemingly failing to qualify either as theological or as profane, nor yet, although it gets a brief mention, as belonging to the vernacular.[28] The verses, 3,062 of them, are written in the fifteen-syllable metre of the romances and other vernacular narratives, but in the 'middle' language register, although with many allusions to the linguistic style of the romance, notably in the coinage of new compound words after the vernacular fashion. Commonly described as a 'moral allegory',[29] its unique mixture of the didactic and the encyclopedic with topoi drawn from the romances, in which a surprising number of Western elements are grafted in an entirely new way on to Byzantine stock, is well analysed by Cupane.[30] Considered as a reading of at least three vernacular romances which are also known to us, however, this work is better understood as parody.[31]

In its structure the poem amounts to a recondite form of literary striptease. A prologue, whose polemical content has been generally noticed but not its comical style and allusions, attacks the falsehood of fictional entertainment and promises pure truth instead. What follows is not, of course, 'truth' at all but fiction, a fiction which both depends upon and inverts the conventions of the romance. The main body of the text consists of a prodigious series of *ekphraseis*, in the course of which veil after veil is stripped away from the elaborate outworks surrounding the beautiful, and by definition untouchable, heroine: Chastity. Although she is introduced into the narrative early on to act as the hero's Beatrice in guiding him through the perils and marvels of her castle, the formal *ekphrasis* of the girl is saved until last,[32] to be followed only by her allegorical exegesis of all that the hero–narrator has seen,[33] and the prayer of the latter with which the work ends.[34]

192

The prologue inveighs against all literature of entertainment on the traditional grounds that fables (μῦθοι) are untrue. The only examples named are the fables of Aesop and the eleventh-century Greek translation of the Arabic *Kalilah va Dimnah: Stephanites and Ichnelates*.[35] Since both the main target and the principal vehicle for the parody which follows will turn out to be the romances, both Byzantine and Western, written between the twelfth and the fourteenth century, this is valuable evidence for the generic affiliations of the romance that were recognized at this time. The comic tone of this prologue is revealed in two ways: first by the gross catachresis of the device, traditional to the vernacular romances, of coining new and improbable compound words, especially on favourite roots like ἔρως (love) and πόθος (desire). Meliteniotes in the thirty-one lines of his prologue produces no fewer than seven compounds of the roots μῦθος (fable) and ψευδο- (false), two of which occur twice,[36] while simple words derived from these roots occur a further nine times. Elsewhere in *To Chastity* the same device is extensively and obviously parodied in the creation of compounds which are meaningless or absurd.[37]

The other indication in the prologue that its invective is partly comic in intent consists of its allusions to the comical begging poems in the vernacular attributed to Theodore Prodromos, which represent some of the earliest uses of the spoken language at the Byzantine court. Meliteniotes' versified subtitle

> Ἐρωτικὴ διήγησις, ἀλλά σωφρονεστάτη,
> μέτρον τι καθηδύνουσα τοὺς ἐραστάς τῶν λόγων.[38]

> A tale of love, but most modest/chaste [a pun on the title]
> gratifying in verse/with moderation lovers of tales.

seems to be modelled on Prodromos' playful introduction of his vernacular verses to the emperor:

> Τί σοι προσοίσω, δέσποτα ...
> εἰ μή τινας πολιτικοὺς ἀμέτρους πάλιν στίχους,
> συνεσταλμένους, παίζοντας, ἀλλ᾽ οὐκ ἀναισχυντῶντας,
> παίζουσι γὰρ καὶ γέροντες, ἀλλὰ σωφρονεστέρως.[39]

> What can I offer you, master ...
> if not once more some immoderate/unmetrical everyday verses,
> restrained, playful, but not disgusting,
> for old men may play, but in a more modest/chaste way.

And the disclaimer that what follows is no fable but the pure truth had also appeared in two others of these poems in words very similar to those used by Meliteniotes; and there, too, in order to introduce stories which are no less fictional in themselves, albeit told for a serious purpose.[40] The lines also have a more distant affinity with a similar disclaimer in another twelfth-century text, the E version of *Digenes Akrites*.[41]

A parodic intention will also account for some of the incongruities noted by Cupane which arise from the apparently indiscriminate juxtaposition of different kinds of sources.[42] Of the vernacular Greek romances these include *Kallimachos, Belthandros* and *Libistros*. *Kallimachos* is alluded to in the description of the dragon's heads with hideous faces which decorate the columns in the heroine's four-story 'chamber'[43] and of its painted roof on which the stars and planets are depicted as figures of pagan mythology;[44] *Belthandros* in the account of the first of seven obstacles the hero has to pass before he can enter the castle. This is a river in which Eros bathes naked with the flaming torch that is part of his Hellenistic accoutrements:

ποτὲ μὲν τούτοις κολυμβῶν καὶ πρὸς τὸ βάθος δύων,
ποτὲ δὲ τρέχων ἄνωθεν ὥσπερ αἰθεροδρόμος.
καὶ πυρακτῶν τὸν ποταμὸν καὶ καίων καὶ φλογίζων.[45]

now swimming and diving to the bottom,
now rising to the top like one floating in the upper air,
and setting the river on fire and burning and making it fiery.

The description is clearly indebted to the account of the fiery river in the romance. Finally, specific allusions to *Libistros* can be seen in the use of a first-person narrative, and in the supernatural device of the flying horse with which the girl assists the hero to cross the moat into her castle.[46] A less specific allusion to this group of romances can be seen in the description of Eros as an emperor holding sway over the entire natural world.[47] Here the shift from the boy deity of the Hellenistic romances to the king/emperor of the fourteenth-century romances is fully allowed for, although many of the older traditional attributes of Eros remain in Meliteniotes' description.

But beyond these parodic echoes of targets which were obviously close at hand, the range of Melieniotes' allusions is truly remarkable for a Byzantine author of the late fourteenth century. References have been detected in *To Chastity* to Achilles Tatios, Eustathios Makrembolites, *Digenes Akrites*, the thirteenth-century historian Niketas Choniates, the Greek bestiary (*Physiologos*) and Athenaios among Greek authors, but also to Pliny, whose *Natural History* provides the source for a lengthy digression on precious stones, and to Western secular writing including the *Roman de la Rose*, Boccaccio's *Amorosa visione* and some Western 'visionary' literature including Dante's *Commedia*.[48] Cupane is surely right to see these allusions as evidence for a more general assimilation of Western literature of these types, rather than as imitations of specific texts,[49] but it is of considerable significance that so much secular and vernacular literature from the West was known at all in

RECEPTION

Constantinople at this time. The extent of Meliteniotes' overt use of such sources greatly strengthens the argument proposed in Chapter 10, that the Constantinopolitan writers of romance, whose work he parodies, were more steeped in the comparable literature of the West than they overtly confess. But it also raises an important point about the way in which the Greek romances were read: not just alongside older Greek fictions like those of Aesop or the translated *Stephanites*, but in close relation to works in Latin, French and Italian which are either secular or use a naturalistic narrative style for the purposes of religious allegory.

This in turn raises the question of Meliteniotes' hostility to the romance. The author of this text is surprisingly well read in a type of literature he affects to despise, and he has gone to considerable lengths both to emulate and even to outdo some of its most characteristic effects. The 'assimilation and adaptation' that, according to Cupane, he has applied to bring Western literary trends within the Byzantine fold, could be extended to his treatment of the whole genre of the romance. The serious purpose of Meliteniotes' parody is not so much to debunk the romance, or indeed the related Western literature of which his audience must be assumed to have had some knowledge, as to edge its writing and interpretation further in the direction hinted at by Andronikos Palaiologos at the end of *Kallimachos* and developed by Philes in his epigram, towards spiritual allegory. Such a role little befits the most commonly presumed author of the poem, Theodore Meliteniotes, a writer on astronomy and of large-scale religious works, who was moreover dogmatically anti-Latin.[50] More plausible is the suggestion of Erich Trapp that the author of *To Chastity* is to be identified with a contemporary of the same family, Demetrios Meliteniotes, who is mentioned as belonging to the imperial household in 1370.[51] This identification of the author does not significantly revise Dölger's date for the composition of the work, between 1355 and 1395, although it very slightly increases the probability of an earlier rather than a later date within that span.[52]

Narrative poetry in related genres

Further testimony to the reading of romances by writers in other genres, not necessarily linked to Byzantine court circles, can be found in a range of texts from the late fourteenth to the late fifteenth century. The earliest of these, and also the closest in manner to the allegorizing court poetry just discussed, is the anonymous *Consolation concerning Ill Fortune and Good Fortune*.[53] The older of the two manuscripts in which the text has been transmitted has recently been dated convincingly, on the basis of watermarks, to the period 1354–74,[54] which makes the poem at least as old as the parody by Meliteniotes. Indeed the inclusion in the manuscript of an epilogue by the copyist, which alludes clearly to the topoi of the contemporary romance, provides important confirmation for the dating of the original romances

195

proposed here.[55] This vernacular narrative of a little over 700 lines contains nothing of Meliteniotes' humour or extravagance. The poem begins with a prologue of the 'come all ye' type, promising an edifying tale, told to the author–narrator by an 'unfortunate', about how ill fortune turned to good. The second-level narrative which follows is told, like that of *Libistros* and *To Chastity*, in the first person. The unnamed unfortunate has been so dogged by ill fortune that he decides to set out and seek the Castle of Ill Fortune from which his troubles have emanated. On the way he meets the personified figure of Time, who is unhelpful; an old woman in the service of the Queen of Ill Fortune, who is a little more encouraging; and finally the beautiful daughter of the Queen of Good Fortune, who has good news for him. He then visits three castles in turn: the octagonal castle of Time, who is given the imperial title (βασιλεύς) but is in fact a vassal, and the castles of his twin overlords, the sister queens of Ill and Good Fortune. All three castles are described in turn. A letter from Time, interceding on the narrator's behalf, persuades the aged, black-clad but not ill-favoured Queen of Ill Fortune to release him.[56] His reception by her beautiful sister, Good Fortune, is tinged with the bureaucratic, as he has first to produce his discharge papers from his former patroness and is almost summoned back again over a procedural impropriety.[57] The text ends with the author drawing attention to the tale's moral and, in the Leipzig version, with an apparent addition by the scribe, who refers to the whole text, in terms drawn from the romances, as a 'fable of love' (μῦθος ἔρωτος).[58]

Perhaps the most interesting connection with the romance here is the folk-tale beginning of this poem, with the unfortunate setting out to seek the source of his ill fortune,[59] which recalls the similar use of folkloric material in *Kallimachos*. Beyond that the text seems merely to confirm the esteem in which the romances, with their conventions of allegorical castles, beautiful heroines and extended *ekphraseis*, were held at the time when this poem was written. Its relative lack of sophistication or reference to a comparable range of sources when compared to Meliteniotes' poem incline one to believe that it may have been addressed to a less sophisticated audience, and this impression is confirmed by its straightforward didacticism, more reminiscent of that found in the later *Tale of Troy*, *Belisarios* and the interpolated ending of the *Tale of Achilles* than of the recondite pleasures invoked by Philes and Meliteniotes.

Narratives in a more 'heroic' vein are also clearly influenced by the romance: its verseform, and some elements of its language, are adopted in a retelling, in over 6,000 lines, of the popular Alexander story dated fairly reliably to 1388.[60] Unlike most of the romances, however, this text seems to have been little read and was apparently unknown to the author of the much more influential rhymed version printed in Venice in 1529.[61]

A more revealing case is provided by the *Tale of Belisarios*.[62] This much-fictionalized story of Justinian's general in the sixth century (who in the *Tale* is made to wage successful military campaigns against England and Persia), is presented in the form of a warning of the political and personal dangers of envy (φθόνος) and a diatribe against the sycophantic nobility who brought about the downfall of the incomparable hero. As such it has no intrinsic connection with the romance. However, in the several forms in which it has come down to us (the poem's most recent editors have identified four distinct redactions), its language and style are heavily influenced by the *Tale of Achilles* and *Imperios*, and one redaction at least concludes with a statement identifying its intended audience, which is almost identical to that contained in the *Tale of Troy*.[63] If the editors are right in identifying three layers of accretion behind all four versions, going back to the decade of the 1390s then probably all the points of contact with the romances would have come about through the activity of later scribes and redactors.[64] Right from its inception, though, this tale must have had a strongly populist cast, and it draws, like the late *Tale of Troy*, on mainly twelfth-century 'middlebrow' sources.[65] The fact that such sources are used by a writer who, in at least one version, is deliberately 'writing down' to a popular audience confirms Van Gemert's intuition that the nucleus of the poem is literary rather than oral, but also raises the possibility that even the original version belongs to a popularizing movement which may have gained momentum in the fifteenth century. It is certainly interesting that the four detectable redactions were all made within a small number of years after 1453, while we have no independent evidence for the existence of the poem before that date.

Another text to have undergone a new redaction at this time is *Digenes Akrites*. The version of this poem now known as 'Z' is a fifteenth-century compilation of two older manuscripts, one in all probability the Escorial (E) manuscript that we now possess, the other closely related to the Grotta-ferrata (G) version.[66] Michael Jeffreys has successfully proved that the opening section of this 'Z' version, to which our oldest witness is the Athens manuscript of the poem,[67] was the invention of the fifteenth-century compiler, and has shown in some detail how he must have gone about his task.[68] Essentially the compiler has supplied the text with a beginning by duplicating incidents already there. The situation that he had to lead up to, in which the brothers of the girl who will later become the hero's mother are engaged in combat with her abductor, the emir, he has assumed was similar to that which leads up to Digenes' abduction of his own bride later in the story. So the hero's mother, like his bride, is shut away from the eyes of the world in a secluded chamber (κουβούκλιον). But in elaborating this theme into the 279 lines that make up the first book of the 'Z' version, he has had copious recourse to narrative topoi that are foreign to *Digenes*, but belong instead to the vernacular romances of his own day.

The longing of the parents, who already have five sons, for a daughter is a variation of the more familiar topos of parents who long for a son, found in the *Tale of Achilles*, *Phlorios* and *Imperios*.[69] The chain of events which follows is inaugurated by a prophecy of all that does indeed happen to the girl down to her marriage to the emir, but her father is advised to prevent this by sealing her up in a splendid palace.[70] The closest parallel to this in the romances is to be found in the *Tale of Troy*, which begins with the prophecy that Paris will bring destruction to his city and includes, among several failed expedients to avert this, his seclusion in a specially built and highly ornate castle.[71] The prophecy of future events in the story is paralleled in *Belthandros* and *Libistros* and perhaps goes back to Xenophon's *Ephesiaka*. The splendours of the girl's palace are directly inspired by the *ekphraseis* of Digenes' own palace later in the text, but in points of detail, and particularly in the intrusion of compound coinages characteristic of the fourteenth-century romance, it comes closer to the world of *Libistros*.[72]

The description of the girl herself at the age of 12 owes much to similar *ekphraseis* in all the romances, but especially to that in the *Tale of Achilles*.[73] It is also more appropriate to the conventions of the romance genre than to the supposed purpose for which the palace has been built, that it should be decorated with paintings of Eros.[74] Just as in *Hysmine and Hysminias*, the king of love duly appears in person in a dream.[75] In the same vein is the girl's formal submission before the painting of Eros.[76] The book ends with a renewed *ekphrasis* of the girl, which turns into something very like a folk-song in rhymed eight-syllable trochaic couplets.[77] Although the intention in writing this book was clearly to pave the way for the beginning of the text proper as he had it before him, the compiler was still faced with a difficult job, in the first forty-three lines of his second book, to effect the transition. The girl's abduction takes place on a picnic, in circumstances which blatantly conflict with the seclusion earlier described, and the emir who will abduct her is only perfunctorily introduced,[78] until with an almost audible sigh of relief the compiler reaches the first line of the E manuscript, in the middle of a speech of exhortation to the girl's brothers to recapture her, which he has wrongly guessed is to be attributed to the mother.[79]

Michael Jeffreys is perhaps rather hard on this compiler in describing him, after a hint by Grégoire, as a 'forger' and his work as a 'rather miserable piece of literature'.[80] But he has been the first to discuss it as a distinct piece of literature at all. Its level of expertise, and the motives of its author, may be compared to those of the probably contemporary *Tale of Troy*. The compiler's stated aim is to write down *everything* that is known of the adventures of Digenes, and he addresses (in an opening formula derived from the much-copied 'advice to a young man' known as 'Spaneas') a youthful reader who does not apparently have access to the older texts himself.[81] This policy is confirmed in practice by his habit of placing the variant readings of his sources consecutively whenever he possibly can. This state of affairs has several interesting consequences. First, it helps explain why so many of our manuscript copies of the romances date from the hundred years after the fall of Constantinople: the manuscripts of *Digenes* available to the compiler at that time were no more numerous nor much better than those we possess today. (In one respect they were inferior, in that neither contained the beginning of the poem.) But a demand existed, the compiler tells us, among a public not especially educated, to preserve these stories. Second, the activity in which this 'forger' has been detected gives the strongest proof yet of the overlap in function between authors and copyists: a copyist finding a lacuna in the text before him apparently sees nothing unusual, still less reprehensible, in filling it with a composition of his own. And, third, the strong infusion of language and topoi from the vernacular romances into this fifteenth-century prologue to the tale of Digenes shows to what extent that genre had become standard fare for copyists, and presumably also for readers and audiences, of any vernacular Greek literature at this date.

Cretan Renaissance literature

The 'common' mixed language and the verseform of the unrhymed fifteen-syllable line that unite all the texts so far discussed in this period were eventually superseded by a developing literary idiom based on the dialect of Crete, and a variety of verseforms among which the fifteen-syllable line remained predominant, but now with the obligatory addition of rhyme. Traces also remain of parallel developments in Rhodes[82] and Cyprus[83] up to the time of these islands' capture by the Ottomans in 1522 and 1571 respectively. In the late sixteenth century and until the Turkish conquest of the island was completed in 1669, Crete under Venetian rule was the only sizeable outpost of Greek speakers not under Ottoman control. The literary tradition based on the Cretan dialect seems to have reached its peak around the turn of the seventeenth century, with the dramas after the style of Italian Mannerism by Georgios Chortatses and (probably) the romance *Erotokritos*. A marked decline sets in after the 1630s, or perhaps a little earlier.[84] Much of this literature, when it became the object of enthusiastic scholarly attention at the turn of the twentieth century, was at first seen as an offshoot of popular folk-poetry. Although it has been recognized for some time that these works are in fact part of a literary tradition with close links to Renaissance and post-Renaissance writing in Italy, the full literary sophistication of Chortatses' plays and Kornaros' romance *Erotokritos*, and the direct involvement of their authors with the literary and scholarly pursuits of the ruling Venetians, are only now being given their due.[85] A consequence of this welcome revision, however, is that much less attention has been given recently to links between this literature and earlier vernacular writing in Greek. This is not the place to do more than touch upon this large question. But it is appropriate that this book should end by looking at the legacy of the medieval Greek romance to the literary tradition of Crete that outlived it.

The Cretan tradition overlaps historically with that of the romances and other literature in the 'common' literary vernacular to a greater extent than used to be realized. The writing career of Stephanos Sachlikes, the first known poet to introduce the Cretan dialect into his language, and rhyme into his verseform, has now been dated to the second half of the fourteenth century.[86] The satirical and didactic autobiographic poems of Sachlikes introduce a new kind of comic gusto into Greek literature, particularly in their extravagant accounts of the real and fantastic activities of the whores of Candia, of the narrator's own ill-advised dealings with them, and the crude realities of prison to which they brought him. There is much more of the spirit of Boccaccio here than of the appeal from prison by Michael Glykas, or of the low-life comedy of the vernacular poems attributed to Prodromos, although all these twelfth-century texts need to be recognized as forerunners of Sachlikes. But for all the difference in style and outlook between Sachlikes and his contemporaries in Constantinople and the Frankish-held Peloponnese, it is worth remembering that at least three of the five original romances, and the oldest of the translated romances, were probably written during his lifetime.[87]

The evidence that Sachlikes knew any of the vernacular Greek romances is slight but worth noting. Sachlikes' *Extraordinary Tale*, a loosely connected series of short episodes, some autobiographical, some imaginary, ends with a 'Parliament of Whores', followed by a 'Tournament of Whores' and, in one of the three extant manuscripts, a parodic hymn of praise to the arch-procuress who is greater than them all.[88] The 'Parliament' and 'Tournament' have many parallels in late medieval Western literature,[89] but the female warrior had also made an earlier appearance in Greek in *Digenes*,[90] and a clear parodic echo of that poem has been noted in the beginning of the section praising the arch-procuress. Some of the names of the combatants in the tournament, which seem to be designed to add an obscene or debunking *double entendre* to the names of real people, are reminiscent in their construction of the names of romance heroes and heroines.[91] A similar effect must surely have been intended in the name of the arch-procuress, whose real-life counterpart seems to have belonged to the Giustinian family: Ποθοτσουτσουνιά (pricktease), and whose name has been derived in the same way as the many compounds of πόθος (desire) in the romances, particularly in *Libistros*.[92] The possibility that this episode also draws on the beauty contest in *Belthandros* cannot be discounted.[93]

A more sophisticated literary personality upon the Cretan scene is Marinos Falieros, a wealthy member of the Catholic ascendancy, educated in Italian and Latin, but a native speaker of the Cretan dialect of modern Greek. Born shortly before 1397 (about the time of Sachlikes' death) he had a varied and unusually well-documented career until his death in 1474. He seems to have taken up literature, as a hobby only, in early life. His five surviving poems, in rhyming, fifteen-syllable verse, were all apparently written in the decade 1420–30.[94] Two of these will concern us here: *Story and Dream* and *Love Dream*.[95]

The first of these is presented, unusually for a Greek text of this period, in dramatized form, and tells how Falieros[96] was awakened in a dream by his personal fate (Μοῖρα), who, after some badinage, persuaded him to go to the house of the girl he loves, Athousa ('flowering'): his fate has arranged for him a night of bliss. The greater part of the text is taken up with a dialogue between Falieros and the girl through her barred window, with his 'fate' and the personified 'desire' (ποθούλα) interceding on his behalf. His pleas range from the florid to the coarsely impatient. At last the girl makes him swear an oath of fidelity (marriage is not mentioned), and the poem ends with the dreamer's frustration as at the crucial moment he is bitten by a flea and wakes. This dream occupies 758 lines.

The second is much shorter, at only 130 lines, some of which the poems' editor believes have been interpolated under the influence of the previous poem. The form here is conventional narrative, in contrast to the dramatized speeches of narrator and characters in *Story and Dream*. The narrator is visited in his sleep by a girl whose advances he had rejected, but she has with her an armed escort in the form of a boy Cupid, an emissary of Eros, the awesome king of love. As these two debate which part of his anatomy ought to receive the Cupid's arrow, the terrified dreamer (still in his dream) awakes and agrees to give in gracefully. The Cupid then tells how the girl had come with her complaint to the Empire of Love ('Ερωτοκρατία) and enlisted the support of its ruler, the First Eros (ὁ Πρῶτος "Ερωτας). As he is about to obey Eros' command and make love to the girl the cock crows and the dreamer awakes disappointed. The two poems are thus complementary, the fictional situations they describe being opposite to one another. In *Story and Dream* it is the narrator who is in love and enlists the support of mythological helpers to gain his ends, while in *Love Dream* it is the girl who has been rejected and has recourse to the mythological Empire of Love.

In his meticulous introduction to these poems, Arnold van Gemert has concentrated most of his attention on finding Western precedents for Falieros' work, the most interesting of which, he is obliged to admit, come from Holland and northern Germany and are unlikely to have had any direct bearing on the creation of these poems.[97] While acknowledging that Falieros' literary dreams must have some connection with the corresponding episodes of *Hysmine and Hysminias* and *Libistros and Rhodamne*, he places the emphasis on the radical departure from the medieval Greek conventions signalled by these poems: 'the atmosphere is no longer chivalric, the chivalric vocabulary is still used for the personification [of Eros] . . ., but the world has changed. The personification no longer inspires terror or awe, but has been demythologised'.[98] Important though this change is, the originality and the nature of Falieros' poems can be better appreciated through recognizing them for what they are: parodic readings of *Hysmine*, *Libistros* and also *Belthandros*, by a Greek writer whose education belonged to the thought-world of the Renaissance.

This dependence seems to have been recognized by manuscript copyists working about a century after the poems were written. Of the three early sixteenth-century manuscripts which contain the poems, one is the notorious Naples manuscript that also includes the *Tale of Achilles*, *Belisarios* and *Imperios*, although Falieros' poems were bound into it some decades after the copying of these texts; while another includes the twelfth-century romance *Hysmine and Hysminias*, with which Falieros' love-dreams have most in common.[99] The most significant resemblance to the romances lies in the teasing nature of the whole text: the build-up to sexual gratification described culminates at the most risqué moment in the dreamer's awakening and frustration. Such dreams seem to have been discussed outside fiction in the twelfth century, and probably the earliest literary one is to be found in the corpus of ceremonial 'begging' poetry addressed to the emperor Manuel I, possibly by Prodromos, probably in the 1150s.[100] The famous dream in which Hysminias, now more than reconciled to Hysmine's love, has his way with her in a garden has been well described by Margaret Alexiou. Hysminias, however, is not baulked of his desire by awaking.[101] Libistros, in a similar situation, is awakened by the strength of his passion and, like Shakespeare's Caliban, 'cries to dream again'.[102]

The whole situation of Falieros' second poem, in which Eros threatens to punish the narrator's rejection of the girl, is taken direct from Hysminias' *first* dream in Makrembolites' romance. There, after the hero has rather rudely rejected the heroine's advances over dinner, he dreams that Eros with all his royal train sweeps into his bedroom and denounces him 'for bringing shame on my friend [/client?] Hysmine'.[103] The unusual narrative device, common to both Falieros' poems, whereby the dreamer is awakened by a supernatural visitant *within* his dream, is most likely to have had its origin in the third of the hero's dreams in *Libistros*, in which he dreamt that Eros woke him to urge haste in his suit to Rhodamne.[104]

There are more specific allusions to the romances, too, in Falieros' love-dreams. The intervention of a personalized 'fate' to bring about the lovers' meeting in *Story and Dream* can be paralleled only in *Kallimachos and Chrysorrhoe*, where the hero's own 'fate' exerts herself to find his brothers and appears tó them in a dream to inform them of his predicament.[105] The language in which his 'fate' announces to Falieros that the hard-hearted Athousa will finally yield to him alludes directly to a striking image from Libistros' love-correspondence with Rhodamne:

ΜΟΙΡΑ: ... Πούρι ὁ σταλαγμὸς τοῦ πόθου βάρει βάρει
νὰ τρύπησε τὸ μάρμαρο, νὰ 'λυσε τὸ λιθάρι;[106]

FATE: ... Can it be that the steady dripping of desire
has worn a hole in the marble, has softened the stone?

Libistros begins a letter to Rhodamne:

Λέγουν εἰς πέτρα ἂν σταλαγμὸς συχνάσῃ νὰ σταλάζῃ,
κἂν οἷος ἔνι ὁ σταλαγμὸς καὶ οἷον τὸ λιθάριν,
ἐκ τοῦ δαρμοῦ πρὸς τὸν δαρμὸν τρυπᾶ το τὸ λιθάριν,
ἐκ τοῦ νεροῦ τὸν σταλαγμὸν τὸν ἔχει ἀπαραιτήτως.[107]

They say that if a drip drops habitually on a stone,
despite the nature of the dripping and the nature of the stone
from the beating on the beating it will pierce the stone,
from the dripping of the water it is inevitable.

The forwards-and-backwards exchange between Falieros and Athousa, with the intermediaries of personified fate and desire, has something in common with the whole lengthy exchange of letters and tokens in *Libistros* from which this passage comes. Certainly the injunction not to tarry but to act at once to gain the object of his desire, appears to be a verbal echo of advice given to Libistros in a comparable context.[108]

In the second poem, *Love Dream*, the allusions are even more evident. The girl is led into the dreamer's presence by a boy-Cupid, just as the boyish face of the grotesque composite Eros in *Libistros* was predominant in the hero's second dream, in which he meets Rhodamne for the first time.[109] A curious and uncharacteristically ferocious addition to the traditional Western attributes of this boy-Cupid is a quiver full of arrows:

ὡς ἔδειξαν μ' ἐφάνησαν νὰ ἦσαν αἱματωμένες,
ὅλες ἐξ αἵματος καρδιᾶς μ' ἐφάνησαν ὅτ' ἦσαν.[110]

as I saw them they appeared to be bloodied,
all of them, with the heart's blood, they appeared to be.

Van Gemert is at a loss to find a Western parallel for this, and also notes an unusual linguistic archaism in these lines.[111] They are probably best taken as an allusion to the description in *Belthandros* of the allegorical statue of a man wounded to the heart by an arrow of love, whose gushing blood pours out to form the fiery element of the mysterious river. Finally, in the dialogue between the Cupid and the girl it emerges that the dreamer had previously sworn allegiance to Eros, in just the manner that Hysminias, Belthandros and Libistros had all done.[112]

The whole tone of these poems is playful and urbane. Certainly the elements they draw from the romances are put to new use, even parodied. But Falieros' humour and lightness of touch are not unlike those of Makrembolites in the twelfth-century: no real awe is felt by the author/narrator in the face of the supernatural powers that wake him from sleep in Falieros' poems, but nor are we to take Hysminias' panic for the response of the author of the romance, or indeed for the one expected from the reader. Not least of the distinctive achievements of Falieros' poems is to revitalize the spirit of playful humour that is an important component of the twelfth-century romances, especially of *Hysmine and Hysminias*, but that had largely disappeared from the later romances in the vernacular. Falieros' Renaissance reading of medieval texts is probably closer to the kind of reading envisaged by Makrembolites than to that of the writers of vernacular romances; it is certainly poles apart from the readings by Philes and Meliteniotes at the Constantinopolitan court not long previously.

The extent to which any of the medieval romances were known in Crete during the 'golden age' around the turn of the seventeenth century remains extremely uncertain. It is likely that the highly individual twist given to Italian pastoral when it arrived in Crete at that time may owe something to the older Greek tradition, at least in the way that Eros is represented.[113]

Parodic allusions to *Digenes Akrites* are found in two sophisticated Cretan comedies of the seventeenth century, but by this time the allusion is as likely to be to popular balladry, in which the name 'Digenes' was already current, as to the text of the medieval 'proto-romance'.[114] But the largest unanswered question concerns the giant, in every sense, of the Greek romances, *Erotokritos*. Written by a descendant of a Venetian noble family, Vitsentzos Kornaros, between 1590 and 1610,[115] it is the only one to have gained a secure place in the estimation of modern readers, and that only really in the twentieth century. In its language, style and amplitude (it runs to just over 10,000 lines), it seems in many ways the acme of the later Greek verse romance; however, its five-part form, reminiscent of Renaissance drama, and its long speeches probing the inner workings and motives of individual characters, reveal it as very much a work of the later Renaissance. Although his principal model was the French *Paris et Vienne*, Kornaros is a Greek Tasso or Ariosto much more than he is a Greek Pierre de la Cypède.

None the less there are curious throwbacks to the earlier Greek tradition in points of detail. Such is the opening formula with which the narrative proper begins, which seems distantly related to the opening formulae we noted in many of the medieval romances in Chapter 11:

Στοὺς περαζόμενους καιροὺς ποὺ οἱ Ἕλληνες ὁρίζα . . .
Ρήγας μεγάλος ὅριζε τὴν ἄξα χώρα ἐκείνη
μ' ἄλλες πολλές, κ' εἰς ἀντρειὲς ἐξακουστὸς ἐγίνη·[116]

In times long past when the [pagan] Hellenes ruled . . .
there ruled a king over that fine land [*sc.* Athens]
and many others too, and for his deeds of valour came to be renowned . . .

Then, as has often been noted, there is the introductory theme of the childlessness of the royal couple which Kornaros has added to his source. Elements of the plot such as the hero playing music outside the palace where the heroine lives, the tournament which takes up much of Book II, the secret exchanges of rings in Book III, and the hero's return in disguise in Book IV, can all be paralleled in the earlier romances, but none is unique to that tradition. More revealing perhaps is the pagan setting in which the characters worship only the sun and moon as gods,[117] and the seemingly artful creation of a composite historical world of the Greek East. As the poem's most recent editor puts it:

> With the anachronisms, omissions and the appropriate use of a variety
> of literary themes, Kornaros aimed to create a composite mythical and
> poetical world, placed in the environment of Greece, a world created
> out of elements selected for the purpose and with full awareness of
> different historical periods .... In this way was created an ideal world
> of the Greek East, corresponding to that which Kornaros had come to
> know in the world of Ariosto.[118]

Just such an amalgam of historical epochs with a geographical centre of the eastern Mediterranean seems to have been pursued by all the writers of vernacular romances in the later Middle Ages; and they too, as we saw, attempted a similar integration of Western literary precedents within their own geographical and cultural sphere. But perhaps most tantalizing of all is Kornaros' choice of source. *Paris et Vienne* is a late French romance, in theme and setting closely linked to *Floire et Blancheflor Pierre de Provence*, the sources respectively of the Greek *Phlorios* and *Imperios*. It shares with *Floire* the theme of the young lovers, one of royal birth, the other a commoner, brought up together and falling in love against the wishes of the king, and with both of these other romances it also shares the travels of the pair from France to the eastern Mediterranean.

One of the changes that Kornaros made, probably more with an eye to the Aristotelian unities than to the moral standards of his time, was to suppress the elopement and send the exiled hero no further than Negroponte (Euboea). It may not be entirely accidental that in doing so he also obscured the motive that had drawn him to this source in the first place: like *Pierre*, this French text too had linked the Western romance tradition with the geographical centre of the *Greek* romance since Hellenistic times. Such a reason for choosing *Paris et Vienne* also assumes that Kornaros knew that the two comparable French romances had already been translated into Greek. Although he may not have known very much of the earlier Greek tradition in any detail, Kornaros' choice of source would none the less have been dictated by exactly the same criteria as directed the medieval Greek translators of Western romances to their sources. If, as has been persuasively argued, the Greek literature that Kornaros knew at first hand was what was available in print, then he would have known of the earlier romances only the *Theseid* and the rhymed version of *Imperios*.[119] All the points of contact between *Erotokritos* and the earlier romances could in fact be accounted for with reference to these two late texts. And a knowledge of these, together with an intuition of their translators' concerns to incorporate Western models into an emergent, native tradition, would probably suffice to place *Erotokritos* at the fulcrum between the medieval Greek romance and modern Greek literature.

AFTERWORD:
THE MEDIEVAL GREEK
ROMANCE SINCE 1987

Since the first edition of this book was completed (in 1987), the subject of the medieval Greek romance has attracted a great deal of scholarly interest among Byzantinists – although not, so far as I am aware, among classicists or students of Western medieval literature, at whom this book is equally aimed.[1] It is a welcome sign of the times that much of the new work that has appeared since the late 1980s has been conceived independently of my own, and so has already laid the basis for the kind of further dialogue envisaged in the original preface to the book. Latterly, it has also been gratifying to see how scholars working in different areas of Byzantine studies have engaged with the ideas presented in this book: several of them in reviews, others in discussions embedded in articles and books of their own.

The purpose of this Afterword is to bring the foregoing discussion as far as possible up to date (to the end of 1994). Rather than present a bald summary of the work published in the intervening period, I have preferred to focus on the most important issues that have attracted the attention of scholars. The headings in what follows, although they do not, as a consequence, correspond to the chapter divisions of the main body of the text, should be self-explanatory.

RESPONSES TO *THE MEDIEVAL GREEK ROMANCE*

The response of reviewers to the first edition has been overwhelmingly positive. The most conspicuous general feature of this scholarly response is that it has been largely concentrated in journals dealing with Hellenic and Byzantine studies.[2] There has been a markedly smaller, though no less positive response, in 'general', or Western, medieval circles.[3]

The specific comments, and points of agreement and disagreement, in these reviews, as well as in a number of specific discussions of the book embedded in other studies,[4] may be left for the interested reader to evaluate. A number of minor corrections arising from these, as indicated in the Preface to the present edition, have been incorporated into the main body of the text. Here I shall take issue only with the two most substantial reviews which have appeared, and only insofar as they touch on the underlying premises on which this study is based, where it seems to me that some clarification may be useful to the reader.

George Kechayoglou offers a detailed exposition of the content of the book, a generous evaluation, and a considered assessment of many of its arguments, as well as pointing out minor corrections, the great majority of which have been adopted in this edition. He takes issue with the book's overall conception on two counts: first, what he calls 'the choice of a title broader than the subject matter of the book' and second, the (related) neglect of the impact of Arabic and Persian narrative literature in Greek in the later Middle Ages.[5]

The first of these is based on a misunderstanding of the book's title, which should perhaps have been clarified. In an English-language context the term 'medieval romance' is synonymous with the tales of love and chivalry, in prose and verse, written in the Western vernaculars between the twelfth and the sixteenth century. It is on the grounds of thematic contiguity that the term 'romance' is also commonly extended, in the English bibliography, to the Hellenistic novel (as in this book). Neither in its title nor in any other way does the present study aspire to cover the whole range of narrative fiction in Greek during the Middle Ages. It is, instead, the study of a thematically and structurally cohesive body of texts which make up, although never strictly defined as such, a distinct genre: the Greek equivalent of the romances of the medieval West. Underlying this whole study is the definition of the French term *roman* advanced by Daniel Huet in 1670: 'ce que l'on appelle proprement Romans sont des fictions d'aventures amoureuses, écrites en Prose avec art, pour le plaisir & l'instruction des Lecteurs',[6] and especially as modified to the Greek context by Adamantios Koraes in his definition of the Greek term he proposed, in 1804, to correspond to it, *mythistoria*. The subject of this book is therefore the *erotic literature* of the period, perceived as a more or less coherent genre, and not fiction in a more general sense.

Kechayoglou's second criticism concerns my neglect or undervaluation of fiction translated from Arabic and Persian in the Greek literature of the time. I must confess that the decision to exclude the tales of *Barlaam*, of *Stephanites and Ichnelates* and of *Syntipas*, together with such later Eastern-inspired tales as the *Ptocholeon* was taken at an early stage and on grounds both generic and (more questionably, as I now perceive) of their integration into original writing in Greek. I now believe that the importance of translated literature may be greater than the sum of directly observable influences,[7] and in any case the separateness of this strand in Greek fiction, which is rather taken for granted in the present study, has yet to be proved. The best that I can offer in extenuation is the 'chivalrous' confession that I am not in a position to add anything to the study of this particular group of texts beyond the excellent work of Professor Kechayoglou himself.

* * *

Very different is the second extended review, by Panagiotis Agapitos and Ole Smith.[8] Presented in book form, with 113 pages of text and an extensive bibliography, this is a somewhat extravagant format for a review. However, as the reviewers explain in their preface, the division into chapters is not their own but follows the chapters of *The Medieval Greek Romance*, with the exclusion of two of the most important ones, on the revealing grounds that 'a critique of Beaton's interpretations ... would result in a large-scale interpretation of our own which is not the purpose of the present monograph [*sic*]'.[9] What the purpose of the two reviewers, or authors, is, soon becomes clear. *The Study of Medieval Greek Romance* is a modern essay in the Byzantine rhetorical exercise of *psogos*, or speech of blame, and in a very similar way a high degree of scholastic endeavour is directed towards an end which hardly seems worthy of the means employed. To justify the scale of their rebuttal, the authors might have been expected to advance some coherent opinions of their own, or at the very least to engage critically with the ideas put forward in the present book. Instead, their attack is dogged but piecemeal.[10] Most of their objections to the present book are palaeographical or codicological, and it is at this level that Agapitos and Smith come nearest to arguing, although unsystematically throughout their text, a consistent case which might merit further discussion.

The reviewers' case can conveniently be summarized in the form of a syllogism: (1) we do not have adequate published texts of the medieval Greek romances; (2) Beaton has based his study on the published texts; therefore (3) Beaton's book is inadequate – and indeed should not have been written![11] As with most syllogisms, the first two premises are perfectly sound; it is only the third that is objectionable. I am well aware of the deficiencies of the editions on which all but the most highly specialized reader of the medieval Greek romances is bound to depend. There is undoubtedly much that can yet be learnt from careful palaeographical study of the surviving manuscripts – and (*pace* Agapitos and Smith) nothing in the present book to suggest that I believe otherwise. But I hold to what I wrote in the Preface to the first edition: that we are unlikely to make significant further progress in confronting the textual problems raised by the surviving witnesses unless we can first gain a clearer idea of the nature of the literary works contained in them. Agapitos and Smith in their review have abundantly, if unwittingly, confirmed the validity of this position. There is nothing anywhere in their review to suggest why anyone might ever want to read any of these romances, and therefore what the purpose of all this editorial and codico-logical industry might be. The reviewers seem never to have asked themselves this fundamental question – which is, for better or for worse, the subject of the present book.[12]

THE TWELFTH-CENTURY ROMANCES

Our understanding of the cultural background out of which the 'proto-romance', *Digenes Akrites*, and the romances proper of the twelfth century emerged, has increased considerably in recent years. The old terminology of 'enlightenment or repression', within which my own discussion in Chapter 1 was conducted, has given way to a recognition that the two forces co-existed and competed during the Komnenian 'long twelfth century'. This shift in perspective is amply demonstrated by the papers given at an international conference on the reign of Alexios I, held in Belfast in April 1989,[13] and by the magisterial survey, nominally of the reign of Manuel I, but in practice of the whole Komnenian century, by Paul Magdalino.[14] As Magdalino succinctly sums up this new understanding: 'there could be no repression without enlightenment, just as there could be no social snobbery without social mobility'.[15] The picture that he paints of the 130 years that separate the battle of Manzikert from the fourth crusade is one of significant realignment at the top of Byzantine society, in which the traditional 'guardians of Orthodoxy' (in a cultural and social as much as specifically religious sense) found themselves vying for the favours of a new and exclusive ruling class centred upon the Komnenian dynasty. Both the unprecedented quantity of surviving literature, and the high degree of complexity and subtlety manifest in it, Magdalino persuasively attributes to the interaction of these two factors. Developments in literary taste, he concludes, are 'neither wholly dictated by the lords of the Komnenian system, nor wholly monopolised by the guardians of rhetorical Orthodoxy, but shaped by the tense and fertile encounter of the two groups'.[16] Out of this tension, and particularly from the strains attendant on the 'ambivalent social status, of those educated Byzantines who did not belong to the Komnenian nobility' grew a network of patronage which in its turn made possible a flowering of the literary and visual arts such as cannot be paralleled until the Italian Renaissance of two centuries later.[17]

The powerful historical synthesis proposed by Magdalino, together with the studies collected by Mullett and Smythe, make unprecedented use of the literary evidence for the period, including the romances. And here, at last, the historian has penetrated well beyond the *Aktualisierungsversuch* of a previous generation. At least a third of Magdalino's book is devoted to literature, rhetoric and the (again largely written) evidence for the visual arts of the period. This literature he is prepared to discuss on its own terms, and the results of doing so are impressive indeed. Magdalino's conclusion is that the reign of Manuel I represented '*in some sense* the high point of medieval Greek civilisation'.[18] The complexity of the picture he paints of twelfth-century Byzantine civilisation is perhaps one of the reasons for the hesitancy betrayed in the phrase I have italicized (tellingly repeated, in a similar context, in the very last sentence of the book). Magdalino is to a degree an apologist for Manuel and the civilization whose workings he unravels so well. But whether or not one is fully convinced by his book's larger claims, his is a reading of that civilization that is likely to be authoritative for a long time to come; and it is a reading to which the twelfth-century romances are indispensable. It also, in its turn, sheds much light on the phenomenon of the texts that are discussed in the first part of the present book.

Turning now to the twelfth-century texts, both Prodromos' and Eugenianos' romances have now become available in modern editions.[19] Only *Hysmine and Hysminias*, of the four twelfth-century romances, still awaits a modern editor.[20]

Recent work has returned to the question of the dating and cultural context of these romances, which in its turn also involves a reconsideration of their relation to Western literature of the twelfth century. The most radical proposal so far has been put forward by Karl Plepelits, the German translator of *Hysmine and Hysminias*. Basing his argument solely on an ingenious decoding of the name of the fictional addressee of Hysminias' narrative, Plepelits identifies this figure with the Caesar John Doukas, brother of Constantine X, who died *c.* 1083. On this evidence the romance becomes not only the earliest of the four but a product of the age of Psellos.[21] Specialists in the twelfth century, in the meantime, have not lent support to this view. Suzanne MacAlister has devoted two substantial and well-documented articles to refining and restating the case first put by Polyakova, and discussed on pp. 80–1 of the present book, namely that Makrembolites' romance predates the second crusade.[22] But central to MacAlister's argument for an earlier dating of *Hysmine and Hysminias* is the detailed evidence she adduces to show that the writers of the romances 'were working closely within the same milieu, and possibly even in collaboration with each other'.[23] Basing her arguments on a detailed examination of a single (important) theme, that of the dream, in the four romances, and tracing the interrelations among each of the twelfth-century texts and with the theories of Aristotle on which all of them have drawn, MacAlister makes a case for a sequence of composition beginning with Makrembolites and ending with Eugenianos. Although Plepelits' arguments were clearly not available to her at the time of writing these articles, everything in them works to rule out an *eleventh*-century context for any of the romances.

The close links among the four romances are also emphasized, from a rather different perspective, by Magdalino. Although he does not tackle the *relative* chronology of the four, Magdalino, too, makes a strong case that to detach *Hysmine and Hysminias* from the other three romances even as far as the traditional dating of the 1180s is to do violence to its known affinities not just with the romances of the mid-century, but also with the themes, style and preoccupation of a wealth of rhetorical literature from the early years of the reign of Manuel.[24] My own (tentative) suggestion that *Hysmine and*

Hysminias might, as a logical consequence of accepting Cupane's studies on Western influences, have had to be seen as a work of the thirteenth century rather than of the twelfth is strongly and persuasively contested by both these scholars, and has been deleted from the present edition.

The crux of the argument on the date of Makrembolites' romance is the provenance of the highly developed iconography of Eros the King in *Hysmine and Hysminias*. It is on these grounds that I remain unconvinced by MacAlister's arguments that this romance was written first. At least as clear a line of retrospective allusion and development as she discerns in the presentation of dream material, can be seen to run from Prodromos to Eugenianos to Makrembolites in the representation of the all-important figure of Eros. But my reluctance to accept in full the arguments of Cupane, discussed in Chapter 10, that this iconography is a Western importation and could not have developed independently in the Byzantine world has been strengthened in the meantime by the studies just mentioned. Magdalino argues in detail for a developing concept of Eros in just these terms in the early years of the reign of Manuel, which he persuasively links to the impact of the second crusade and Manuel's *Westpolitik*.[25]

In the light of this recent work, I now believe that the Western elements in *Hysmine and Hysminias* are certainly less than Cupane has claimed.[26] I now believe that all four Byzantine romances may have been composed between (at the earliest) 1140 and abut 1160. In particular, the possibility, raised tentatively by Magdalino, that Makrembolites was a pupil of Nikephoros Basilakes (and not, as Polyakova thought, the other way about) deserves very serious consideration.[27] I still adhere to the traditional sequence of writing (Prodromos, Eugenianos, Makrembolites, with Manasses' fragmentary romance fitting in somewhere in the 1150s). But in the light of our greatly increased understanding of the literary currents and interests of the mid-twelfth century in Byzantium, the question addressed by Elizabeth Jeffreys, and implicitly also by Magdalino, should now be taken up once again: namely the phenomenon of the near-simultaneous appearance, fully fledged in both East and West, of the 'romance of antiquity'.[28] And it might also be fruitful, in such a context, to consider in the same light the roughly coincidental appearance, in written, more or less literary form, of the epic-style heroic narratives in both halves of Christendom, among which *Digenes Akrites* has so often been numbered.

Aside from questions of dating and of the theme of sexuality (on which see below), literary investigation of the twelfth-century romances in recent years has focused on *Drosilla and Charikles*, which had previously been, in my opinion unjustly, relatively neglected, and on *Hysmine and Hysminias*. With primary reference to the former, separate studies by Conca and Jouanno have adopted a new and sophisticated approach to the relation of a twelfth-century romance to its sources.[29] Jouanno, in particular, has shown impressively how the selection of an antique topos (in this case that of the barbarous foreigner) may metaphorically but quite precisely allude to contemporary anxieties.[30]

Makrembolites' romance has provoked more radical reinterpretations. The French translation, which includes an introduction in chatty style that assumes little previous knowledge of Byzantium or Byzantine literature, devotes welcome attention to the text's structure and its use of rhetoric. But the provocative title under which the romance has been presented to French-speaking readers, *Les Amours homonymes*,[31] picks up a characteristic of the romance which had also fascinated its German translator, to whose inter-pretation we now come.

The translation into German by Plepelits is preceded by a long introduc-tion. As well as proposing a radical (and in my view unacceptable) new dating for the romance, already discussed, this introduction proceeds to a thorough-going reinterpretation of *Hysmine and Hysminias*, on two levels. In deciphering what Plepelits calls the 'literal meaning', he removes the fictional masks behind the geographical names in the romance, so that Eurykomis, Aulikomis, Daphnepolis and Artykomis reveal, respectively, Alexandria, Constantinople, Antioch and Ephesos.[32] The evidence for this, drawn from conventional and mythical associations of the fictional places in the text, and the real places in Hellenistic literature, is far from persuasive; and at this level it is hard to see what has been added to our understanding of the romance by the unmasking of these fictional names. Had Makrembolites wished to set the scene for his romance in the real world, the world he describes is in any case so far (and explicitly) removed in time from the present, that no possible embarrassment could have arisen from using real place-names, as indeed Prodromos, Eugenianos and Manasses all did. The names actually used in the romance, as Plepelits is not the first to point out, certainly have symbolic connotations, but it seems perverse, having granted this, then to seek for real places to which they might also, allusively, refer.

The second, and longer, part of Plepelits' re-interpretation deserves more serious consideration. According to this, *Hysmine and Hysminias* functions simultaneously at a literal and at an allegorical or, as Plepelits puts it, 'mystical' level.[33] At this second level, the story of the hero's love for Hysmine represents 'the vocation of a worldly man to the monastic life'.[34] This mystical meaning turns out, however, to be an unstable or multi-layered one. Hysmine's home town of Aulikomis (Constantinople, according to the 'literal' interpretation) is successively equivalent to Paradise, the Heavenly Jerusalem, a monastery or a monk's cell,[35] and the heroine, Hysmine, is subject to a similar, bewildering series of transfigurations, to be identified in turn with nothing less than the Church, Christian learning and the 'Hypostasis of Christ'.[36]

All this reveals an allegorizing zeal worthy of a Manuel Philes in the fourteenth century, or a Reinhard Merkelbach in the twentieth.[37] As was said in Chapter 4 of this book, and in a different context again in Chapter 12, the existence and proliferation of allegorical readings of romance literature testify to a significant potential always latent within the genre itself. On the other hand, no convincing case has yet been made for a conscious and systematically worked-out use of allegory in *any* work of Greek erotic literature, other than Meliteniotes' parody, *To Chastity*. If Makrembolites' romance was read (and perhaps even written) with a spiritual dimension in mind, the very looseness of the allegory that Plepelits identifies should warn us that we are dealing with something very different in kind from the *Roman de la Rose* or the *Vita nuova*.

One clue to which Plepelits, alone, so far as I am aware, among modern commentators, has drawn attention is the name of the heroine, which he links with the more frequently remarked, and unusual, homonymy of the romance's two protagonists: Hysmine and Hysminias. The Homeric term ὑσμίνη, Plepelits reminds us, has the meaning of 'fight, battle, combat'. To revive this long-obsolete term in the twelfth century would have been a deliberately recondite act, and not all readers then, as now, would have 'got the point'. But the kind of allusion contained in such an act of naming is entirely consonant with twelfth-century practice and does most certainly, through the metaphorical connotations of the Homeric term, add something to our understanding of the romance. The idea of 'strife' is inherent throughout the whole genre, both as antithesis and obstacle to love and even as inbuilt within it. The *amours homonymes* in this way become a symbolic (not an allegorical) account of the strife, both internal and external to the homonymous pair, that will eventually result in their (longed-for) salvation in the 'imperishable monument' of the text itself.[38]

DIGENES AKRITES

Of all the texts discussed in this book none has had such dense and complex fortunes in the intervening years as the 'proto-romance', *Digenes Akrites*. In the wake of Stylianos Alexiou's edition of the long-neglected Escorial version,[39] a series of important studies has gone a long way towards vindicating the once discredited stance of the Greek folklorist Stilpon Kyriakidis and the Belgian Byzantinist Henri Grégoire on the close links between this version and the oral songs recorded in later times. The distinguished Homeric scholars Bernard Fenik and Gregory Sifakis have, in complementary ways, drawn convincing parallels between the diction and style of the Escorial *Digenes* on the one hand and, on the other, the traditional style of heroic oral poetry both ancient and modern.[40] Also drawing on a sophisticated grasp of Homeric scholarship, David Ricks has proposed to break down the Escorial *Digenes* into its constituent 'lays',[41] and has also provided the first English translation of that version, based on Alexiou's edition, with accompanying Greek text, introduction and notes.[42] We also now have a well-produced bilingual Greek and Spanish text by

AFTERWORD

Miguel Castillo Didier, based on Alexiou's text and including the Armoures and Andronikos poems, with a detailed and perceptive introduction which broadly endorses Alexiou's approach.[43] Finally, from a linguistic viewpoint, Peter Mackridge has further been able to demonstrate that the language of the E version is not the hotchpotch that has usually been assumed but actually obeys a consistent set of rules, for which a living analogue can be found in the modern dialect of Cyprus.[44]

As a result of these and other studies, Alexiou's new text has won wide recognition as a fairly authentic record of an earlier stage in the development of the formulaic style of modern Greek oral poetry. However, Alexiou's arguments for the dating of this text to the first years of the twelfth century have not found favour with historians. Although the counter-arguments of Magdalino and Galatariotou are not conclusive either,[45] Alexiou's dating can no longer be taken for granted, and it must be accepted that, in the present state of our knowledge, neither the language of the E version nor the world it reflects can be placed with confidence in *any* securely identifiable historical period. By contrast, recent work on the G manuscript by Elizabeth Jeffreys has shown convincingly that the version contained in G can be dated between the beginning and the middle of the twelfth century,[46] confirming the views of those historians who have had some success in establishing a credible context for this version.[47] A new edition of *Digenes Akrites*, in the E and G versions, based on a re-examination of the manuscripts, has been announced by Professor Jeffreys, to appear in the bilingual Medieval Classics series of Cambridge University Press,[48] and a further research tool will shortly be available in the form of computer concordances to both versions.[49]

The vexed question of primacy between these two versions, which was discussed in Chapter 3 of the present book, is by no means resolved as a result of these researches. Further comparison of the two has shown significant instances where, it now seems to me, the author/editor of G has filled in gaps in E, or replaced material in his source, in a manner strikingly (and surely deliberately) close to that of the mid-twelfth-century romances. At the same time, I am struck by the evidence for progressive accretion in the tradition represented by the E manuscript.[50] What in Chapter 3 I had termed the 'original *Digenes*' I now think can better be termed the common 'core' of (written) narrative underlying the two versions.[51]

It is this 'core', which could have been quite a short text, that I now believe may have first achieved written form in the early years of the twelfth century. Whether or not this happened in Constantinople, this poem was certainly known there in time to be parodied in the first of the *Poems of Poor Prodromos*, addressed to the Emperor John II. But even this core, in the earliest discernible form underlying our two extant witnesses, must already have been in important respects a 'proto-romance'. Its longest and most developed episode, the 'Lay of the Emir', is a bipartite tale in which love overcomes not just armies but the symmetrically threatened curses of a Christian and a Muslim mother. And this tale in turn leads into a hero-narrative in which the power of love is scarcely less evident, and is explicitly signalled in both our surviving witnesses. The elaboration of this core (in a rudimentary way in E, more copiously in G) would have come about later, perhaps in response to the mid-century revival of the fully fledged romance.[52]

BYZANTINISCHES EROTIKON

Since the appearance of Beck's monograph with this title,[53] the sexual mores presented in the romances have come under renewed scrutiny. Certainly in the context of the several studies devoted to this subject in the last ten years, my own brief remarks in Chapter 7, together with comments passed on several of the individual romances, now seem rather laconic.

The sexual symbolism of the Byzantine garden, with copious references to the evidence of the romances, has been explored, from an art-historical perspective, by Charles Barber.[54] Studies by A. R. Littlewood, on the *real* gardens that Byzantine authors could have known, with some rare illustrations,[55] and on the symbol of the apple, from its beginnings in the Palaiologan romances through to later Greek popular tradition,[56] add consistently to our understanding of the common topoi of the *locus amoenus* in the twelfth-century romances, and the magic castle in the later ones.

To Caroline Cupane we owe two studies, more or less directly in response to Beck, in which she argues that there occurred in the Greek romance a (literary) relaxation of sexual conduct in response to Western (literary) practice.[57] This view has since been challenged by Panagiotis Agapitos, with particular reference to the erotic bathing-scene in *Kallimachos*.[58] The question of Western 'influence' will be discussed below. Suffice it to note here that the scene in *Kallimachos* of explicit erotic foreplay in the bath followed by full sexual intercourse on the bathside is no less original (and 'daring') whether one tries to place it in the context of previous Greek or of Western literature.

But the fullest study of the developing presentation of sexuality in the romances, from the twelfth century to the fifteenth, and even including *Digenes Akrites*,[59] is by Lynda Garland.[60] This study has the particular merit of treating the vernacular romances of the fourteenth and fifteenth centuries as, in this respect, the continuators of a tradition begun in the twelfth century. The line of development is well summed up by Garland: 'whereas the learned romances specialise in erotic innuendo without the accompanying action, the popular [i.e. vernacular] romances in general prefer the action without the innuendo'.[61] There are no very reliable grounds, however, for supposing that this change came out about either because the later, vernacular (δημώδεις) romances were *popular* (δημοφιλεῖς), a common misconception in the older bibliography, or because specifically Western models had modified the literary tastes (not necessarily the sexual behaviour, of course) of readers.

THE VERNACULAR ROMANCES

The texts

Although the well-known problems of textual criticism raised by the manuscripts and existing editions of the romances have been aired quite extensively in recent years, the actual crop of new editions is disappointing. Aside from the bilingual (Greek and English) *Digenes* in the E version,[62] the only vernacular romance to have appeared in a new edition is the abbreviated Oxford version of the *Tale of Achilles*.[63] In addition we now have an Italian verse translation of the *Tale of Troy*, which also contains the fullest introduction and notes to that poem available so far.[64] Panagiotis Agapitos has announced a forthcoming integrated edition of the three manuscripts of *Libistros* that he terms the α group, namely N, P and S;[65] and Tina Lendari has completed a doctoral thesis for the University of Cambridge based upon the *editio princeps* of the V manuscript of the same romance.[66] Again on *Libistros*, the King's College 'Medieval Greek Database Project' has so far produced lemmatized concordances on computer file for four of the five versions, based on a systematic re-editing of the manuscripts by Tina Lendari.[67] Finally, 1994 saw appearance of the first ever English version of any of the vernacular romances, containing *Kallimachos*, *Belthandros* and *Libistros*.[68]

Several of these are interim results of longer-term projects. The complete edition of all three versions of the *Tale of Achilles*, announced by Ole Smith, has been frustrated by that scholar's untimely death in 1995. On *Libistros*, it will clearly be some time before a usable alternative to Lambert's edition is available in print. The *editio princeps*, by Elizabeth Jeffreys and Manolis Papathomopoulos, of the *War of Troy*, by far the single largest surviving specimen of medieval Greek verse in the vernacular, is still awaited. The publication date for the new edition of *Digenes Akrites* by Elizabeth Jeffreys has yet to be announced. The slow progress of new editions is no doubt a reflection of the methodological (not to say practical) problems involved. But more often than not these problems have been tackled recently in print only insofar as they impinge upon the specific readings of a particular text.[69] Not the least of the lessons from the Second International Congress, 'Neograeca Medii Aevi', held in Venice in 1991, was the significant lack of agreement which still exists among specialists on the editorial principles appropriate to new editions of these texts.[70]

Most of the scholarly discussion on editorial matters assumes principles which derive from nineteenth-century textual criticism; some scholars have made more or less dogmatic statements about the standards and procedures they would wish to see adopted by editors. But what has not been sufficiently considered is that different editorial principles and practices are surely appropriate to different *uses*. For certain purposes a more or less diplomatic transcript of the contents of each manuscript may be desirable or necessary. This has been the policy of the King's College London 'Medieval Greek Database Project' in its handling of *Libistros* (though not of *Digenes Akrites*), of Smith in his editions of the *Tale of Troy*, and more recently of the O version of the *Tale of Achilles*,[71] of Agapitos in his doctoral thesis,[72] and of the announced new edition of *Digenes Akrites*.[73] If the intention is to analyse the contents of a *manuscript* or to compare it with other manuscripts, then this is surely the best course. There is undoubtedly much still to be learnt from the manuscripts of the vernacular romances: about the date and place of copying,[74] but also about linguistic norms and copying-practice at the time when each manuscript was produced.[75] However, if these texts are worth studying as literature, as I believe they are, in their literary, historical and cultural context, it is essential that we also have editions which, despite their necessary imperfections, can be used by scholars and readers outside the palaeography seminar room. After all, this has long ago been done for Aeschylus and Shakespeare, although no one pretends that every word of the *Persians* or *King Lear* as it came from its author's pen is recoverable.

It seems to me that study of the manuscripts is an essentially different task from the production of usable modern editions; and the tendency of some editors and commentators to conflate them, and assume that an edition is the same thing as a transcript of the contents of a manuscript, only hinders a better understanding of the romances and the processes of their transmission.[76] Given that in the case of four out of the five original romances, and at least the oldest and longest of the translated romances, the extant witnesses were copied some two centuries after the composition of the texts, we should be wary of investing the manuscripts which happen to survive with a spurious authority to which they have no claim.[77]

The manuscripts provide, obviously, the only evidence we have for the older texts that they transmit. But the scribes, copyists, recensors or even editors of the late fifteenth and early sixteenth century were clearly no less fallible than their modern successors, and in many respects a great deal more so.[78] I do not believe that usable editions can be based on the manuscript readings alone. Rather than 'definitive' critical editions which, the more definitive they are, the more bulky and the less readable they will in most cases be, I would prefer to see available a choice of editions, each representing a *reading* of the text with which today's readers and scholars might in turn engage critically.[79]

The value of further systematic study of the manuscripts, on which most scholars in the field rightly insist, may now lie in what they have to tell us not about the *texts* that these manuscripts transmit but, rather, about the process of transmission itself. This latter field of enquiry should certainly not be neglected. If there is no very good reason for supposing that faithful attention to the manuscript copies of the fifteenth and sixteenth centuries will unlock previously undiscovered secrets of texts that may first have been composed two hundred years before, it is none the less increasingly coming to be realized today that the process whereby literary fiction in both vernacular and 'learned' Greek came to be copied and read between the fifteenth and the eighteenth century, is to a large extent synonymous with the formation of a modern literary tradition in Greek.[80]

East meets West? Dating and context of the romances

The case for recognizing Western cultural and literary borrowings in the original romances of this period has continued to be pressed by Carolina Cupane and, less controversially, for the translated romances, by Giuseppe Spadaro.[81] The question of where the impetus for particular words, motifs and narrative devices in the romances comes from is more open than ever. Undoubtedly Western traces are discernible in all but *Kallimachos*. But how deep do they go, and in particular how far can they be attributed to the process of transmission of the texts rather than to their first composition? My own view, developed beyond what is said in Chapter 10 and based, in particular, upon an analysis of the proper names and fictional geography of *Belthandros* and *Libistros*, remains that 'Byzantine writers of romance acknowledged the part played by the crusader states in the East, in transmitting a vitalizing, but to the Byzantines always subordinate, element from the courtly romances of the West'.[82]

On *Belthandros*, both Garland and Agapitos, in separate studies, have discerned references to imperial Byzantine ritual of the late thirteenth century (even though the former writes from the perspective of Cupane's 1983 paper, which sees the romance as a 'byzantinization' or 're-byzantinization' of a previously Frankish tale); and Agapitos has also proposed a radically new chronological sequence for the three original romances of Constantinople.[83] It says much for the state of studies in the field that at the congress in Venice mentioned above proposals were heard to redate the composition of *Libistros* to periods as much as a century and a half apart! Agapitos' proposal is for a sequence *Libistros*, *Belthandros*, *Kallimachos*, with a terminus of a kind given by the allusions to Byzantine ritual in *Belthandros* mentioned above. On this dating, both *Libistros* and *Belthandros* would be works of the thirteenth century, with only *Kallimachos* remaining close to its traditional date in the early fourteenth (though not for the traditional reason, since Agapitos rejects the ascription to Andronikos Palaiologos). In the opposite direction, Dimitris Michailidis has proposed a quite precise date for *Libistros* in the first decade of the *fifteenth* century, based on art-historical realia.[84]

The juxtaposition of these radical departures is probably more instructive than the specific case made by either one of them. The evidence presented by Michailidis is highly persuasive, but as it refers to only a single detail of the text (admittedly one well attested throughout the five manuscripts) it still seems more probable that the 'Frankish haircut' attributed to the hero is a later accretion to the text, than that this, the most 'Byzantine' of the vernacular romances (as Agapitos rightly insists), was written as late as the reign of Manuel II – and where? In the other direction, it is quite true that *Libistros* has much more in common with the twelfth-century romances and even their ancient precursors than any other text in vernacular Greek. But this in itself is not a reason for supposing that it was written first, just as the greater closeness of Makrembolites' twelfth-century romance to the ancient genre is not in itself a reason for dating it before the verse romances of Prodromos and Eugenianos.

Many readers of *Belthandros*, myself included, have been intrigued by the hybrid names of its principal characters and its unmistakably crusader geography, which seems to stem from the thirteenth century if not, even, the twelfth. (The political geography of this romance is in many respects congruent with that of the reign of Manuel I.)[85] If there were any solid evidence to support an earlier date, and a credible cultural context into which its composition could be put in the thirteenth century or even the twelfth, I would see no insurmountable obstacle to such a dating on internal, literary grounds. But the evidence has yet to be presented. In the meantime if we were seriously to seek a context for this romance in the thirteenth century, consideration might be given to the *Latin* empire of Constantinople, with its byzantinizing veneer and Greek-speaking population. It is hard to see, however, how this context might fit any of the other original romances – and such a dating would surely be too early to provide a credible context for any of the known translations of Western originals.

Narrative structure

This has proved to be one of the least controversial of the topics addressed in the present book. No doubt owing to the general acceptance accorded the pioneering work of Aleksidze,[86] several quite independent studies in recent years have contributed to a consensus that the romances, and particularly the trio made up of *Kallimachos*, *Belthandros* and *Libistros*, are tightly structured and built out of complex and often symmetrical patterns. Following the example set by Aleksidze, some scholars have adopted the morphological scheme of Vladimir Propp. This has the advantage of allowing quite complex structural patterns to emerge without necessarily attributing these to the conscious craftsmanship of the authors of the romances.[87] Lars Nørgaard does not use Propp as a model but bases himself in part on older perceptions of the romances, and *Belthandros* in particular, as popular literature, close to epic and amenable to analysis in terms of 'motif-indexes', although the particular patterns he discerns he ascribes (rightly, in my view) to 'conscious composing by the author' and 'the poet's conscious attempt of [*sic*] originality'.[88]

The other structural element of the romances which has drawn the attention of scholars recently is the function of the narrator within the text. Useful and well-tabulated analyses of self-referential comments in the romances and of explicit references to the narrator and the addresses in *Digenes Akrites* have been produced as postgraduate dissertations at the University of Thessaloniki.[89] Finally, all these subjects have been (independently) examined at length by Panagiotis Agapitos in his doctoral thesis on the three Constantinopolitan romances.[90] Agapitos starts out from the welcome premise: 'The romances have to be understood in [*sic*] their own terms in order to be appreciated better as literary products',[91] and proceeds to subject the texts to a fairly rigorous analysis of their formal features and organization, paying particular attention to self-referential devices,[92] what he calls 'aspects of narrative sequence',[93] and the narrative organization of time and space.[94] The most striking parts of the argument are, first, the structural, stylistic and organizational *differences* that he detects among the three romances under consideration,[95] and, second, the revision and reformulation of the outmoded views of Sigalas and Schreiner that the text of *Belthandros* as we have it is seriously corrupt.[96]

The distinctions Agapitos draws between one romance and another are worth drawing, though it needs to be more clearly stated that these are *divergences* within a common pattern. Certainly, the three romances can in no sense be regarded as 'one unit'.[97] But their real differences need to be seen in the context of variations (no doubt conscious ones) upon a shared, underlying pattern. (The same holds good for the twelfth-century romances too.)

On *Belthandros*, Agapitos' proposal is that there is no disruption in the narrative *sequence* of the text as transmitted (a view confirmed by the other studies mentioned above under this heading, as well as by Chapter 8 of the present book) but that the text as we have it has been systematically abbreviated. The evidence for this is intriguing, but not conclusive. Agapitos attaches great significance to the rubrics in red ink which are to be found in most of the fifteenth- and sixteenth-century manuscripts in which the texts are preserved.[98] His argument that these are in almost all cases integral to the texts is not persuasive, although the possibility cannot be excluded that they go all the way back to the original composition (more likely, surely, to the first copying for formal presentation, the equivalent of publication, rather than to an autograph). In any case, the rubrics function in a similar way to the chapter-titles in eighteenth- and nineteenth-century fiction. Their absence from *Belthandros* (though to confuse matters there are in fact two in the manuscript) is only a weak indication in support of the drastic pruning proposed by Agapitos. More telling is his examination of speech-frames (where it may well be the case that speeches present in an earlier version have been excised), and of the deployment of narrative 'models' which reveals significant departures from that found in the other two romances.[99]

Agapitos sums up his view of the narrative structure of *Belthandros*: 'The overall impression given by the text stands much closer to the epic cycle of the *akritika tragoudia* than the Komnenian novels. In my opinion, all of this indicates that the text was shortened, possibly to produce this very effect.'[100] I agree with Agapitos about the effect. But if this effect was *intentionally* produced, why not attribute it to the author? The deviations from the 'norm' (i.e. the practice observed in the other two romances examined by Agapitos) are so systematic that they could as well represent the stylistic choice of an author as pruning by a copyist or editor.

THE ORAL SUBSTRATUM OF THE VERNACULAR ROMANCES

The role and extent of oral tradition in the composition and transmission of medieval Greek literature in the vernacular, the subject of Chapter 11, have continued to provoke scholarly debate. Several of those whose views are summarized and discussed in that chapter have continued to restate and refine the broad positions taken up in previous work.[101] The whole question of orality in medieval and modern Greek literature was aired at a colloquium in Oxford in 1989, which included discussion of the Jeffreys' and Spadaro's proposals.[102] At that colloquium I gave a paper which extends the discussion of Chapter 11 and separately examines the case for orality in each of the processes of composition, performance and transmission in the romances and other texts in the medieval Greek vernacular. I quote at length from the conclusion of that paper, since the view expressed there is the one that I still hold:

> Firstly, oral precedents play a part, in varying degrees, in the composition of the texts; but only 'The Song of Armoures' can be regarded as the product of oral composition, and only *Digenes* is based substantially on an oral source. Secondly, oral performance of written texts of this type was common, but ... this took the form of reading aloud rather than a memorised or improvised performance .... It is not until the mid fourteenth century that vernacular texts come to be addressed to a less educated public; and only in manuscript interpolations of the late fifteenth and early sixteenth centuries is there any evidence that such texts were orally presented to a popular audience. Finally, oral transmission does not have to be invoked to account for variants in the manuscript tradition of these texts, and in some cases can be ruled out or relegated to a very minor role. But one case can very probably be substantiated – the manuscripts of Sachlikis – and further examination of individual manuscripts ... may reveal others.[103]

Since then Gregory Sifakis has entered the debate with the proposal that 'the key here is not the oral but the traditional'.[104] Although formulated independently of my own and drawn from a different perspective, Sifakis' conclusions are broadly congruent with the proposals in Chapter 11. Although he tends to emphasize *collective* processes where I have preferred to stress the self-consciousness of the writers of romance, I none the less find myself in broad agreement with his definition of tradition.[105]

None of the work so far mentioned takes the form of an explicit reply to the arguments of the present book. These have, however, been addressed in print by Michael Jeffreys in two papers, to which I now turn.[106] Like the other participants in the debate mentioned above, Jeffreys sets out to restate and refine an earlier position (in this case set out by himself and Elizabeth Jeffreys in the articles discussed in Chapter 11). The first thing to be said is that I recognize the difficulty of entering the oral debate without imposing an artificial duality: *either* a text is thought of as oral (or 'oral-generated' in the phrase of John Miles Foley),[107] *or* it is written and therefore 'purely' literary. I agree that this polarity is misleading and has tended to distort previous discussions of the subject, not just in the field of medieval Greek.[108] Moreover, I am conscious of having allowed it a place in my own discussion of the subject. The aim of Chapter 11 of this book is to show that an oral tradition consisting of long narratives, distinct from the later *dimotiko tragoudi*, did not *have* to exist in the fourteenth century for the surviving literary texts to have been composed in the way they were. This is not to say that an oral tradition of this sort *did not* exist. I agree that such a negative conclusion could not be proved,[109] and I have no interest in trying to prove it. I certainly accept that there was an oral substratum among Greek-speakers of the fourteenth century, and no doubt earlier too, which could have been drawn on at will by writers of romance and other kinds of vernacular literature in verse. But our best evidence for what that oral substratum might have been like, in my opinion, remains the Escorial version of *Digenes Akrites*, 'Armoures' and, *mutatis mutandis*, the oral songs recorded in the nineteenth and twentieth centuries.

The counter-argument that a 'ballad' tradition is unlikely to have existed in the Greek world as early as the twelfth century, given that 'all over Europe, roughly from the twelfth to the fifteenth centuries, narrative-type poetry was giving way to ballads'[110] is hard to accept. The history of the *written* vernaculars throughout Europe certainly reveals this trend, but this has surely more to do with the circumstances in which these vernaculars first acquired written, literary form than with a contemporary evolution from epic-style narrative (ballads are narrative too!) to ballad traditions. Much scholarship devoted to epic, going back to the Homeric Analysts, has sought the origins of the first (written) epics in brief oral narratives, and certainly the nearest Byzantine equivalent to the 'epic', *Digenes Akrites*, has recently begun to yield to a variety of 'analytic' approaches.[111]

In conclusion, I should like to propose that the characteristics of the Palaiologan romances that have provoked this particular debate can best be understood as the result of a conscious process of establishing a *vulgaris eloquentia* in medieval Greek. The motivation for this development may have come, as we saw in the previous section, from the example of the West, both directly in Western-ruled regions and, more distantly, by emulation at the Byzantine court. The first step towards the creation of such a literary idiom, in any society, is bound to be the search for precedents. To the Greek writers of romances and other vernacular literature of the fourteenth and fifteenth centuries these precedents in their own language were not many: a handful of short poems from the twelfth century, the vernacular version of *Digenes Akrites*, nothing in prose. In such a situation it would be remarkable if these writers had not turned to the oral narrative poetry that, in some form, must have existed around them, and of which clear traces have come down to us in the songs of Armoures and Andronikos. To that extent, the Greek oral tradition of the period must surely represent a vital substratum in the literary achievements of these writers. But we need not suppose either that, as writers, they consciously tried to reproduce the patterns and phrases of the oral poetry they knew, or that they found themselves incapable of composing in a form of the vernacular without subconsciously reproducing these same patterns and phrases. Rather, we must suppose that the writers of the Palaiologan period drew on the precedent of oral tradition in the same way as Vitsentzos Kornaros and other literary writers of the Cretan Renaissance did and as, *mutatis mutandis*, the first poets of independent Greece set out to do, in full consciousness of what they were doing, in the early nineteenth century.

RECEPTION OF THE ROMANCES

Chapter 12, in the first edition of this book, began with a short section entitled 'The Audience in the Text', in which I examined the ways in which the later romances refer to their addressees: whether as audience or as (silent) readers, as singular or plural. The evidence is notoriously contradictory, from which I drew the conclusion that more than one type of reception was probably envisaged for these texts: that, in effect, the ambivalence of the references to the addressee in the text reflected an ambivalence about the ways in which the text would really have been presented. In addition, I drew attention to two fictional narrating instances in the romances. One was the description of the foreign king in *Kallimachos* who, footloose and fancy-free, likes to be entertained by recitations of 'marvellous tales'.[112] The other was the fictional situation at the beginning and end of *Libistros*, according to which the whole tale is being narrated by Klitobos before his lady, Myrtane, in front of the whole court, consisting quite specifically of young and old of both sexes.[113]

Carolina Cupane has now presented this evidence more fully, and drawn rather different conclusions from it.[114] Beginning from an aside in Niketas Choniates' thirteenth-century *History*, in which the historian addresses a public far more humble than could possibly have grappled successfully with his erudite, Attic Greek, Cupane makes the case that the exordium to the public was a conventional topos in late Byzantine literature, inbuilt, in other words, into the tradition discussed in the previous section, and therefore wholly unreliable as a guide to the reality of the romances' reception. She also, entirely properly, draws a distinction between the evidence of a manuscript colophon (a written comment entirely external to the fictional world of the text) and the prologues and other intratextual indications which I had examined.[115] On this evidence, writing (obviously) and reading of manuscripts of this type are attested historically. But on what other evidence may we legitimately draw? Cupane's conclusion is, perhaps, sensibly, downbeat. As she puts it, 'the Byzantine public for vernacular literature remains faceless, the modes of communication and reception hypothetical'.[116]

Here it might be useful to set out upon a different tack. Recent examination of a wide range of ceremonial literature from the twelfth century has placed new emphasis on the act of performance. Although we do not know precisely what was meant in the twelfth century by a *theatron*, or whether such things continued in existence in the fourteenth, it is becoming clear that a significant component of Byzantine court ceremonial consisted of the *performance* of poetic texts, composed by a skilled *rhetor*, in front of a powerful official or member of the imperial family. The romances, of course, differ considerably from such poetry in their much greater length; on the other hand, all the twelfth-century writers of romances were also active in writing for, and presumably also performing at, court ceremonial, and it is perfectly possible that the same was true in the fourteenth century.[117] On this evidence, it is at least likely that romances of this later period, like their predecessors of the twelfth century, would have been read aloud for the admiration of the writer's peers as well as to impress a more dignified personage, by whom he might hope to be rewarded. This is precisely the situation envisaged in the fictional narrating instance of *Libistros*, with the recognizable displacement that the 'patron' is not a lord or emperor but a woman, and that the implied 'reward' to be earned by the narrator is her favours.

Such evidence must certainly be approached with caution, but (*pace* Cupane) I would propose that the model of oral presentation before a *theatron*, as in the twelfth century, should be extended to the fourteenth and may fruitfully help us to envisage the circumstances for which at least *Kallimachos*, *Belthandros*, *Libistros* and Meliteniotes' parody, *To Chastity*, may first have been composed. In this case the fictional narrating instances in *Kallimachos* and *Libistros* would have been based on a reality which the first hearers and/or readers of these romances would have recognized, but with systematic transformations to suit the fictional situations invoked. How long this kind of public occasion would have lasted, or whether anything comparable to it might have existed outside Constantinople, and particularly at the courts of Western rulers, is difficult to say. But most of the prologues or asides to the audience which specify the *dulce et utile* formula, and particularly those in which a writer–narrator claims only a limited education, and to be exerting himself for the benefit of those less educated still, can be dated to the fifteenth century and later.[118]

THE LEGACY OF THE MEDIEVAL GREEK ROMANCES

One of the most remarkable developments of recent scholarship has been that the story of the romances' reception does not end, where I rather modestly left it in Chapter 12, at the end of the sixteenth century, with *Erotokritos*. Indicatively, I had myself written some years ago: 'The Greek novel when it reappears after 1834 is imported wholesale from the West.'[119] Research over the last few years has shown that this is not entirely the case, and the full extent of the legacy of the medieval (and Hellenistic) Greek romance to the re-emergent Greek prose fiction in the nineteenth century has yet to be established. Suffice it here to draw attention to a number of significant pointers.

An important place in the leisure reading of educated Greeks in the late eighteenth century (chiefly in Constantinople and the Danubian principalities of Moldavia and Wallachia) was occupied by new editions of the Hellenistic and Byzantine (learned) romance, all from leading Greek publishers in Vienna and Venice: Heliodoros in 1790, Makrembolites in 1791, *Daphnis and Chloe* in 1792, Xenophon's *Ephesiaka* in the following year.[120] This in itself helps to explain the curious fact that the series of highly influential editions of ancient texts inaugurated by Adamantios Koraes, the 'father of the Modern Greek nation' in the early 1800s, began with *Daphnis and Chloe* (1802) and continued with the *Aithiopika* (1804). Koraes' preface to the latter text has long been cited for the views it expounds on the modern Greek language. What has scarcely been noticed is that the *context* of these views is the edition of an ancient work of prose fiction. And before turning to his linguistic theories, Koraes begins his preface by claiming (legitimately) that prose fiction such as was by then widely written and read throughout Europe was in fact a Greek invention, of which Heliodoros' *Aithiopika* is presented as the prime specimen. Koraes further notes that, although the French (among whom he lived for most of his life) had long had a word for this literary genre, *roman*, no such generic term existed among the Greeks who had originated it. This deficiency he proposed to rectify, and so was born the modern Greek term *mythistoria*.[121] More important even than the term is Koraes' proposed definition of it, which is only slightly adapted from that of Daniel Huet, dating from 1670, for the *ancient* romances: 'a fictional, but plausible story of sufferings in love, written with artistry and dramatically, for the most part in prose'.[122]

It used to be asserted that the first modern Greek fiction in the nineteenth century was the historical novel. This generalization has been overturned as several of the early novels from this revival have been rescued from the obscurity in which they had languished for many years.[123] One conclusion that is beginning to emerge from this reassessment is that most if not all of these novels (called *mythistoria* by their authors, after Koraes) conform to his definition of the genre, which is in essence a definition of the Hellenistic and medieval novel, or romance.[124]

In this way, through the mediation of Koraes, the latest stage of reception of the medieval Greek romance must be the tales of love and adventure set in the more or less contemporary world, by Panayotis Soutsos, I. Pitsipios, Grigorios Palaiologos, in the 1830s and 1840s, by Alexandros Rizos Rangavis and Pavlos Kalligas in the 1850s – a type of narrative wickedly and memorably parodied by Emmanuel Roidis in *Pope Joan* (1866). Through an understanding of the poetics of the medieval Greek romance, which is what this book has tried to achieve, we might even hope to identify and understand better those aspects of contemporary fiction in Greek which set it apart from its Western-dominated context.

NOTES

INTRODUCTION

1 This situation is slowly beginning to change; see, e.g., Garland 1990, and the attention paid to the twelfth-century predecessors of the Palaiologan romances by Agapitos (1991), discussed in the 'Afterword'.
2 Dunlop 1888: 77–82.
3 Rohde 1960: 525, 535–7.
4 Valetas 1964: 1247.
5 Psichari 1886–9.
6 Mango 1980: 237; Trypanis 1981: 488.
7 Beck 1978: 131; Hunger 1980: 11.
8 Browning 1980: 152.
9 Hunger 1978: II, 119–42; Beck 1971: 151–3.
10 Dimaras 1975: 19–30; cf. Kechayioglou 1980; Politis 1975; Mastrodimitris 1984.
11 See Kriaras 1951: 92–3; Beck 1978: 151; Eideneier 1985b and the contributions of Savvidis, Eideneier, Vitti and Alexiou to Panayotakis 1993.
12 E. and M. Jeffreys 1983a: ii; cf. Beck 1978: 148.
13 Beck 1971: 11.
14 M. Jeffreys 1974b: 192.
15 Aleksidze 1979: 3–4, 305.
16 Jauss 1982a; 1982b.

1 THE TWELFTH-CENTURY BACKGROUND

1 Bryer 1981: 97.
2 Mango 1980: 1; cf. Kazhdan and Franklin 1984: 14.
3 Mango 1980: 22–9, 233.
4 Clucas 1981: 161; on the trial, see ibid.: 26–73. This picture may well turn out to be over-simplified, but is widely endorsed among modern historians. See Angold 1984: 115–18; Shepard 1984; Kazhdan and Epstein 1985: 127–8, 158–9; Magdalino 1993a: 268–9.
5 Browning 1975: 23. Among contemporary judgements, Anna Komnene on her father Alexios I, and Ioannes Kinnamos on Manuel are examples of a strongly favourable line, endorsed in modern times by, e.g., Ostrogorsky (1968: 351–417). Negative criticisms are voiced in the twelfth and thirteenth centuries respectively by Ioannes Zonaras and Niketas Choniates, discussed by Magdalino (1983; 1993a *passim*), and in modern times by Browning (1975; 1980); and by Kazhdan

and Constable (1982: 136–7). The best modern accounts of the history of the period are Angold (1984) and Magdalino (1993a). See also Hunger 1968b; Kazhdan and Franklin 1984. For a radical approach to the intellectual history of the twelfth century, see Mullett 1984.

6 Jauss 1982a: 35.
7 Cf. E. Jeffreys 1980: 483n.
8 For bibliography on these and other vernacular Greek texts of the period which lie outside the scope of this book, see Chapter 6, and Beck 1971.
9 See Browning 1978a: 122; Beck 1975: 72–3; 1978: 148; Kriaras 1959; 1976; Ševčenko 1982: 174–7; 1985; Beaton 1987a: 8–12.
10 Ševčenko 1982; Markopoulos 1983: 282.
11 Curtius 1953: 383–7; Dronke 1970: 2–8; 1973; 1976; 1982.
12 Curtius 1953: 26.
13 Cf. Patlagean 1979; Lyons 1981: 24–7.
14 Mango 1980: 60–87; 1981.
15 Mango 1980: 236–7; 241.
16 Margaret Mullet puts it, with admirable caution and a string of references to recent scholarship, which space forbids my reproducing here, like this: 'If . . . the cost of books is thought to be beyond the pocket of a minor civil servant, if chronicles are thought of as light reading for the court, if the vernacular experiments are seen as a literary game of the learned classes, if *Digenes Akrites* was written for a learned Constantinopolitan audience, and above all if lower-style metaphrases were used for reading other people's books while you yourself wrote in high style, it is conceivable that the readership of Byzantine literature was no wider than its audience, an audience comprising the sum of all contemporary *theatra* .... It may well be that audience and readership were simply two sides of the same coin' (Mullett 1984: 180).
17 Wilson 1975; Mango 1980: 253; Jenkins 1963: 40.
18 Kazhdan and Constable 1982: 104.
19 Browning 1978b.
20 Bowie 1985: 684.
21 AT 16.
22 Beck 1984: 133.
23 Beaton 1981a: 15–16.
24 Browning 1962–3; Ostrogorsky 1968: 328; Southern 1982.
25 Curtius 1953: 383–8.
26 Dronke 1982: 582–3. 'What can hardly be denied . . . is the common intellectual origin of the interpretative nature of the romance on the one hand and of the exegetic tradition on the other. Both reflect the teaching provided by the great cathedral schools of France in the twelfth century' (Vinaver 1971: 18).
27 On satire, see Robinson 1979: 68–81; M. Alexiou 1982–3. On the 'begging topos' and particularly its relation to Prodromos, see M. Alexiou 1986; Beaton 1987a.
28 Cf. Browning's comments on similarities between intellectual developments in East and West, which he argues are not causally related. 'Surely', he goes on, 'the explanation lies in the development of urban life and the growing complexity of commercial relations in both East and West' (Browning 1975: 21).
29 E. Jeffreys 1980: 483.
30 The role of this somewhat shadowy figure as an influential patroness is further discussed by E. Jeffreys 1982; M. and E. Jeffreys 1994.
31 Dronke 1970: 33–65; Ryding 1971: 135.
32 Bury 1911: 16; cf. Faral 1913.
33 Deligiorgis 1975: 28.

34 Pecoraro 1982.
35 Cf. Beaton 1980: 116–20. The origin of the two later romances which, translated into Greek from Italian and French respectively, preserve Arabic story elements, will be discussed in Chapter 9.

2 THE LITERARY TRADITION

1 Mango 1980: 241.
2 The norms against which (as they see it) progressive twelfth-century authors were tempted to rebel are well described by Kazhdan and Franklin (1984: 185): 'The repetitive formulae are essential to the didactic purpose of Byzantine literature, whose aim is not to reproduce reality but to convey a set idea, not to communicate or stimulate fresh impressions but to state the case correctly.'
3 Beck 1969; Kustas 1973: 149; cf. Lodge 1977. A similar point has been made by Lemerle for Byzantine art. There: 'ce qui demeure essentiel et permanent, c'est l'effort pour dépasser l'homme et l'accident, l'individuel et le passager; pour atteindre quelque chose que par définition on ne serait nommer, que l'on appelle le surhumain, l'impersonal, l'intemporel, l'éternel, le sacré: tous ces termes conviennent et en même temps sont insuffisants' (Lemerle 1967). Tanaşoca (1979) develops this with regard to the ideological function of Byzantine literature in upholding an ideal and demonstrating its permanence.
4 See W. B. Yeats, 'Sailing to Byzantium' (1928) and 'Byzantium' (1933). Cf. Kazhdan and Epstein (1985: 139): 'Byzantine imitative literature did not avoid vital contemporary questions, and used antique expressions to comment upon social and ideological phenomena in the Byzantine world. This art was in a sense an art of allusion.'
5 Kennedy 1980: 40.
6 Jenkins 1963: 43–6; cf. Mango 1975: 1. A subtler view of 'creative imitation', at least in the twelfth century, is advanced by Hunger (1969–70); see also Kazhdan 1967: 112. For a partial revaluation of the literature of the second sophistic, several of the essays edited by Winkler and Williams (1982) are instructive.
7 Kennedy 1980: 163–4.
8 Kustas 1973: 22–3.
9 *Mythos*, which one might have expected to play a part, is defined as what we would call a fable ('not true but of some utilitarian value') by Hermogenes (Herm. *Prog.* I), and always exemplified in Aphthonios and his successors by a moral tale in the Aesopian manner. Such fables seem to have been continuously popular in Byzantium (Beck 1971: 25–38), but it is not until the fourteenth century that we find allegories from the world of nature that go beyond a simple didactic structure and purpose.
10 Aphth. *Prog.* II.
11 Kennedy 1980: 164; Ryding 1971: 66–82; Dronke 1973.
12 Pignani (Ed.) 1983.
13 Pignani 1983: 79–100.
14 Herm. *Prog.* II.
15 Kustas 1973: 41–2n.; Kennedy 1963: 92.
16 Herm. *Prog.* IX.
17 Aphth. *Prog.* XI.
18 Bas. *Prog.* VII.
19 Bas. *Prog.* VII 27; cf. Hunger 1969–70: 21 and n.
20 Bas. *Prog.* VII 26. For Nikolaos, see Walz 1832: 381–94.

21 The numerous verbal correspondences between Basilakes and Makrembolites' romance are noted by Pignani (1983: 41–2) and documented in her footnotes to the text of the *progymnasmata*, as well as by Polyakova (1969: 122–3; 1979: 25–32). For discussion of the latter's argument that it was Basilakes who drew on the romance, see p. 80. See now Magdalino 1992, and Afterword.

22 Danae addresses Zeus: πάλαι σὲ ὡς ὄρνιν ἔρως ἐπτέρωσε ... καὶ νῦν ὡς χρυσὸν ἐπέχρωσε καὶ ὡς ἕδνον ἐπέδωκεν ('Eros once gave you wings like a bird of prey ... [and] now has coloured you with gold and offers you as a wedding gift) (Bas. *Prog.* vii 17, lines 37–40). Cf. *HH* iv 21, 2.

The seduction by the deceitful Goth is described by his victim: τὴν παρθενίαν ἐσύλησε ... τὴν παρθενίαν ἐσκύλευσεν ('he ransacked [my] virginity ... he defiled [my] virginity') (Bas. *Prog.* vii 27, lines 2–3).

23 Bas. *Prog.* vii 17, 25; cf. Beck 1984: 113.

24 Bas. *Prog.* vii 22.

25 Bas. *Prog.* vii 26; cf. Littlewood 1979; Polyakova 1976.

26 There are remarkable correspondences between this piece and the episode of *Kallimachos and Chrysorrhoe* in which the hero, disguised as a gardener, has to draw water for the bath by means of which the king hopes to quench Chrysorrhoe's obstinate longing for Kallimachos, and the two are reunited through the heroine's stratagem of hanging her ring in a tree (*Kall.* 1566–1824); and also with the imagery of love-songs in the modern Greek oral tradition (see Beaton 1980: 58–64).

27 Herm. *Prog.* x; Aphth. *Prog.* ii.

28 Hunger 1978: I, 170–88, II, 110–11. An interesting exception is provided by the *ekphraseis* of gardens and apples by John Geometres in the tenth century (Littlewood 1972), which anticipate some of the descriptions in the later vernacular romances (cf. Littlewood 1974). On the *ekphrasis* of the garden and its relevance to the romances, see Littlewood 1979; for the development of this type of *ekphrasis* and its relation to rhetorical theory, see Schissel 1942.

29 Kazhdan and Constable 1982: 61; Nikolaos, *Prog.* vii 7 = Walz 1832: 406; cf. AT ii 3.

30 Cupane 1984.

31 Maguire 1974.

32 Curtius 1953: 485.

33 Hanning 1977: 1; cf. Benton 1982.

34 Compare the following account of how matters stood in the West: 'The figure of the author–writer came into existence in the years around 1170 after a gestation that had lasted several decades. It is a remarkable fact that he did not spring directly from the flourishing oral traditions, Germanic, French, or Celtic, and their precedents for fictional narrative: it was the scholarly writer who groped his way toward fiction, not the oral storyteller who simply resorted to writing' (Nykrog 1982: 594). See also Shepherd 1979.

35 Kazhdan and Franklin (1984: 188) cite, as an example of 'mundane minutiae' and a writer's perception of 'particular reality', a passage by Eustathios of Thessalonica in which the writer describes being unable to sleep because of mice, and the impudence with which the mouse effected its escape when he attempted to stalk it. But how can we be sure that Eustathios is really describing nature, and not adding his playful variation to a literary topos which made much of the *adoxon*, that is of devoting the highest rhetorical skills to the lowest possible subject? Mice by the late twelfth century had become something of a mini-topos of their own, as developed by Prodromos in the 'Battle of Cat and Mice' (Hunger 1968c) and Σχέδη μυός (Papademetriou 1969), as well as in the anonymous satire

Timarion (= Romano 1974: 136; cf. Lambakis 1982: 101–2 n. 19). It may, rather, be the new, mock-heroic cast given to an old literary topos by Prodromos that represents the real innovation in his younger contemporary Eustathios' little anecdote.

3 THE 'PROTO-ROMANCE', *DIGENES AKRITES*

1   It is claimed by Kazhdan and Constable (1982: 113), that the 'embryonic plot' of the twelfth-century romances is prefigured in Nikephoros Bryennios' historical *Commentaries*, written earlier in the same century, in which 'the center of the narrative is formed by the marriage of Alexios Comnenos and Irene Doukaina'. As in romance, the pair 'succeed in surmounting various obstacles' (cf. Kazhdan and Epstein 1985: 202). Attention has also been drawn to the passage in which the thirteenth-century historian Niketas Choniates apparently echoes Prodromos' romance (Hunger 1968b: esp. 70), but such cross-fertilizations are apparently rare.

2   Ševčenko (1982: 13) even links the saint's life with the romance as 'one of the two Byzantine equivalents of modern novel'; cf. Beck 1977.

3   Hunger 1978: II, 123; cf. Hägg 1983: 154–65.

4   Mango 1980: 247–8.

5   Mango 1980: 249; Browning 1980: 153. One reason for the parallel development of the romance in East and West may be the existence of a common substratum of saints' lives, many of which in the West, like the *Life of St Alexis* (adapted from Latin into French *c.* 1050), derive from the Greek or Syriac East and preserve something of an exotic setting. This is particularly evident in Anglo-Saxon saints' lives, several of which (St Juliana, St Helen, St Andrew) are accepted as deriving, via Latin, from early Greek hagiography (Legouis and Cazamian 1967: 44; cf. Boitani 1982: 37).

6   Hörandner 1974: 45.

7   Beck 1971: 25–38, 145; Kechayoglou 1982b; 1988.

8   In the *Tale of the Four-Footed Beasts*, *Poulologos*, *Oporikologos* and the *Tale of the Donkey*; and in the relatively independent reworkings of the Alexander story in successive versions from the fourteenth to the sixteenth centuries. *Barlaam* makes a brief reappearance in the introductory section of Bergades' dream-poem about the underworld, *Apokopos*, in Crete in the mid-fifteenth century. *Stephanites and Ichnelates* may have been expanded with further translations in the fourteenth century, and was twice paraphrased into modern Greek in Phanariot circles in the seventeenth and early eighteenth centuries (Beck 1971: 43); while *Syntipas* also underwent paraphrases in the sixteenth and seventeenth centuries (Beck 1971: 47; Kechayoglou 1982b; 1988). I am grateful to David Holton for drawing my attention to what may have been the last Venetian reprinting of this text, in 1848. See also Afterword.

9   But see Ro>ché (1988) for the possibility that powerful families may have commissioned their own partisan chronicles in an 'epic' style, later to be drawn on by eleventh- and twelfth-century historians.

10   The thematic independence of the two component parts of *Digenes* was first noted by Beck (1971: 68–87; cf. 1984: 105–6), who christened them respectively the 'Lay of the Emir' and the 'Romance of Digenes', and assigned their original composition to different periods (see his stemma for the original composition, 1971: 71); and this model for the formation of the poem was adopted by Huxley (1974) and Oikonomidès (1979). On bipartite structure in Western medieval narrative, briefly

discussed in the case of Digenes by Kastner (1976: 36), see Jackson 1960: 56–7; Vinaver 1971: 33–52; Ryding 1971: 25–7, 117–35. For the importance of this structural principle in the later Greek romances, see Chapter 8.

11 Beaton 1981a: 18–19.

12 For the relation of *Digenes* to Arabic literature, see Grégoire 1975; Christides 1979. On parallels with the *Cid*, see Martino 1986; Hook in Beaton and Ricks 1993.

13 The poem was, however, translated (very loosely) into Russian, probably at a fairly early date (Graham 1968). Although no direct evidence for a translation into a Western language survives, the name 'Digenes' is cited as that of a legendary hero 'who suffered for love' in a vernacular Dutch poem of 1271 (S. Alexiou 1985: cxx–cxxi) and may also be reflected in Boccaccio's choice of name for his 'knight of Mars', Arcita, in the *Theseid* (Kahane 1945; see p. 142).

14 There are two English translations of the Grottaferrata (G) version. Mavrogordato's (1956) is printed facing the Greek text and is scholarly and generally accurate, if often quaint. The translation and introduction by Hull (1972) make no pretensions to scholarship. On the bilingual (Greek and English) edition of the Escorial (E) version by Ricks (1990), and a forthcoming critical edition of both versions by E. Jeffreys, see Afterword.

Because of the special editorial problems posed by the different versions, which will be discussed below, there is no single edition to which reference can be made. All citations in this chapter give line numbers for the two earliest versions, preceded by their initial letters, E and G. Where only one version is cited, the locus is absent from the other. Line references to E refer to the edition of S. Alexiou (1985), and quotations adopt the readings of that edition. References to G, in the form of book number (in roman) followed by line number, are to Mavrogordato 1956, although the text has been silently emended to incorporate the readings of Trapp (1971a). Separate references to Trapp's synoptic edition are not given, as the line numbers of earlier editions (also retained by Alexiou) are given there alongside Trapp's own numbering. Although the reader may in practice find it easier to refer to the synoptic edition, which gives the two versions side by side, it is simpler to find a reference in Trapp's edition from the line numbers of the separate editions than to do the reverse. For the limitations of Trapp's edition, see E. Jeffreys (1972); M. Jeffreys (1975a; 1976). For responses to Alexiou's edition of the E version, see Beaton 1986a; 1987b, and several of the papers collected in Beaton and Ricks 1993.

15 E 73 ≈ G I 224.

16 Respectively by Mavrogordato 1956; cf. the novel by Patrick White, *The Twyborn Affair*, published in 1979; and Hull 1972.

17 M. Jeffreys 1975a; 1976. On the long-running controversy about the relation of the poem to oral folk-songs collected in modern times, see Grégoire 1932; 1941; 1942; Kyriakidis 1958; Fletcher 1977; Herzfeld 1980; Beaton 1981b. On the Russian versions see Graham 1968 and the papers by Saunier and Mackridge in Beaton and Ricks 1993.

18 For bibliography, and the form of citations to the text in the present discussion, see n.14 above.

19 The third version, whose earliest form has also been lost, is preserved with significant divergences of style and language register in four manuscripts of the sixteenth and seventeenth centuries. Following the publication of Trapp's synoptic edition, which attempts to collate these manuscripts to recover their lost archetype 'Z', which is then printed in parallel with the E and G versions,

it has been generally accepted that this 'Z' version represents a compilation of the available versions made in the fifteenth century (Trapp 1971a: 26–9; for a negative view, see L. Politis 1973a). The sources behind this compilation identified by Trapp (1971a: 29–33) have been reduced to only two through the astute detective work of Michael Jeffreys (1975a; 1976), who has shown that the fifteenth-century compiler had before him only a version very similar to our G (but lacking some pages at the beginning), and the very copy of the E version that has come down to us. Trapp's somewhat overburdened stemma (1971a: 46) can as a result be greatly simplified. The new opening to the work supplied by the compiler in the fifteenth century, as preserved by the Athens manuscript (A) and edited by Trapp as 'Z' 1–290, will be discussed separately in Chapter 12. Many new proper names seem also to have been introduced into the work by the fifteenth-century compiler, to flesh out the uncompromising anonymity of such roles as Digenes' wife and mother in the older versions, and these names have often crept into modern commentaries. The present discussion is strictly confined to the older versions.

20   Karayianni 1975; S. Alexiou 1979; 1982; 1983; 1985: liv–lxiii.
21   S. Alexiou 1985: cxxi–cxxiii.
22   E 619.
23   E 620–701.
24   G IV 33–5.
25   Morgan 1960: 54; 58–68; Lord 1954; 1960: 207–20; Beaton 1981a: 22–3.
26   S. Alexiou 1979: 35–42; 1985: lxxiii–lxxvii.
27   Bäuml 1984: 43.
28   S. Alexiou 1985: cxxxvii–cxxxix. The Pontic thesis is proposed by Prombonas 1985; Trapp 1971c.
29   S. Alexiou 1985: viii; xix–xx.
30   G IV 965–71.
31   G VII 5–7.
32   The original form of this scene, and the political attitude implied by it, are discussed by Trapp (1971a: 58–62; 1971b). Kazhdan and Epstein (1985: 117–18) make the telling point that the emperor's homage to the hero follows a topos common in earlier saints' lives.
33   On the episode of Digenes' first adultery with the daughter of Haplorrhabdes, see Beaton 1981b: 35–6; Dyck 1983; Galatariotou 1987: 57–9.
34   Trapp 1971a: 69–70.
35   G VI 836–8 and see Mavrogordato 1956: lvi. These are the line numbers of Mavrogordato's edition only, as his numbering allows for a manuscript page of forty lines that is missing just before this. Trapp (1971a) numbers the same passage VI 796–8, and has also emended the punctuation to conform to Mavrogordato's translation of the lines. Unlike Mavrogordato, however, I take μοιχείαν to be used in its normal sense of 'adultery', not 'adulteress', which is nowhere attested (Mavrogordato had noted this difficulty). The interpretation of the lines proposed here requires the comma at the end of line 837, as it is found in Mavrogordato's edition. For the importance of the episode in this version of the poem as a whole, see Galatariotou 1987: 59–62.
36   MacAlister 1984. The compiler's manuscript of the G version did, however, contain a leaf in Book VI detailing the hero's dalliance with Maximou, and seemingly removed from our exemplar (Mavrogordato 1956: 210–13; G VI 786–826; cf. E 1575–8). This is the only point at which the manuscripts of the 'Z' group provide a unique witness to the original.
37   First demonstrated by Kastner 1976.

38 G IV 4–64 ≈ E 703–41.
39 G IV 65–253 ≈ E 724–91.
40 G IV 254–964 ≈ E 793–1088.
41 G IV 965–1093 only.
42 G IV 241–53.
43 G IV 254.
44 Cf. E 835.
45 G I 30.
46 Tiftixoglu 1974; M. Alexiou and Holton 1976.
47 S. Alexiou 1979: 57–77; 1985: xcv–xcvii.
48 For the results of a new and more rigorous comparison between the versions, assisted by computer-produced concordances, see Beaton 1993a; 1993b.
49 Grégoire's most important contributions to the study of *Digenes* are collected in Grégoire 1975; see also 1942. In recent years the most productive attempts to uncover the historical background of the eastern frontier, from which the original story must have derived, have been made by Pertusi (1970; 1976); Huxley (1974); M. Jeffreys (1978) and Oikonomidès (1979). It should be emphasized that all these studies focus on the story-*material* on which the literary work is based. None of these writers draws a clear distinction between story-material and background on the one hand, and the creation of a self-conscious literary work on the other. See also Afterword.
50 Bouvier 1960: 87.
51 Academy of Athens 1962: 59–63; S. Alexiou 1990: 175–94.
52 See n. 17 above and the excellent discussion of S. Alexiou (1985: cviii–cxiii), whose criticism of my own former negative view (Beaton 1980: 78–82) I now accept (cf. Beaton 1981b). For a revival of interest in this subject, see Afterword.
53 S. Alexiou 1985: 157–89.
54 Cf. Beaton 1980: 77, 154; S. Alexiou 1985; cviii–cx.
55 1985: cii–cxx.
56 Mavrogordato 1956: 265–6; Trapp 1971a: *passim*.
57 Kazhdan and Epstein 1985: 117–18.
58 See further Trapp 1976; 1993: 120–1. Compare the incorporation of hagiographic elements in the *Cid* (West 1983).
59 G IV 4–36 ≈ E 702–22.
60 On the *ekphraseis* of Digenes' palace and garden in G, and their relation to ancient literary models, see Andronikos 1969; Xyngopoulos 1973.
61 Digenes' deeds are compared to Alexander's in the prologue to Book IV (G IV 29); the warrior-maiden Maximou is said to be descended from the Amazons encountered by Alexander (G VI 397), whose adventures are among those depicted on the walls of Digenes' palace (G VII 90–4).
62 E 1695–1786 ≈ G VIII 1–210.
63 G VIII 7, 31–6.
64 Σφοδρόν (here: intensity of pain), G VIII 37; Mavrogordato 1956: 234–5n.
65 On the relation between the Alexander 'romance' and *Digenes* more generally, see Veloudis 1968: 265; Moennig in Beaton and Ricks 1993.
66 E 712–19.
67 G IV 26–35.
68 Beaton 1981a: 17–21.
69 A proposal along these lines was first made, it turns out, by Grégoire (1932), who does not seem to have followed it up; cf. Beaton 1993: 44, 49–50.
70 This had been Grégoire's position: see also Mavrogordato (1956). It was subsequently restated by Beck (1971), and elaborated by Huxley (1974: see n. 49

above). The genesis of the poem outlined here effectively rules out any such process: we need to find a date and place for the decisive act of grafting together the literary and oral traditions underlying the work in its present form.

71 Angold 1984: 218–19; S. Alexiou 1985: liv–lxiv; Mullett 1984: 180.
72 See, e.g., N. Politis 1906; 1911; Hesseling 1911; Beck 1971: 94–8; 1984: 105–6.
73 Mavrogordato 1956: xiv–xv; contrast lxxix.
74 Trapp 1972; S. Alexiou 1985: xlviii–liii.
75 On the reception of the poem in the later Middle Ages, but more particularly in modern times, see Kechayoglou 1986a and Kechayoglou 1993.
76 G IV 956–64.
77 Galatariotou 1987: 65–6: ἵνα σὲ ἐκκερδήσω.

4 THE RENAISSANCE OF A GENRE

1 Perry 1967: 103; Hägg 1983: 73–80.
2 Hilberg 1876: xxvi–xlvii; Hunger 1980: 10.
3 Rohde 1960: 521–37.
4 H.-G. Beck notes that the setting of these romances in space and time represents an 'alienation effect' rare in the literature of any period before the twentieth century, but makes no attempt to account for the phenomenon (Beck 1984: 117; cf. Hunger 1980: 34).
5 On the emergence of the genre and its likely date see Hägg 1987; 1988. The five extant romances are: Chariton of Aphrodisias, *Chaireas and Kallirrhoe* (Char.) = Molinié 1979 (with French translation); Xenophon of Ephesos, *Ephesiaka* (Xen.) = Papanikolaou 1973; Longos, *Daphnis and Chloe* (*Daphn.*) = Dalmeyda 1960; Achilles Tatios, *Leukippe and Kleitophon* (AT). Gaselee 1969 (with English translation); Heliodoros, *Aithiopika* (Hel.) = Rattenbury and Lumb 1960.

All five, together with the papyrus fragments of several other romances, can be found in English translation in Reardon 1989.

A useful table giving details of all the extant and known Hellenistic romances, with their probable dates of composition, is given by Bowie (1985: 684). For a bibliography of work on the ancient and Byzantine romances up to 1960, see Mazal 1965; see also Afterword.
6 There is a good deal of evidence that the last two named were read extensively during the Byzantine period: Heliodoros' romance is the object of a résumé and commentary, along with Iamblichos' romance which is now lost, by Photios in the ninth century; it is also discussed, in comparison with *Leukippe and Kleitophon*, by Psellos, and on its own by Philip the Philosopher and Ioannes Eugenikos. All these commentaries are concerned with rhetorical style, and with a moral–allegorical interpretation of content (Gärtner 1969). Heliodoros' romance is also echoed by Psellos and Michael Glykas, who repeat the digression on the flooding of the Nile found in the *Aithiopika*, and another digression in the same romance is echoed elsewhere by Psellos (Gärtner 1969: 55 n.). In the twelfth century, alongside the revival of the romance, we find a spate of allusions to its themes, for example in the occasional poetry of Theodore Prodromos and 'Manganeios' Prodromos (E. Jeffreys 1980: 478–82). Finally, such information as we possess on the contents of private libraries owned by Byzantines at various periods includes several references to Achilles Tatios and Heliodoros (Vryonis 1957; Lemerle 1977: 15–63). For an overview of the reception of these and other ancient 'erotica' between the ninth century and the eleventh, see Beck 1984: 87–96.

7 The case for a residue of ancient myth and cult underlying the ancient romances, earlier proposed by Kerényi and Merkelbach, has been daringly restated, with new supporting evidence, by Graham Anderson (1984). But Anderson's 'sources' for the romances in Sumerian baked tablets uncovered in the twentieth century cannot have been used *directly* by the Greek writers of romance, who in any case are unlikely to have had a historical perception of the popular story motifs on which they drew as deriving from the religious myths of a remote civilization. More probable is that the debris of myths, which have lost the meaning and power once conferred on them by a former set of institutions and system of belief, is intuitively recognized in an era which itself is searching for a myth, and thrown together with many other heterogeneous elements in the process of *bricolage* out of which a new myth, with usage and repetition, emerges. The same model, interestingly enough, can be applied to the relation between Arthurian romance and Celtic mythology.

8 Dodds 1965; Bowie 1985: 687–8.

9 Perry 1967: 124; Reardon 1969: 294.

10 Bloom 1973.

11 *The Ordeal of Gilbert Pinfold* (Harmondsworth: Penguin Books, 1967), p. 9.

12 C. W. Müller was the first to describe this relationship in terms of 'reception aesthetic' (Müller 1976; 1981); see also Perry 1967: 3–43; Reardon 1969; Steiner 1969; Hägg 1971: 334–5. For a somewhat different view of the ancient romances' relation to the past, see Anderson 1984: *passim*.

13 *DC* VI 329–558.

14 In the pathetic appropriation: Γυνὴ γὰρ εἶ σύ – γνῶθι τὴν σαυτῆς φύσιν (*DC* VI 420) [you are a woman know thy own nature]).

15 *DC* VI 640–1. The parody in Longos from which this derives is quoted and discussed by Hägg (1983: 38–9).

16 *HH* V 2–5; cf. M. Alexiou 1977: 34.

17 *HH* VII 13–14; cf. M. Alexiou 1977: 37.

18 οὓς γὰρ θεὸς συνῆψε, τίς διασπάσοι; (*DC* III 12, VII 264); Kazhdan 1967.

19 ὅμως κἄν τούτῳ νικῶ (*HH* III 7).

20 Müller 1976: 132.

21 Hägg 1971: 23.

22 Perry 1967: 153–67; Maehler 1976; Hägg 1987; 1988; cf. Treu 1984.

23 At III 5: the coast of Egypt was 'then' infested with robbers; for VII 12 and Gaselee (1969: 367 n.), cf. Hägg 1971: 63. Hel. I 9–10: Knemon is outlawed by a classical Athenian lawcourt. Hel. II 24, V 8, VI 13, etc.: Persian rule in Egypt.

24 *Sic* in the manuscripts and quite reasonably retained by Papanikolaou (1973), though more usually 'corrected' to Habrokomes. Compare the way in which similarly 'meaningful' names in modern literature are often spelt.

25 *Daphn.* I 7, II 5, II 7, III 12.

26 *RD* VIII 191–209; *DC* II 125–43; *AK* Frs 8, 21, 22, 64, 95, 117; *HH* II 11–12, 14, III 1, XI 14.

27 *AT* V 25.

28 *RD* VII 5–15.

29 He is like a dragon or serpent (*DC* II 217, 222) and, as well as carrying the traditional torch, actually breathes fire (*DC* VI 595–7); he has the hundred hands of Briareus (*DC* III 114); he is despicable, like a leech (*DC* IV 399–403); he ensnares mortals in his web like a spider (*DC* IV 409).

30 Ἔρωτι δόξαν τῷ τυράννῳ (*DC* III 17); παντάναξ (*DC* II 135); δοῦλος ἄθλιος ... ὁλοσχερῶς Ἔρωτι θητεύων βίᾳ (*DC* VI 339–40).

31 Cupane 1974b: 250–61; see also Chapter 10.

32   Compare the fragment from Iamblichos cited in this connection by Hunger: 'Eros when he becomes jealous is no longer a king (βασιλεύς) but a tyrant (τύραννος)' (Hunger 1980: 24 and n.). See also Afterword.

33   This reading of *HH* III 1 confirms the intuition of Aleksidze that slavery in this romance is accorded an importance not found in the other ancient and Byzantine romances where the theme also appears (Aleksidze 1965: 12; cf. contra Hunger 1978: II, 141 n.). But it is unnecessary to account for this by attributing a political ideology of more recent times to Makrembolites. Rather, the romance explores the nature of love, and the salvation it traditionally offers in the genre, by analogy first with the emperor/subject relationship (in the hero's subjection to Eros and king) and, second, with that between masters and slaves (in the third part of the romance).

34   παλιγγενεσία (Char. I 8).

35   Xen. III 6–8.

36   Xen. V 2.

37   *Daphn.* III 4.

38   AT II 23, III 15–16, III 20–2.

39   AT V 7; VII 3. Cf. Anderson's apt characterization of Achilles as an 'erotic entertainer with a learned flourish to a vicious streak' (1984: 74).

40   AT III 17.5, V 11.6, V 19.2, V 26.4, VII 6.

41   Hel. VI 14–15; cf. Gärtner 1969.

42   Anderson (1984: 34) neatly captures Heliodoros' idiosyncrasy as 'wry religiosity'. Elsewhere in the same book he comments on Heliodoros' 'ambiguity and mystification' (ibid.: 36) and remarks: 'If Heliodoros has a belief, it might be in equivocation in all things' (ibid.: 83).

43   *RD* IV 209–42.

44   *RD* VI 225–36, VIII 441–86.

45   *DC* II, 169–85, II 245–6; cf. VI, 589, 592. In post-Byzantine Greek, Χάρων becomes Χάρος and ousts Hades and Thanatos to become the single personification of death (M. Alexiou 1978). (See Chapter 11, n. 52).

46   *HH* VII 12ff., IX 9.

47   διὰ σὲ θανάτου γευσαμένη πικροῦ καὶ τέλος αἰχμάλωτος καὶ δούλη νῦν ... (*HH* IX 9).

48   *HH* IX 22.

49   Char. VII 5–6.

50   AT II 23–31.

51   Xen. III 6–8, V 7.

52   e.g. Hel. I 22, 26.

53   Hel. IV *passim*, V 13, V 30.

54   Gaselee 1969: 390–1; AT VIII 10.

55   Kleitophon's original fiancée is abducted by mistake for Leukippe (AT II 16–18); a rival lover is disposed of just in time by the fortunes of war (IV 14); shortly afterwards Leukippe goes temporarily mad, the result, we learn, of an *accidental* overdose of magic by another would-be suitor (IV 15); the entire wanderings of the lovers would have been unnecessary but for a few hours' delay in the delivery of a letter (V 10); Leukippe's father, arriving in Ephesos where all the principals have now gathered in preparation for the denouement, misses her by minutes (VII 13–14).

56   AT II 27, III 2. The theme is not, of course, confined to *Leukippe and Kleitophon*; and even Chariton's romance, which partially transcends it, makes extensive use of it in the *chance* meeting (ἐκ τύχης) of the lovers arranged by Eros (Char. I 1); in the hero's frequent attempts at suicide (e.g. V 10); the explicit intervention of

chance in stirring up a timely rebellion in Egypt (VI 8) and finally in arranging for the happy ending (VIII 1). In the *Ephesiaka* Abrokomes boasted that he was immune to love, and Eros and fate (εἱμαρμένη) set an ambush for him (Xen. I 10); sold into slavery, he can still boast 'they have power over my body, but I have a soul that is free' (Xen. II 4), only to fall abjectly at the feet of his master Apsyrtos under torture a few paragraphs later (Xen. II 10). Abrokomes only wins through thanks to divine providence (πρόνοια) and the solicitous interventions of the homosexual pirate Hippothoos. In *Daphnis and Chloe* divine providence is replaced by a fundamentally beneficent Nature, but the events in the romance still happen at random and almost invariably happen *to* the main characters: Daphnis' rival for Chloe's love is conveniently killed by brigands (*Daphn.* I 29); the supernatural takes a hand to turn back the Methymnaians' ship with Chloe on board (*Daphn.* II 26–7); riches fall, almost literally, from heaven (*Daphn.* III 27); and the happy ending is accounted a change in the 'will of Chance' (*Daphn.* IV 24). Heliodoros in the *Aithiopika* twice has Charikleia devise a stratagem with no other object than to gain time so that chance (αἱ τύχαι) may produce something better (Hel. I 26, VII 21); in other crises the pair seem anaesthetized by the effects of chance (Hel. II 15, V 6).

57 Char. I 1; cf. Parthenios, Frs: Introduction (text in Gaselee 1969). There may even on occasion be a deliberate play on the opposite meanings of πάθος ('suffering, experience') and δρᾶμα ('something done') in *Leukippe and Kleitophon* (for references, see Müller 1976: 116, where a different but compatible interpretation is proposed) and in *Hysmine and Hysminias*, which is called a δρᾶμα but is in fact the story of *passive* experience. This seems to be explicit at *HH* VI 13: the abduction of Hysmine first mooted between Hysminias and his confidant Kratisthenes. The hero makes a joking reference to the value of friendship in ancient tragedy, and his friend picks up the allusion in a partial pun: ἐγώ σοι καθυπηρετήσω τῷ δράματι 'I shall assist you in the drama/action' (VI 13).

58 Kazhdan and Franklin 1984: 180–1.

59 Hörandner 1974: no. LXIX.

60 See, e.g., *RD* I 222, 331, VII 125, 197–9, VIII 145, IX 182; *DC* I 52, 220, 301, VII 206–7, IX 42; *AK* Frs 49, 54, 59, 137, 159; *HH* II 13, VI 11, VII 12, VIII 11, IX 3, 7. Fate in the twelfth-century romances is either the fickle goddess Chance (Τύχη) or the thread of destiny spun by the three Fates (Μοῖραι), as also in the ancient romances. Alongside these traditional attributes Manasses for the first time in the Greek romances introduces the 'wheel of Fortune' (ὁ τροχὸς τῆς Τύχης), which in time became a commonplace of Greek as well as Western literature in the later Middle Ages and the Renaissance (*AK* 49, 54). On the visual representation of the wheel of Fortune in Greek texts, see Davies 1978.

61 Cf. Hunger 1980: 18–19.

62 *RD* III 73–5, 125–6, VI 264–403, VIII 529–30; *DC* V 188–9, VII 186, 208; cf. Kazhdan 1967.

63 *HH* VI 18.

64 *HH* IX 20–3; see p. 86 below.

65 *RD* II 253–78.

66 *DC* III 53–64. Kazhdan argues that these attributes are intended to undermine the character as a serious romantic hero; but they are paralleled by Psellos' accounts of the leisure pursuits of the 'military' emperor Isaac Komnenos (*Chron.* VII 73), as well as by the early exploits of Digenes Akrites.

67 *RD* II 381–454; *DC* III 351–411, *HH* VI.

68 *RD* III 500ff.; *DC* V 98–102.

69 *HH* VI–VIII.

70 *HH* viii 9.
71 μᾶλλον παθὼν καὶ κολασθεὶς ἢ δράσας καὶ κολάσας (*AK* Fr. 33, 1. 2).
72 Anderson 1982; Winkler and Williams 1982; Hägg 1983.
73 Char. i 1; iii 6; vi 7; viii 5; i 1; cf. Steiner 1969: 124–50.
74 Xen. i 1–2.
75 Hel. iii 1–4; ix 14–15; iv 3.
76 AT iii 7–8, v 3; cf. viii 5; cf. Davison 1977.
77 *Daphn.* iv 2–3; AT i 15; cf. Littlewood 1979.
78 Hel. iii 17.
79 Hel. i 1, iii 1–4; cf. Palm 1967, cit. Hägg 1983: 66.
80 *DC* i 77–107. The choice of vocabulary further emphasizes the technical skill of the sculptor and so, by analogy, of the description itself: τεχνικῶς ('artfully') (*DC* i 94), εὐτέχνως ('with fine artistry') (98), ἀγαλματουργίαν ('sculpture') (104), κατεσκεύαστο ('assembled') (107).
81 *DC* iii 83–9.
82 *DC* ii 85.
83 Καὶ γὰρ ἡ φύσις/ . . . ἀγαλματοῖ σε λευκερυθροφωσφόρον (*DC* ii 246–8).
84 Cf. AT i 14–15.
85 *DC* vi 568–88.
86 *RD* i 39–60; cf. vii 238.
87 *RD* ii 249–50.
88 *RD* iv 163–5; see further.
89 *RD* iv 331–411; cf. AT ii 3, Herodotos i 25.
90 *RD* ix 320, 324–8, 335–8.
91 *HH* 1 5; cf. *DC* i 77–107.
92 *HH* viii 7.
93 *HH* ix 22.
94 See note 20.

5 THE TWELFTH-CENTURY TEXTS

1 Marcovich 1992.
2 This view has not been shared by scholars working in the former USSR, who have dated Makrembolites' romance to the early part of the twelfth century (Polyakova 1969; 1971; 1976; 1979: 84–124; Kazhdan and Epstein 1985: 202 and these views have been recently revived. On the dating of Makrembolites' romance, see pp. 79–80 and Afterword.
3 Hörandner 1974: 22, 32; Hunger 1978: ii 114; Kazhdan and Franklin 1984: 92–100.
4 E. Jeffreys 1980: 475–6; Kazhdan and Franklin 1984: 101.
5 E.g. Beck 1978: 131; 1984: 125–7.
6 Hörandner 1974: 55–6.
7 For this term, equivalent to 'flashback' but more precisely defined, see Genette · 1980: 40, and pp. 129–33.
8 Xen. iv 2.
9 There is a similar wry reversal for the author's own art in the *Aithiopika* (Hel. x 18.2; cf. Anderson 1984: 45 and n. 14).
10 Hunger 1968b; 1972; 1978: II 128–33.
11 See n. 16.
12 *RD* i 372–404; Cupane 1974a.
13 Ἕλλην ἐκ Κύπρου (*RD* i 36); Ἕλλην θεοὶ σωτῆρες, οὗτος ὁ ξένος,/Ἕλλην;

(*RD* I 153–4). Contrast *DC* IX 4, where Kleandros' body is burnt 'according to the custom of the Hellenes [= pagans]'.

14 *RD* VI 8–24, 32–8; Hunger 1972; 1980: 12–13.

15 *RD* VI 11–12.

16 Hel. IX 3–5. Details of this episode are repeated in the account by the emperor Julian of a historical siege which took place in AD 351, and the assumption that Heliodoros has incorporated a real event into his narrative provides the only basis for the traditional dating of his romance to the fourth century. Intriguingly, the possibility that Julian's account was based instead on Heliodoros' fiction has been raised, and a measure of support for it is lent by a new awareness of Heliodoros' proximity in style and interests to the second sophistic, which ended in the third century (Bowie 1985: 696). A comparable topos also appears in *Leukippe and Kleitophon*: 'land-battles on water, sea-fights on land' (AT III 2ff., IV 14; cf. Anderson 1984: 56 and n. 75).

17 Cf. Petronius, *Satyricon* 40; Hunger 1978: II 131.

18 Note a further allusion here to Petronius' sinister banquet in the *Satyricon*.

19 *RD* IV 313; cf. AT III 20–2.

20 *RD* IV 122–308.

21 See Hunger 1968b; 1978: II, 131–2; cf. Kazhdan 1967: 111; Koder and Weber 1980.

22 *RD* III 265–93, 319–404.

23 I Kings X 18–20; Herodotos VII 27; Brett 1954.

24 Conca 1990.

25 Kazhdan (1967) assumes that Drosilla was modelled on the bride of Stephanos Komnenos for whom the epithalamium was written, and therefore that the romance must have been written after it. In fact the highly stylized nature of the description makes it just as probable that the flattering picture of a royal bride was modelled on that of the idealized heroine of the romance. In view of what has already been said on the nature of Byzantine description, the goal of both passages would probably have been the approximation to an ideal, rather than real portraiture. This piece of evidence cannot be used to date the romance with any precision.

26 In the Paris MS: Ποίησις κυροῦ Νικήτου τοῦ Εὐγενιανοῦ κατὰ μίμησιν τοῦ μακαρίτου φιλοσόφου τοῦ Προδρόμου (Conca 1990: 30).

27 Petit 1902.

28 Kazhdan 1967; Hunger 1978: II 133–6; cf. Deligiorgis 1975.

29 *DC* VIII 185; contrast AT I 12, I 34; Hel. I 30–1, II 3; *RD* I 195.

30 *DC* VIII 311–16.

31 *DC* VII 280–95.

32 Examples are: πτηνοτοξοπυρφόρε (epithet of Eros: 'with wings, bow and fire') (*DC* II 143); λευκερυθροφωσφόρον (of Kalligone: 'iridescent in white and red') (II 248); πετροκάρδιος ('stony-hearted') (II 256); δακνοκαρδία ('biting into the heart') (II 271; VI 34); ὁπλοτοξότης ('armed archer') (III 140); κρυσταλόστερνε (of the heroine: 'crystal-breasted') (IV 120; cf. 80–1, 83, 149, 375, 382); λεπτολεύκοις (of fingers: 'fine and white') (IV 153); ἐρωτοληψία ('falling in love') (IV 253; cf. VI 625); αἰθεροκράτορ οὐρανοκράτορ (addressed to Zeus: 'lord of the upper air; the heavens') (V 108); ἐρωτοτόκου ('giving birth to love') (VI 210); σκληροπετρόστερνος ('hard/stony-hearted') (VI 270); ἐρωτομανίας ('love-passion') (VII 59).

33 *DC* I 77–107; III 65–100, IV 225–64, 330–41, VI 568–73 (parodied), VIII 2–130.

34 Mazal 1967; Tsolakis 1967. The two modern attempts at reconstruction were produced independently and adopt different principles in the arrangement and

numbering of the lines. References to the text here, for the sake of economy, give only the fragment number of Mazal's edition followed, where appropriate, after a point by a line number within the fragment.

35   E. Jeffreys 1980; Mullett 1984.
36   E. Jeffreys 1980: 476–7; Hunger 1978: II 128; cf. Tsolakis 1967: 15–20.
37   Cf. Tsolakis 1967: 47–8.
38   Anastasi 1969.
39   Mazal 1967: 84–152; Tsolakis 1967: 48–50; Hunger 1978: II 126–7.
40   Frs 80, 110, 161.
41   Fr. 36 and *passim*; Mazal 1967: 35; Hunger 1978: II 128.
42   Cf. Mazal 1967: 11, 155.
43   The line 'Ὁρᾷς τὰ δένδρα τὰ μακρὰ τὰ παρὰ τοῖς χειμάρροις; ('Do you see those trees far off by the ravines?') (Fr. 85) is reminiscent of a series of formulae from oral songs recorded in the nineteenth and twentieth centuries. And, like Eugenianos, Manasses uses new vernacular compounds: ἀνδροκάρδιον ('having a man's heart') (Fr. 51); βλοσυροβλέφαρον ('with cruel eyelids') (Fr. 52, line 15); ἐρωτολήπτου ('a man who has fallen in love') (Fr. 97, line 1); ἐρωτοκεντήτοις ('those stung by love') (Fr. 111, line 2); καρδιοκράτωρ (epithet of beauty: 'lord of the heart') (Fr. 116, line 1); ἐρωτόξεστον ('touched by love') (Fr. 141, line 5); δρακοντογνώμονος ('of ogreish opinion') (Fr. 153, line 2); ἐρωτοκρατούντι ('in the sway of love') (Fr. 163, line 5).

  Contact with Western literature is discernible only in the references to the 'wheel of Fortune' (τροχὸς τῆς Τύχης), previously unknown in the Greek romance.
44   Hilberg 1876; for translations, see Plepelits 1989 (German); Meunier 1991 (French).
45   See Chatzis 1950, refuted by M. Jeffreys 1976.
46   *HH* VIII 9, X 15; cf. M. Alexiou 1977; 35 and n.
47   Polyakova 1969; 1971.
48   Polyakova 1976; 1979: 84–124; Kazhdan and Epstein 1985: 202.
49   Cupane 1974b: 245–81.
50   Cupane 1978: 251 n. 84.
51   Hult 1986: 15–16.
52   Cf. E. Jeffreys 1980.
53   At this point I have deleted a paragraph from the 1st edition which attempted to identify a small number of Western-derived elements in *HH*, and gave serious consideration to the possibility of a thirteenth-century date. For an explanation of this change of heart see the Afterword.
54   Dunlop 1888: 81. Hysminias does, as a matter of fact, tell us whom he is addressing (*HH* I 2) and why – see the passage from XI 22 quoted on p. 86.
55   Gigante 1960; M. Alexiou 1977.
56   Müller's detective work (1976) on the allusions in Chariton's romance produces results uncannily similar to those of Gigante for Makrembolites.
57   Gigante 1960: 169 (my italics), 170.
58   Hunger 1968b: 74; cf. MacAlister 1985.
59   M. Alexiou 1977: 32.
60   M. Alexiou 1977: 42.
61   M. Alexiou 1977: 25 and n. 12; 43; cf. Hunger 1980: 24–6, 34.
62   Hägg 1983: 75.
63   A full summary of the plot is given by M. Alexiou (1977: 26–9).
64   M. Alexiou 1977: 29–30.
65   M. Alexiou 1977: 29.

NOTES

66 *HH* VIII 16.
67 *HH* VIII 20–1.
68 Stern 1955: 173–5; Webster 1938: 37–41, 111–13. Prodromos, *Verses on the Twelve Months* = Keil 1889: 113–15; cf. Hörandner 1974: 55; Eideneier 1979: 370–3. All the later *ekphraseis* on this theme (Eideneier 1979) can plausibly be derived from Makrembolites.
69 *HH* IV 16.
70 Stern 1955: 182.
71 *HH* IV 17. Χρόνος by the twelfth century could be used in its modern sense as 'year'. But the banal statement that the pictures represent the whole *year* would hardly suffice to deflect Hysminias' thoughts from Hysmine. In classical Greek (on which Makrembolites' language is modelled) the word always means 'time' in the broad sense, and also had the sense of 'lifetime' or 'age', which is surely relevant here.
72 διὰ κόρης ἁπαλόχροος οὐ διάησι, τροχαλὸν δὲ γέροντα τίθησιν (*HH* IV 18, cf. *Works and Days* 518–19).
73 *HH* II 7–10.
74 *HH* III 5–7, cf. M. Alexiou 1977: 41.
75 *HH* IV 21–3.
76 ὑπὲρ παίδων ὀλλυμένων οἰκτρῶς ἐν ἔαρος ἀκμῇ, ἐν ἀτρυγήτῳ λειμῶνι καὶ μέσῃ νεότητι (*HH* X 12).
77 Explicitly at IX 3 = I 3, and X 5 = V 6.
78 *HH* XI 20.
79 *HH* XI 22.

6 THE FIRST 'MODERN GREEK' LITERATURE

1 Nicol 1972: 150–6, 203–5, 208–10.
2 For the range of fourteenth-century writings and a discussion of the backgrounds and interests of writers, see Ševčenko (1976), who highlights the small proportion of the total output which is written in the vernacular.
3 Schmitt 1904. On the date and primacy of the Greek version, see M. Jeffreys 1975b; for general introduction and older bibliography, see Beck 1971: 157–9.
4 Schirò 1975; see also Nicol 1984: 164–7, 183–93, 248–9.
5 Text and English translation = Dawkins 1932; cf. Beck 1971: 160–1.
6 M. Jeffreys 1973.
7 See Beck 1971: 173–9.
8 This had been the view of Jean Psichari, one of the first European-trained linguists to study the historical development of modern Greek (1886–9). Although Psichari produced good evidence for a progressive tendency to use more modern forms in the texts of the period, Georgios Chatzidakis was able to prove that most of these developments had taken place in the spoken language many centuries earlier (1905).
9 Browning 1983: 69–87; E. and M. Jeffreys 1979.
10 Beck 1971: 9; 1975: 48.
11 Mackridge 1985: 326–31.
12 *Ach.* N 813, 816–20.
13 *Phlor.* 190–4.
14 For other examples between the twelfth and the fifteenth century, and comment, see Browning 1983: 84–5.
15 Majuri 1919: lines 5–14.

243

16 Majuri 1919: lines 36–52. Whether or not the word ζουγλός used here in reference to Prodromos' imagined rival refers specifically to a *jongleur*, as proposed by Angold (1984: 218), or merely means someone 'not quite all there', as has been inferred from later usage (Kriaras 1968– : *ad loc.*), it is clear that this supposed substitute is intended to mimic or parody Prodromos' gifts for the emperor's amusement.

17 The four *Poems of Poor Prodromos* (Πτωχοπροδρομικά) are published by Hesseling and Pernot (1910). For a radically new edition, with German translations and full bibliography, see Eideneier 1991a. For additional discussion in M. Alexiou 1986; Beaton 1987a; 1988b; and the Introduction to Eideneier 1991a.

18 Best exemplified by the 144 poems of the 'Mangana Codex' which may also be the work of Prodromos (partially edited by Bernardinello, 1972, and listed in full with summary contents by Magdalino 1993a: Appendix) the *Synopsis Historike*, or *Chronicle* of Manasses and allegorical exegeses of Tzetzes (discussed by M. Jeffreys 1974a).

19 See further Beaton 1988b. Eideneier's edition (1991) reverses the sequence of Poems III and IV as edited by Hesseling and Pernot.

20 Kazhdan and Epstein 1985: 161.

21 Glykas' plea, entitled 'Verses Written while Held Imprisoned', is edited by Tsolakis (1959); on this and the collection of proverbs, see Beck 1971: 206–7.

22 See Spadaro 1982–3; 1987; Danezis 1987.

23 A proposal that the passage in *Phlorios*, usually thought to derive from it, was on the contrary the *source* of the self-contained poem of advice in the vernacular (Fyrigos 1985) is plausible only in the explanation it offers for the enigmatic title of the poem in some of the manuscripts: 'Εκ τοῦ Σπανέα (From 'Spaneas'). Fyrigos points out that the advice in *Phlorios* is given by the king of *Spain*, Σπανία in the romance. The poem must have had a separate existence before the romance, but could none the less have derived its popular title from having been quoted in the latter text.

24 Cf. Beck 1975; Browning 1980: 195–7. Even Eideneier, who believes that the *Poems of Poor Prodromos* were transposed from an originally learned form to a popular level in the fourteenth century (1982–3: 140–1; 1985a; 1987a; 1991a: 25–40), accepts that the vernacular was first used in the twelfth century by a learned writer, Glykas, although his reading of the evidence places a much smaller emphasis on twelfth-century developments than is proposed here (1982–3: 144–5). For additional evidence of attitudes to the vernacular among twelfth-century writers, see Beaton 1987a: 8–12.

25 Beck 1975; 1976; cf. Browning 1980: 197.

26 The transposition of the 'Spaneas' poem may be an exception, if Spadaro is to be believed (1982). It may be of some significance for this general picture that the thirteenth-century vernacular versions to which Spadaro draws attention were the product of the local literary 'renaissance' of that century among the Greek-speaking community of southern Italy.

27 The traditional literary-historical equation of a national literature with the acceptance of a vernacular as the national language has been restated in modern theoretical terms by Franz Bäuml (1980), who argues that the concept of 'fiction', as a category distinct from 'truth' and 'falsehood', could gain wide currency only when the conventions of writing in the learned language came to be superimposed on the different 'structure' and greater immediacy of a vernacular previously used only in oral contexts.

28 Symeonidis 1981.

29 M. Jeffreys 1974a: 144–58.
30 The exceptions are the tale, of Eastern origin, of *Ptocholeon* or 'Poor Lion' (Kechayoglou 1978) and the vernacular paraphrase of the *Iliad* by Konstantinos Hermoniakos, a court poet to the Despot of Epiros in the first half of the fourteen century (see E. Jeffreys 1975), both of which are written in eight-syllable iambic lines.
31 Beaton 1980: 75–7.
32 Ševčenko 1970; M. Jeffreys 1974a: 169–70; Koder 1972.
33 M. Jeffreys 1974a: 144.
34 It seems not to have been until Planoudes' time that a half-hearted attempt to reconcile 'political' verse with an ancient precedent was undertaken. Planoudes, in the passage cited by M. Jeffreys above (1974a: 144–5) tries to connect it with the catalectic tetrameter that had been defunct for a thousand years. Despite the obviously factitious nature of this derivation, it has often been repeated by serious scholars in the nineteenth and twentieth centuries.
35 See M. Alexiou and Holton 1976.
36 Kyriakidis 1926; 1947; Baud-Bovy 1935: 39–122; 1973.
37 L. Politis 1970; Koder 1972; M. Jeffreys 1974a: 173–95; Stathis 1977: 36–43; Koder 1983.
38 Maas 1912; L. Politis 1975: 173–4.
39 L. Politis 1981: 226.

7 THE ORIGINAL ROMANCES: THE TEXTS AND THEIR STORIES

1 Curtius 1953: 30–3.
2 Genette's distinction is parallel to but more rigorously defined than that between 'story' and 'plot' or, in the parlance of the Russian formalists, between *fabula* and *sjužet*. Compare the distinction of Seymour Chatman: 'Following such French structuralists as Roland Barthes, Tzvetan Todorov, and Gérard Genette, I posit a *what* and a *way*. The what of narrative I call its "story"; the way I call its "discourse"'(Chatman 1978: 9).
3 Genette 1980: 27.
4 We now have English translations of three of these romances, *Kallimachos*, *Belthandros*, and *Libistros* (Betts 1994). For summaries in English, see also the relevant chapters of: L. Politis 1973; Dimaras 1975; Trypanis 1981; and (for *Belthandros* only) Vasiliev 1952: II, 557–8. A detailed summary of *Kallimachos*, as well as a parallel French translation, is to be found in Pichard 1956. Lambert (1935: 2–8) gives a full summary in French, with line references, of *Libistros*. Plot summaries of all the original romances except *Troy* can be found in German in Beck 1971, and of *Kallimachos* and *Belthandos* in Greek in Kriaras 1955. A detailed summary of The *Tale of Troy* is given (in English) by Dedes (1971: 49–60), but this work is not generally available. Italian translations exist of three of the romances: *Achilles* (Stomeo 1959), *Libistros* (Rotolo 1965) and *Troy* (Lavagnini 1989).
5 Chatziyiakoumis 1977: 247–9.
6 Hesseling 1919; Smith 1990.
7 For different views on the dating on the poem, see Hesseling 1919: 15 (early fifteenth century); Mitsakis 1963: 72–3 (second half of the fourteenth century). See also Beck 1971: 129–32; Smith 1988; 1993.
8 It has been proposed that the author of this text knew the fourteenth-century

Greek translation of the *Roman de Troie*, *The War of Troy* (Spadaro 1978b), but the evidence for this is refuted below: see pp. 173–4.

9 Lambros 1913. The dating of Cod. Florent. Laurent. Conv. Soppr. 16, which contains the fragment, is based on the conjecture of Lambros' informant, who copied the lines for him. Lambros himself had not seen the manuscript and rather cautiously described it as being 'written ... in a hand of approximately the thirteenth century' (1913: 144). This conjecture does not seem to have been re-examined since Lambros' time (cf. Mitsakis 1963: 46–7; Beck 1971: 132).

10 See, e.g., the cautious remarks of Beck (1971: 132). Mitsakis (1963: 46–7) suggests that the poem as we know it may have been preceded by a 'romance of Achilles' in the learned language written in the thirteenth century; but so far as I know it has not previously been suggested that the fragment published by Lambros may represent a transposition 'upwards' of an early text in the vernacular. On all these questions we lack firm evidence for more drastic conclusions. This is why, no doubt, the secondary literature on *Achilles* has in general been disappointingly inconclusive. See, e.g., Hesseling 1919: 3–15; Beck 1971: 129–32; 1984: 140–2; Keydell 1979; and the papers by Smith cited in n. 7 above.

11 Cod. Neap. graec. III B 27 (251), published by Hesseling (1919); see also the emendations and comments of Lavagnini (1969–70). The date of 5 May 1520, written on this manuscript and often cited as the date of copying of *Achilles*, as well as of *Imperios* and the *Tale of Belisarios* also contained in it, has been shown not to refer to that part of the manuscript volume at all. Van Gemert has satisfactorily redated the folios containing these texts, on the evidence of the watermark, to the period 1460–75 (Van Gemert 1980a: 50 n. 6; cf. Smith 1987: 316–17).

12 British Library (Additional MSS no. 8241), published by Hesseling (1919: 91–125) together with N.

13 Cod. Bodl. Misc. auct. 5, 24 = Sathas 1879: 126–75; Lambros 1921: 367–408; Smith 1990. See also Hesseling 1919: 15–23; Beck 1971: 129–32.

14 *Ach.* N 1759–1820. Several explanations have been proposed to account for the relation between the two texts, and between both of them and Manasses' chronicle. A small number of lines from the epilogue, not deriving from Manasses, is also found in *Imperios*. Michailidis (1971–2) is probably right to suppose that the interpolation at the end of *Achilles* is modelled on the (later) *Tale of Troy* and represents the work of a copyist. Against this Spadaro has argued in detail that the interpolation in *Achilles* came first, and was used along with other parts of the poem by the author of *Troy* (1978a: 266–79). Nørgaard and Smith propose merely a 'common source not yet discovered' (1975: 13). In the state of our knowledge about the way in which manuscripts of this kind were copied, it must be concluded that we have insufficient evidence to decide among these proposals. See further Chapter 11.

15 Pichard 1956; Kriaras 1955: 19–83. English translation: Betts 1994.

16 The case for Andronikos' authorship is argued by Pichard (1956: xxiii); and minutely but inconclusively scrutinized by Knös (1962). The identification of the author has found fairly widespread acceptance (e.g. Beck 1971: 8, 124–5), which has often been expressed, however, in guarded terms, as if to imply the inherent improbability of an imperial prince dabbling with vernacular entertainment (e.g. Knös 1962: 293–4; Hunger 1968a: 422). In view of the increasing evidence that both the vernacular and literature of entertainment were welcomed at the imperial court in the twelfth century, it should no longer be surprising to find this trend continuing in the early fourteenth. See also Afterword.

17 For contrasting but complementary views of *auctoritas* versus anonymity in

medieval thought, see Minnis 1984; M. Alexiou 1986: 1–5.

18 Manousakas 1952: 77–8; Kriaras 1955: 15–16, 95–6; Beck 1971: 177–24; Cupane 1974b: 282; but see also Afterword.

19 Politi-Sakellariadi 1987: 286.

20 Cod. Scalig. 55; Chatziyiakoumis 1977: 36.

21 Kriaras 1955: 85–130. English translation: Betts 1994.

22 Bibliothèque Nationale: Cod. gr. 2909; Chatziyiakoumis 1977: 213–15.

23 Gidel 1866: 134ff.

24 Sigalas 1956; Schreiner 1959.

25 Kriaras 1955: 89–96; Beck 1971: 120–1; Chatziyiakoumis 1977: 241–3. See, however, Agapitos 1991, and Afterword.

26 Lambert 1935. The spelling λίβιστρος is fairly consistent in the manuscripts, but has on occasion been 'corrected' to λύβιστρος on the evidence of the early fifteenth-century satire in the learned language, 'Mazaris' Stay in Hell' (Maz. 38), which cites the name in a context that has nothing to do with the romance (see Lambert 1935: 45–6). There seems to be no justification for the spelling 'Libystros' given without explanation by Beck (1971: 122–4) and Trypanis (1981: 538).

27 Vat. gr. 2391. An edition now exists in the form of a University of Cambridge doctoral thesis (Lendari 1994). See also Chatziyiakoumis 1977: 80–1, 138–40, 162–3. Cupane discusses and quotes examples of the fuller description of the Castle of Eros given in V (Cupane 1974b: 288–9, 293).

28 Ψ IV 22 which also contains the E version of *Digenes*. See Lambert 1935: 8–28; Chatziyiakoumis 1977: 35–79; cf. Beck 1971: 122–4.

29 Respectively Cod. Neap. III A a 9 and Cod. Scalig. 55, the same manuscript as contains our unique copy of *Kallimachos*.

30 *Lib*. E 1209–2126, 3933–4178.

31 Nørgaard and Smith 1975. The text has also been edited, with introduction, notes and glossary, as an unpublished doctoral thesis of the University of London by Demetrios Dedes (1971).

32 See Nørgaard and Smith 1975: 9–10, 12–13; E. Jeffreys 1978: 116 n. 19; Spadaro 1978a: 246–79; Kambylis 1980; Lavagnini 1988.

33 Edited by Legrand 1890. See also Dedes 1971: 33–5; E. Jeffreys 1978.

34 Dedes 1971: 42–3.

35 Dedes 1971: 45–7; Spadaro 1978a: 253; di Benedetto 1979.

36 Par. Suppl. Gr. 926 of the Bibliothèque Nationale, Paris; see Astruc and Concasty 1960.

37 Lambros 1914: 434–5.

38 Lambros 1914: 436.

39 For Meliteniotes to allude to all three, implying that they were well known at the time when *To Chastity* was written, we have to allow some time for manuscripts to circulate (or public recitals to become common). On the dating of Meliteniotes' allegorical parody between 1355 and 1395 see p. 195. The redating of the allegorical *Consolation concerning Ill Fortune and Good Fortune* to some time before the period 1354–74 (Politi-Sakellariadi 1987: 286) increases the likelihood of an early date for at least some of the romances, as that poem also makes use of romance topoi (see pp. 195–7 below).

40 *Ach*. 1241–2, 1247–51; *Kall*. 771–8, 794–804; *Belth*. 866–8 (cf. the sexual details of 1040–4); *Lib*. E 2211–16; S 1114–16 (the reticence of this passage, which is closer in spirit to the twelfth-century romance, is explained by the fact that Libistros is here relating his exploits to his friend Klitobos); *Troy* 712–13; cf. 723–7. See also Beck 1984: 148–57; and Afterword.

41 Hippothoos in *Ephesiaka*, Satyros in *Leukippe and Kleitophon*, Kalasiris in *Aithiopika*, Gnathon in *Drosilla and Charikles*, Kratisthenes in *Hysmine and Hysminias*.

42 On the folk-tale elements peculiar to this romance see Megas 1956; Diller 1977; Aleksidze 1982.

43 Pichard 1956: 91 n. 2. An instance has been noted in the reign of Alexios I, two hundred years before the romance was written (Pieler 1971: 198).

44 *Belth.* 721–4. On the relation of this episode to Byzantine imperial ceremonial, see Hunger 1965; Pieler 1971: 201–2; Garland 1989. For the specifically literary transformations undergone by these realia, see Cupane 1983.

45 Or perhaps, on the same principle of correspondence between the hero's name and that of his homeland as applied in the case of Libistros, this should be Klitobia, a form actually used at N 2315, 3638.

46 E. Jeffreys 1978; Nørgaard and Smith 1975.

47 Spadaro 1978a: 247 n. 1; Nørgaard and Smith 1975: 8.

8 THE ORIGINAL ROMANCES: NARRATIVE STRUCTURE

1 *Ach.* N 1–19; 1563–1759.
2 *Ach.* N 20–606.
3 *Ach.* N 1248–52.
4 *Ach.* N 1089–1548.
5 *Ach.* N 1295–1359; 1455–1509.
6 Apostolopoulos 1984.
7 ἔρωτος γλυκοπικράς ὀδύνας (*Kall.* 21).
8 *Kall.* 843–5.
9 *Kall.* 24–840.
10 *Kall.* 842–2605.
11 *Kall.* 1293–1323.
12 *Kall.* 25–268, 1329–1466.
13 Aleksidze, whose discussion of the structure of this romance gives more weight to the affiliations of its story material with the folk tale than I have done, was the first to attempt a structural analysis of *Kallimachos*, which he sees as tripartite (Aleksidze 1979: 270–81, 314–15; cf. Kechayoglou 1982).
14 *Kall.* 1659–68.
15 *Kall.* 925–7.
16 *Kall.* 2082–7.
17 *Kall.* 2451–83; cf. II *Kings* xii; Pichard 1956: 87 n. 1.
18 *Kall.* 1550–64; cf. 1430; Pichard 1956: 51–3 n. 3.
19 *Kall.* 1722–1813.
20 *Kall.* 1572–1600.
21 *Kall.* 443–69, esp. 460–1, quoted on p. 149.
22 For bibliography and discussion, see Kriaras 1955: 99–100. The formal coherence of this romance as it stands has been convincingly demonstrated by Aleksidze (1979: 281–90, 314–15). But see now Agapitos 1991, and Afterword.
23 *Belth.* 642–61.
24 *Belth.* 662–76.
25 *Belth.* 677–719. On a strict line count the midpoint of the poem occurs at line 674, just before Belthandros begins his speech to Eros. Exact mathematical correspondences in numbers of lines would be suspect, however, since there

could have been no question of an author mechanically counting the lines of his text. In any case we know that the nature of the manuscript tradition makes line-for-line copying unlikely as a general principle. What is at stake in the present discussion is not arcane mathematical properties of the text, but larger (and rougher) proportions which would have been fully perceptible to a writer, reader or even hearer.

26 *Belth.* 486–536; 760–6.
27 *Belth.* 320–742; 781–1089.
28 *Belth.* 403–18; 1041–4.
29 *Belth.* 484–6. The syntax and punctuation of line 485 are not clear. The general sense may be either as rendered here or, alternatively, if line 485 is taken together with the following line, the sense of 'in order to' must be supplied, perhaps by substituting πρός for καί in line 485.
30 *Belth.* 1090–3.
31 *Belth.* 236–425.
32 *Belth.* 1101–1205.
33 *Belth.* 240, 293, 317, 518.
34 *Belth.* 1206–26.
35 *Belth.* 1096–1122.
36 *Belth.* 1114–1203.
37 *Belth.* 72–235; 1226–1315.
38 The bipartite model adopted here is essentially similar to that proposed by Aleksidze (1979: 281–90, 314–15), who also concludes his discussion of this romance with a diagram. My own reading differs from his in points of detail and takes the basic principle of symmetrical organization further. I also differ from Aleksidze in attributing these formal properties to the designs of a fully self-conscious author, rather than to the legacy of folk narrative, which both he and Popova (1985) emphasize in their studies of these romances.
39 *Belth.* 236–42; cf. lines 254, 271, 371, 520, 666.
40 The details of this scene present several difficulties of interpretation, some of which have been highlighted by the ingenious reading of Kahane and Kahane (1983), in support of their contention that the whole romance is a symbolic reworking of the Narcissus myth. While they are surely right to conclude that the first statue is that of a woman, other interpretations are more problematic. The two statues described in lines 369–416 are not the same as those more cursorily described at 339–65. The transition from the one passage to the other is not effected by Belthandros 'returning for a closer scrutiny' (1983: 201). First he takes in the decoration of the sides of the banqueting hall, which consists of representations of the punishment meted out by Eros to young men and women who have disdained love; then (369) he turns his attention to the top end of the room, where he sees the two statues that are the source of the river. The suggestion that these two statues are intended as symbolic representations of Belthandros and Chrysantza themselves is intriguing, but in that case the legends on the statues would have to have been reversed (either by the author for a complex but not wholly convincing effect, or by a copyist). Only the second, whose subject is Chrysantza, is grammatically in the form of a caption, such as we find in *Hysmine and Hysminias* and in *Libistros*. The first is a vatic statement in the present tense, whose subject is Belthandros. But it is the probably *female* statue whose legend names the hero first, and the certainly *male* statue (404; cf. 414–16) whose legend begins with the name of the heroine. It is not in fact clear whether the name of Chrysantza, without a main verb, in the accusative case, is intended as a caption to the statue or, rather, as an answer to the rhetorical

question prompted by the sight: 'Who could have shot the arrow, if not a woman's desire?' (Τίς τὴν σαΐτταν ἔρριψεν ἐπάνω τοῦ ζῳδίου/ κ' ἐποῖκεν καρδιοκοπετόν; Οὐχὶ πόθος γυναίου;) (417–18).

41   *Belth.* 637–40.

42   *Belth.* 841–2.

43   *Belth.* 231–2; 1286.

44   *Belth.* 384–8, 421–5.

45   *Belth.* 389–4, 426–39, 730–9.

46   *Belth.* 1116–17.

47   *Lib.* E 540–55.

48   As well as in *Leukippe and Kleitophon*, framing, or at least a 'Chinese box' effect of different narrative levels, had also been used in Hellenistic fiction in the lost *Invisible beyond Thule* by Antonios Diogenes and in the *Babyloniaka* of Iamblichos, both of the second or third century (Bowie 1985: 686), but the way in which these devices are exploited, by Diogenes at least, is quite different from the innovative technique of *Libistros*. In any case, it is not very likely that the author of *Libistros* would have known these works.

On the other hand a possible source for the first-person narrative might have been (as happened both in the eighteenth-century English novel and in the Greek novel of the nineteenth century) the epistolary novel. Some such fictional source has been posited for the Hellenistic Alexander 'romance' and for the lost early romance *Chion* (Hägg 1983: 126–7).

49   See p. 31. A detailed account of the reception of these collections of Eastern tales in Greek can be found in Kechayoglou 1988. See also Afterword.

50   *Lib.* N. 3–26. The main witness to this prologue is the Naples MS. E, which will be used in this chapter as the standard for the *organization* of the text (while N and S give superior *readings* throughout) has lost the two outer folios of its first quire, containing between forty and seventy lines, corresponding to the prologue and the opening of the main narrative (Chatziyiakoumis 1977: 71). It has been shown that the incomplete P version must originally also have contained a version of this prologue (Lambert 1935: 16–17; Chatziyiakoumis 1977: 61–2), of which a slightly expanded form is additionally given by the unpublished V text (Chatziyiakoumis 1977: 139; Lendari 1994).

Generally in this chapter I shall cite line references to the E version first, as this is the only way to observe the place of a particular passage in the text as a whole, followed by a reference to the corresponding lines of N or S, except for the poem's first 35 lines, for which N alone will be cited.

51   *Lib.* E 4384–6 ≈ S 3240–3. Libistros and Rhodamne are, of course, living when the narrative leaves them, but a shared death has been prophesied to them in the Castle of Eros ([E 554 ≈] N 345).

52   *Lib.* E 82–2606 ≈ N 101–2293; cf. S 1–1148.

53   *Lib.* E 2669–4360 ≈ N 2358–3795 ≈ S 1521–3213.

54   A more precise line count would be pointless in view of the state of the texts as transmitted, and in any case it must be remembered that we are dealing with large proportions, such as would be perceptible to writers, readers and listeners.

55   *Lib.* E 2195–2210 ≈ N 1934–48: the E text contains 4,407 lines, the N text 3,840.

56   *Lib.* E 2684–2723 ≈ S 1537–74.

57   *Lib.* E 174–569, 615–85, 816–30. The first of these passages, describing Libistros' dream visit to the palace of Eros, is presented with a different order of episodes and some gaps in N 190–466b. Cf. N 502–60, 693–706.

58   *Lib.* E 100–21 ≈ N 119–36.

59   Compare in particular E 4049–56 (≈ S 2858–66) with N 27–52 (cf. E 1–20).

60   *Lib.* E 1209–2126 ≈ S 82–1053; E 3933–4173 ≈ S 2779–3005.
61   *Lib.* E 4158–65 ≈ S 2982–93.
62   *Lib.* N 44–7.
63   E 248–54; N 291–2; N 614; N 781; S 599–600; S 662; S 749; S 769; S 891; S 1038;
     E 2211–16 (cf. S 1114–18); S 1147–8; S 1198–9; S 1202; S 1211; S 1261–6; S
     1309–11; S 1341; S 1370.
64   *Lib.* E 837–41 ≈ N 713–17. On this passage see pp. 156–8.
65   *Lib.* E 866–74 ≈ N 733–6.
66   *Lib.* E 2611–64 ≈ S 1467–1516.
67   *Lib.* E 2659–62 ≈ S 1511–14.
68   *Lib.* E 2665 = S 1517.
69   *Lib.* E 3490–3530 ≈ S 2308–43.
70   *Lib.* E 3531–82 ≈ S 2344–99.
71   *Lib.* E 4361–4407 ≈ S 3214–62.
72   Genette 1980: 227–31.
73   The valid theoretical distinction between 'real' and 'implied' author and reader
     (see, e.g., Booth 1961; Iser 1974) need not be insisted upon here. The only
     consequence of doing so would be to duplicate this narrative level. Notionally
     the fictive discourse in which the implied author addresses the implied reader
     would have to be seen as 'framed' by the real discourse of real author to real
     reader.
74   The theoretical terminology for designating a hierarchy of narrative levels is not
     entirely satisfactory. In particular Genette's definition that *'any event a narrative
     recounts is at a diegetic level immediately higher than the level at which the
     narrating act producing this narrative is placed'* (1980: 228; his italics) is one of
     his least lucid, and his terms are cumbersome to use, as well as ambiguous, when
     dealing with a narrative that involves more than three levels. Todorov (1977:
     70–3) refers to stories 'embedded to an nth degree'. For present purposes I
     envisage a descending hierarchy with the author at the top, designated by an
     ascending series of numbers. 'Level 4' indicates a narrative 'embedded to the
     fourth degree' (Todorov) or a 'meta-metadiegetic' narrative (Genette).
75   There is no distinction to be made here between direct and indirect speech or, in
     Genette's terms, between 'reported' and 'transposed' speech (Genette 1980:
     170).
76   *Lib.* 1313–72 ≈ S 190–246.
77   *Lib.* E 3602–35 ≈ S 2424–68.
78   *Lib.* E 1318–69 ≈ S 196–246.
79   *Lib.* E 1320–35 ≈ S 197–214.
80   Cf. Beck 1971: 123; Aleksidze 1979: 291.
81   'To study the temporal order of a narrative is to compare the order in which
     events or temporal sections are arranged in the narrative discourse with the order
     or succession these same events or temporal segments have in the story' (Genette
     1980: 35). Anachrony is then defined as 'the various types of discordance
     between the two orderings of story and narrative' (ibid.: 35–6).
82   Defined as 'any evocation after the fact of an event that took place earlier than
     the point in the story where we are at any given moment' (Genette 1980: 40).
83   Cf. Genette 1980: 231–2.
84   *Lib.* E 540–54 ≈ N 336–45.
85   '... any narrative manoeuvre that consists of narrating or evoking in advance an
     event that will take place later' (Genette 1980: 40).
86   For the technical sense of this term and the distinction between 'reach' and
     'extent', see Genette 1980: 48.

87 *Lib.* E 2552–3 ≈ S 1403–4.
88 *Lib.* E 2671–2727 ≈ S 1523–78.
89 Cf. Beck 1971: 123.
90 *Lib.* E 2879 ≈ S 1713.
91 *Lib.* E 3092 ≈ S 1929.
92 *Lib.* E 4174–5 ≈ S 3006–7; cf. E 4290 ≈ S 3134.
93 *Lib.* E 2892.
94 *Lib.* E 3051 ≈ S 1892.
95 *Lib.* E 3434–9.
96 Homeric details appear to be: Achilles hiding in his tent for love of Chryseis/Briseis; and the same hero's transvestism (rather ludicrously transposed to the scene in his tent) (E. Jeffreys 1978: 116 n. 19; Nørgaard and Smith 1975: 12).
97 *Troy* 445–52, 583–608; cf. 836–77.
98 *Troy* 760.
99 *DA* G v 66–149.
100 Beaton 1980: 128–35.

9 TRANSLATIONS AND ADAPTATIONS OF WESTERN ROMANCES

1 See Bury 1911; Kriaras 1955; E. Jeffreys 1979; Aleksidze 1979. Καβαλάρης in the strict sense of 'knight' appears only in the *War of Troy, Phlorios, Imperios* and the *Theseid*. The idiosyncratic fragment *The Old Knight* is the only one to transpose the loan-word καβαλάρης into the learned register as ἱππότης, although in the standard histories of modern Greek literature the similarly learned term ἱπποτικά μυθιστορήματα (lit. 'novels of chivalry') has prevailed. In the original romances καβαλάρης means simply 'horseman'.
2 E. Jeffreys 1976.
3 Cf. E. and M. Jeffreys 1986: 528.
4 E. Jeffreys (ed.) and Papathomopoulos: forthcoming.
5 Cf. Highet 1949: 50–5.
6 Cf. Curtius 1953: 30–3.
7 E. Jeffreys 1980 and Ch. 1 above.
8 E. Jeffreys 1978: 113 n. 5.
9 E. Jeffreys 1976.
10 E. Jeffreys 1978: 113–14.
11 E. Jeffreys 1978: 126, 128.
12 E. Jeffreys 1978: 113 n. 7, 129 n. 84. The sheer size of the project, together with the editorial niceties of balancing divergent manuscript readings against a known original in another language, have contributed to unforeseen delays in the appearance of the *editio princeps* of this work, which was first announced in 1971 (= E. Jeffreys 1976). I am grateful to both editors for many illuminating conversations about the project over the years, and for allowing me to read a representative section of the established text in advance of its publication.
   Extracts totalling about 1,000 lines, from individual manuscripts, have been published by Mavrofrydis (1866: 183–211); Gidel (1866: 197–229) and L. Politis (1969). Brief extracts are also published, with commentary, by L. Politis in the second edition of his *Anthology* (1975: 134–7). On the manuscripts and textual problems, see E. Jeffreys 1976; Papathomopoulos 1987; on aspects of the content, see E. Jeffreys 1978; on the poem's style, see E. and M. Jeffreys 1979. Cf. Beck, 1971: 138–9.

13 E. Jeffreys 1976.
14 Kriaras (ed.) 1955: 131–96.
15 Crescini 1899; Kriaras 1955: 137–9; Spadaro 1966a. On the date of the Italian and Greek versions, see Spadaro 1966a: 14–15; Kriaras 1955; 1959; 1960.
16 See Spadaro 1966a: 14; Beck 1971: 142–3. For a further possible connection between this poem and Boccaccio, see Garufi Italia 1982–3.
17 In several instances in the manuscripts the Italian termination has even been retained, in the form Πλάτζια-Φλώρε, unaltered to fit the patterns of Greek morphology (e.g. *Phlor.* 188); in the genitive we find both Πλάτζια-Φλώρης and Πλάτζια-Φλώρας (title and apparatus criticus).
18 εἰς πίστιν τὴν καθολικὴν Ρωμαίων ὀρθοδόξων (*Phlor.* 1841).
19 *Phlor.* 36; cf. Spadaro 1966b.
20 *Phlor.* 1843.
21 Cf. Pieler 1971: 212.
22 See, e.g., *Phlor.* 33, 1461.
23 On this poem and its relation to the romance see p. 96 above.
24 Kriaras (ed.) 1955: 197–249.
25 The best account of this romance, its relation to its source, and the editorial problems it presents, is by M. and E. Jeffreys (1971). See also E. Jeffreys 1974; Kriaras 1955: 199–214; Beck 1971: 143–7.
26 M. and E. Jeffreys 1971: 127.
27 Schreiner 1930; 1960; Loenertz 1976.
28 Cf. Pichard 1952.
29 For older bibliography on this proposal, see Kriaras 1955: 136 n. The idea has since been revived by Deligiorgis (1975) and Pecoraro (1982).
30 Voutieridis 1924: 145–6; 159–61; Pecoraro 1982: 310.
31 Loenertz 1976.
32 Cf. Hägg 1986.
33 For this date (corrected from 1553), see Layton 1981: 133. The Greek translation of the *Theseid* was also printed in Venice, in 1529 (Beck 1971: 140), but the work itself was not 'updated' in this way for its wider dissemination. The later rhymed versions of *Apollonios* and the Alexander 'romance' were produced directly without reference to the earlier unrhymed versions of these poems (Beck 1971: 137–8, 133–4; cf. Holton 1974: 7–8). The rhymed version of the *Tale of Belisarios*, which is based closely on an earlier unrhymed recension, has been dated between 1453 and 1490 (Bakker and van Gemert 1988).
34 Wagner (ed.) 1870: 63–90.
35 Μεταγλώττισμα ἀπὸ λατινικὸν εἰς Ρωμαϊκόν (Beck 1971: 136–7; cf. Gidel 1870).
36 *Apol.* 1–2.
37 *Apol.* 809–10.
38 *Apol.* 798–800.
39 *Apol.* 821–3.
40 Cf. Frye 1976: 48–50.
41 Perry 1967: 294–329.
42 Kechayoglou 1987. Until recently the Venetian edition of 1553 was thought to represent the first appearance of this new version, and a facsimile of the printed text was republished by Kechayoglou (1982c). See also Beck 1971: 136, 138. For details of two earlier printings, dated respectively to 1524–6 and 1534, see Layton 1979; Kechayoglou 1986b.
43 Follieri 1953; Beck 1971: 139–40.
44 Follieri 1959.

45   Marshall 1930; Follieri 1953.
46   *Thes.* IV 1.1–6.
47   Follieri 1958: 296.
48   *Thes.* I 6; cf. Follieri 1958: 294; Spadaro 1977. The significance of this correspondence is discussed on pp. 171–6.
49   By Kahane and Kahane (1945); see also Chapter 3.
50   See Breillat 1938: 215–16. The sources he cites – the chronicles of Boustronios (in Greek) and Amadi (in French) – date from the following two centuries.
51   Loomis 1936: 10.
52   Koder 1976.
53   Pelaez 1929.
54   Breillat 1938: 326–40. The manuscript had earlier been edited, with a German translation, by Ellissen (1846), who, however, failed to correct the sequence of the folios (Breillat 1938; Pontani 1950; Garzya 1983).
55   Breillat 1938: 310–11; Beck 1971: 138. For a summary of the compilation, its date and its relation to the romances of Tristan and Palamedes/Guiron, see Löseth 1890: 423–73.
56   Breillat 1938: 318–19, 319–22; cf. *OK* 156–8; Rizzo Nervo 1985.
57   Breillat 1938: 323 n. 2.
58   Breillat 1938: 324.
59   Cf. Beck 1971: 138.
60   *OK* 95–8.
61   Cf. E. Jeffreys 1979: 33 n. 1.
62   Garzya 1983; contrast Beck 1971: 138.
63   Rizzo Nervo 1985.
64   See Mitsakis 1966; refuted by E. Jeffreys 1968; Michailidis 1971–2.
65   *OK* 28–9.
66   Lathuillère 1966: 16–17.
67   Löseth 1890: xxiv and *passim*.

10 GENEALOGY

1   See in particular Jenny 1982.
2   Eliot 1932: 13–22.
3   Cf. Jauss 1982a: 35.
4   Cf. Paul de Man, who proposes to 'document the emergence of the genetic pattern within the Romantic movement and Romantic rhetoric.... Such a study', continues de Man, '... would show that a dialectical conception of time and history can very well be genetic and that the abandonment of an organic analogism by no means implies the abandonment of a genetic pattern.... The allegorization and ironization of the organic model leaves the genetic pattern unaffected' (1979: 80). It seems to me that this point is worth emphasizing, even though the thrust of de Man's reading of Nietzsche is to 'deconstruct' the latter's reading of history and to expose the 'genetic' component of 'genealogy' as the reflection of Romantic rhetoric, and not therefore inherent in historical data themselves.
5   Pichard 1956: notes *passim*; Hunger 1968a.
6   Cupane 1974b.
7   Sigalas 1956; Schreiner 1930.
8   H. and R. Kahane 1983: 218–19. This conclusion deserves to be accepted, although I am not persuaded that the Kahanes were looking in the right place for

proof, in sketching a tenuous, Frazerian link with the Narcissus myth (cf. Chapter 8, n. 40).

9   Hesseling 1919: 9–12; Mitsakis 1963: 48–63.
10 The influence of Manasses' Chronicle on vernacular writing in the fourteenth and fifteenth centuries has been ably demonstrated by E. Jeffreys (1975: 127; 1978).
11 E.g. Littlewood 1979.
12 *Ach.* N 795–830: see line 800.
13 *Kall.* 819–20; 826; cf. *HH* IX 3; noted by Pichard 1956: 30 n.
14 *Belth.* 647–57; cf. 677–719.
15 ἀχειροποίητα ἀγάλματα Κυρίου: *Ach.* N 794. The epithet ἀχειροποίητος is normally attributed to icons fashioned directly by God.
16 χέρια ζωγράφου . . . τὸ ἐποίκαν (*Lib.* N 193–4).
17 παράξενος πετρολιθοξύστης (*Lib.* N 959–60).
18 *Kall.* 300–3.
19 E.g. *Belth.* 376.
20 *Belth.* 286–90.
21 *Lib.* S 2432–63.
22 *Kall.* 449–55.
23 *Ach.* N 661–2. I have silently corrected τῆς of Hesseling's edition.
24 *Lib.* S 1922–8 (slightly edited).
25 E.g. *Kall.* 703–22; *Lib.* S 1145–6; *Belth.* 734–9; *Troy* 361–2.
26 *Kall.* 1310–20, 1686, 1809; *Belth.* 1107–1202; *Lib.* S 1400–12.
27 Further comparisons between the two texts, in terms of their general structure, specific episodes, and individual lines, have been noted by Mitsakis (1963: 52–63).
28 Cf. Mitsakis (1963: 50–2), who also suggests that the series of love-letters in this romance may derive from *Drosilla and Charikles*.
29 *Kall.* 1388, 1393. Compare respectively Nausikles (Hel.) and Dosikles (*RD*), Leukippe (AT) and Hippothoos (Xen.).
30 Lambert 1935: glossary; Pichard 1956: 83 n.; Kriaras 1968– : *ad loc.*
31 AT 17.
32 οὕτω τυραννεῖς ὃν κρεμώμενον λάβῃς (*DC* VI 414; cf. 462).
33 κρεμωμένην (*DC* II 69, IV 231).
34 δρακοντώδης γόνος (*DC* II 216–19).
35 Megas 1956.
36 *Kall.* 768–96; *HH* V 1.
37 Cf. Cupane 1974b.
38 *Belth.* 299–315; *HH* I 5; *DC* I 93–9.
39 *Belth.* 467–72; cf. *DC* III 85–9. Cf. also *Ach.* N 739–54; *Kall.* 317–18.
40 Cf. *DC* III 90ff.
41 *DC* II 382, IX 90; cf. V 22; *RD* VIII 225.
42 *Belth.* 456; *DC* VI 473–85.
43 *HH* III–IV; *Lib.* N 801–979; S 1–36.
44 *Lib.* S 3251–62.
45 *Lib.* S 1538–48.
46 *DA* E 318–31; G II 134–52.
47 For an exaggerated and often inaccurate picture of the dependence of Greek vernacular literature on Western models and influences, see Gidel 1866; Setton 1956: 38–40; Irmscher 1979. More balanced, but lacking in detail, is the treatment by Knös (1952).
48 Ostrogorsky 1968: 380; Kazhdan and Epstein 1985: 109.

49 Kazhdan and Franklin 1984: 109.
50 *HH* III 1. The verb δουλογραφῶ used here reappears in the vernacular romances: *Kall.* 2168; *Belth.* 360.
51 *Belth.* 770–9; cf. Psellos, *Chron.* VII 72.
52 φράγκικα κουρεμένα (*Ach.* N 102; *Lib.* N 38).
53 *Ach.* N 80; *Lib.* S 1072.
54 *Lib.* E 540; S 202.
55 Cf. Lambert 1935: 45.
56 Cupane 1974b.
57 *HH* II 7, 9; Cupane 1974b: 245–61.
58 Cupane 1974b: 257. More fully documented for the romances by Steiner (1969: 136), who additionally cites Char. VI 3.2; *Daphn.* II 7.2; AT I 5.7; Hel. IV 10.5; cf. ch. 4, n. 132.
59 See respectively: *DC* II 135 (παντάναξ); *DC* III 147; cf. II 227; IV 412 (ὁ τῶν βροτῶν τύραννος αὐτοδεσπότης); *DC* III 17 (Ἔρωτι δόξαν τῷ τυράννῳ).
60 *AK* Fr. 165: οὕτως οὐδὲν ἀτόλμητον Ἔρωτι τῷ τυράννῳ ... καὶ δοῦλός τις γενόμενος ταῖς Ἔρωτος παλάμαις.
61 Cupane 1974b: 288–91.
62 *Lib.* N 293–304. Lambert in her apparatus proposes two emendations to this passage, suggested by the E version, which while perfectly possible do not seem to me necessary: τρυφεροῦ for φοβεροῦ in line 295, and ὅλον for ἄλλον in line 303. I have silently corrected the spelling of στρογγυλόν in line 299.
63 Cupane 1974b: 290–1.
64 *Lib.* N 504–31.
65 Cupane 1974b: 290.
66 *Lib.* N 506; N 528–9.
67 *Lib.* N 300–1.
68 *Lib.* N 516, 528–9; cf. N 302–5.
69 *Lib.* N 693–706.
70 *Lib.* N 713–17.
71 *Lib.* E 844–62, abbreviated in N 720–9.
72 E for once has the better text. See in particular E 840 ≈ N 716; E 844 ≈ N 720; E 847–50; E 855–7; E 862 = N 729.
73 Cupane 1978: 241; 264–5.
74 *DA* E 1620–94; G VII 1–108.
75 *DA* G VII 15–16; E 1621; E 1630–1; Cupane 1978: 234–6.
76 Cupane follows Xyngopoulos (1948) in believing this episode to be a later interpolation in *Digenes Akrites*. However, its presence in the two oldest witnesses, E and G, and its structural importance, discussed in Chapter 3, make this in my view most improbable. To complicate matters, Cupane quotes from MS T, which derives from the fifteenth-century compilation known as 'Z', and which *does* include a brief interpolated description of a castle or tower (πύργος) apparently within the walls of Digenes' palace ('Z' 3837–48 = T 2760–9, in Trapp 1971a). These details are confusing, but the conclusion to emerge does not differ greatly from Cupane's. The description of the tower in the 'Z' group of manuscripts is almost certainly inspired by the fourteenth-century romances; on the other hand, the passing references to fortifications surrounding Digenes' palace in E and G reveal that this was an element of the original early twelfth-century composition. There is no reason to disagree with Cupane that this vestigial castle has no structural role to play in *Digenes*, other than perhaps a realistic one. But its presence, even in a minor role, in an earlier Greek text which was known to the writers of the later romances, was almost certainly a factor

which assisted these writers in their task of naturalizing the Western motif of the castle into the Greek tradition.

77 Cupane 1978: 236–41.
78 Cupane 1978: 241–6.
79 *Ach.* N 606–1260; *Troy* 487, 600–763.
80 *Kall.* 510–15, 694–9, 763–5, 779–80; *Ach.* N 843–78.
81 *Troy* 479–528.
82 Cf. Cupane 1978: 246–60.
83 Cf. Lambert 1935: 48.
84 *Lib.* N 786–9, 799–800.
85 *Lib.* N 746–51.
86 *Lib.* N 759–80.
87 *Lib.* S 61–3; E 1192; S 65–8. I have followed Lambert's emendation of S 63, with the addition of ἡ following E 1191. Line S 64 (replaced here by E 1192) is corrupt.
88 In addition to the symbolism of this passage discussed here, there may well be a sexual innuendo in some of its vocabulary. As well as the verb ἐμπέσῃς, whose possible sexual innuendo can be conveyed in translation, πουλί ('bird') in colloquial Greek today means 'penis', and τὰ ἀχαμνά (cf. ἄχαμνα, 'low down') are 'testicles'.
89 *Lib.* S 278–99.
90 *Lib.* S 285–7; 295–6.
91 *Ach.* N 1024–7 = L 720–3.
92 Cupane 1978: 245.
93 *Belth.* 384–8, 421–5, 730–5.
94 *Ach.* N 1072–4, 1194–7.
95 *Kall.* 271–9, *Belth.* 847.
96 *Troy* 600–14, 629–39.
97 Bas. *Prog.* 27, II. 24–7 = Pignani 1983.
98 *HH* III 7.
99 ἄχρις ἂν τὴν τῆς γραμματικῆς καταλάβῃς ἀκρόπολιν (Podestà 1945: 248).

11 ORALITY

1 For bibliography on the Jeffreys' work, see below. Their approach builds systematically on scattered suggestions made previously by Hesseling 1919: 12–14; Morgan 1960; Trypanis 1963; Steryelis 1967.
2 Following suggestions by Wartenberg 1900: 197; Schmitt 1893; Kriaras 1955: 205; 1960; and Mitsakis 1963: 67.
3 Schreiner 1959; 1962; van Gemert and Bakker 1981; Bakker 1987; cf. Bakker and van Gemert 1988.
4 M. and E. Jeffreys 1971.
5 M. Jeffreys 1973; 1987.
6 M. Jeffreys 1973: 193–4; 1974a: 174–8.
7 Parry 1930: 80; cf. Lord 1960: *passim.*
8 E. and M. Jeffreys 1979: 138.
9 See, in particular, E. Jeffreys 1979; 1981.
10 E. and M. Jeffreys 1983b: 317.
11 E. and M. Jeffreys 1986: 536.
12 M. Jeffreys 1987: 161.
13 Trypanis 1981: 535–43; Eideneier 1982; 1982–3; 1984; 1987a.

14   Eideneier 1987a; 1991, for the *Poems of Poor Prodromos*; Smith 1987; 1988, for the *Tale of Achilles*.
15   Spadaro 1966; cf. Schreiner 1958; 1962.
16   Spadaro 1975; 1976b.
17   Spadaro 1976a. For *Belisarios*, which is not, in terms of genre, a romance, see Chapter 12.
18   Spadaro 1978a.
19   Respectively: Spadaro 1977; 1978b; 1981; cf. 1987.
20   Spadaro 1977: 160; cf. 1976a: 310.
21   Van Gemert and Bakker 1981; Bakker 1987; Bakker and van Gemert 1988. On the interpolation in the Naples MS of *Ach*. N see Michailidis 1971–2: 274; but cf. Spadaro 1978a: 266–79.
22   E. and M. Jeffreys 1983b: 331 n. 66; 332.
23   Bakker and van Gemert 1988: 71–80.
24   E. and M. Jeffreys 1983b: 318–33.
25   Spadaro 1975: 307–9. E. and M. Jeffreys 1983b: 320–1.
26   Spadaro 1976a; 1981; Michailidis 1971–2.
27   Cf. Mitsakis 1963: 68–9 on correspondences with *Imperios*.
28   Spadaro 1977; 1978a; 1978b.
29   Spadaro 1977: 158. Spadaro gives lines 1–10 of the Coislin MS with, in a footnote, an apparatus from the Bologna MS. The differences between Spadaro's text and the reading of the edition by Jeffreys and Papathomopoulos are minor and affect neither Spadaro's argument nor the conclusions proposed here.
30   *Roman de Troie* 715–32; cit. Spadaro 1977: 158.
31   Spadaro 1977: 159; 1978b: 3.
32   *Thes.* I 6, cit. Spadaro 1977: 159; after Follieri 1958.
33   *Ach*. N 20–1; cf. O 1–2.
34   Spadaro 1977: 159; 1978b: 3–4.
35   Compare, e.g., Michailidis 1971–2 with Spadaro 1978a: 266–79.
36   *Ach*. N 20–8.
37   *Kall*. 25–30.
38   *Belth*. 25–9.
39   *Troy* 4–10.
40   Some of the correspondences discussed here were earlier noted by Mitsakis (1963: 14–15), whose conclusion, however, anticipates Spadaro's, that *Achilles* drew on the *War of Troy* (ibid.: 16).
41   E. and M. Jeffreys 1983b: 327.
42   *DA* G I 30–1. Only the G text preserves the original beginning of the poem (see Chapter 3). On the interpolated opening of the fifteenth-century compilation 'Z', see Chapter 12.
43   M. Jeffreys 1973; E. and M. Jeffreys 1979.
44   Beaton 1980: 175–6, 209; cf. 1986b: 125–6.
45   E. and M. Jeffreys 1979: 119–20.
46   Mohay 1974–5; 178–9.
47   Eideneier 1982: 302.
48   In the twelfth century the Cypriot saint Neophytos the Recluse quoted and then paraphrased a traditional song lamenting the plight of the exile, which he says he heard (M. Jeffreys 1974a: 160). The fifteenth-century examples are the two very similar manuscript versions of the heroic 'Song of Armoures' and the 'Son of Andronikos' discussed in Chapter 3, one of them dated to 1461; the seventeenth-century songs are in a brief collection with music published by Bouvier (1960). For discussion of these examples and the earliest history of the

modern song tradition, see Beaton 1980: 74–86.

49 Beaton 1980: 209.

50 Examples have been documented by, among others, Kriaras 1955; Megas 1956; Steryelis 1967.

51 A bird addresses a human character μὲ ἀνθρώπινην λαλίαν ('with human speech') (*Ach*. N 993); ἀνάθεμα καὶ τὸν καιρόν, ἀνάθεμα τὴν ὥραν ('cursed be the time, cursed be the hour') (*Ach*. N 1667 = *Kall*. 1643); a character with supernatural powers is described as τῆς ἀστραπῆς ὁ σύντροφος καὶ τῆς βροντῆς ἡ μάννα ('companion of the lightning and mother of thunder') (*Kall*. 1305); ἐχάραζεν ἡ ἀνατολὴ καὶ ἀνέτειλεν ἡ ἡμέρα ('the east was lightening and day was breaking') (*Lib*. S 1445; cf. *Phlor*. 33; 1480); the emotional centre of a character's being is called φύλλα ἀπὸ τὴν καρδίαν μου ('leaves of my heart') (*Lib*. S 2924 = *Phlor*. 469); a girl's graceful bearing is described by the almost untranslatable stock phrase of folk-song τὸ σεῖσμα καὶ τὸ λύγισμα (cf. modern Greek σειέμαι καὶ λυγιέμαι, 'I put on coquettish airs') (*Ach*. N 825; *Belth*. 645); καὶ ἀφ' τὴν θλίψιν τὴν πολλὴν κ' οἱ πέτρες ἐρραγίσαν ('and from so much sorrow the stones cracked') (*Belth*. 1279); ὁ Φλώριος ἔν' φρόνιμος, φρόνιμα ἀπιλογήθην ('Phlorios was prudent, prudently he replied') (*Phlor*. 766 = 1396; cf. 1630; cf. *Ach*. N 308; *Imp*. 438; *Troy* 629).

52 *Ach*. N 1619–24; 1651; *Kall*. 235; 2390; *Lib*. S 3224. On the evolution of the modern popular representation of Charos by conflation of the ancient divinities of Hades, Thanatos and Charon, see M. Alexiou 1978.

53 Especially evident in *Belth*. (e.g. 864–5, 1119ff., 1279, 1302); cf. also *Lib*. S 2631.

54 Bäuml 1984; cf. Miletich 1981: 194: 'Thus, I would like to suggest that between the orally-composed *Bagdad* song and the highly polished literary epic which draws to some extent on the oral tradition, there exists a form of epic composed in writing which is aimed at an audience accustomed to oral presentations and which is orally diffused for the consumption of such an audience. A genre such as this shares to some extent the features of oral-traditional song as well as those of learned writing.... It is not an overlay of learned elements in an orally-composed text, but rather a blend or fusion of techniques with its own separate poetics.' See also Ong 1986.

55 E. Jeffreys 1981: 123.

56 E. and M. Jeffreys 1983b: 320–1. Since then the Jeffreys have gone some way towards accepting that purely literary factors could have been involved: 'Spadaro's work is a useful counterbalance to those who might feel that the hypothesis of the influence of an oral tradition prevents any further investigation of links between the texts under discussion. It is plain that connections can be established in several cases among those texts he examines, whether they result from common authorship, similar circumstances of composition, or even the conventional literary influence which Spadaro assumes' (E. and M. Jeffreys 1986: 530). It should also be emphasized that their detailed work on the *War of Troy* has consistently ruled out any *direct* intervention of oral processes in favour of constructing a conventional stemma for the surviving witnesses (e.g. ibid.: 533).

57 See E. and M. Jeffreys 1979: 124; 1986: 530.

58 E. Jeffreys 1978: 113 n. 7.

59 Spadaro's comments have already been cited. The Jeffreys no less subjectively associate literary merit in medieval texts with the 'liveliness' of oral tradition: 'It is unfortunate that most of the early remains of demotic Greek survive in a literary (not to mention linguistic) form which is neither easy to evaluate nor attractive to the twentieth-century reader. The lack of literary originality in plot and use of language is rarely compensated by signs of non-literary liveliness and

inspiration such as seem to survive in much Western medieval poetry. The reason, we would suggest, is that these poems are rarely directed based on genuine oral material' (E. and M. Jeffreys 1979: 139).

60 Cf. Emrich 1982 on *Kallimachos*.
61 Eideneier 1982–3.
62 Hult 1986: 94–5.
63 Translated by Hult (1986: 35), who also gives the French text and follows it with a detailed discussion of the significance of Gui's explicit intervention in the text which is strongly suggestive for the case of the Greek scribes too (Hult 1986: 32–55).
64 Vincent 1970.
65 Politis 1964; Vincent 1980.
66 Beck 1971: 9; 1975: 48.
67 Beck 1971: 1–11; 1975; 1976.
68 Kriaras 1976: 221, 234–5.
69 E. Jeffreys 1979: 23.
70 Browning 1983: 74; E. and M. Jeffreys 1986: 523.
71 The key point of Beck's explanation is the *inability* of learned writers to use the vernacular consistently. Browning considers alternatives, both expressed in terms of disparagement: either a common spoken language is '*reflected, however imperfectly*, in the language of early vernacular poetry'; alternatively, 'do these poets write in an artificial amalgam of forms belonging to different dialects, which they have heard on the lips of uneducated speakers? In other words, is their poetry a kind of *incompetent attempt to imitate* living speech by men whose only familiar mode of expression was the literary language?' (Browning 1983: 82; my italics).
72 Cf. Chatziyiakoumis 1977: 247–8.
73 The difficulty has been recognized, although not in quite these terms, by the Jeffreys: 'The disconcerting feature is that it is the translations, particularly the distorted Homeric material in the *War of Troy*, the French *Imperios and Margarona* ... and the Italian *Phlorios and Platzia-Phlora* ... which produce, in our opinion, the best reflection of the Greek oral style.... Only with the *Achilleis* [*Tale of Achilles*] and the [*Tale of Troy*] do the original Greek works reach the same impression of oral authenticity as the translated romances mentioned above' (E. and M. Jeffreys 1986: 528).
74 Chatzidakis 1905: 482.
75 Beck 1971: 7.
76 Browning 1978a: 108.
77 S. Alexiou 1980: lx–lxii; Holton 1991; Bancroft-Marcus forthcoming.

12 RECEPTION

1 I have omitted from the present edition the first section of this chapter, entitled 'The Audience in the Text' (pp. 184–9 of the first edition), which dealt with the audience, or readership, implied within the texts, and attempted to extrapolate from this information a view of the real manner of reception of these texts between the fourteenth and the sixteenth century. This subject has now been dealt with more fully by Carolina Cupane (1994–5). See also Afterword.
2 Pernot 1931, see Hesseling and Pernot 1913; cf. Beck 1971: 183–6.
3 Legrand 1891; on the attribution to Prodromos; Hörandner 1974: 65–7.
4 Tselikas 1974.

5 Siapkaras-Pitsillidis 1976.
6 Ἐπίγραμμα εἰς Ἐρωτικὸν Βιβλίον τοῦ Ἐξαδέλφου τοῦ Αὐτοκράτορος (Martini 1896); text reprinted and discussed by Knös 1962: 280–4.
7 Phil. 14–19.
8 Phil. 47–83.
9 Cf. Pichard 1956: xxi–xxiii.
10 Phil. 48–9.
11 Phil. 16–21.
12 Phil. 86–9.
13 Phil. 90–7.
14 Phil. 99–103.
15 ὁρμάς ... φιληδόνους (Phil. 98, 102–3).
16 Phil. 104–6, cf. 53, 65.
17 Phil. 106.
18 ἡ θεία χάρις (Phil. 110).
19 συζύγῳ (Phil. 112).
20 Phil. 107–15.
21 Phil. 116–50.
22 Knös 1962: 289.
23 Beck 1975: 57.
24 Cf. Cupane 1994–5: 152.
25 *Kall.* 2601–5. There is no reason to doubt that these lines belong to the poem's original author. The same probably does not apply to the versified headings in red ink which punctuate the manuscript, one of which, in terms of conventional piety, takes up the last two lines of the text (2606–7).
26 Phil. 110.
27 Στίχοι τοῦ Μελιτηνιώτου εἰς τὴν Σωφροσύνην (Miller 1858).
28 See Beck 1971: 125, 147.
29 Beck 1971: 125; Trypanis 1981: 521.
30 Cupane 1978: 248–60.
31 The most detailed study of Meliteniotes' poem remains the unpublished doctoral thesis of Franz Dölger (1919), the main conclusions of which are summarized in Dölger 1934 and endorsed by Cupane, whose discussion of the work in relation to its central symbol of the allegorical castle represents the only attempt in recent years to come to terms with the literary status of the text (Cupane 1978: 246–60; cf. Hunger 1978: II, 119). *To Chastity* has also been discussed, in terms of its relation to *Digenes* and the development of the fifteen-syllable verseform, by Tiftixoglu 1974, and textual emendations have been proposed by Kambylis 1975. The only (brief) discussion in English is to be found in Trypanis 1981: 521.
32 Mel. 2810–62.
33 Mel. 2872–3016.
34 Mel. 3017–62.
35 Mel. 9, 15–19.
36 Μυθολογογράφοι (3; cf. 9), ψευδομυθοπλάττουσι (4), ψευδοσυνθέτους (4, 23), ψευδεπιπλάστους (10), ψευδοκομπορρήμονα (17), ψευδολογήσαντας (23), ψευδοκομπόμυθοι (29).
37 χρυσοπρασινίζουσα ('becoming gold and green') (Mel. 46, 82); λευκομελανίζουσαν ('becoming white and black') (84); λαμπροφωνίαν ('bright speech') (109); βαθμιδοσιδηρόστρωτος ('layered in steps of iron') (230); βατραχοσαυροφάγοι ('frog and lizard eating') (338); μελανοχιονῶδες ('the colour of black snow') (877); χρυσοχυτοξανθότριχον ('blonde haired of poured gold') (2828).

38   Mel. 1–2.
39   *Ptochopr.* I 1, 9–11; ed. Eideneier 1991.
40   *Ptochopr.* (ed. Eideneier 1991a) IV 29–35; III 47–54 (= Hesseling and Pernot 1910: III 23–9; IV luu–lbbb). On the fictional content of these poems, see M. Alexiou 1986; Beaton 1987a; 1988b.
41   *DA* E 717–22.
42   Cupane 1978: 248–9.
43   κουβούκλιον (Mel. 899–903; cf. *Kall.* 189–93).
44   Mel. 978–87; cf. *Kall.* 420–47.
45   Mel. 351–3; cf. *Belth.* 238: οὐρανοδρόμον ἀστέρα.
46   Mel. 635–41.
47   αὐτοκράτωρ, μονοκράτωρ (Mel. 402–6).
48   Dölger 1934; cf. Cupane 1978: 249–56.
49   Cupane 1978: 250–1.
50   Dölger 1934: 330; Beck 1959: 792–3; Hunger 1978: II, 253–4.
51   Trapp 1976–94: nos. 17848–51.
52   Except that the date of Theodore Meliteniotes' death is now put at 1393 (Trapp 1976–   : nos 17848–51).
53   Λόγος Παρηγορητικὸς περὶ Δυστυχίας καὶ Εὐτυχίας (Lambros 1906).
54   Politi-Sakellariadi 1987: 286.
55   *Dyst.* L 748–56. This fourteenth-century manuscript in the Leipzig University Library was published by Lambros (1906). The sixteenth-century Oxford version, which differs from it principally in using a more archaic linguistic register, was also published by Lambros (1880: 289–311). On the respective merits of the two versions, see Svoronos (1937), whose views have now been confirmed by Politi-Sakellariadi (1987). The last named has also announced a new edition of the poem. See also Beck 1971: 147–78; Dölger 1934; Cupane 1978: 260–1. The representation of the 'wheel of Fortune' in this poem is discussed in relation to surviving visual depictions of the theme in Davies 1978: 121–6.
56   *Dyst.* L 586–90.
57   *Dyst.* L 685–716.
58   *Dyst.* L 748–56.
59   See Megas 1953.
60   Reichmann 1963; cf. Beck 1971: 133–5; Holton 1974: 7–8.
61   Holton 1974: 25–40. This was also the fate of the unrhymed translation of *Apollonius*, which was unknown to the translator of the rhymed version of the late fifteenth century (Kechayoglou 1987).
62   Bakker and van Gemert 1988.
63   See *Troy* 886–8, 1062–3; van Gemert 1987: 136.
64   van Gemert and Bakker 1981: 95; van Gemert 1987: 123; Bakker and van Gemert 1988: 81–95.
65   van Gemert 1987: 136.
66   M. Jeffreys 1975a; 1976.
67   Text published by Kalonaros 1941: I.
68   M. Jeffreys 1976; cf. MacAlister 1984.
69   *DA* A 31–40; cf. Kalonaros 1941: I, 15n. The substitution of a daughter for a son is, of course, dictated by the compiler's circumstances: he has to tell a story about a girl in order to link up with the rest of the text before him. Sanction for this less usual form of the topos, however, also comes from the folk tradition: the song of the 'Dead Brother' begins with a mother who has nine sons but cannot bear to be parted from her only daughter (Academy of Athens 1962: 309–19; for discussion, see M. Alexiou 1983).

70 *DA* A 45–123; that is, only up until the first significant event of the story proper. The compiler respects the rather different conventions of the older poem (which contains no prophecies) by not allowing his prophet, drawn from the later romances, to anticipate the course of events beyond the material that he himself has devised.

71 *Troy* 101–9, 349–62.

72 E.g. ἐρωτοληψία ('falling-in-love') (*DA* A 76, 85, 123).

73 *DA* A 124–57; cf. Kalonaros 1941: I, 20 n. Either from there (*Ach.* N 820 ≈ L 555) or from *Belthandros* (705) must be derived the striking compound coinage στρογγυλοευμορφοπώγωνον ('round-beautiful-chinned') (*DA* A 153).

74 *DA* A 162–8.

75 *DA* A 200–25; cf. *Ach.* N 989–1018; *Lib.* S 196–212.

76 *DA* A 234–47; cf. *Ach.* N 850–8.

77 *DA* A 255–79.

78 *DA* A 280–322.

79 *DA* A 323 = E 1; cf. M. Jeffreys 1976: 396–7.

80 M. Jeffreys 1976: 389; cf. Grégoire 1941: 98.

81 *DA* A 1–7.

82 This development is centred, as far as narrative poetry is concerned, on the figure of Emmanuel Georgillas or Limenites, who was active around the year 1500. Spadaro has shown that *Achilles* and *Phlorios*, as well as *Belisarios*, were known to Georgillas and are further reflected in the love-poems, the 'Kataloyia', which are also thought to have originated in the Dodecanese (Spadaro 1985).

83 See Siapkaras-Pitsillidis 1976.

84 The only works certainly dated after this are the tragedies *Rodolinos* and *Zeno* and the derivative comedy *Fortounatos*. Uncertainty still surrounds the date of the romance *Erotokritos*, on which see below, and to a lesser extent of the religious play *Abraham's Sacrifice*, which was certainly in existence by 1635. On all these questions, see Holton 1991. For a chronology of Cretan literature, see Bakker and van Gemert 1983.

85 S. Alexiou 1980; Holton 1991; Bancroft-Marcus forthcoming.

86 Manousakas and van Gemert 1981; van Gemert 1980b.

87 Sachlikes was born in 1331/2; *Kallimachos*, the earliest of the datable fourteenth-century romances, was written between 1310 and 1340; while the first of the translations, the *War of Troy*, belongs to the mid-century. Meliteniotes, whose parody makes use of *Kallimachos*, *Belthandros* and *Libistros*, was probably an exact contemporary of Sachlikes.

88 Ἀφήγησις Παράξενος. Two manuscripts are published by Wagner (1874: 62–105), the third by Papadimitriu (1896). A new 'synoptic' edition has been announced by Nikos Panayotakis (1987), who includes the newly edited text of the 'Tournament of Whores' as a specimen (1987: 238–9). For further discussion of the texts, see Morgan 1960: 69–86.

89 Panayotakis 1987: 247–54.

90 Cf. Panayotakis 1987: 252; van Gemert 1980b: 73.

91 Such are Ἀειδού (cf. Ἀηδία, 'disgust') (2); Πορδομάραινα ('fart-withering'?) (4); κοπελομοσκάρα (as an epithet: 'bullcalf-girl') (21); and Πορδομίλαινα ('fart-speaking') (42). Line numbers refer to Panayotakis 1987: 238–9.

92 Beck (1971: 201) and van Gemert (1980b: 68–9, 74) are among modern scholars who accept that this was the form of the name in the original text. Insisting on the readings of the single manuscript which preserves this episode, Panayotakis takes it to be a real name, for which he cites analogues from Venetian archives: Πόθα Τζουστουνιά (Panayotakis 1987: 225–7). While Panayotakis is surely right

to detect a real family name beneath the sobriquet, it would surely be out of
character for Sachlikes to have missed the possibilities of playing on such a
name in such a context.

93   Cf. Panayotakis 1987: 278.
94   van Gemert 1977; 1980a; van Gemert in Holton 1991: 58–61.
95   Ἱστορία καὶ Ὄνειρο Ἐρωτικὸν Ἐνύπνιον (van Gemert 1980a).
96   The author introduces himself by name as one of the four *dramatis personae* of
     the work.
97   van Gemert 1980a: 42–5.
98   van Gemert 1980a: 37–8.
99   van Gemert 1980a: 49–52.
100 *De Mang.* VII = Bernardinello 1972; cf. Beaton 1987a: 24.
101 *HH* v 1–2; cf. M. Alexiou 1977.
102 *Lib.* N 504–60.
103 τὴν ἐμὴν φίλην Ὑσμίνην αἰσχύναντα (*HH* III 1).
104 *Lib.* N 698.
105 *Kall.* 1329–41; here called ἡ τύχη του, not Μοῖρα or Ριζικό.
106 Fal. *Ist.* 25–6.
107 *Lib.* S 524–5; E 1630; S 526.
108 Μηδὲν ὀκνῆς καὶ κάμε το ('Don't delay but do it') (Fal. *Ist.* 421); πλὴν τοῦτο
     σὲ συμβουλεύγομαι, ποίησέ το, μην τὸ ὀκνήσῃς ('but this I advise you, do it,
     don't delay') (*Lib.* S 60). Other verbal echoes of the romances in this text can
     be seen in the compounds; Ἐρωτοκρατίας ('Empire of Love') (1; cf. *Enypn.*
     67); ποθοκρατούντας ('those in a state of desire') (289); ποθομολογᾶται
     ('confess to desire') (678); ἐκαρδιοδάκασε ('wounded the heart') (751).
109 Fal. *Enypn.* 13–14; *Lib.* N 504–60.
110 Fal. *Enypn.* 18–19.
111 ἐξ αἵματος (van Gemert 1980a: 171; *Belth.* 409–13). Another reference to the
     same romance can be seen in the name used for the King of Love, or 'Sovereign
     Eros': τὸν Πρῶτον Ἔρωτα (Fal. *Enypn.* 54, 68), ὁ Πρῶτος τῶν Ἐρώτων
     (*Enypn.* 81, cf. *Belth.* 365).
112 Fal. *Enypn.* 23, 47; cf. *Lib.* N 217, 314–16; *Belth.* 495–6, 508.
113 Cf. Spadaro 1978a: 241 on 'The Shepherdess'.
114 Cf. Beaton 1981a: 23–4 and n.
115 The controversy over the date of this poem is summarized by Holton (1988;
     1991: 211–12).
116 *Erotokritos* I 19, 27–8.
117 Cf. *Kall.* 1692–92; *Lib.* S 2898.
118 S. Alexiou 1980: lxiv–lxv.
119 Holton 1988.

AFTERWORD

1   This despite the continuing and impressive revaluation of the *ancient* Greek
    novel, in which the vital role of rhetoric and self-conscious allusion is now
    widely accepted (see, e.g., Bartsch 1989; Reardon 1991; Gill and Wiseman 1993;
    Létoublan 1993). The 'afterlife' of the Greek romance in Byzantine times is
    barely mentioned in these studies, however. Notable exceptions to this general
    neglect are the abstracts of the 1989 Dartmouth conference on the ancient novel
    (Tatum and Vernazza 1990), which included a panel on 'The Novelists of
    Byzantium and Modern Greece', and the edition of Achilles Tatios by Yoryis

Yatromanolakis, which as well as an elegant rendition of the text into Modern Greek, touches in its long and detailed introduction on the later Greek reception of the text (Yatromanolakis 1990: 185–92). In France, too, a multi-author overview of the ancient novel includes at least a brief summary of the salient facts about the medieval Greek romance, though based on a sketchy bibliography (Arrignon and Duneau 1992).

2 See the following (excluding brief bibliographical entries or summaries): Kechayo-glou 1990; Jouanno 1991; Wouters 1991; Mackridge 1992a; Kotzamanidou 1992.
3 See Robinson 1991; Philippides 1993.
4. See in particular Mullett 1990: 271–3; Macrides and Magdalino 1992: 148–52; Magdalino 1992: 198; 1993a: 398–402; M. Jeffreys 1993b; Cameron 1992: 22.
5 Kechayoglou 1990 (citation from p. 159).
6 Huet 1966: 4; and see below.
7 In principle, at least, I admire the categorical view of the poet and critic Nasos Vayenas (1989: 91): 'A history of literature which does not include translations is a deficient history', although I think that realistic considerations of space (and of the patience of readers!) make this an ideal rather than a real goal. Faced, as in the present book, with a choice between original and translated literature, I would still place the emphasis on the former.
8 Agapitos and Smith 1992; now in its turn the subject of a detailed review by Kechayoglou (1994). See also p. xviii above.
9 Agapitos and Smith 1992: 8.
10 I confine myself to a single example, to illustrate the reviewers' method. On p. 46, quoting my remark in Chapter 6 that the 'vernacular' is not identical to 'the spoken language transferred to parchment', Agapitos and Smith interject a parenthesis: 'somewhat maliciously one might object that no vernacular text was ever written on parchment'. The 'malice' must be presumed to lie in the imputation that I do not know that the surviving copies are written on paper. But this trivial jibe is overshadowed by the enormous arrogance of the statement itself: given that we possess no autographs, or in most cases even manuscripts written less than a century after the composition of the texts they transmit, how could Agapitos and Smith possibly know this?
11 Agapitos and Smith 1992: 58–9, 66–7, 90–1, 112.
12 And this, disappointingly, despite the apparently more open-minded remarks of Agapitos in the Preface to his doctoral thesis (1991: vii).
13 Due to be published in two volumes as Mullett and Smythe 1996.
14 Magdalino 1993a.
15 Magdalino 1993a: 392.
16 Magdalino 1993a: 356.
17 Magdalino 1993a: 339.
18 Magdalino 1993a: xi (my italics).
19 Prodromos = Marcovich 1992; Eugenianos = Conca 1990, to which all citations in the present edition of this book have been updated to refer, replacing the references to the 1859 texts of both romances by R. Hercher.
20 It has, however, been translated into both German (Plepelits 1989; review by Cupane (1992)) and French (Meunier 1991).
21 Plepelits 1989: 3–6. This dating has been, surprisingly, accepted by Trapp (1993: 118). Trapp rightly rejects Plepelits' further contention, that John Doukas, the fictional addressee of the narrative, was actually the *author* of the romance, who concealed himself behind the pseudonym of Eustathios Makrembolites.
22 MacAlister 1990; 1991. These arguments were first advanced in an unpublished doctoral thesis (MacAlister 1987). Although I have not seen this thesis, I am

grateful to Dr MacAlister for several stimulating discussions on the subject.

23 MacAlister 1991: 209.
24 Magdalino 1992.
25 See the analysis in depth in Magdalino 1993a: 46–76.
26 In the same spirit I have withdrawn from the present edition the proposal of tenuous, but none the less intriguing, links between this romance and the French *romans d'antiquité* in terms of allusions to proper names and places (pp. 78–9 of the first edition).
27 Magdalino 1992: 203.
28 E. Jeffreys 1980; Magdalino 1992.
29 Conca 1986 (not accessible to me at the time of preparing the first edition); Jouanno 1989; 1992.
30 Jouanno 1992. I have not seen this scholar's doctoral thesis (Jouanno 1987). Something of its scope can presumably be gleaned from the articles mentioned, as well as from the published abstract of her paper at the 1989 conference on 'The Ancient Novel' (Jouanno 1990). The main argument of this abstract, too, is that the revival of the timeless and 'permanent' genre of description in the twelfth century may be seen, (paradoxically, but by no means unreasonably) as a response to the new anxieties of the age.
31 Meunier 1991. The author is cited as 'Eumathios', an alternative to 'Eustathios' found in the manuscripts but not sanctioned by the text's (nineteenth-century) editors.
32 Plepelits 1989: 23–9.
33 Plepelits 1989: 29–69.
34 Plepelits 1989: 38.
35 Plepelits 1989: 38–46.
36 Plepelits 1989: 55–61.
37 Indeed, Plepelits points to Philes on *Kallimachos* among a number of late medieval allegorical interpretations of older romances (1989: 29–30). However, as we saw in the case of *Kallimachos*, the existence of allegorical interpretations does not make a text in itself, necessarily, allegorical.
38 I have been privileged to see in draft a new reading of this romance by Margaret Alexiou, which both draws on and criticizes that by Plepelits. While I have not, so far as I am aware, drawn on that reading in what is said here, I agree with Alexiou that a new symbolic reading should now be attempted, and look forward to seeing her work in print.
39 S. Alexiou 1985; updated with new introductory material as S. Alexiou 1990.
40 Fenik 1991; Sifakis 1989; 1992.
41 Ricks 1989.
42 Ricks 1990.
43 Castillo Didier 1994.
44 Mackridge 1993a; 1995.
45 Magdalino 1993b; Galatariotou 1993.
46 E. Jeffreys 1993a.
47 Angold 1989; Magdalino 1989.
48 See E. Jeffreys 1993a.
49 Part of the 'Medieval Greek Database Project' initiated by the Department of Byzantine and Modern Greek Studies, King's College London, and funded by the British Academy, in 1989. For a printed concordance to the E version of *Digenes* see Beaton, Kelly and Lendari (1995). It is hoped to make the G concordance available on computer file. On these concordances, and preliminary conclusions for the versions of *Digenes*, see also Beaton 1993a; 1993b; Kelly 1993.

50 Cf., but in a slightly different spirit, Ricks 1990: *passim*.
51 For a fuller statement of this position, and a sample of the likely contents of this 'core' for the 'Lay of the Emir', see Beaton 1993a. On the dating and cultural context of the 'original' *Digenes*, see (written before the essays mentioned above) Beaton 1996.
52 For the present state of debate on this and other aspects of Byzantine heroic poetry, see the essays collected in Beaton and Ricks 1993, which also includes an up-to-date bibliography.
53 Beck 1984; cf. Beck 1986.
54 Barber 1992.
55 Littlewood 1992.
56 Littlewood 1993.
57 Cupane 1986; 1987. Neither of these was available to me before the first edition of this book went to press.
58 Agapitos 1990b; 1991: 110–14, 292–6.
59 On the peculiar sexual mores of *Digenes*, touched on in Chapter 3, see Mackridge (1992b; 1993b), who emphasizes that the central theme of this poem, in any of its versions, is neither more nor less than the abduction and holding of women by men, an observation which places *Digenes* closer to the ethos of later Greek balladry than that of the romances.
60 Garland 1990.
61 See the passage in *Kallimachos*, especially lines 771–804; cf. Garland 1990: 103.
62 Ricks 1990.
63 Smith 1990.
64 Lavagnini 1988.
65 Agapitos 1992. In the course of this work Agapitos has also identified and published a number of short extracts from *Libistros* in other manuscripts, which he connects with this group (Agapitos 1991–2; 1993b).
66 Lendari 1994 (unpublished); cf. her published comments in Lendari 1993.
67 Cf. Lendari 1993. For technical aspects of the project, see Kelly 1993. On the concordances to *Digenes*, see n. 49 above.
68 Betts 1994.
69 See Spadaro (1989a; 1990) on (essentially) *Digenes Akrites*; Agapitos (1990) on *Kallimachos*, and (1992) on *Libistros*; di Benedetto Zimbone (1990) on *Phlorios*; Olsen (1990; 1993) on the *Theseid*; Smith (1988; 1993) on the *Tale of Achilles*.
70 See, e.g., the diametrically opposite approaches favoured by Garantoudis (1993) and by Kambylis (1993) on the role of metrical criteria in establishing a text; the proposals put forward by Mackridge (1993a) on permissible degrees of linguistic intervention; and the continuing debate on stemmatics (Papathomopoulos 1993; Tsavari 1993), all in the proceedings of that congress.
71 Nørgaard and Smith 1975; Smith 1990.
72 Agapitos 1991.
73 See E. Jeffreys 1993a.
74 Demonstrated by Elizabeth Jeffreys for *Digenes Akrites* (1993a), the *War of Troy* and the *Iliad* of Hermoniakos (1993b).
75 Cf. M. Jeffreys 1993b.
76 See, e.g., Smith 1990, which prints a text that the editor elsewhere concedes is incoherent as it stands (1988: 259–60), with only a four-page preface, a limited apparatus, and an index. Even the confessedly minimalist practice of this edition as set out in its preface (Smith 1990: 7–8) has proved impossibly elusive in practice (see the review by Eideneier 1992).
77 This is the extreme position adopted by Agapitos (1990a; 1991). But there is little

point in invoking fidelity to the manuscript as a firm principle if the result is to produce a text which makes no sense (see, e.g., the rearrangement of *Kall.* 793–5 in Agapitos 1990a: 38, 1991: 112, 114 n. 199).

78 The argument put forward by Agapitos and Smith (1994) that the manuscripts we possess are the work of professional scribes who knew their job and operated no differently from the copyists of classical or Byzantine texts at the same period seems perversely to miss the point. *Somebody* was responsible for the variations among the texts that have come down to us, variations of a type and on a scale unmatched in texts in the ancient/learned language, but closely paralleled by vernacular texts in Western languages. It follows, therefore, that *some other method* than conventional, professional copying was *also* used to reproduce texts of this kind, and not the least of its consequences is the unreliability of the surviving manuscripts as witnesses to the original texts composed up to two centuries before.

79 Exemplary in this respect (whether or not one happens to endorse the particular readings that result) are the editions of *Digenes Akrites* by Alexiou (1985; 1990) and Ricks (1990), and, outside the field of the romance but of great importance for the study of medieval Greek literature in the vernacular, of the *Poems of Poor Prodromos* by Eideneier (1991a).

80 The evidence for this is well presented by Kechayoglou (1993).

81 Cupane 1986; 1992; 1993; Spadaro 1989b; 1992. A more cautious approach, for both groups but primarily the former, had earlier been taken by Conca (1986).

82 Beaton 1989: 354.

83 Garland 1989; Agapitos 1993a.

84 Michailidis 1993.

85 See Magdalino 1993a: 69–78.

86 Aleksidze 1979.

87 This is the approach of Koliadimou (1988); cf. Kechayoglou 1990: 166.

88 Nørgaard 1989: 279, 293.

89 Respectively by Karyianioti (1992) and Giannou (1993). I am grateful to Professor G. Kechayoglou and the authors of the dissertations mentioned for making these available to me and for permission to refer to them here.

90 Agapitos 1991. For an extended review, see Kechayoglou 1994.

91 Agapitos 1991: 64; cf. vii, 12–13.

92 Agapitos 1991: 74–128.

93 Agapitos 1991: 129–222.

94 Agapitos 1991: 223–333.

95 Agapitos 1991: 64, 199, 319–20.

96 Agapitos 1991: 26–8, 68–72.

97 The phrase occurs several times in Agapitos' book; but surely no one has proposed to see the three romances in this way?

98 Agapitos 1991: 95–103.

99 See Agapitos 1991: 69–70, and especially *Belth.* 110–13. In this instance Agapitos is right that the manuscript as it stands does not make sense. An alternative solution to supposing that a speech has been omitted would be to reverse the order of lines 111–12. Later, concluding his discussion of 'narrative modes' in the three romances, Agapitos again singles out *Belthandros*: 'The passage from *Belthandros* presents us with a text fairly disjunct and "abbreviated", although the basic constituent parts are there in logical order, this being the result of some kind of shortening of the original version' (Agapitos 1991: 158).

100 Agapitos 1991: 199.
101 Eideneier 1991b; Spadaro 1989a; 1993; Smith 1993.
102 Mackridge 1990a; 1990b.
103 Beaton 1990: 182.
104 Sifakis 1993: 283.
105 Cf. Sifakis 1993: 278n.
106 M. Jeffreys 1993a; 1993b.
107 Comparative work on the applications of the 'oral-formulaic theory' to both written and oral literature has been greatly facilitated by the compendious studies of Foley. For anyone with an interest either in the theory or in the possibility of applying it to any particular field, including that of medieval Greek, Foley 1988 is essential reading; see also Foley 1991.
108 Cf. the arguments of Ruth Finnegan (1988).
109 M. Jeffreys 1993b: 265–6.
110 M. Jeffreys 1993a: 63.
111 See Dyck 1983; 1987; Ricks 1989; Beaton 1993a.
112 ξενόχρους ἀφηγήσεις (*Kall.* 858–9).
113 *Lib.* N 3–20.
114 Cupane 1994–5.
115 See esp. Cupane 1994–5: 165–6; cf. 152–3. The difficulty of extrapolating from the fictional world within the text to the practice of reading or reciting in the real world outside had also been pointed out by Agapitos and Smith (1992: 107–8), who have, however, no alternative proposal to offer (cf. Cupane 1994–5: 153 n. 31).
116 Cupane 1994–5: 167.
117 Magdalino 1993a: 353–5, 407–8; cf. Mullett 1984.
118 The earliest to use this type of exordium is the *Tale of the Four-Footed Beasts*, probably composed in 1364 (Tsiouni 1972), but such expressions only become common in the fifteenth century and into the sixteenth, for example in *Imperios*, the *Tale of Belisarios*, the *Tale of Troy* (see 886–8, 1062–3) and the interpolated ending of the *Tale of Achilles* (N). In line with this view, although I confess I can adduce no corroborative evidence, I believe the 'come-all-ye' prologue to *Belthandros* (from which Cupane takes the title for her article) to be an interpolation not much older than the sixteenth-century manuscript we possess.
119 Beaton 1988a: viii.
120 Angelou 1989: 33–4.
121 Valetas 1964: A 832–9. The now standard term μυθιστόρημα seems to have gained currency only after 1865.
122 πλαστήν, ἀλλά πιθανὴν ἱστορίαν ἐρωτικῶν παθημάτων, γραμμένην ἐντέχνως καὶ δραματικῶς, ὡς ἐπὶ τὸ πλεῖστον εἰς πεζὸν λόγον (Valetas 1964: A2, 833). For the original French formulation (Huet 1966: 4), see p. 208 above.
123 Denisi 1990; 1992; Kechayoglou 1991a; 1991b.
124 Cf. Beaton 1994: 51–3, 56.

REFERENCES

MEDIEVAL AND ANCIENT TEXTS

The following is an alphabetical list of all medieval and ancient texts cited, together with, in square brackets, abbreviated forms of reference used in citations in the notes. For cross-references by author or under alternative forms of the title see the index. This list gives author/date references for the most recent critical editions. For full bibliographical references see the next section.

[*Ach.*] *Achilles, Tale of*: Versions N and L = Hesseling 1919; Version O = Smith 1990

[Hel.] *Aithiopika* (Heliodoros) = Rattenbury and Lumb 1960

Alexander, Tale of: Byzantine metrical version = Reichmann 1963; rhymed version = Holton 1974

[Aphth. *Prog.*] Aphthonios (see *Progymnasmata*)

[*Apol.*] *Apollonios of Tyre*: unrhymed version = Wagner 1870: 63–90; rhymed version = Kechayoglou 1982c

[*AK*] *Aristandros and Kallithea* (Konstantinos Manasses) = Mazal 1967; Tsolakis 1967

AT (see *Leukippe and Kleitophon*)

Bas. *Prog.* (see *Progymnasmata*)

[*Belth.*] *Belthandros and Chrysantza* = Kriaras 1955: 85–130

[*Bel.*] *Belisarios, Tale of*: Naples manuscript = Follieri 1970; synoptic edition = Bakker and van Gemert 1988

[Char.] *Chaireas and Kallirrhoe* (Chariton) = Molinié 1979

[Mel.] *Chastity, To* (Meliteniotes) = Miller 1858

[*Chron.*] *Chronographia* (Psellos) = Renauld 1926

[*Dyst.*] *Consolation concerning Ill Fortune and Good Fortune* = Lambros 1880, 1906

[*Daphn.*] *Daphnis and Chloe* (Longos) = Dalmeyda 1960

[*De Mang.*] *De Manganis* (Prodromos?) = Bernardinello 1972; for summary and dating of all 144 poems see Magdalino 1993a: 494–500

[*DA*] *Digenes Akrites*:
  Version A = Kalonaros 1941: I
  Version E = S. Alexiou 1985, 1990
  Version G = Mavrogordato 1956
  Synoptic edition: Trapp 1971a

[*DC*] *Drosilla and Charikles* (Eugenianos) = Conca 1990

Dyst. (see *Consolation* ...)
[Xen.] *Ephesiaka* (Xenophon) = Papanikolaou 1973
Epigram on *Kall.* (see Philes)
[Fal. *Ist.*; *Enypn.*] Erotic Dreams (Falieros) = van Gemert 1980a
Hel. (see *Aithiopika*)
[Herm. *Prog.*] Hermogenes (see *Progymnasmata*)
[*HH*] *Hysmine and Hysminias* (Makrembolites) = Hilberg 1876 (see also Hercher 1859: 159–286)
[*Imp.*] *Imperios and Margarona* = Kriaras 1955: 197–249
[*Kall.*] *Kallimachos and Chrysorrhoe* = Pichard 1956; Kriaras 1955: 17–83
[AT] *Leukippe and Kleitophon* (Achilles Tatios) = Gaselee 1969
[*Lib.*] *Libistros and Rhodamne* = Lambert 1935
Logos Paregoretikos ... (see *Consolation* ...)
[*Maz.*] *Mazaris' Stay in Hades* = Barry, Share, et al. 1975
Mel. (see *Chastity*)
[*OK*] *Old Knight, The* = Breillat 1938
[Phil.] Philes (Epigram on *Kall.*) = Martini 1896; Knös 1962
[*Phlor.*] *Phlorios and Platzia-Phlora* = Kriaras 1955: 131–96
[*Ptochopr.*] *Poems of Poor Prodromos* = Eideneier 1991; Hesseling and Pernot 1910
[Aphth. *Prog.*] *Progymnasmata* (Aphthonios) = Walz 1832
[Herm. *Prog.*] *Progymnasmata* (Hermogenes) = Walz 1832
[Bas. *Prog.*] *Progymnasmata* (Nikephoros Basilakes) = Pignani 1983
Ptochoprodromika (see *Poems of Poor Prodromos*)
[*RD*] *Rhodanthe and Dosikles* (Prodromos) = Markovich 1992
[*Thes.*] *Theseid* = Follieri 1959 (Book I only)
[*Tim.*] *Timarion* = Romano 1974
[*Troy*] *Troy, Tale of* = Nørgaard and Smith 1975 (see also Dedes 1971; Lavagnini 1988)
[*WT*] *War of Troy* = E. Jeffreys and Papathomopoulos, forthcoming
Xen. (see *Ephesiaka*)

PRINTED PUBLICATIONS

The list of publications which follows is not intended to be a complete bibliography of the subject. For texts in the learned language the older bibliography is fully presented by Hunger (1978), and for texts in the vernacular by Beck (1971), and I have not sought to duplicate these monumental works by referring to the secondary literature or to older published editions except where they have been directly relevant to the arguments presented here.

However, for the period following the appearance of Hunger's and Beck's studies I have made a point of including references to *all* the secondary literature relevant to the romances, so that the list given here may be used as a supplement to the bibliographies of Beck and Hunger for the period up to 1994.

Academy of Athens 1962. Ἑλληνικὰ δημοτικὰ τραγούδια. Athens.
Agapitos, P. 1990a. 'Textkritisches zu *Kallimachos und Chrysorrhoe*.' Ἑλληνικά 41: 33–41 = *Byzantion* 62 (1992): 34–44.
——— 1990b. 'The erotic bath in the Byzantine vernacular romance *Kallimachos and*

REFERENCES

Chrysorrhoe.' Classica et mediaevalia 41: 257–73.

——— 1991. *Narrative structure in the Byzantine vernacular romances: a textual and literary study of Kallimachos, Belthandros and Libistros* (Miscellanea Byzantina Monacensia, no. 34), Munich.

——— 1991–2. Ἡ ἔμμεση παράδοση τοῦ δημώδους μυθιστορήματος *Λίβιστρος καὶ Ροδάμνη. Ἑλληνικά* 42: 61–74.

——— 1992. 'Libistros und Rhodamne: Vorläufiges zu einer kritischen Ausgabe der Version α.' *Jahrbuch der Österreichischen Byzantinistik* 42: 191–208.

——— 1993a. Ἡ χρονολογικὴ ἀκολουθία τῶν μυθιστορημάτων *Καλλίμαχος, Βέλθανδρος καὶ Λίβιστρος,* in Panayotakis 1993: II, 97–134.

——— 1993b. Ἕνα ἀκόμη σπάραγμα τοῦ μυθιστορήματος *Λίβιστρος καὶ Ροδάμνη:* ὁ βατικανὸς κώδικας Barb. Gr. 172. *Ἑλληνικά* 43: 337–59.

Agapitos, P., and Smith, O. 1992. *The study of medieval Greek romance.* Copenhagen.

——— 1994. 'Scribes and manuscripts of Byzantine vernacular romances: palaeographical facts and editorial implications.' *Ἑλληνικά* 44: 61–71.

Aleksidze, A. 1965. Византийский роман XII века. Tbilisi.

——— 1979. Мир греческого рнцарского романа (XIII–XIV вв). Tbilisi.

——— 1982. 'Каллимах и Хрисорроя: проблема шанра.' *Jahrbuch der Österreichischen Byzantinistik* 32/3: 93–9.

Alexiou, M. 1977. 'A critical reappraisal of Eustathios Makrembolites' *Hysmine and Hysminias.' Byzantine and Modern Greek Studies* 3: 23–43.

——— 1978. 'Modern Greek folklore and its relation to the past: the evolution of Charos in Greek tradition', in S. Vryonis (ed.), *Βυζαντινὰ καὶ Μεταβυζαντινά,* Vol. I, pp. 211–26. Malibu, Calif.

——— 1982–3. 'Literary subversion and the aristocracy in twelfth-century Byzantium: a stylistic analysis of the *Timarion* (ch. 6–10).' *Byzantine and Modern Greek Studies* 8: 29–45.

——— 1983. 'Sons, wives and mothers: reality and fantasy in some Modern Greek ballads.' *Journal of Modern Greek Studies* 1: 73–111.

——— 1986. 'The poverty of écriture and the craft of writing: towards a reappraisal of the Prodromic poems.' *Byzantine and Modern Greek Studies* 10: 1–40.

Alexiou, M., and Holton, D. 1976. 'The origins and development of politikos stichos: a select critical bibliography.' *Μαντατοφόρος* 9: 22–34.

Alexiou, S. 1979. Ἀκριτικά – τὸ πρόβλημα τῆς ἐγκυρότητας τοῦ κειμένου Ε – χρονολόγηση – ἀποκατάσταση χωρίων – ἑρμηνευτικά. Heraklion, Crete.

——— 1980. Ἐρωτόκριτος: κριτικὴ ἔκδοση, εἰσαγωγή, σημειώσεις, γλωσσάριο. Φιλολογικὴ Βιβλιοθήκη, ἀρ. 3. Athens. (Reprinted in paperback with some additions, 1985.)

——— 1982. Παρατηρήσεις στὸν Ἀκρίτη. Ἀριάδνη 1: 41–57.

——— 1983. Ὁ Διγενὴς Ἀκρίτης τοῦ Ἐσκοριάλ. Πρακτικὰ τῆς Ἀκαδημίας Ἀθηνῶν 58: 68–83.

——— 1985. Βασίλειος Διγενὴς Ἀκρίτης (κατὰ τὸ χειρόγραφο τοῦ Ἐσκοριὰλ) καὶ τὸ Ἄσμα τοῦ Ἀρμούρη. Athens.

——— 1990. Βασίλειος Διγενὴς Ἀκρίτης καὶ τὰ ἄσματα τοῦ Ἀρμούρη καὶ τοῦ Υἱοῦ τοῦ Ἀνδρονίκου. Athens.

Anastasi, R. 1969. 'Sul romanzo di Costantino Manasse.' *Rivista di cultura classica e medioevale* 11: 214–36.

Anderson, G. 1982. *Eros sophistes: ancient novelists at play.* American Classical Studies, no. 9. Chico, Calif.

——— 1984. *Ancient fiction: the novel in the Graeco-Roman world.* London and Sydney.

Andronikos, M. 1969. Τὸ παλάτι τοῦ Διγενὴ Ἀκρίτα. Ἐπιστημονικὴ Ἐπετηρὶς τῆς

REFERENCES

Φιλοσοφικῆς Σχολῆς τοῦ Πανεπιστημίου Θεσσαλονίκης 11: 5–15.

Angelou, A. 1989. Εἰσαγωγή, in G. Palaiologos, *Ὁ Πολυπαθής*. Athens.

Angold, M. 1984. *The Byzantine empire, 1025–1204: a political history*. London and New York.

—— 1989. 'The wedding of Digenes Akrites: love and marriage in Byzantium in the eleventh and twelfth centuries', in *Πρακτικὰ τοῦ Α´ Διεθνοῦς Συμποσίου, Ἡ Καθημερινὴ Ζωὴ στὸ Βυζάντιο*, pp. 201–15. Athens.

Apostolopoulos, Ph. 1984. *La langue du roman byzantin 'Callimaque et Chrysorrhoé.'* Athens.

Arrignon, J.-P., and Duneau, J.-F. 1992. 'Le roman byzantin: permanence et changements', in M.-F. Baslez et al. (eds.), *Le monde du roman grec*, pp. 283–90. Paris.

Astruc, C., and Concasty, M. L. 1960. *Catalogue des manuscrits grecs III. Le supplément grec, t. III, nr. 926*. Paris.

Babbi, A. M., Pioletti, A., Rizzo Nervo, F., and Stevanoni, C. 1992 (eds). *Medioevo romanzo e orientale: testi e prospettive storiografiche (Colloquio Internazionale, Verona, 4–6 aprile 1990)*. Verona and Messina.

Bakker, W. 1987. 'The transition from unrhymed to rhymed: the case of the Βελισαριάδα', in Eideneier 1987b: 25–51.

Bakker, W., and van Gemert, A. 1983. Χρονολογικὸς πίνακας τῶν ἔργων τῆς κρητικῆς λογοτεχνίας κατὰ τὴν περίοδο τῆς Βενετοκρατίας. *Μαντατοφόρος* 22: 79–87.

—— 1988. *Ἱστορία τοῦ Βελισαρίου. Κριτικη ἔκδοση τῶν τεσσάρων διασκευῶν μὲ εἰσαγωγή, σχόλια καὶ γλωσσάριο*. Βυζαντινὴ καὶ Νεοελληνικὴ Βιβλιοθήκη. Thessaloniki.

Bancroft-Marcus, R. forthcoming. *The plays of Georgios Chortatsis: introduction, text, translation and glossary*. Oxford.

Barber, C. 1992. 'Reading the garden in Byzantium: nature and sexuality.' *Byzantine and Modern Greek Studies* 16: 1–19.

Barry, J. N., Share, M. J., et al. 1975. *Ἐπιδημία Μάζαρι ἐν Ἄδου: introduction and text*. Arethusa Monographs, no. 5 (Seminar Classics, no. 609), Buffalo, NY.

Bartsch, S. 1989. *Decoding the ancient novel: the reader and the role of description in Heliodorus and Achilles Tatius*. Princeton, NJ.

Baud-Bovy, S. 1935. *Chansons du Dodécanèse*, 2 vols. Athens.

—— 1973. Ἡ ἐπικράτηση τοῦ δεκαπεντασύλλαβου στὸ ἑλληνικὸ δημοτικὸ τραγούδι. *Ἑλληνικά* 26: 301–13.

Baugh, A. C. 1959. 'Improvisation in the Middle English romance.' *Proceedings of the American Philosophical Society* 103: 418–54.

—— 1967. 'The Middle English romance: some questions of creation, presentation and preservation.' *Speculum* 42: 1–31.

Bäuml, F. H. 1980. 'Varieties and consequences of medieval literacy and illiteracy.' *Speculum* 55: 237–65.

—— 1984. 'Medieval texts and the two theories of oral-formulaic composition: a proposal for a third theory.' *New Literary History* 16/1: 31–49.

Beaton, R. 1980. *Folk poetry of modern Greece*. Cambridge.

—— 1981a. 'Was *Digenes Akrites* an oral poem?' *Byzantine and Modern Greek Studies* 7: 7–27.

—— 1981b. '*Digenes Akrites* and modern Greek folk song: a reassessment.' *Byzantion* 51: 22–43.

—— 1986a. [Review of S. Alexiou 1985] *Journal of Hellenic Studies* 106: 271–3.

—— 1986b. 'The oral traditions of modern Greece: a survey.' *Oral Tradition* 1: 110–33.

—— 1987a. 'The rhetoric of poverty: the lives and opinions of Theodore

Prodromos.' *Byzantine and Modern Greek Studies* 11: 1–28.

—— 1987b. Ἀκρίτης καὶ οἱ κριτικοί: φιλολογικὰ καὶ ἐκδοτικὰ προβλήματα, in Eideneier 1987b: 73–84.

—— (ed.) 1988a. *The Greek novel, A.D. 1–1985*. London and Sydney.

—— 1988b. '*De vulgari eloquentia* in twelfth-century Byzantium', in J. Howard-Johnston (ed.), *Byzantium and the west: c. 850–c. 1250*, pp. 261–8. Amsterdam.

—— 1989. 'Courtly romances in Byzantium: a case study in reception.' *Mediterranean Historical Review* 4: 345–55.

—— 1990. 'Orality and the reception of late Byzantine vernacular literature.' *Byzantine and Modern Greek Studies* 14: 174–84.

—— 1993a. 'An epic in the making? The early versions of *Digenes Akrites*', in Beaton and Ricks 1993: 55–72.

—— 1993. '*Digenes Akrites* on the computer: a comparative study of the E and G versions', in Panayotakis 1993: II, 42–68.

—— 1994. *An introduction to modern Greek literature*. Oxford.

—— 1996. 'Cappadocians at court: Digenes and Timarion', in Mullet and Smythe 1996.

Beaton, R., and Ricks, D. 1993 (eds). *Digenes Akrites: new approaches to Byzantine heroic poetry*. London.

Beaton, R., Kelly, J., and Lendari, T. 1995. *Concordance to Digenes Akrites, Version E*. Heraklion and Rethymnon.

Beck, H.-G. 1959. *Kirche und theologische Literatur im byzantinischen Reich*. (Byzantinisches Handbuch). Munich.

—— 1969. 'Antike Beredsamkeit und byzantinische Kallilogia.' *Antike und Abendland* 15: 91–101.

—— 1971. *Geschichte der byzantinischen Volksliteratur* (Byzantinisches Handbuch). Munich.

—— 1975. 'Der Leserkries der byzantinischen "Volksliteratur" im Licht der handschriftlichen Überlieferung', in *Byzantine Books and Bookmen*, Dumbarton Oaks Colloquium, pp. 47–67. Washington, DC.

—— 1976. 'Die griechische Volksliteratur des 14. Jahrhunderts', in *XIVe Congrès International des Etudes Byzantines (Bucarest 1971): Rapports*, Vol. I, pp. 67–83. Bucharest.

—— 1977. 'Marginalia on the Byzantine novel', in Reardon 1977: 59–65.

—— 1978. *Der byzantinische Jahrtausend*. Munich. (Paperback 1982.)

—— 1984. *Byzantinisches Erotikon: Orthodoxie – Literatur – Gesellschaft* (Bayerische Akademie der Wissenschaften, philosophisch–historische Klasse, Sitzungsberichte: Jahrgang 1984, no. 5). Munich.

—— 1986. 'Ortodossia ed erotismo. Marginalia alla letteratura erotica bizantina', in Beck et al. 1986: 13–32.

Beck, H.-G., Conca, F., and Cupane, C. 1986 (eds). *Il romanzo tra cultura latina e cultura bizantina (testi della III Settimana Residenziale di Studi Medievali, 17–21 ottobre 1983)* (Biblioteca dell'Enchiridion, no. 5). Palermo.

Benson, R. L., Constable, G., and Lanham, C. D. 1982. *Renaissance and renewal in the twelfth century*. Oxford.

Benton, J. 1982. 'Consciousness of self and perceptions of individuality', in Benson et al. 1982: 263–95.

Bernardinello, S. 1972. *Theodori Prodromi de Manganis* (Studi bizantini e neoellenici, no. 4). Padua.

Betts, G. 1994 (trans.). *Three medieval Greek romances* (Garland Medieval Library). New York.

Bloom, H. 1973. *The anxiety of influence: a theory of poetry*. Oxford.

Boitani, P. 1982. *English medieval narrative in the thirteenth and fourteenth centuries*, trans. J. K. Hall. Cambridge.

Booth, W. 1961. *The rhetoric of fiction*. Chicago, Ill.

Bouvier, B. 1960. *Δημοτικὰ τραγούδια ἀπὸ χειρόγραφο τῆς Μονῆς τῶν Ἰβήρων*. Athens.

Bowie, E. L. 1985. 'The Greek novel', in P. E. Easterling and B. M. W. Knox (eds), *The Cambridge History of Classical Literature*, Vol. I: *Greek Literature*, pp. 683–94. Cambridge.

Breillat, P. 1938. 'La table ronde en orient. Le poème grec du vieux chevalier.' *Mélanges d'archéologie et d'histoire* 55: 308–40.

Brett, G. 1954. 'The automata in the Byzantine "Throne of Solomon".' *Speculum* 29: 477–87.

Browning, R. 1962–3. 'The Patriarchal School at Constantinople in the twelfth century.' *Byzantion* 32: 167–201; 33: 11–40.

—— 1975. 'Enlightenment and repression in Byzantium in the eleventh and twelfth centuries.' *Past and Present* 69: 3–23.

—— 1978a. 'The language of Byzantine literature', in S. Vryonis (ed.), *Βυζαντινὰ καὶ Μεταβυζαντινά*, Vol. I, pp. 103–33. Malibu, Calif.

—— 1978b. 'Literacy in the Byzantine world', *Byzantine and Modern Greek Studies* 4: 39–57.

—— 1980. *The Byzantine world*. London.

—— 1983. *Medieval and modern Greek* (revised edn). Cambridge.

Bryer, A. 1981. 'The first encounter with the west, A.D. 1050–1204', in P. Whitting (ed.), *Byzantium: an introduction* (revised edn), pp. 83–110. Oxford.

Bury, J. B. 1971. *Romances of chivalry on Greek soil*. Oxford.

Cameron, A. 1992. *The use and abuse of Byzantium: an essay on reception* (inaugural lecture, King's College London). London.

Castillo Didier, M. 1994. *Poesia heroica griega: epopeya de Diyenís Akritas. Cantares de Armuris y de Andrónico*. Santiago.

Chatman, S. 1978. *Story and discourse: narrative structure in fiction and film*. Ithaca and London.

Chatzidakis, G. 1905. *Μεσαιωνικὰ καὶ νέα ἑλληνικά, Τόμ. Α΄*. Athens.

Chatzis, A. 1950. *Εὐστάθιος Μακρεμβολίτης καὶ Ἀκριτηίς*. *Ἀθηνᾶ* 54: 184–226, 317–18.

Chatziyiakoumis, M. 1977. *Μεσαιωνικὰ ἑλληνικὰ κείμενα*. Athens.

Christides, V. 1979. 'Arabic influence on the akritic cycle.' *Byzantion* 49: 94–109.

Clucas, L. 1981. *The trial of John Italos and the crisis of intellectual values in Byzantium in the eleventh century* (Miscellanea Byzantina Monacensia, no. 26). Munich.

Conca, F. 1986a. 'Il romanzo nell'età dei Paleologi: temi e strutture', in Beck et al. 1986: 33–45.

—— 1986b. 'Il romanzo di Niceta Eugeniano: modelli narrativi e stilistici.' *Siculorum Gymnasium*, n.s., 39: 115–26.

—— 1990. *Nicetas Eugenianus, de Drosillae et Chariclis amoribus* (London Studies in Classical Philology, no. 24). Amsterdam.

Crescini, V. 1899. *Il cantare di Fiorio e Biancifiore*. Bologna.

Crosby, R. 1936. 'Oral delivery in the Middle Ages.' *Speculum* 11: 88–110.

Culler, J. 1983. *On deconstruction: theory and criticism after structuralism*. London.

Cupane, C. 1974a. 'Un caso di giudizio di Dio nel romanzo di Teodoro Prodromo.' *Rivista di studi bizantini e neoellenici*, nuova serie, 10–11: 147–68.

—— 1974b. '"Ἔρως-Βασιλεύς": la figura di Eros nel romanzo bizantino d'amore.' *Atti del Accademia di Arti di Palermo*, serie 4, 33/2: 243–97.

——— 1978. 'Il motivo del castello nella narrativa tardo-bizantina. Evoluzione di un' allegoria.' *Jahrbuch der Österreichischen Byzantinistik* 27: 229–67.

——— 1983. 'Il "concorso di bellezza" in Beltandro e Crisanza sulla via fra Bisanzio e l'Occidente medievale.' *Jahrbuch der Österreichischen Byzantinistik* 33: 221–48.

——— 1984. '"Natura formatrix". Umwege eines rhetorischen Topos', in W. Hörandner, J. Koder, O. Kresten, and E. Trapp (eds), Βυζάντιος. *Festschrift für Herbert Hunger zum 70. Geburtstag*, pp. 37–52. Vienna.

——— 1986. 'Topica romanzesca in oriente e in occidente: "avanture" e "amour"', in Beck et al. 1986: 47–72.

——— 1987. 'Byzantinisches Erotikon: Ansichten und Einsichten.' *Jahrbuch der Österreichischen Byzantinistik* 37: 213–33.

——— 1992a. [Review of Plepelits 1989]. *Jahrbuch der Österreichischen Byzantinistik* 42: 384–90.

——— 1992b. 'Concezione e rappresentazione dell'amore nella narrativa tardo-bizantina. Un tentativo di analisi comparata', in Babbi et al. 1992: 283–305.

——— 1993. 'Note su Fortuna nella letteratura greca medievale', in Panayotakis 1993: I, 413–37.

——— 1994–5. 'Δεῦτε, προσκαρτερήσατε μικρόν, ὦ νέοι πάντες. Note sulla ricezione primaria e sul pubblico della letteratura greca medievale', in Δίπτυχα Ἑταιρείας Βυζαντινῶν καὶ Μεταβυζαντινῶν Μελετῶν 6, pp. 147–68.

Curtius, E. R. 1953. *European literature and the Latin Middle Ages*, trans. W. R. Trask. London.

Dalmeyda, G. 1960. *Longus: Daphnis et Chloé* (2nd edn). Paris.

Danezis, G. 1987. 'Das Vorbild des Spaneas: ein neuer Vorschlag und die Folgen für die Edition des Textes', in Eideneier 1987b: 89–100.

Davies, S. 1978. 'The wheel of fortune: the picture and the poem.' *Revue des études sud-est européennes* 16: 121–38.

Davison, M. 1977. 'The thematic use of ekphrasis in the ancient novel', in Reardon 1977: 32–3.

Dawkins, R. M. 1932. *Leontios Makhairas: Recital concerning the sweet land of Cyprus entitled Chronicle*, 2 vols. Oxford.

Dedes, D. 1971. 'An edition of a mediaeval Greek poem on the Trojan War (Διήγησις τῆς Τρωάδος).' University of London: unpublished Ph.D. thesis.

Deligiorgis, S. 1975. 'A Byzantine romance in international perspective: the Drosilla and Charikles of Niketas Eugenianos.' *Neo-Hellenika* 2: 21–32.

de Man, P. 1979. 'Genesis and genealogy (Nietzsche)', in his *Allegories of reading: figural language in Rousseau, Nietzsche, Rilke, and Proust*, pp. 79–102. New Haven and London.

Denisi, S. 1990. Γιὰ τὶς ἀρχὲς τῆς πεζογραφίας μας. Ὁ Πολίτης 109: 55–63.

——— 1992. Οἱ ἀρχὲς τοῦ ἑλληνικοῦ ἱστορικοῦ μυθιστορήματος. Διαβάζω 291: 28–34.

di Benedetto, A. 1979. [Review of Nørgaard and Smith 1975]. Ἑλληνικά 31: 236–41.

di Benedetto Zimbone, A. 1990. 'Note critiche al testo di Φλόριος καὶ Πλατζιαφλόρε.' Ἰταλοελληνικά (Naples) 3: 197–204.

Diller, I. 1977. 'Märchenmotive in Kallimachos und Chrysorrhoe.' *Folia neohellenica* 2: 25–40.

Dimaras, K. Th. 1975. Ἱστορία τῆς νεοελληνικῆς λογοτεχνίας: ἀπό τὶς πρῶτες ρίζες ὡς τὴν ἐποχή μας, 6th edn. Athens.

Dodds, E. R. 1965. *Pagan and Christian in an age of anxiety*. Cambridge.

Dölger, F. 1919. 'Quellen und Vorbilder zu dem Gedicht des Meliteniotes: Εἰς τὴν Σωφροσύνην. Mit einer Einleitung über die Person des Dichters.' Doctoral dissertation. Munich.

—— 1934. 'Die Abfassungszeit des Gedichtes des Meliteniotes, Auf die Enthalt-samkeit.' *Annuaire de l'Institut de Philologie et d'Histoire Orientales (Mélanges Bidez), de l'Université Libre de Bruxelles* 2: 315–30.

Dronke, P. 1970. *Poetic individuality in the Middle Ages: new departures in poetry, 1000–1150*. Oxford.

—— 1973. 'Medieval rhetoric', in D. Daiches and A. Thorlby (eds), *Literature and western civilisation*, Vol. II, pp. 315–45. London. (Reprinted in Dronke 1984: 7–38.)

—— 1976. 'Learned lyric and popular ballad in the early middle ages.' *Studi medievali* (Spoleto), 3a serie 17/1: 1–40. (Reprinted in Dronke 1984: 167–207.)

—— 1982. 'Profane elements in literature', in Benson et al. 1982: 569–92.

—— 1984. *The medieval poet and his world* (Storia e letteratura, raccolta di studi e testi, no. 164). Rome.

Dunlop, J. C. 1888. *History of prose fiction* (rev. H. Wilson), Vol. I. London.

Dyck, A. 1983. 'On *Digenis Akritas*, Grottaferrata version Book 5.' *Greek, Roman and Byzantine Studies* 24: 185–92.

Eideneier, H. 1979. 'Ein byzantinisches Kalendargedicht in der Volkssprache.' Έλληνικά 33: 368–419.

—— 1982. 'Zum Stil der byzantinischen Tierdichtung.' *Jahrbuch der Österreichischen Byzantinistik* 32/3: 301–6.

—— 1982–3. 'Leser- oder Hörerkreis? Zur byzantinischen Dichtung in der Volkssprache.' Έλληνικά 34: 119–50.

—— 1984. 'Ausläufer byzantinischer Dichtung in zypriotischen Volksliedern. Beweis mündlicher Überlieferung?' in Ἀντίχαρη. Ἀφιέρωμα στὸν καθηγητὴ Σταμάτη Καρατζᾶ, pp. 97–109. Athens.

—— 1985a. 'Sinnvolles Verhörer im Ptochoprodromos III.' Έλληνικά 36: 78–101.

—— 1985b. Ὁ προφορικὸς χαρακτήρας τῆς νεοελληνικῆς λογοτεχνίας. Δωδώνη: Φιλολογία 14: 39–53.

—— 1987a. 'Der *Ptochoprodromos* in schriftlicher und mündlicher Überlieferung', in Eideneier 1987b: 101–19.

—— 1987b (ed.). *Neograeca Medii Aevi: Text und Ausgabe. Akten zum Symposion Köln 1986*. Cologne.

Eideneier, H. 1991a. *Ptochoprodromos* (Neograeca medii aevi no. 5). Cologne.

—— 1991b. 'Byzantinische volkssprachliche Schriftkoine und mündliche Überlieferung.' *Mandatoforos* 33: 7–10.

—— 1992. [Review of Smith 1990]. Έλληνικά 42: 226–8.

Eideneier, H. and N. 1979. 'Zum Fünfzehnsilber der Ptochoprodromika', in Ἀφιέρωμα στὸν καθηγητὴ Λίνο Πολίτη, pp. 1–7. Thessaloniki.

Eliot, T. S. 1932. *Selected essays*. London.

Ellissen, A. 1846. Ὁ πρέσβυς ἱππότης. *Ein griechisches Gedicht aus dem Sagenkreis der Tafelrunde*. Leipzig.

Emrich, G. 1982. 'Erzählformen in Kallimachos und Chrysorrhoe.' *Jahrbuch der Österreichischen Byzantinistik* 32/3: 289–99.

Faral, E. 1913. *Recherches sur les sources latines des contes et romans courtois au moyen âge*. Paris.

Fenik, B. 1991. *Digenis: epic and popular style in the Escorial version*. Heraklion and Rethymnon.

Finnegan, R. 1988. *Literacy and orality: studies in the technology of communication*. Oxford.

—— 1990. 'What is orality – if anything?' *Byzantine and Modern Greek Studies* 14: 130–49.

Fletcher, R. 1977. 'The epic of Digenis Akritas and the akritic songs: a short guide to bibliography.' Μαντατοφόρος 11: 8–12.

Foley, J. M. 1988. *The theory of oral composition: history and methodology.* Bloomington and Indianapolis.

—— 1991. *Immanent art: from structure to meaning in traditional oral epic.* Bloomington and Indianapolis.

Follieri, E. 1953. 'La versione in greco volgare del Teseida del Boccaccio.' *Rivista di studi bizantini e neoellenici* 7: 67–77.

—— 1958. 'Gli elementi originali nella versione neogreca del Teseide del Boccaccio', in Πεπραγμένα τοῦ Θ′ Διεθνοῦς Βυζαντινολογικοῦ Συνεδρίου, Τόμ. Γ′ pp. 292–8 = Ἑλληνικά, Παράρτημα, ἀρ. 9. Thessaloniki.

—— 1959. *Il Teseida neogreco. Libro I. Saggio di edizione.* Rome.

—— 1970. 'Il poema bizantino del Belisario', in *Atti del Convegno Internazionale sul Tema: La Poesia Epica e la sua Formazione* (Accademia Nazionale dei Lincei, Quaderno 139), pp. 583–661. Rome.

Frye, N. 1976. *The secular scripture: a study of the structure of romance.* Cambridge, Mass.

Fyrigos, A. 1985. 'Σπανίας Σπανέας. Proposta per una interpretazione del termine e ipotesi sulla datazione dell'omonimo poema.' *Bollettino della Badia Greca di Grottaferrata*, nuova serie, 39: 39–56.

Galatariotou, C. 1987. 'Structural oppositions in the Grottaferrata *Digenes Akrites.' Byzantine and Modern Greek Studies* 11: 29–68.

—— 1993. 'The primacy of the Escorial *Digenes Akrites*: an open and shut case?', in Beaton and Ricks 1993: 38–54.

Gärtner, H. 1969. 'Charikleia in Byzanz.' *Antike und Abendland* 15: 47–69.

Garufi Italia, S. 1982–3. 'Sui rapporti tra il *Filocolo* di Giovanni Boccaccio e il romanzo greco-medievale *Florio e Plaziaflora.' Δίπτυχα Ἑταιρείας Βυζαντινῶν καὶ Μεταβυζαντινῶν Μελετῶν* 3: 283–304.

Garzya, A. 1983. '"Matière de Bretagne" a Bisanzio', in A. Garzya, *Il Mandarino e il Quotidiano: Saggi sulla Letteratura Tardoantica e Bizantina*, pp. 263–81. Naples.

Gaselee, S. 1969. *Achilles Tatius* (Loeb Classical Library). London and Cambridge, Mass.

Garantoudis, E. 1993. Προβλήματα περιγραφῆς καὶ ἀνάλυσης πρωτονεοελληνικῶν δεκαπεντασυλλάβων, in Panayotakis 1993: I, 188–227.

Garland, L. 1989. 'The "βεργὶν τρίκλωνον" of Belthandros and Chrysantza: a note on a popular verse romance and its sources.' *Byzantinische Zeitschrift* 62: 87–95.

—— 1990. 'Sexual morality in Byzantine learned and vernacular romance.' *Byzantine and Modern Greek Studies* 14: 62–120.

Genette, G. 1980. *Narrative discourse.* Oxford.

Giannou, T. 1993. Σήματα τοῦ ἀφηγητῆ καὶ τοῦ δέκτη στὶς παραλλαγὲς τοῦ Διγενῆ Ἀκρίτη. Unpublished thesis, University of Thessaloniki.

Gidel, C. 1986. *Etudes sur la littérature grecque moderne.* Paris.

—— 1870. 'Etude sur Apollonius de Tyr. Roman écrit en grec et en vers politiques, d'après une version latine', in Wagner 1870: 91–101.

Gigante, F. 1960. 'Il romanzo di Eustathios Makrembolites.' *Akten des XI. internationalen Byzantinistenkongresses (München 1958)*, pp. 168–81. Munich.

Gill, C., and Wiseman, T. P. 1993. *Lies and fiction in the ancient novel.* Exeter.

Graham, H. F. 1968. 'The tale of Devgenij.' *Byzantinoslavica* 29: 51–91.

Grégoire, H. 1932. 'Autour de Digénis Akritas. Les cantilènes et la date de la récension d'Andros-Trébizonde.' *Byzantion* 7: 287–302.

—— 1941. 'Notes on the Byzantine epic: the Greek folk-songs and their importance for the classification of the Russian version and of the Greek manuscripts.' *Byzantion* 15: 92–103.

—— 1942. Ὁ Διγενὴς Ἀκρίτας. New York.

—— 1975. Autour de l' épopée byzantine (Variorum Reprints). London.

Hägg, T. 1971. Narrative technique in ancient Greek romances. Stockholm.

—— 1983. The novel in antiquity. Oxford.

—— 1986. 'The oriental reception of Greek novels.' Symbolae Osloenses 61: 99–131.

—— 1987. 'Callirhoe and Parthenope: the beginnings of the historical novel.' Classical Antiquity 6/12: 184–204.

—— 1988. 'The beginnings of the historical novel', in Beaton 1988a, pp. 169–81.

Hanning, R. W. 1977. The individual in twelfth-century romance. New Haven and London.

Herzfeld, M. 1980. 'Social borderers: themes of conflict and ambiguity in Greek folksongs.' Byzantine and Modern Greek Studies 6: 61–80.

Hesseling, D. C. 1911. 'Le roman de Digénis Akritas d'après le manuscrit de Madrid.' Λαογραφία 3: 557–604.

—— 1919. L'Achilléïde byzantine, avec une introduction, des observations et un index. Amsterdam.

Hesseling, D. C., and Pernot, H. 1910. Poèmes prodromiques en grec vulgaire. Amsterdam.

—— 1913. Ἐρωτοπαίγνια: Chansons d'amour. Paris and Athens.

Highet, G. 1949. The classical tradition: Greek and Roman influences on western literature. Oxford.

Hilberg, I. 1876. Εὐσταθίου Πρωτονωβελεσίμου τοῦ Μακρεμβολίτου τῶν καθ' Ὑσμίνγν καὶ Ὑσμινίαν λόγοι ια'. Vienna.

Holton, D. 1974. Διήγησις τοῦ Ἀλεξάνδρου: the tale of Alexander. The rhymed version. Critical edition with an introduction and commentary (Βυζαντινὴ καὶ Νεοελληνικὴ Βιβλιοθήκη, ἀρ. 1), Thessaloniki.

—— 1988. 'Erotókritos and Greek tradition', in Beaton 1988a: 144–55.

—— 1991 (ed.) Literature and society in Renaissance Crete. Cambridge.

Hörandner, W. 1974. Theodoros Prodromos. Historische Gedichte (Wiener Byzantinistische Studien, no. 11). Vienna.

Huet, Pierre Daniel 1966. Traité de l'origine des romans, facsimile reprint. Stuttgart. (First published 1670.)

Hull, D. B. 1972. Digenis Akritas: the two-blood border lord. The Grottaferrata version translated with an introduction and notes. Athens, Ohio.

Hult, D. F. 1986. Self-fulfilling prophecies: readership and authority in the first 'Roman de la Rose'. Cambridge.

Hunger, H. 1965. 'Die Schönheitskonkurrenz in "Belthandros und Chrysantza" und die Brautschau am byzantinischen Kaiserhof.' Byzantion 35: 150–8. (Reprinted in Hunger 1973.)

—— 1968a. 'Un roman byzantin et son atmosphère: Callimaque et Chrysorrhoé.' Travaux et mémoires 3: 405–22. (Reprinted in Hunger 1973.)

—— 1968b. Die byzantinische Literatur der Komnenenzeit. Versuch einer Neubewertung (Anzeiger philosophisch–historische Klasse, Österreichische Akademie der Wissenschaften, no. 105). Graz, Vienna and Cologne. (Reprinted in Hunger 1973.)

—— 1968c. Der byzantinische Katz–Mäuse-Krieg. Graz, Vienna and Cologne.

—— 1969–70. 'On the imitation (mimesis) of antiquity in Byzantine literature.' Dumbarton Oaks Papers 23–4: 17–38. (Reprinted in Hunger 1973.)

—— 1972. 'Byzantinische "Froschmänner"?' in Antidosis. Festschrift Walter Krauss zum 70. Geburtstag, pp. 183–7. Vienna.

—— 1973. Byzantinistische Grundlagenforschung. Gesammelte Aufsätze (Variorum Reprints). London.

—— 1978. *Die hochsprachliche profane Literatur der Byzantiner,* 2 vols (Byzantinische Handbuch). Munich.

—— 1980. *Antiker und byzantinischer Roman* (Sitzungsberichte der Heidelberger Akademie der Wissenschaften, Philosophisch–historische Klasse, no. 3: Abhandlung). Heidelberg.

Huxley, G. 'Antecedents and context of *Digenes Akrites.*' *Greek, Roman and Byzantine Studies* 15: 317–38.

Irmscher, J. 1979. 'Les Francs – représentants de la littérature en grec vulgaire.' *Byzantinische Forschungen* 7: 57–66.

Iser, W. 1974. *The implied reader: patterns of communication in prose fiction from Bunyan to Beckett.* Baltimore and London.

—— 1978. *The act of reading: a theory of aesthetic response.* Baltimore and London.

Jackson, W. Y. H. 1960. *The literature of the Middle Ages.* New York.

Jauss, H. R. 1982a. 'Literary history as a challenge to literary theory', in his *Toward an Aesthetic of Reception,* pp. 3–45. Brighton and Minnesota.

—— 1982b. 'Theory of genres and medieval literature', in his *Toward an Aesthetic of Reception,* pp. 76–110. Brighton and Minnesota.

Jeffreys, E. 1968. 'Further notes on Palamedes.' *Byzantinische Zeitschrift* 61: 251–3.

—— 1972. [Review of Trapp 1971a]. *Journal of Hellenic Studies* 92: 253–5.

—— 1974. 'Some comments on the manuscripts of Imberios and Margarona.' Ἑλληνικά 27: 39–49.

—— 1975. 'Constantine Hermoniakos and Byzantine education.' Δωδώνη 4: 81–109. (Reprinted in E. and M. Jeffreys 1983a.)

—— 1976. 'The manuscripts and sources of the War of Troy', in *Actes du XIVe Congrès International des Etudes Byzantines (Bucarest 1971),* pp. 91–4; figs 1–5. Bucharest.

—— 1978. 'The judgement of Paris in later Byzantine literature.' *Byzantion* 48: 112–31. (Reprinted in E. and M. Jeffreys 1983a.)

—— 1979. 'The popular Byzantine verse romances of chivalry. Work since 1971.' Μαντατοφόρος 14: 20–34.

—— 1980. 'The Comnenian background to the romans d'antiquité.' *Byzantion* 10: 455–86. (Reprinted in E. and M. Jeffreys 1983a.)

—— 1981. 'The later Greek verse romances: a survey', in E. and M. Jeffreys and A. Moffatt (eds), *Byzantine Papers* (Byzantina Australiensia, no. 1), pp. 116–27. Canberra.

—— 1982. 'The Sevastokratorissa Eirene as literary patroness: the monk Iakovos.' *Jahrbuch der Österreichischen Byzantinistik* 32/3: 63–71.

—— 1993a. 'The Grottaferrata version of *Digenes Akrites*: a reassessment', in Beaton and Ricks 1993: 26–37.

—— 1993b. 'Place as a factor in the edition of early demotic texts', in Panayotakis 1993: I, 310–24.

Jeffreys, E. and M. 1979. 'The traditional style of early demotic Greek verse.' *Byzantine and Modern Greek Studies* 5: 115–39. (Reprinted in E. and M. Jeffreys 1983a.)

—— 1983a. *Popular literature in late Byzantium* (Variorum Reprints). London.

—— 1983b. 'The style of Byzantine popular poetry: recent work', in *Okeanos: Essays Presented to Ihor Ševčenko* (Harvard Ukrainian Studies, no. 7), pp. 309–43.

—— 1986. 'The oral background of Byzantine popular poetry.' *Oral Tradition* 1/3: 504–47.

Jeffreys, E. and Papathomopoulos, M. forthcoming. Ὁ Πόλεμος τῆς Τρωάδος: *critical edition with introduction, notes and glossary* (Βυζαντινὴ καὶ Νεοελληνικὴ Βιβλιοθήκη). Athens.

Jeffreys, M. 1973. 'Formulas in the Chronicle of the Morea.' *Dumbarton Oaks Papers* 27: 165–95. (Reprinted in E. and M. Jeffreys 1983a.)

—— 1974a. 'The nature and origins of the political verse.' *Dumbarton Oaks Papers* 28: 141–95. (Reprinted in E. and M. Jeffreys 1983a.)

—— 1974b. 'The literary emergence of vernacular Greek.' *Mosaic* (Manitoba) 8: 171–93.

—— 1975a. '*Digenis Akritas* manuscript Z.' *Δωδώνη* 4: 163–201. (Reprinted in E. and M. Jeffreys 1983a.)

—— 1975b. 'The Chronicle of the Morea: priority of the Greek version.' *Byzantinische Zeitschrift* 68: 304–50.

—— 1976. 'The astrological prologue of *Digenis Akritas*.' *Byzantion* 46: 375–97. (Reprinted in E. and M. Jeffreys 1983a.)

—— 1978. 'Digenis Akritas and Commagene.' *Svenska Forskningsinstitutet i Istanbul, Meddelanden* 3: 5–28.

—— 1987. 'Η γλῶσσα τοῦ Χρονικοῦ τοῦ Μορέως – γλῶσσα μιᾶς προφορικῆς παράδοσης;, in Eideneier 1987b: 139–63.

—— 1993a. 'Early Modern Greek verse: parallels and frameworks.' *Modern Greek Studies (Australia and New Zealand)* 1: 49–78.

—— 1993b. 'Proposals for the debate on the question of oral influence in early Modern Greek poetry', in Panayotakis 1993: I, 251–66.

Jeffreys, M. and E. 1971. 'Imberios and Margarona: the manuscripts, sources and edition of a Byzantine verse romance.' *Byzantion* 41: 122–60. (Reprinted in E. and M. Jeffreys 1983a.)

—— 1994. 'Who was the Sevastokratorissa Eirene?' *Byzantion* 64: 40–68.

Jenkins, R. 1963. 'The Hellenistic origins of Byzantine literature.' *Dumbarton Oaks Papers* 17: 37–52.

Jenny, L. 1982. 'The strategy of form', in T. Todorov (ed.), *French literary theory today*, pp. 34–62. Cambridge and Paris.

Jouanno, C. 1987. 'L'ekphrasis dans la littérature byzantine d'imagination.' Unpublished doctoral dissertation, Université de Paris IV.

—— 1989. 'Nicétas Eugénianos, un heritier du roman grec.' *Revue des études grecques* 102: 346–60.

—— 1990. 'L'univers des déscriptions romanesques byzantines, ou le règne du faux-semblant', in Tatum and Vernazza 1990: 119–20.

—— 1991. [Review of Beaton, *The medieval Greek romance*.] *Revue des études grecques* 104: 672–3.

—— 1992. 'Les barbares dans le roman byzantin du XIIe siècle. Fonction d'un topos.' *Byzantion* 62: 264–300.

Kahane, H. and R. 1945. 'Akritas and Arcita, a Byzantine source of Boccaccio's *Teseida*.' *Speculum* 20: 415–25.

—— 1983. 'The hidden Narcissus in the Byzantine romance of Belthandros and Chrysantza.' *Jahrbuch der Österreichischen Byzantinistik* 33: 199–219.

Kalonaros, P. 1941. *Βασίλειος Διγενὴς Ἀκρίτας: τὰ ἔμμετρα κείμενα*, 2 vols. Athens.

Kambylis, A. 1975. 'Textkritische Bemerkungen zum Gedicht des Theodoros Meliteniotes', in *Φίλτρα: Τιμητικὸς τόμος Σ. Γ. Καψωμένου*, pp. 227–42. Thessaloniki.

—— 1980. 'Beiläufiges zur Byzantinischen Ilias des cod. Paris Suppl. Gr. 926.' *Jahrbuch der Österreichischen Byzantinistik* 29: 263–73.

—— 1993. Κριτικὴ τῶν κειμένων καὶ μετρικὴ [abstract], in Panayotakis 1993: I, 309.

Kapsomenos, E. 1985. 'Η δομὴ τῆς ἀφήγησης στὸν "Ἐρωτόκριτο" in *Πεπραγμένα τοῦ Εʹ Διεθνοῦς Κρητολογικοῦ Συνεδρίου*, Vol. II, pp. 164–81. Heraklion, Crete.

REFERENCES

Karyianioti, E. 1992. Ποιητικὰ αὐτοσχόλια στὶς βυζαντινὲς δημώδεις ἐρωτικές μυθιστορίες. Unpublished dissertation, University of Thessaloniki.

Karayianni, I. 1975. Ὁ ‘Διγενὴς Ἀκρίτας’ τοῦ Ἐσκοριάλ. Συμβολή στὴ μελέτη τοῦ κειμένου (Μελέτες στὴ Νέα Ἑλληνικὴ Φιλολογία, ἀρ. 1), Ioannina.

Kastner, G. 1976. ‘Narrative unity in the Digenes Akrites,’ in J. W. Barker (ed.), *Second Annual Byzantine Studies Conference, University of Wisconsin: Abstracts*, pp. 35–6. Madison, Wis.

Kazhdan, A. 1967. ‘Bemerkungen zu Niketas Eugenianos.’ *Jahrbuch der Österreichischen Byzantinischen Gesellschaft* 16: 101–17.

Kazhdan, A., and Constable, G. 1982. *People and power in Byzantium: an introduction to modern Byzantine studies*. Washington, DC.

Kazhdan, A., and Epstein, A. W. 1985. *Change in Byzantine culture in the eleventh and twelfth centuries*. Berkeley, Los Angeles and London.

Kazhdan, A., and Franklin, S. 1984. *Studies on Byzantine literature of the eleventh and twelfth centuries*. Cambridge and Paris.

Kechayoglou, G. 1978. Κριτικὴ ἔκδοση τῆς ἱστορίας Πτωχολέοντος. Ἐπιστημονικὴ (Ἐπετηρὶς τῆς Φιλοσοφικῆς Σχολῆς τοῦ Πανεπιστημίου Θεσσαλονίκης, Παράρτημα, ἀρ. 22). Thessaloniki.

—— 1980. Οἱ ἱστορίες τῆς νεοελληνικῆς λογοτεχνίας. *Μαντατοφόρος* 15: 5–66.

—— 1982a. Ἡ λογικὴ τῆς διήγησης στὰ βυζαντινὰ δημώδη ἀφηγηματικὰ κείμενα: προβλήματα μεθόδου. *Jahrbuch der Österreichischen Byzantinistik* 32/3: 267–76.

—— 1982b. Ὁ Βυζαντινὸς καὶ μεταβυζαντινὸς Συντίπας: γιὰ μιὰ νέα ἔκδοση. *Graeco-Arabica* 1: 105–30.

—— 1982c. Ἀπόκοπος – Ἀπολώνιος – Ἱστορία τῆς Σωσάννης (Λαϊκὰ Λογοτεχνικὰ Ἔντυπα, ἀρ. 1). Athens.

—— 1986a. Τύχες τῆς Βυζαντινῆς ἀκριτικῆς ποίησης στὴ νεοελληνικὴ λογοτεχνία: σταθμοὶ καὶ χρήσεις. Ἀποτιμήσεις. Ἑλληνικά 37: 83–109.

—— 1986b. Πρῶτες ἐκδόσεις τοῦ Ἀπολλωνίου: νέα στοιχεία. Ἑλληνικά 37: 145–59.

—— 1987. Γιὰ μιὰ νέα ἔκδοση τοῦ Ἀπολλωνίου: παρατηρήσεις καὶ προτάσεις, in Eideneier 1987b: 179–203.

—— 1988. ‘Translations of eastern “novels” and their influence on late Byzantine and modern Greek fiction (11th–18th centuries)’, in Beaton 1988a: 156–66.

—— 1990. [Review of Beaton, *The medieval Greek romance*]. Ἑλληνικά 41: 158–71.

—— 1991a. 1790–1800: γέννηση, ἀναβίωση, ἀνατροφοδότηση ἢ ἐπανεκτίμηση τῆς ἑλληνικῆς ἐρωτικῆς πλασματικῆς πεζογραφίας; *Synkrisi/Comparaison* (Athens) 2–3: 53–62.

—— 1991b. Νεοελληνικὰ λογοτεχνικὰ λαϊκὰ βιβλία: προκαταρκτικὰ γραμματολογικὰ-εἰδολογικὰ καὶ βιβλιογραφικὰ ζητήματα. Ἐπιστημονικὴ Ἐπετηρίδα Φιλοσοφικῆς Σχολῆς Πανεπιστημίου Θεσσαλονίκης (Τμῆμα Φιλολογίας) 1: 249–60.

—— 1993. ‘*Digenes Akrites* in prose: the Andros version in the context of modern Greek literature’, in Beaton and Ricks 1993: 116–30.

—— 1994. [Review of Agapitos 1991; Agapitos and Smith 1992.] Ἑλληνικά 44: 200–23.

Keil, B. 1889. ‘Die Monatscyclen der byzantinischen Kunst in spätgriechischer Literatur.’ *Wiener Studien* 11: 94–142.

Kelly, J. 1993. ‘*Digenes* and *Livistros* on the computer’, in Panayotakis 1993: I, 129–35.

Kennedy, G. 1963. *The art of persuasion in Greece*. London.

REFERENCES

—— 1980. *Classical rhetoric and its Christian and secular tradition*. Chapel Hill, NC.

Keydell, R. 1979. 'Achilleis. Zur Problematik und Geschichte einer griechischen Romans.' *Byzantinische Forschungen* 6: 83–99.

Knös, B. 1952. 'A propos de l'influence française sur la littérature néohellénique du moyen âge', in *Mélanges de Philologie Romane offerts à Karl Michaëlsson*, pp. 281–91. Gothenburg.

—— 1962. 'Qui est l'auteur de Callimaque et Chrysorrhoé?' Ἑλληνικά 17: 274–95.

Koder, J. 1972. 'Der Fünfzehnsilber am kaiserlichen Hof um das Jahr 900.' *Byzantinoslavica* 33: 214–9.

—— 1975. 'Fata Morgana in Negroponte. Spüren des Artusstoffes auf Euboia im 14. Jahrhundert.' *Jahrbuch der Österreichischen Byzantinistik* 24: 129–36.

—— 1983. 'Kontakion und politischer Vers.' *Jahrbuch der Österreichischen Byzantinistik* 33: 45–56.

Koder, J. and Weber, T. 1980. *Liutprand von Cremona in Konstantinopel*. Vienna.

Koliadimou, S. 1988. Ἡ μορφολογικὴ ἀνάλυση τοῦ Βλαντίμιρ Πρόπ καὶ τὸ βυζαντινὸ ἐρωτικὸ ἱπποτικὸ μυθιστόρημα. Ἀπόπειρα ἐφαρμογῆς. Unpublished dissertation, University of Thessaloniki.

Kotzamanidou, M. 1992. [Review of Beaton, *The medieval Greek romance*.] *Journal of Modern Greek Studies* 10: 276–8.

Kriaras, E. 1951. Ἡ μεσαιωνικὴ ἑλληνικὴ γραμματεία (τὰ ὅρια – μερικὰ χαρακτηριστικά). Ἀγγλοελληνικὴ Ἐπιθεώρηση 5: 92–6.

—— 1955. Βυζαντινὰ ἱπποτικὰ μυθιστορήματα (Βασικὴ Βιβλιοθήκη, ἀρ. 2), Athens.

—— 1959. 'Die Besonderheiten der letzten Periode der mittelalterlichen griechischen Literatur.' *Jahrbuch der Österreichischen Byzantinistische Gesellschaft* 8: 69–85.

—— 1960. 'Die zeitliche Einreihung des "Phlorios und Platzia-Phlora" - Romans in Hinblick auf den "Imberios und Margarona" - Roman', in *Akten des XI. internationalen Byzantinistenkongresses (München 1958)*, pp. 269–72. Munich.

—— 1968– . Λεξικὸ τῆς μεσαιωνικῆς ἑλληνικῆς δημώδους γραμματείας: *1100–1669*. Thessaloniki. (12 vols so far published.)

—— 1976. Ἡ διγλωσσία στὰ ὑστεροβυζαντινὰ γράμματα καὶ ἡ διαμόρφωση τῶν ἀρχῶν τῆς νεοελληνικῆς λογοτεχνίας. Βυζαντινὰ 8: 213–43.

Krumbacher, K. 1897. *Geschichte der byzantinischen Literatur*. Munich. (Reprinted New York, 1970.)

Kustas, G. 1973. *Studies in Byzantine rhetoric* (Ἀνάλεκτα Βλατάδων, ἀρ. 17). Thessaloniki.

Kyriakidis, S. P. 1926. Ὁ Διγενὴς Ἀκρίτας. Ἀκριτικὰ ἔπη – ἀκριτικὰ τραγούδια – ἀκριτικὴ ζωή. Athens.

—— 1947. Ἡ γένεσις τοῦ διστίχου καὶ ἡ ἀρχή τῆς ἰσομετρίας. Thessaloniki. Reprinted in Τὸ δημοτικὸ τραγούδι: συναγωγὴ μελετῶν, (Νεοελληνικὰ Μελετήματα, ἀρ. 3), pp. 209–80. Athens.

—— 1958. 'Forschungsbericht zum Akritas-Epos,' in *Berichte zum XI. Internationalische Byzantinistenkongresses*, II/2. Munich.

Lambakis, S. 1982. Οἱ καταβάσεις στὸν κάτω κόσμο στὴ Βυζαντινὴ καὶ στὴ μεταβυζαντινὴ λογοτεχνία. Athens.

Lambert, J. A. 1935. *Le roman de Libistros et Rhodamné, publié d'après les manuscrits de Leyde et de Madrid avec une introduction, des observations grammaticales et un glossaire* (Verhandelingen der Koninklijke Akademie van Wetenschappen te Amsterdam, Afdeeling Letterkunde, Nieuwe Reeks, no. 35). Amsterdam.

Lambros, S. 1880. *Collection de romans grecs en langue vulgaire et en vers*. Paris.

283

—— 1906. Λόγος Παρηγορητικὸς περὶ Δυστυχίας καὶ Εὐτυχίας κατὰ τὸν κώδικα τῆς Λειψίας. *Νέος Ἑλληνομνήμων* 3: 402–32.

—— 1913. Λείψανον στίχων ἐξ Ἀχηλληίδος. *Νέος Ἑλληνομνήμων* 10: 144–6.

—— 1914. Εἰκονογραφημένοι λογοτεχνικοὶ κώδικες. *Νέος Ἑλληνομνήμων* 11: 433–40.

—— 1921. Ἀχηλληίς. *Νέος Ἑλληνομνήμων* 15: 367–408.

Lathuillère, R. 1966. *Guiron le Courtois: étude de la tradition manuscrite et analyse critique* (Publications romanes et françaises, no. 86). Geneva.

Lavagnini, R. 1969–70. 'Note sull' Achilleide.' *Rivista di studi bizantini e neoellenici* 6–7: 165–79.

—— 1988. *I fatti di Troia. L'Iliade bizantina del cod. Paris Suppl. Gr. 926. Introduzione, traduzione e note* (Quaderni dell'Istituto di Filologia Greca della Università di Palermo, no. 20). Palermo.

Layton, E. 1979. 'Greek bibliography. Additions and corrections (c. 1471–1829).' *Θησαυρίσματα* 16: 89–112.

—— 1981. 'Notes on some printers and publishers of 16th century Greek books in Venice.' *Θησαυρίσματα* 18: 119–44.

Legouis, E., and Cazamian, L. 1967. *A history of English literature*. London.

Legrand, E. 1890. *La guerre de Troie* (Bibliothèque grecque vulgaire, no. 5). Paris.

—— 1891. 'Poésies inédites de Théodore Prodrome.' *Revue des études grecques* 4: 70–3.

Lemerle, P. 1967. *Le premier humanisme byzantin*. Paris.

—— 1977. *Cinq études sur le XIe siècle byzantin*. Paris.

Lendari, S. 1994. *Livistros and Rodamne: a critical edition of Vat. gr. 2391*. Unpublished doctoral dissertation, University of Cambridge.

Lendari, T. 1993. '*Livistros and Rodamne*, manuscript V', in Panayotakis 1993: II, 135–47.

Létoublan, F. 1993. *Les lieux communs du roman grec: stéréotypes d'aventure et d'amour* (*Mnemosyne* suppl.). Leiden.

Littlewood, A. R. 1972. *The Progymnasmata of Ioannes Geometres*. Amsterdam.

—— 1974. 'The symbolism of the apple in Byzantine literature.' *Jahrbuch der Österreichischen Byzantinistik* 23: 33–59.

—— 1979. 'Romantic paradises: the rôle of the garden in the Byzantine romance.' *Byzantine and Modern Greek Studies* 5: 95–114.

—— 1992. 'Gardens of Byzantium.' *Journal of Garden History* 12: 126–53.

—— 1993. 'The erotic symbolism of the apple in late Byzantine and meta-Byzantine demotic literature.' *Byzantine and Modern Greek Studies* 17: 83–103.

Lodge, D. 1977. *The modes of modern writing*. London.

Loenertz, R.-J. 1976. 'La Belle Maguelone [*sic*] ou le fondement historique d'un roman de chevalerie.' *Θησαυρίσματα* 13: 40–6.

Loomis, R. 1936. 'The Modena sculpture and Arthurian romance.' *Studi medievali*, nuova serie, 9: 1–17.

Lord, A. B. 1954. 'Notes on *Digenis Akritas* and Serbocroatian epic.' *Harvard Slavic Studies* 2: 375–83.

—— 1960. *The singer of tales*. Cambridge, Mass.

—— 1977. 'Parallel culture traits in ancient and modern Greece.' *Byzantine and Modern Greek Studies* 3: 71–80.

Löseth, E. 1890. *Le roman en prose de Tristan, le roman de Palamède et la compilation de Rusticien de Pise* (Bibliothèque de l'Ecole des Hautes Etudes, no. 82). Paris.

Lyons, J. 1981. *Language and linguistics: an introduction*. Cambridge.

Maas, P. 1912. 'Metrische Akklamationen der Byzantiner.' *Byzantinische Zeitschrift* 21: 28–51.

MacAlister, S. 1984. 'Digenis Akritas: the first scene with the apelatai.' *Byzantion* 54: 551–74.

―― 1985. 'The dream tradition in the Byzantine learned romance: a revival.' *Byzantine Studies in Australia. Newsletter* 16: 13–14.

―― 1990. 'Aristotle on the dream: a twelfth-century romance revival.' *Byzantion* 60: 195–212.

―― 1991. 'Byzantine twelfth-century romances: a relative chronology'. *Byzantine and Modern Greek Studies* 15: 175–210.

Mackridge, P. 1985. *The modern Greek language: a descriptive analysis of Standard Modern Greek.* Oxford.

―― 1990a (ed.). *The Oxford colloquium on orality in medieval and modern Greek poetry* (= *Byzantine and Modern Greek Studies* 14), pp. 121–239.

―― 1990b. 'Orality in medieval and modern Greek poetry', in Mackridge 1990a: 123–8.

―― 1992a. [Review of Beaton, *The medieval Greek romance.*] *Journal of Hellenic Studies* 112: 224–5.

―― 1992b. 'Bride-snatching in *Digenes Akrites* and Cypriot heroic poetry.' Ἐπετηρὶς τοῦ Κέντρου Ἐπιστημονικῶν Ἐρευνῶν (Nicosia) 19: 617–22.

―― 1993a. 'An editorial problem in medieval Greek texts: the position of the object clitic pronoun in the Escorial *Digenes Akrites*', in Panayotakis 1993: I, 325–42.

―― 1993b. '"None but the brave deserve the fair": abduction, elopement, seduction and marriage in the Escorial *Digenes Akrites* and Modern Greek heroic songs', in Beaton and Ricks 1993: 150–60.

―― 1995. Ἡ θέση τοῦ ἀδύνατου τύπου τῆς προσωπικῆς ἀντωνυμίας στὴ μεσαιωνικὴ δημώδη ἑλληνική. *Studies in Greek Linguistics, Proceedings of the XVth Annual Meeting*, pp. 906–29. Thessaloniki.

Macrides, R., and Magdalino, R. 1992. 'The Fourth Kingdom and the rhetoric of Hellenism', in P. Magdalino (ed.), *The Perception of the Past in Twelfth-Century Europe*, pp. 117–56. London.

Maehler, H. 1976. 'Der Metiochos-Parthenope-Roman.' *Zeitschrift für Papyrologie und Epigraphik* 23: 1–20.

Magdalino, P. 1983. 'Aspects of twelfth-century Byzantine *Kaiserkritik*.' *Speculum* 58: 326–48.

―― 1989. 'Honour among Romaioi: the framework of social values in the world of Digenes Akrites and Kekaumenos.' *Byzantine and Modern Greek Studies*, 13: 183–218. (Reprinted in P. Magdalino, *Tradition and Transformation in Medieval Byzantium*, London, 1991).

―― 1992. 'Eros the King and the king of *Amours*: some observations on *Hysmine and Hysminias*', in A. Cutler and S. Franklin (eds), *Homo Byzantinus: Papers in Honor of Alexander Kazhdan* (= *Dumbarton Oaks Papers* 46), pp. 197–204.

―― 1993a. *The empire of Manuel I Komnenos, 1143–1180.* Cambridge.

―― 1993b. '*Digenes Akrites* and Byzantine literature: the twelfth-century background to the Grottaferrata version', in Beaton and Ricks 1993: 1–14.

Maguire, H. 1974. 'Truth and convention in Byzantine descriptions of works of art.' *Dumbarton Oaks Papers* 28: 111–40.

Majuri, A. 1919. 'Una nuova poesia di Teodoro Prodromo.' *Byzantinische Zeitschrift* 23: 397–407.

Mango, C. 1975. *Byzantine literature as a distorting mirror.* Oxford. (Reprinted in C. Mango, *Byzantium and its image: history and culture of the Byzantine empire and its heritage*, (Variorum Reprints), pp. 3–18. London.

―― 1980. *Byzantium: the empire of New Rome.* London.

—— 1981. 'Daily life in Byzantium.' *Jahrbuch der Österreichischen Byzantinistik* 31: 337–53.

Manousakas, M. 1952. 'Les romans byzantines de chevalerie et l'état présent des études les concernant.' *Revue des études grecques* 10: 70–83.

Manousakas, M. and van Gemert, A. F. 1981. Ὁ δικηγόρος τοῦ Χάντακα Στέφανος Σαχλίκης: ποιητὴς τοῦ ΙΔ´ καὶ ὄχι τοῦ ΙΕ´ αἰῶνα, in *Πεπραγμένα τοῦ Δ´ Διεθνοῦς Κρητολογικοῦ Συνεδρίου (1976)*, Vol. II, pp. 215–31. Athens.

Marcovich, M. 1992. *Theodori Prodromi, de Rhodanthes et Dosiclis amoribus libri IX.* Stuttgart.

Markopoulos, A. 1983. 'Sur les deux versions de la Chronographie de Syméon Logothète.' *Byzantinische Zeitschrift* 76: 279–84.

Marshall, F. H. 1930. 'The Greek Theseid.' *Byzantinische Zeitschrift* 30: 131–42.

Martini, E. 1896. 'A proposito d'una poesia inedito di Manuele File.' *Reale Istituto Lombardo di Scienze e Lettere: Rendiconti*, serie 2, 29: 460–71.

Martino, A. B. 1986. 'Mío Cid y Dighenis Akritas en la tradición juglaresca (aportes para una comparación)', in M. Criado de Val (ed.), *La juglaresca: actas del I Congreso Internacional sobre la Juglaresca*, pp. 191–213. Madrid.

Mastrodimitris, P. D. 1984. *Νεοελληνικὴ γραμματεία, Τόμ. Α´: Ἡ ποίηση τῶν πρωτονεοελληνικῶν χρόνων. Εἰσαγωγή – ἀνθολογία – ὑπομνήματα – γλωσσάριο.* Athens.

Mavrofrydis, D. I. 1866. *Ἐκλογὴ μνημείων τῆς νεωτέρας ἑλληνικῆς γλώσσης, Τόμ. Α´.* Athens.

Mavrogordato, J. 1956. *Digenes Akrites, edited with an introduction, translation and commentary.* Oxford.

Mazal, O. 1965. 'Der griechische und byzantinische Roman in der Forschung von 1945 bis 1960.' *Jahrbuch der Österreichischen Byzantinischen Gesellschaft* 14: 83–124.

—— 1967. *Der Roman des Konstantinos Manasses. Überlieferung, Rekonstruktion, Textausgabe der Fragmente* (Wiener Byzantinistische Studien, no. 4). Vienna.

Megas, G. 1953. Ὁ λόγος παρηγορητικὸς περὶ εὐτυχίας καὶ δυστυχίας [sic] καὶ τὰ παραμύθια τῆς πρὸς τὴν τύχην ὁδοιπορίας. *Λαογραφία* 15: 3–43.

—— 1956. Καλλιμάχου καὶ Χρυσορρόης ὑπόθεσις, in *Mélanges Merlier*, Vol. II, pp. 147–72. Athens.

Meunier, F. 1991. *Eumathios: les amours homonymes.* Paris.

Michailidis, D. 1971–2. 'Palamedes rediens – la fortuna di Palamede nel medioevo ellenico.' *Rivista di studi bizantini e neoellenici* 8–9: 261–80.

—— 1993. Νέες χρονολογήσεις μεσαιωνικῶν δημωδῶν κειμένων, in Panayotakis 1993: II, 148–55.

Miletich, J. 1981. 'Repetition and aesthetic function in the *Poema de mio Cid* and south-Slavic oral and literary epic.' *Bulletin of Hispanic Studies* 58: 189–96.

Miller, E. 1858. 'Poème allégorique de Meliténiote', in *Notices et extraits des manuscrits de la Bibliothèque Impériale*, Vol. XIX, part 2, pp. 1–138. Paris.

Minnis, A. J. 1984. *Medieval theory of authorship.* London.

Mitsakis, K. 1963. *Προβλήματα σχετικὰ μὲ τὸ κείμενο, τὶς πηγὲς καὶ τὴ χρονολόγηση τῆς Ἀχιλληΐδος.* Thessaloniki.

—— 1966. 'Palamedes.' *Byzantinische Zeitschrift* 59: 5–7.

Mohay, A. 1974–5. 'Schriftlichkeit und Mündlichkeit in der byzantinischen Literatur.' *Acta classica* (Debrecen) 10–11: 175–82.

Molinié, G. 1979. *Chariton: le roman de Chairéas et Callirhoé.* Paris.

Morgan, G. 1960. *Cretan poetry: sources and inspiration* (offprint from *Κρητικὰ Χρονικά* 14). Heraklion.

Müller, C. W. 1976. 'Chariton von Aphrodisias und die Theorie des Romans in der

Antike.' *Antike und Abendland* 22: 115–36.

—— 1981. 'Der griechische Roman', in E. Vogt (ed.), *Griechische Literatur* (Neues Handbuch der Literaturwissenschaft, no. 2), pp. 377–412. Wiesbaden.

Mullett, M. 1984. 'Aristocracy and patronage in the literary circles of Comnenian Constantinople', in M. Angold (ed.), *The Byzantine aristocracy: IX to XIII centuries* (B. A. R. International Series, no. S 221), pp. 173–201. Oxford.

—— 1992. 'Dancing with deconstructionists in the gardens of the Muses: new literary history vs ?' *Byzantine and Modern Greek Studies* 14: 258–75.

Mullett, M., and Smythe, D. 1996 (eds). *Alexios I Komnenos*, 2 vols (Belfast Byzantine Texts and Translations). Belfast.

Nicol, D. M. 1972. *The last centuries of Byzantium, 1261–1453*. London. (Revised edn Cambridge, 1993.)

—— 1984. *The despotate of Epiros, 1267–1479: a contribution to the history of Greece in the Middle Ages*. Cambridge.

Nørgaard, L. 1989. 'Byzantine romance – some remarks on the coherence of motives.' *Classica et mediaevalia* 40: 271–94.

Nørgaard, L., and Smith, O. 1975. *A Byzantine Iliad: the text of Par. Suppl. Gr. 926, edited with critical apparatus, introduction and indexes* (Museum Tusculanum: Opuscula Graecolatina, no. 5). Copenhagen.

Nykrog, P. 1982. 'The rise of literary fiction', in Benson et al. 1982: 593–612.

Oikonomidès, N. 1979. 'L'épopée de Digénis et la frontière orientale de Byzance aux Xe et XIe siècles.' *Travaux et mémoires* 7: 375–97.

Olsen, B. 1990. 'The Greek translation of Boccaccio's *Theseid* Book 6.' *Classica et mediaevalia* 41: 273–301.

—— 1993. 'The model and translation method of the Greek *Theseid*', in Panayotakis 1993: II, 313–18.

Ong, W. J. 1986. 'Text as interpretation: Mark and after', in J. M. Foley (ed.) *Oral tradition in literature: interpretation in context*, pp. 147–69. Columbia, Mo.

Ostrogorsky, G. 1968. *History of the Byzantine state*, trans. J. Hussey, 2nd edn. Oxford.

Palm, J. 1967. 'Bemerkungen zur Ekphrase in der griechischen Literatur,' in *Kungliga Humanistiska Vetenskaps-Samfundet i Uppsala, Årsbok 1965–6*, pp. 108–211. Stockholm.

Panayotakis, N. 1987. 'Sachlikisstudien', in Eideneier 1987b: 219–78.

—— 1993 (ed.). Ἀρχὲς τῆς νεοελληνικῆς λογοτεχνίας (Πρακτικὰ τοῦ δεύτερου διεθνοῦς συνεδρίου "Neograeca Medii Aevi", Βενετία, 7–10 Νοεμβρίου 1991). 2 vols. Venice.

Papademetriou, J.-Th. 1969. Τὰ σχέδη τοῦ μυός: new sources and text,' in *Classical Studies Presented to Ben Edwin Perry* (= *Illinois Studies in Language and Literature* 58), pp. 210–22.

Papadimitriu, S. 1896. Стефан Сахликис. Odessa.

Papanikolaou, A. D. 1973. *Xenophon Ephesius Ephesiacorum*. Leipzig.

Papathomopoulos, M. 1987. 'L'édition critique du Πόλεμος τῆς Τρωάδος: problèmes méthodologiques', in Eideneier 1987b: 279–84.

—— 1993. Τὸ στέμμα καὶ ἡ ἔκδοση τῆς Βελισαριάδας, in Panayotakis 1993: I, 349–57.

Parry, M. 1930. 'Studies in the epic technique of oral verse-making, I: Homer and the Homeric style.' *Harvard Studies in Classical Philology* 41: 73–147.

Patlagean, E. 1979. 'Discours écrit, discours parlé. Niveaux de culture à Byzance aux VIIIe–XIe siècles.' *Annales économies sociétés civilisations* 2: 264–78.

Pecoraro, V. 1982. 'La nascita del romanzo moderno nell'Europa del XIIo secolo: le sue origini orientali e la mediazione di Bisanzio all'Occidente.' *Jahrbuch der*

Österreichischen Byzantinistik 32/3: 307–19.

Pelaez, M. 1929. 'Un frammento del romanzo francese in prosa di Tristano.' *Studi medievali*, nuova serie, 2: 198–204.

Pernot, H. 1931. *Chansons populaires grecques des XVe et XVIe siècles*. Paris.

Perry, B. E. 1967. *The ancient romances: a literary-historical account of their origins*. Berkeley and Los Angeles.

Pertusi, A. 1970. 'La poesia epica bizantina e la sua formazione: problemi sul fondo storico e la struttura letteraria del "Digenis Akritas"', in *Atti del convegno internazionale sul tema: La poesia epica e la sua formazione* (Accademia Nazionale dei Lincei, Quaderno 139), pp. 481–549. Rome.

—— 1976. 'Tra storia e leggenda: akrítai e Ghâzi sulla frontiera orientale di Bisanzio', in *XIVe Congrès International des Etudes Byzantines (Bucarest 1971), Rapports*, Vol. II, pp. 27–72. Bucharest.

Petit, L. 1902. 'Monodie de Nicétas Eugénianos sur Théodore Prodrome.' Византийский Временник 9: 452–63.

Philippides, M. 1993. [Review of Beaton, *The medieval Greek romance*.] *Speculum* 68: 105–6.

Pichard, M. 1952. 'Sur les fondements historiques des romans d' "Imbérios et de Margarona" et "de Pierre de Provence et la belle Maguelonne".' *Revue des études byzantines* 10: 84–92.

—— 1956. *Le roman de Callimaque et de Chrysorrhoé: texte établi et traduit*. Paris.

Pieler, P. 1971. 'Recht, Gesellschaft und Staat im byzantinischen Roman der Palaeologenzeit.' *Jahrbuch der Österreichischen Byzantinistik* 20: 189–22.

Pignani, A. 1983. *Niceforo Basilace, Progimnasmi e monodie. Testo critico. Byzantina et Neo-Hellenica Neapolitana* (Collana di Studi e Testi, no. 10). Naples.

Plepelits, K. 1989. *Eustathios Makrembolites: Hysmine und Hysminias. Eingeleitet, übersetzt und erläutert* (Bibliothek der griechischen Literatur, no. 29). Stuttgart.

Podestà, G. 1945. 'Le satire lucianesche di Teodoro Prodromo.' *Aevum* 19: 239–52.

Politi-Sakellariadi, N. 1987. Προβλήματα τῆς ἔκδοσης τοῦ "Λόγου Παρηγορητικοῦ περὶ Δυστυχίας καὶ Εὐτυχίας", in Eideneier 1987b: 285–94.

Politis, L. 1964. *Γεωργίου Χορτάτση: Κατζούρμπος, κωμωδία.* (Ἑταιρία Κρητικῶν Ἱστορικῶν Μελετῶν: Κρητικὸν Θέατρον, ἀρ. 1). Heraklion, Crete.

—— 1969. Δύο φύλλα ἀπό χειρόγραφο τοῦ "Πολέμου τῆς Τρωάδος". Ἑλληνικά 22: 227–34.

—— 1970. 'L'épopée byzantine de Digénis Akritas; problèmes de la tradition du texte et des rapports avec les chansons akritiques,' in *Atti del convegno internazionale sul tema: La poesia epica e la sua formazione* (Accademia Nazionale dei Lincei, Quaderno 139), pp. 551–81. Rome.

—— 1973a. 'A propos de la nouvelle édition de l'épopée byzantine.' *Scriptorium* 27: 327–51.

—— 1973b. *A history of modern Greek literature*. Oxford.

—— 1975. *Ποιητικὴ ἀνθολογία, βιβλίο πρῶτο: Πρὶν ἀπὸ τὴν Ἅλωση*, 2nd edn. Athens.

—— 1981. Νεώτερες ἀπόψεις γιὰ τὴ γέννηση καὶ τὴ δομὴ τοῦ δεκαπεντασύλλαβου. *Πρακτικὰ τῆς Ἀκαδημίας Ἀθηνῶν* 56: 211–28.

Politis, N. G. 1906. Περὶ τοῦ ἐθνικοῦ ἔπους τῶν νεωτέρων Ἑλλήνων. Athens. (Reprinted in *Λαογραφικὰ Σύμμεικτα, Τόμ. Α΄*, pp. 237–60. Athens, 1920.)

—— 1911. Τὸ ἐθνικὸν ἔπος τοῦ Διγενῆ Ἀκρίτου. *Λαογραφία* 3: 217.

Polyakova, S. V. 1969. 'К вопросу о датировке романа Евматия Макремводита.' Византийский Временник 30: 113–23.

────── 1971. О хронологической последовательности романов Евматия Макремволита и Феодора Продрома.' Византийский Временник 32: 104–8.

────── 1976. 'К вопросу о византино-французских литературных связях.' Византийский Временник 37: 114–22.

────── 1979. Из историй византийского романа. Moscow.

Pontani, F. M. 1950. 'Note al Πρέσβυς Ἱππότης.' *Aevum* 24: 236–52.

Popova, T. 1985. Византийская народная литература: история жанровых форм зпоса и романа. Moscow.

Prombonas, I. K. 1985. 'Ἀκριτικά Α'. Athens.

Psichari, J. 1886–9. *Essais de grammaire néogrecque*, 2 vols. Paris.

Rattenbury, R. M., and Lumb, T. W. 1960. *Héliodore, les Ethiopiques*, 2 vols. Paris.

Reardon, B. 1969. 'The Greek novel.' *Phoenix* 23/3: 291–309. (Reprinted in H. Gärtner (ed.), *Beiträge zum griechischen Liebesroman* (Olms Studien, no. 20), pp. 218–36. Hildesheim, Zurich and New York.

────── 1977 (ed.) *Erotic antiqua: acta of the international conference on the ancient novel (Bangor, 1976)*. Bangor.

────── 1988. 'The form of ancient Greek romance', in Beaton 1988a: 205–16.

────── 1989 (ed.) *Collected ancient Greek novels*. Berkeley, Calif.

────── 1991. *The form of Greek romance*. Princeton, NJ.

Reichmann, S. 1963. *Das byzantinische Alexandergedicht nach dem Codex Marcianus 408* (Beiträge zur klassischen Philologie, no. 13). Meisenheim.

Renauld, E. 1926. *Michel Psellos: Chronographie*. Paris.

Ricks, D. 1989. 'Is the Escorial *Akrites* a unitary poem?' *Byzantion* 59: 184–207.

────── 1990. *Byzantine heroic poetry*. Bristol.

Rizzo Nervo, F. 1985. 'Il "mondo dei padri" nella metafora del Vecchio Cavaliere', in *Studi di filologia bizantina III = Quaderni del Siculorum Gymnasium* (Università di Catania) 15: 115–28.

Robinson, C. 1979. *Lucian and his influence in Europe*. London.

────── 1991. [Review of Beaton, *The medieval Greek romance*.] *Medium Ævum* 60: 142–3.

Rohde, E. 1960. *Der griechische Roman und seine Vorläufer*, 4th edn. Hildesheim.

Romano, R. 1974. *Pseudo-Luciano: Timarione* (Byzantina et neo-hellenica neapolitana, no. 2). Naples.

Rotolo, V. 1965. *Libistro e Rodamne, romanzo cavalleresco bizantino*. Athens.

Roueché, C. 1988. 'Byzantine writers and readers: storytelling in the eleventh century', in Beaton 1988a: 123–33.

Ryding, W. 1971. *Structure in medieval narrative*. The Hague and Paris.

Sathas, K. 1879. 'L'Achilléide byzantine.' *Annuaire de l'Association pour l'Encouragement des Etudes Grecques* 13: 126–75.

Schirò, G. 1975. *Cronaco dei Tocco di Cefalonia di anonimo* (Corpus Fontium Historiae Byzantinae, no. 10). Rome.

Schissel, O. 1942. *Der byzantinische Garten* (Akademie der Wissenschaften in Wien, Philosophisch–historische Klasse, Sitzungsberichte, no. 221/2). Vienna.

Schmitt, J. 1893. 'Zu Phlorios und Platziphlora.' *Byzantinische Zeitschrift* 2: 212–30.

────── 1904. *The Chronicle of Morea*. London. (Reprinted Groningen, 1967.)

Schreiner, H. 1930. 'Neue Quellen zur Komposition und Entstehungsgeschichte des mittelgriechischen Romans Imberios und Margarona.' *Byzantinische Zeitschrift* 30: 121–30.

────── 1959. 'Zerrissene Zusammenhänge und Fremdkörper im Belthandros-Text.' *Byzantinische Zeitschrift* 52: 257–64.

REFERENCES

―――― 1960. 'Der älteste Imberios-Text,' in *Akten des XI. Internationalen Byzantinistenkongresses (München 1958)*, pp. 556–62. Munich.

―――― 1962. 'Die zeitliche Aufeinanderfolge der im Cod. Vindob. Theol. Gr. 244 überlieferten Texte des Imberios, des Belisar und des Florios und ihr Schreiber.' *Byzantinische Zeitschrift* 55: 213–23.

Setton, K. 1956. 'The Byzantine background to the Italian Renaissance.' *Proceedings of the American Philosophical Society* 100: 1–76.

Ševčenko, I. 1970. 'Poems on the deaths of Leo VI and Constantine VII in the Madrid manuscripts of Scylitzes.' *Dumbarton Oaks Papers* 23–4: 185–228.

―――― 1976. 'Society and intellectual life in the XIVth century', in *XIVe Congrès International des Etudes Byzantines (Bucarest 1971): Rapports*, Vol. I, pp. 7–30. Bucharest.

―――― 1982. 'Storia letteraria – conclusion générale', in *Università degli studi di Bari, Centro di Studi Bizantini, corsi di studi III, 1978: La civiltà bizantina dal XII al XV secolo*, pp. 170–88. Rome.

―――― 1985. 'Three Byzantine literatures: a layman's guide.' *Journal of Modern Hellenism* 2: 1–20.

Shepard, J. 1984. [Review of Clucas 1981.] *English Historical Review* 99: 409–10.

Shepherd, G. T. 1979. 'The emancipation of story in the twelfth century', in *Medieval Narrative: a Symposium*, pp. 44–57. Odense.

Siapkaras-Pitsillidis, Th. 1976. Ὁ πετραρχισμὸς στὴν Κύπρο: Ρίμες ἀγάπης, ἀπό χειρόγραφο τοῦ 16ου αἰῶνα μὲ μεταφορὰ στὴν κοινή μας γλῶσσα. Athens.

Sifakis, G. M. 1989. Ζητήματα ποιητικῆς τοῦ Διγενῆ Ε καὶ τῶν ἀκριτικῶν τραγουδιῶν. *Ariadne* (Heraklion) 5: 125–39.

―――― 1992. 'Homeric survivals in the medieval and modern Greek folksong tradition?' *Greece and Rome*, 39/2: 139–54.

―――― 1993. Τὸ πρόβλημα τῆς προφορικότητας στὴ μεσαιωνικὴ δημώδη γραμματεία, in Panayotakis 1993: I, 267–84.

Sigalas, A. 1956. Τὸ μυθιστόρημα "Βέλθανδρος καὶ Χρυσάντζα" καὶ ἡ ἀποκατάστασή του, in *Mélanges Merlier*, Vol. II, pp. 355–77. Athens.

Smith, O. 1987. 'Versions and manuscripts of the *Achilleid*', in Eideneier 1987b: 315–25.

―――― 1988. 'Notes on the Byzantine Achilleid: the Oxford version.' *Classica et mediaevalia* 39: 259–72.

―――― 1990. *The Oxford version of the Achilleid*. Copenhagen.

―――― 1993. 'Literary and ideological observations to the *Achilleid*', in Panayotakis 1993: II, 182–7.

Southern, R. W. 1982. 'The schools in Paris and the school of Chartres', in Benson et al. 1982: 113–37.

Spadaro, G. 1966a. *Contributo sulle fonti del romanzo greco-medievale 'Florio e Plaziaflora'* (Κείμενα καὶ Μελέται Νεοελληνικῆς Φιλολογίας, ἀρ. 26), Athens.

―――― 1966b. "Εἰς πίστιν τὴν καθολικὴν Ρωμαίων ὀρθοδόξων". *Byzantion* 36: 535–43.

―――― 1975. 'Problemi relativi ai romanzi greci dell'età dei Paleologi, I. Rapporti tra Ἰμπέριος καὶ Μαργαρῶνα e Φλώριος καὶ Πλατζιαφλόρε.' Ἑλληνικά 28: 302–27.

―――― 1976a. 'Problemi relativi ai romanzi greci dell'età dei Paleologi, II. Rapporti tra la Διήγησις τοῦ Ἀχιλλέως, la Διήγησις τοῦ Βελισαρίου e l' Ἰμπέριος καὶ Μαργαρῶνα.' Ἑλληνικά 29: 287–310.

―――― 1976b. '"Imberio e Margarona" e "Florio e Plaziaflore"', in *Miscellanea neogreca, atti del I Convegno Nazionale di Studi Neogreci (Palermo 1976)*, pp. 181–6. Palermo.

—— 1977. 'Sul Teseida neogreco.' *Folia neohellenica* 2: 157–60.

—— 1978a. 'Problemi relativi ai romanzi greci dell'età dei Paleologi, III. *Achilleide, Georgillàs, Callimaco, Beltandro, Libistro, Florio, Imperio* e Διήγησις γεναμένη ἐν Τροία.' Ἑλληνικά 30: 223–79.

—— 1978b. 'L'inedito Polemos tis Troados e l'Achilleide.' *Byzantinische Zeitschrift* 71: 1–9.

—— 1981. 'L' "Achilleide" e la Ἱστορικὴ Ἐξήγησις περὶ Βελισαρίου di Gheorghillàs.' Δίπτυχα Ἑταιρείας Βυζαντινῶν καὶ Μεταβυζαντινῶν Μελετῶν 2: 23–41.

—— 1982. 'Due redazioni inedite di Spaneas.' *Jahrbuch der Österreichischen Byzantinistik* 32/3: 277–88.

—— 1982–3. 'Il Πρὸς Δαμονικόν pseudoisocrateo e Spaneas.' Δίπτυχα Ἑταιρείας Βυζαντινῶν καὶ Μεταβυζαντινῶν Μελετῶν 3: 143–59.

—— 1985. 'Problemi di poesia greca medievale rodia', in *Studi di filologia bizantina III* = *Quaderni del Siculorum Gymnasium* (Università di Catania) 15: 129–37.

—— 1987. 'Edizioni critiche di testi greci medievali in lingua demotica: difficoltà e prospettive', in Eideneier 1987b: 327–56.

—— 1989a. 'Tra innovazione e conservazione: problemi di critica testuale inerenti a testi greci medievali', in *Contributi di filologia greca medievale e moderna* (Quaderni del Siculorum Gymnasium, Università di Catania, no. 18), pp. 55–64.

—— 1989b. 'Influssi occidentali in Grecia dalla IV Crociata alla caduta di Creta in mano ai Turchi.' Ἰταλοελληνικά (Naples) 2: 77–101.

—— 1990. Γραφὲς metri causa στὰ μεσαιωνικὰ κείμενα σὲ δημώδη γλῶσσα. *Mandatoforos* 32: 35–44.

—— 1992. 'Originalità e imitazione nei romanzi medievali greci di origine occidentale', in Babbi et al. 1992: 1–18.

—— 1993. 'Oralità nella letteratura greca medievale in demotico?', in Panayotakis 1993: I, 285–305.

Stathis, G. Th. 1977. Ἡ δεκαπεντασύλλαβος ὑμνογραφία ἐν τῇ βυζαντινῇ μελοποιίᾳ. Athens.

Steiner, G. 1969. 'The graphic analogue from myth to Greek romance', in *Classical Studies Presented to Ben Edwin Perry* (= *Illinois Studies in Language and Literature 58*), pp. 123–37.

Stern, H. 1955. 'Poésies et représentations carolingiennes et byzantines des mois.' *Revue archéologique* 45: 141–86.

Steryelis, A. 1967. Τὸ δημοτικὸ τραγούδι εἰς τὸ ἱπποτικὸν μυθιστόρημα Φλώριον καὶ Πλάτζια Φλώρα. *Παρνασσός* 9: 413–23.

Stevens, J. 1973. *Medieval romance: themes and approaches.* London.

Stomeo, P. 1959. 'Achilleide, poema bizantino anonimo.' *Studi salentini* 7: 155–97.

Suleiman, S. R., and Crosman, I. 1980. *The reader in the text: essays in audience and interpretation.* Princeton and Guildford.

Svoronos, N. 1937. Παρατηρήσεις εἰς "Λόγον Παρηγορητικὸν περὶ Δυστυχίας καὶ Εὐτυχίας". Ἀθηνᾶ 47: 117–40.

Symeonidis, Ch. P. 1981. Ἡ ἑρμηνεία τῆς ὀνομασίας "πολιτικός στίχος", in *Μελέτες γιὰ τὴν Ἑλληνικὴ Γλῶσσα. Πρακτικὰ τῆς 2ης Ἐτήσιας Συνάντησης τοῦ Τμήματος Γλωσσολογίας τῆς Φιλοσοφικῆς Σχολῆς τοῦ Ἀριστοτελείου Πανεπιστημίου Θεσσαλονίκης*, pp. 229–43. Thessaloniki.

Tanaşoca, N.-S. 1979. 'La littérature byzantine et le réalisme.' *Etudes byzantines et post-byzantines* (Bucharest) 1: 77–93.

Tatum, J., and Vernazza, G. 1990 (eds). *The ancient novel: classical paradigms and modern perspectives. Proceedings of the international conference, Dartmouth College, Hanover, New Hampshire, July 23–29, 1989.* Hanover, NH.

REFERENCES

Tiftixoglu, V. 1974. 'Digenes, das "Sophrosyne-Gedicht" des Meliteniotes und der byzantinische Fünfzehnsilber.' *Byzantinische Zeitschrift* 67: 1–63.

Todorov, T. 1977. *The poetics of prose*. Ithaca and London.

Trapp, E. 1971a. *Digenes Akrites – synoptische Ausgabe der ältesten Versionen* (Wiener Byzantinistische Studien, no. 8). Vienna.

—— 1971b. 'Hatte das Digenes-Epos ursprünglich eine antikaiserliche Tendenz?' *Βυζαντινά* 3: 203–11.

—— 1971c. 'Pontische Elemente im Wortschatz des Digenes-Epos.' *Revue des études sud-est européennes* 9: 601–5.

—— 1972. 'Digenes Akrites, Epos oder Roman?' in *Studi classici in onore di Quintino Cataudella*, Vol. II, pp. 637–43. Catania.

—— 1976. 'Hagiographische Elemente im Digenes-Epos.' *Analecta Bollandiana* 94: 275–87.

—— 1976–94. *Prosopographisches Lexikon der Palaiologenzeit*, 12 vols. Vienna.

—— 1993. 'Learned and vernacular literature in Byzantium: dichotomy or symbiosis?' *Dumbarton Oaks Papers* 47: 115–29.

Treu, K. 1984. 'Roman und Geschichtsschreibung.' *Klio* 66: 456–9.

Trypanis, C. 1963. 'Byzantine oral poetry.' *Byzantinische Zeitschrift* 56: 1–3.

—— 1973. [Review of Trapp 1971a.] *Gnomon* 45: 614–16.

—— 1981. *Greek poetry: from Homer to Seferis*. London.

Tsavari, I. 1993. Τὸ στέμμα καὶ τὸ κείμενο τοῦ *Πουλολόγου*, in Panayotakis 1993: I, 358–67.

Tselikas, A. 1974. Πέντε ἀνέκδοτα βυζαντινὰ ἐρωτικὰ ποιήματα σὲ μαρκιανὸ κώδικα. *Θησαυρίσματα* 12: 148–54.

Tsiouni, V. 1972. *Παιδιόφραστος Διήγησις τῶν Ζώων τῶν Τετραπόδων: critical edition* (Miscellanea Byzantina Monacensia, no. 15). Munich.

Tsolakis, E. 1959. *Μιχαὴλ Γλυκᾶ στίχοι οὓς ἔγραψε καθ' ὃν κατεσχέθη καιρόν. Κριτικὴ ἔκδοση* ('Επιστημονικὴ 'Επετηρὶς τῆς Φιλοσοφικῆς Σχολῆς τοῦ Πανεπιστημίου Θεσσαλονίκης, Παράρτημα, ἀρ. 5). Thessaloniki.

—— 1967. *Συμβολὴ στὴ μελέτη τοῦ ποιητικοῦ ἔργου τοῦ Κωνσταντίνου Μανασσῆ καὶ κριτικὴ ἔκδοση τοῦ μυθιστορήματός του 'Τὰ κατ' 'Αρίστανδρον καὶ Καλλιθέαν'* ('Επιστημονικὴ 'Επετηρὶς τῆς Φιλοσοφικῆς Σχολῆς τοῦ Πανεπιστημίου Θεσσαλονίκης, Παράρτημα, ἀρ. 10). Thessaloniki.

Valetas, G. 1964. *Κοραῆς: ἅπαντα τὰ πρωτότυπα ἔργα του*, Τόμ Α'. Athens.

van Gemert, A. F. 1977. 'The Cretan poet Marinos Falieros.' *Θησαυρίσματα* 14: 7–70.

—— 1980a. *Μαρίνου Φαλιέρου: ἐρωτικὰ ὄνειρα. Κριτικὴ ἔκδοση* (Βυζαντινὴ καὶ Νεοελληνικὴ Βιβλιοθήκη, ἀρ. 4). Thessaloniki.

—— 1980b. Ὁ Στέφανος Σαχλίκης καὶ ἡ ἐποχή του. *Θησαυρίσματα* 17: 36–130.

—— 1987. 'Die Belisariada: Mündliche Sage oder gelehrte Geschichte als Quelle des Verfassers,' in Eideneier 1987b: 121–37.

van Gemert, A. F., and Bakker, W. 1981. Ἡ 'Αχιλληΐδα καὶ ἡ ἱστορία τοῦ Βελισαρίου. 'Ελληνικά 82–97.

Vasiliev, A. A. 1952. *History of the Byzantine empire*, 2 vols. Madison, Wis.

Vayenas, N. 1989. *Ποίηση καὶ μετάφραση*. Athens.

Veloudis, G. 1968. *Der neugriechische Alexander: Tradition und Wandel* (Miscellanea Byzantina Monacensia, no. 8). Munich.

Vinaver, E. 1971. *The rise of romance*. Oxford.

Vincent, A. L. 1970. 'A manuscript of Chortatses' "Erophile" in Birmingham.' *University of Birmingham Historical Journal* 12: 261–7.

—— 1980. *Μάρκου 'Αντωνίου Φοσκόλου: Φορτουνάτος. Κριτικὴ ἔκδοση*, σημειώσεις, γλωσσάριο (Ἑταιρία Κρητικῶν Ἱστορικῶν Μελετῶν: Κρητικὸν Θέατρον, ἀρ. 2). Heraklion, Crete.

Voutieridis, E. 1924. *Ἱστορία τῆς νεοελληνικῆς λογοετεχνίας ἀπό τῶν μεσῶν τοῦ ΙΕ' αἰῶνος μέχρι τῶν νεοτάτων χρόνων*. Τόμ Α'. Athens.

Vryonis, S. 1957. 'The will of a provincial magnate: Eustathios Boilas (1059).' *Dumbarton Oaks Papers* 11: 263–77.

Wagner, W. 1870. *Medieval Greek texts*. London.

—— 1874. Wagner, G. *Carmina graeca medii aevi*. Leipzig.

Walz, C. 1832. *Rhetores graeci*, Vol. I. Stuttgart.

Wartenberg, G. 1900. 'Die byzantinische Achilleis', in *Festschrift J. Vahlen*, pp. 175–201. Berlin.

Webster, J. C. 1938. *The labours of the months in antique and mediaeval art* (Northwestern University Studies in the Humanities, no. 4). Evanston and Chicago.

West, G. 1983. 'Hero or saint? Hagiographic elements in the *Life of the Cid.*' *Journal of Hispanic Philology* 7: 87–105.

Wilson, N. G. 1975. 'Books and readers in Byzantium,' in *Byzantine Books and Bookmen* (Dumbarton Oaks Colloquium), pp. 1–15. Washington, DC.

Winkler, J., and Williams, G. (eds) 1982. *Later Greek literature* (Yale Classical Studies, no. 27). Cambridge.

Wouters, A. 1991. [Review of Beaton, *The medieval Greek romance.*] *Les études classiques* 59/1: 83–4.

Xyngopoulos, A. 1948. Τὸ ἀνάκτορον τοῦ Διγενῆ Ἀκρίτα. *Λαογραφία* 12: 547–88.

—— 1973. Ἡ ἀρχαία μυθολογία στὸ ἔπος τοῦ Διγενῆ Ἀκρίτα. *Ἐπιστημονικὴ Ἐπετηρίδα τῆς Φιλοσοφικῆς Σχολῆς τοῦ Πανεπιστημίου Θεσσαλονίκης* 12: 415–24.

Yatromanolakis, G. 1990. *Ἀχιλλέως Ἀλεξανδρέως Τατίου: Λευκίππη καὶ Κλειτοφών*. Athens.

INDEX